MW01128768

THE
SINKING
OF THE
BLÜCHER

To
Oberst Birger Kristian Eriksen
and the others who fought and died
in the battle for Norway in 1940.

THE
SINKING
OF THE
BLÜCHER
THE BATTLE OF DRØBAK NARROWS
APRIL 1940

Geirr Haarr and Tor Jørgen Melien

Greenhill Books

The Sinking of the Blücher
First published in 2023 by
Greenhill Books,
c/o Pen & Sword Books Ltd,
47 Church Street, Barnsley,
S. Yorkshire, S70 2AS

www.greenhillbooks.com
contact@greenhillbooks.com

ISBN: 978–1–78438–875–1

CIP data records for this title are available from the British Library

Edited and designed by Donald Sommerville
Typeset in 11/13.5 pt Arno Pro Small Text and Arno Pro Display
Maps by Peter Wilkinson

Printed and bound by CPI Group (UK) Ltd, Croydon, CR0 4YY

Page i: The present-day Oscarsborg Fortress, now a museum
commemorating the events of April 1940.
Page ii: Oberst Eriksen.
Page iii: Blücher immediately before the start of the Norwegian campaign.

Contents

	Acknowledgements	vii
	Picture Credits	ix
	List of Maps	x
	Introduction	xi
Chapter 1	The Ship	1
Chapter 2	The Price of Neutrality	18
Chapter 3	'Winston is Back'	28
Chapter 4	Threat from the North	49
Chapter 5	Let Slip the Dogs of War	71
Chapter 6	No Way Back	100
Chapter 7	Towards Oslo	116
Chapter 8	A Day of Highest Tension	132
Chapter 9	Guns and Forts	162
Chapter 10	Trespassing	174
Chapter 11	Intruders	189
Chapter 12	Improvisations	233
Chapter 13	War in Oslofjord	254
Chapter 14	Aftermath	280
Chapter 15	Homeward Bound	328
Chapter 16	Requiem	340
Chapter 17	Conclusions	350
	Notes	359
Appendix A	Equivalent Naval Ranks, 1940	383
Appendix B	Norwegian Forces	385
Appendix C	German Forces	393
	Bibliography	404
	Index	411

Acknowledgements

Many persons have contributed to this book. Some have helped with an important piece of information or analysis; others have given generously from a lifetime of research. Above all, Erling Skjold, Jan Egil Fjørtoft, Morten Kasbergsen, Andrew Smith, Søren Nørby, Vegar N. Toska and Jonatan Myhre Barlien have contributed information and archive material. Their support and encouragement have been crucial. Håvard Hovdet is thanked for sharing his knowledge of guns, ammunition, torpedoes and fire-control systems in 1940. Kåre Willoch let us have access to his father's diaries and archives. The naval historian and author Frank Abelsen passed away in 2008 – much too early. Most of his work related to the Oslofjord in 1940 has been made available to us by the Naval Museum in Horten. Unfortunately, we cannot thank him in person, but we remember him with esteem and have used his work with respect.

Tom Kristiansen at the University of Tromsø deserves special thanks for immeasurable amounts of help and inspiration. Frode Færøy at Norges Hjemmefrontmuseum and Roald Gjelsten, Rolf Hobson, Sigurd C. Sørlie and the others at the Norwegian Institute for Defence Studies are thanked for challenging inspirational discussions and administrative support. Andrew Lambert, Sönke Neitzel, Nicholas Rodger, Andrew Boyd, Simon Orchard and John Kiszely have all contributed to our understanding of the larger picture. Jens Henrik Andersen, Hans Christian Bjerg, Bjørn Terjesen, Gunnar S. Jensen, Erik Fundingsrud, Bjørn Olsen, Morten Svinndal, Thorsten Reich, Reinhard Huxmann, Atle Wilmar, Jo Olav Bakken, Tore Greiner Eggan, 'PeterK aus Österreich', Urs Hessling, Lennart Berns, Lennart Andersson, Jørgen Johannessen, Jan K. Sommerfelt-Pettersen, Stephan Docksjö, Thor Christian Jevanord and Halvor Sperbund deserve thanks for their contributions. They understand what we are trying to achieve.

Jan Ingar Hansen and Thor Kristiansen at Marinemuseet are thanked for enthusiastic support and access to the huge archives of the Naval Museum in Horten. Øyvind Waldeland at Forsvarsmuseets Billedarkiv and the library in Oslo is thanked for providing many of the photographs. Hjørdis Bondevik and Kristina Tobiassen assisted us at the library of the Norwegian Maritime

Museum. Stian Fosland at Festningsverk.no is thanked for providing excellent photos, as is Anne Sophie Høeg-Omdal at Lillesand by- og sjøfarts-museum. The staff of the National Archives at Kew, Bundesarchiv in Freiburg and Riksarkivet in Oslo deserve thanks for patience and professional dedication. Peter Wilkinson is thanked for drawing the unique maps. Antonio Bonomi and Abram Joslin are thanked for their kind permission to use their outstanding drawings of *Blücher*. Michael Leventhal at Greenhill deserves great thanks for believing in us and giving us the deadlines we needed. Without his support the project might never have seen completion.

And last, but not least, great thanks to our dear life companions Lillian Husby Melien and Gro Larsen who drag us back to real life when we sink too deep into the history.

Geirr H. Haarr   *Tor Jørgen Melien*
Sola, 2023.   Vevelstad, 2023

Picture Credits

The following organisations and individuals kindly supplied the illustrations featured on the pages listed.

J. Bakken collection: 321
Behmüller collection: 63 (top),
Briggs collection: 42, 43, 84, 133
Denham: 109
Dreyer collection, via T. Eggan: 87
A. Duncan via E. Skjold: 36
T. Eggan collection: 113, 295, 296, 325
E. Ettrup collection: 63 (bottom)
Festningsverk collection: 239, 319
Forsvarsgalleriet: 147
Forsvarsgalleriet via Søren Nørby: 120 (all)
Forsvarets museer, Oslo: ii, 90, 167 (both, Regulations for Orograph), 177, 243, 244, 245, 246, 261, 291, 293, 306, 309
Geirr Haarr collection: iii, 2, 4, 5, 6, 7, 8, 9, 10 (both), 19, 20, 29, 31, 35, 39, 44, 45, 50, 52, 56, 59, 65, 74, 79, 88, 100–1, 102, 103, 104, 107, 108, 117, 119, 121, 126, 127, 130, 137, 142, 176, 182, 229, 233, 234–5, 236, 248, 250, 262–3, 269, 275, 278, 290, 292, 313, 314, 315, 317, 318, 320, 322, 323, 324, 328, 331, 333, 334, 335, 337, 339, 340, 341, 343, 344, 345 (both), 347, 357
Hosar collection: 312
H. Hovdet collection: 172
Abram Joslin via Antonio Bonomi: 12–13, 14–15, 210–11

T. Kjosvold/Forsvaret: i, 348
Kit Layman: 134
Lillesand bymuseum: 140, 143
Marinemuseet Horten: 23, 25, 125, 163, 178, 179, 181, 199, 222, 254, 258–9, 260, 261, 264,
Melien/Fjeld collection: 171 (both), 186, 187, 202–3
NARA, Washington DC: 72 (E180-24b); 249 (PG-48289); 285, 289 (both E279-01)
National Archives, Kew: 299 (NA-FO 371/24834)
Normann-Anno Domkirkeodden via Digitalmuseet: 287
NTB: 82, 151, 152, 286
Riksarkivet, Oslo: 129; 205 (RA-PA-1469); 214–15, 216, 219, 220 (both), 223, 224, 227 (RA-PA-1209); 230 (RA-II-C-11 2000)
Royal Navy Submarine Museum, Gosport: 336
E. Skjold collection: 116, 138, 139, 164, 165, 169, 170, 192, 236, 237, 238, 240, 252, 253, 273, 276, 277, 358
Asbjørn Svarstad: 57
Svenska RA, Krigsarkivet, Forshell: 93
Trojmiasto.wyborcza.pl: 141
A. Wilmar collection: 135, 200, 267

Maps

Organisation of the Kriegsmarine, Spring 1940 .... page 3
Trade routes to Germany 32
The Winter War, 1939–1940 47
Group V, 7 April 110
1. R-Boat Flotilla, 7 and 8 April 118
Group V, 8 April 123
The Skagerrak, 8 April 128
Operation *Weserübung* 136
German mines in the Skagerrak, April 1940 159
Oslofjord, Group V 175
Outer Oslofjord, Night of 8–9 April 184
The Drøbak Narrows, 9 April – Morning 191
Oscarsborg Fortress 196
The Drøbak Narrows, 9 April – Afternoon 247
Horten, 9 April 257
Rauøy, 9 April 270
German advances out of Oslo 307
Operation *Weserübung Süd* – Denmark 9 April 310
British Submarines in the Skagerrak and Kattegat, April 1940 316

Introduction

In the darkness of a bitterly cold night in April 1940, the German war machine descended upon Norway. Hitler had made a strategic decision that would change the course of World War 2, one month before his long-planned attack on the Western Front. It was a daring action that required absolute surprise on all levels over a large geographical area. This is an account of what happened in Oslofjord on the night of 9 April and in the days that followed. The German heavy cruiser *Blücher* was sunk on its way to the Norwegian capital and just about everything in that part of the operation went wrong for the German invaders. The book recounts why *Blücher* was there in the first place, why she was sunk and what the disaster led to.

As far as possible, the narrative is based on primary sources. Hours have been spent at various archives and collections, and tens of thousands of document pages have been scrutinised and compared. Published books, accounts and memoirs have only been used as sources after a thorough assessment of their reliability. The research material has come in many languages: Norwegian, German, English, Swedish, and Danish. All translations into English are our own responsibility and where necessary we have striven to maintain the significance of what was said or written rather than create a word-by-word translation. All *Blücher*'s war diaries, logs, signals book and official papers were lost when the ship went down. Most of the accounts of what happened on board are therefore based on memories or compilations rewritten after the survivors had been taken care of and gathered in Oslo – or later.

There were no German plans whatsoever for an attack on Scandinavia in September 1939. The rationale for Hitler to unleash his dogs of war on Norway and Denmark seven months later developed during the winter through a series of inter-twined, concurrent incidents and processes involving a German fear of being outflanked, Norwegian neutrality policy, Allied aspirations to sever Germany's iron ore supply and their wish to establish an alternative front in Scandinavia, using the opportunity of the Soviet attack on Finland. The almost uniform inability to see and understand the warning signals, which were abundantly available, is one of the great enigmas of

Operation *Weserübung*, as Germany's attack on Denmark and Norway was code-named. Dissemination and analysis of intelligence was in its infancy in 1940, in particular in Scandinavia, and there was an intriguing inability to compile and understand what was about to happen. Not only were the signals overlooked in Oslo, they were equally neglected in London, Paris and Copenhagen.

As shown in this account, *Blücher*'s demise was attributable to arrogance, unfortunate planning and poor judgement. Her sinking was to have dramatic long-term effects on the development of the war. First of all, it opened a breach between the German Army and Navy over command of joint operations that would plague the German High Command for a long time. In addition, the outcome of the invasion and unexpected ensuing campaign affected Germany's ability to take the war to Britain later in 1940. Our objective has been to document the events in Oslofjord in April 1940 and their consequences, giving a balanced and factual account, a readable narrative without compromising the demand for research and accurate detail.

Many people have helped us and contributed to our work but responsibility for the interpretations of what happened and why and how this is conveyed is nevertheless ours and ours alone.

Conventions Followed

Place names are given in the local spelling used in 1940 (thus Swinemünde, for example, rather than its modern Polish name of Świnoujście), except for a few places like Gothenburg or Copenhagen where there is an accepted English-language name. Titles and ranks are given in the original language – *see* Appendix A. The three Norwegian letters æ, ø and å are used as in the original language. In the text, Norwegian ranks are written without an initial capital, except when starting a sentence – as is the custom in Norwegian writing.

In Germany, Great Britain was generally known as England in 1939/40, like the Soviet Union was known as Russia. Hence, in translation of German text to English, we have used England where it appears in order to maintain the flavour of the German expression.

German time in April 1940 was one hour ahead of Norwegian and British time. Hence, midnight German time was 23:00 Norwegian time. Unless noted, all times after Group V passed into Norwegian waters are Norwegian time (NoT) and thus one hour behind German time (GeT).

Chapter 1

The Ship

The Kriegsmarine

On 30 January 1933, Adolf Hitler took office as chancellor of a right-wing coalition government in Berlin. The C-in-C of the German Navy, Admiral Erich Raeder, met his new head of government for the first time on 2 February, when Hitler addressed senior officers during a dinner. In a subsequent private meeting some weeks later, Raeder was assured he would have time to re-build the Navy before any war erupted. The two appear to have struck a friendly note at first and the *Führer* was willing to listen to the admiral and accept his advice in naval matters. Arguably not a hardened National Socialist, unlike many colleagues in the senior officer corps, Raeder nevertheless used the powers of the Nazi regime to the utmost for his Navy, realising that he could not have one without the other. Most probably he believed – or at least hoped – that the sharp edges of the new regime would wear off with time. In August 1934, the elderly head of state President Hindenburg died, and Hitler declared himself president in addition to chancellor, combining the two offices of state with full dictatorial powers. A few days later, all officers of the armed forces were paraded and ordered to pledge an oath of allegiance to Hitler in person. In a speech on Heroes' Memorial Day, 16 March 1935, Hitler repudiated the Versailles Treaty and declared that Germany would resume its full sovereign powers. Compulsory conscription and military service for all young men was reintroduced and the resurrection of the German armed forces commenced. Two months later, the Navy was ominously renamed the Kriegsmarine and the German shipyards started to plan for full production.

On 27 January 1938, Hitler issued a decree declaring himself Commander-in-Chief of the armed forces. The authority would be exercised through a new joint high command – Oberkommando der Wehrmacht (OKW) – that oversaw the separate high commands of the country's armed services. OKW was in effect to be Hitler's personal staff, combining strategic, operational and ministerial functions. Generaloberst Wilhelm Keitel was head of OKW with Generalmajor Alfred Jodl as his deputy and leader of the Operations Staff – Führungsstab. In April 1939, Raeder was promoted to *Großadmiral*, Grand Admiral, but it appears that he, and thus the Kriegsmarine, increasingly lost

Commander-in-Chief of the German Navy, Admiral Erich Raeder, Oberbefehlshaber der Marine und Chef der Seekriegsleitung among his men on board *Scharnhorst*.

touch with Nazi reality during this period. The Navy was gradually excluded from the inner circles of the Third Reich and Raeder would only be invited to meetings that had naval affairs on the agenda.[1]

The headquarters of the Navy High Command – Oberkommando der Marine (OKM) including Raeder – had its offices at Tirpitzufer in Berlin, next to the Landwehr Canal. The Naval Warfare Command – Seekriegsleitung (SKL) – responsible for planning and execution of naval operations as well as intelligence, administration and construction, was directly subordinated to OKM. The Chief of Staff of the SKL, Konteradmiral Otto Schniewind, a reserved, analytical and meticulous officer, was Raeder's right-hand man. Under the SKL, Naval Group Command West – Marinegruppenkommando West – with its headquarters at Sengwarden near Wilhelmshaven under the command of Generaladmiral Alfred Saalwächter, oversaw operations in the Heligoland Bight, the North Sea and the Norwegian Sea while Naval Group Command East – Marinegruppenkommando Ost – under Admiral Rolf Carls covered the Baltic from headquarters in Kiel. The naval group commands had on paper operational control within their areas of command, but OKM and SKL would routinely intervene, either directly or through strict, detailed orders. Flottenchef or C-in-C Fleet was Generaladmiral

Hermann Boehm with headquarters in Kiel. During major operations the Flottenchef was usually at sea as task-force commander, on board one of the capital ships. Shortly after the outbreak of war in 1939, Boehm fell out with Saalwächter, and was replaced by Admiral Wilhelm Marschall. At the same time, the command of the Flottenchef was limited to the capital ships and separate commands established for cruisers, destroyers, torpedo boats and other functional groups of ships. The submarine headquarters under Befehlshaber der Unterseeboote (BdU) Konteradmiral Karl Dönitz, also at Sengwarden in early 1940, had significant operational freedom. Most minesweepers and patrol boats were under harbour security command at this stage.

The new ships needed crews, and a large-scale recruitment campaign was initiated while many petty officers and warrant officers were promoted and some commissioned, preparing for expansion. This was good for them, but awkward for the Kriegsmarine, which lost the backbone of its organisation and had to train new petty officers amidst increased competition for the best candidates from the other services. As war drew close, a large number of auxiliaries and support ships were requisitioned, and the lack of experienced officers became even worse.[2]

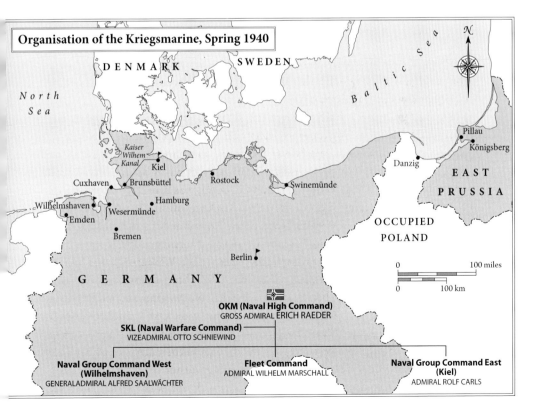

Konteradmiral Otto Schniewind, Chief of Staff of the
SKL or Naval Warfare Command.

Loopholes

The Treaty of Versailles reduced Germany's military forces to a minimum after World War 1. The Navy was reduced to eight out-dated pre-Dreadnought battleships, a similar number of old cruisers and about fifty destroyers, torpedo boats, minesweepers and other smaller vessels. No U-boats were allowed. The programme for new builds was strictly limited, and only in 1927 did the light cruiser *Emden* enter service as the first new ship in a decade. She was robust and functional, but a top speed of 29.5 knots and single 15-cm guns in shielded mountings made her obsolete almost from the day of her launch. The Design Office announced her as displacing 5,400 tons, some 600 tons less than allowed, using all possible loopholes, including the ambiguity between tons and long tons, to the full. In fact, her standard displacement exceeded 6,950 tons, well over the limit. The Allied Control Commission failed to condemn this and, once played successfully, these tricks were exploited in all future designs until limits were altogether ignored.[3]

Designing an efficient capital ship with no more than 28-cm guns within the 10,000-ton displacement limit created even bigger challenges. The first, *Deutschland,* was not only the first German ship to carry triple turrets and aircraft catapults she was also the first capital ship in any navy with solely diesel propulsion: four engines per shaft. It was intended she should outgun all faster ships and outrun any with larger guns, but a maximum speed of only 28 knots would make the latter somewhat of a challenge, even if few Allied capital ships in commission at the time could catch her. Launched in May 1931, *Deutschland* was initially classified by the Kriegsmarine as a *Panzerschiff* or 'armoured ship'. Officially within the 10,000-ton limit, she was nonetheless close to 15,000 tons when loaded. The British Admiralty looked at her with some concern, but though fast, she and her two sisters were not fast enough

The light cruiser *Emden*. She was essentially a WW1 design. Mixed oil and coal firing and a twin-shaft single-reduction geared turbine gave her a mediocre top speed and the eight 15-cm guns in shielded single mountings were an equally antiquated arrangement – but were the only guns available at the time of completion.

and with unreliable engines and poor performance in heavy seas, they never achieved what was expected of them. Up to seven additional similar ships were planned, but only *Admiral Scheer* and *Admiral Graf Spee* were completed. Proper capital ships were needed, and the engineers of the Design Office were sent back to the drawing board. Redesign took time and only in May and June of 1935 were the keels of the battleships *Gneisenau* and *Scharnhorst* laid down. *Bismarck* and *Tirpitz* would follow, but not be operational until 1941 and 1942 respectively, by which time their value was doubtful.[4]

The making of a destroyer force was started with the six ships of the *Raubvogel* class. The first, *Möwe*, was launched in March 1926. Armed with three 10.5-cm guns, six torpedo tubes and capable of a fair 34 knots, they were primarily designed for torpedo attacks but also equipped for mine laying and coastal escort duties. Six subsequent ships of the slightly larger and faster *Raubtier* class were commissioned between October 1928 and August 1929. All these vessels were later reclassified as torpedo boats, *Torpedoboote*. True destroyers would not be available for several years.

For the Kriegsmarine, the war with Britain came several years too early. Raeder had to revise all his plans and accept that resources would have to be spent on building far more U-boats than he had foreseen. The Kriegsmarine could not sustain another humiliating and passive existence as in the previous war. He could not leave the fighting to the Army and Luftwaffe, the new air force. The Royal Navy had been neglected during the 1930s but remained a major challenge, and it would be crucial to find ways of operating with the ships at hand while making those in the pipeline ready for war. If the British

Deutschland in Sognefjord, western Norway, April 1934. Hitler was on board for this voyage. *Deutschland* was renamed *Lützow* after returning from her first war cruise in 1939. Hitler decided it was unacceptable that a ship named 'Germany' might be sunk.

gained the upper hand, the German surface fleet would be degraded to small ships and submarines.

On the eve of WW2, the Kriegsmarine had in commission two battleships, *Scharnhorst* and *Gneisenau*, two old battleships, *Schlesien* and *Schleswig-Holstein*, three *Panzerschiffe* – *Admiral Graf Spee*, *Admiral Scheer* and *Deutschland* – one heavy cruiser, *Admiral Hipper*, six light cruisers, *Emden*, *Leipzig*, *Nürnberg*, *Köln*, *Karlsruhe* and *Königsberg*, thirty-four destroyers and large torpedo boats, fifty-seven U-boats and some forty other small vessels. Within weeks, virtually all building of large surface ships, except those near completion, was suspended to focus on U-boats and smaller vessels. In the end, *Bismarck*, *Tirpitz*, *Blücher* and *Prinz Eugen* were the only ships larger than destroyers to be commissioned by the Kriegsmarine after the outbreak of the war. Germany's first aircraft carrier, *Graf Zeppelin*, was launched in late 1938, but work was suspended in 1940 and she ended up as a useless hulk.[5]

Heavy Cruisers

Most of the German naval staff considered cruisers essential in the Baltic as well as the North Sea and the Atlantic, and vital resources were spent designing and building such ships. The light cruisers *Karlsruhe*, *Königsberg*

Hitler visiting the bridge of *Deutschland* during the 1934 voyage.
He was no naval enthusiast at all, and rumour had it
that he quickly became seasick and locked himself away in his cabin.

and *Köln* commissioned between February 1929 and January 1930, displaced 6,650 tons standard, an undeniable breach of the Versailles Treaty, followed by a further two with modified designs. The Anglo-German Naval Agreement of 18 June 1935 limited the German Navy to 35 per cent of the British strength prescribed by the treaties. This prevented the construction of additional 'armoured cruisers' but allowed for five modern heavy cruisers. Orders for the first two, *Blücher* and *Admiral Hipper*, were placed in secrecy by the Kriegsmarine in October 1934 at Deutsche Werke in Kiel and Blohm & Voss in Hamburg respectively. In parallel, a development and construction contract was awarded to the Krupp company for 20.3-cm (8-inch) main guns and turrets, which was the largest calibre allowed on cruisers according to the Washington Treaty. Following the design specifications of the treaty, *Admiral Hipper* was officially 10,000 tons when taken into service. In reality she had a displacement of 14,247 tons standard and 18,208 tons full load, *Blücher* a few hundred tons more.

Admiral Hipper was commissioned in April 1939. As was the case for most large German ships, the forecastle was found to be very wet, even in moderate seas. During a refit in late 1939, a raked 'Atlantic' clipper bow was fitted, the bridge improved, and a funnel cap added to prevent smoke invading the

The launch of *Blücher* on 8 June 1937.

bridge platforms. This made her a very handsome, efficient-looking ship – and very difficult to distinguish from the battleships at a distance: a problem the Royal Navy and RAF Coastal Command would face several times. These modifications were fitted to *Blücher* before she was commissioned on 20 September 1939. When released from the yard in Kiel on 30 March 1940, *Blücher* displaced 14,224 tons standard, and 18,694 tons fully loaded. She was 195 m (640 ft) long at the waterline and with the clipper bow, her overall length was 205.9 m (676 ft). She was designed primarily for surface warfare, but also had some anti-aircraft, anti-submarine, mine warfare, and signals intelligence capabilities.

Blücher's main armament for surface warfare comprised eight 20.3-cm C/34 guns in twin turrets, *Anton, Bruno, Caesar* and *Dora* from bow to stern in German terminology. All guns were provided with high-explosive, armour-piercing and semi-armour-piercing (HE, AP, SAP) rounds and the magazines for B and C turrets also had star shells. The 122-kg shells were fired using a two-part propellant charge, rate of fire being four rounds per gun per minute with an effective range of 25,000 metres. The turrets revolved electrically, as part of the electro-hydraulic system. Otherwise, turrets, hoists, breeches and loaders were operated hydraulically. Turret *Anton* had restrictions on firing directly ahead at low elevations (for ranges less than 5,000 metres) due to the raised forecastle.

The commissioning of *Blücher* on 20 September 1939. The captain,
Kapitän zur See Woldag, enters his ship in splendid solitude.

Blücher's secondary armament consisted of twelve 10.5-cm C/33 multi-purpose guns in six stabilised twin mountings produced by Rheinmetall. These guns had a maximum range of 17,000 metres, with an effective range of 12,000 metres, using 26.5-kg fixed ammunition with a shell weight of 15.1 kg. The firing rate per gun was 15–18 rounds per minute. Both types of guns were efficient and robust, although the 10.5-cm mounts had some electrical problems due to insufficient attention to watertightness.[6]

Usually, bearing and elevation for the 20.3-cm and 10.5-cm guns were received from one of the centralised, gyro-stabilised fire-control directors or from the centrally controlled data and firing system connected to the calculators. The director was connected to an order-transmission unit and a fire-control transmitter passing information to one of the two fire-control centres, fore and aft. Both centres used a position-keeping calculator and a ballistic calculator, deep in the ship. Any director could provide data to the guns of the main or secondary armament, as well as the torpedoes.

In an emergency the guns could be aimed directly at the target by the trainer at the telescopic sights. B and C turrets had their own rangefinders, but the rest of the guns depended on central rangefinders, or as a last resorts, assessments done by the gun commander supported by telescopic sights or binoculars. There were four 7-metre horizontal, stereoscopic rangefinders,

Top: There were no common canteens or dining rooms on board and men ate and spent off-duty time with their mess or *Korporalschaft*.
Above: Members of each *Korporalschaft* lining up to collect food for the whole group.

one on the foretop tower, one at the aft fire-control and one each on B and C turrets. In addition, one 6-metre rangefinder was in the forward fire-control centre. Switching between directors, calculators and local control was unproblematic. Each fire control could take over from any of the others should they fall out. It was also possible to divide the 20.3-cm battery to engage two targets simultaneously using different directors.

Entering combat, the captain would use a target finder, *Zielsäule,* literally a 'target column' or aiming post, on the open bridge to point out his chosen target to the gunnery officers. The main weapons would be directed by one of the gunnery officers. The First Gunnery Officer, I. Artillerieoffizier or I. AO, was usually in the forward fire-control in the foretop or *Vormarsstand* above the bridge. The navigation bridge, the wheelhouse and the forward fire-control centre were co-located in front of the tower, above the B-turret. Both navigation and combat management took place from the vessel's bridge, either from the open part, the wheelhouse or from inside the armoured citadel. The admiral's bridge was in the middle of the forward tower but had no instruments for navigation or fire-control. The Fourth Gunnery Officer (IV. AO) was in the forward fire-control centre behind the navigation bridge. Outside, between the tower and the fire-control centre, there were on both sides of the ship directors for guns, star-shells, searchlights and torpedoes. The Third Gunnery Officer (III. AO) usually had his station in the aft fire-control centre behind C turret with similar directors as forward. Each gunnery officer handled a *Zielgeber* fire-control director, assisted by two men. Their preferred method was usually salvo-firing and to hit the target, a 'ladder' was first fired – three salvos spaced 400 metres apart – or alternatively ranging shots – 'bracketing'. Rapid salvos were then ordered when the target was straddled or hit.

The 10.5-cm guns were also part of the anti-aircraft system (AA) controlled by the Second Gunnery Officer (II. AO) had his normal position in the anti-aircraft control centre in the tower with two gun-target columns. The forward AA directors for the 10.5-cm guns were designated A (starboard) and B (port), the after directors C (starboard) and D (port). Starboard 10.5-cm mounts were known as Stb I, Stb II and Stb. III – and similarly on the port side. The light anti-aircraft armament included twelve twin-mounted 3.7-cm guns and eight single 2-cm guns, better than many contemporary ships. The 3.7-cm gun was semi-automatic with a rate of fire of up to 80 rounds per barrel per minute. The novel gyro-stabilisation was effective, though not perfect. The 2-cm gun was fully automatic but manually trained and elevated with hand wheels. It had a theoretical rate of fire of 280 rounds per minute. In practice, though, it fired at around 180 rpm due to an inadequate magazine design. The 10.5-cm guns had a rather low rate of fire but, supplemented by 3.7-cm, and 2-cm guns, they gave the cruiser a potent anti-aircraft defence.

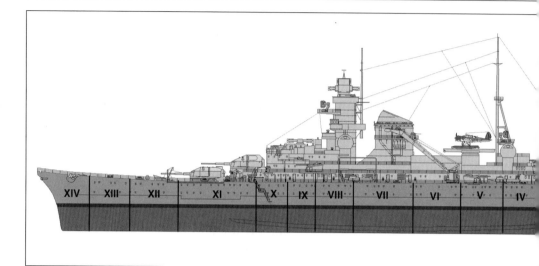

Blücher was equipped with a Funkmess-Ortung radar FuMO22, which was a well-kept secret. The two 6-metre mattress aerials of the FuMO22 set were mounted on the rangefinder cupola above the *Vormarsstand* and could not rotate independently of the cupola. Radar was in its infancy when *Blücher* was built and the type on board could only track one object at a time. Its main use was ranging of targets detected visually. Accuracy was poor and it did not work properly near a coastline or in fjords. Blind-firing by radar was not possible.

Up to three Arado Ar-196 floatplanes could be carried for scouting, reconnaissance and spotting for the artillery. The crew consisted of a pilot and a navigator/gunner. Each aircraft could carry two 50-kg bombs.

There were two separate hydrophone systems on board for passive underwater listening in addition to an active S-Geräte sonar. This was not as effective as the comparable British system known as asdic. Twelve torpedo tubes completed the offensive surface armament in two triple mounts on each side. The torpedoes could be aimed and fired from two torpedo directors in the forward fire-control centre or secondary directors further aft. Each G7a torpedo had a warhead of 280 kg of TNT. At 40 knots, the range was 7,500 metres. Four to six depth-charges on the quarterdeck could be fired electronically. Mines and tracks for minelaying equipment could be carried but were normally kept ashore. Paravanes aboard were for self-protection use in areas threatened by mines.

Signals warfare and intelligence was restricted in 1940. Very High Frequency VHF – Ultrakurzwelle (UKW) – radio-telephone communication between ships had become an integral part of the Kriegsmarine's battle

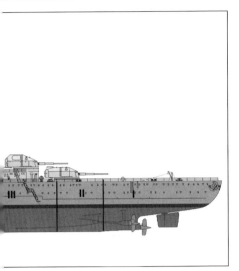

The hull of *Blücher* was subdivided into 14 sections by bulkheads; these sections were numbered from stern to bow.

management. This was normally excellent as it had a very short range and could be used between ships at sea without being intercepted or used for direction-finding by the enemy. *Blücher* was well equipped with electronic equipment and had four radio rooms. Radio room A housed personnel of the cryptanalysis and monitoring service known as the Beobachtungsdienst or B-dienst. Most large ships had B-dienst units on board, which in addition to encoding and decoding own messages were expert in reading enemy signals, monitoring broadcasts, jamming and sending of fake signals.

Blücher's hull was constructed of longitudinal steel frames with an inner and an outer part. There were numerous frames and bulkheads as well as an armoured intermediate deck along the entire length of the ship reinforcing the structure. A double bottom extended over 72 per cent of the keel. The inner hull was separated into fourteen watertight sections by transverse bulkheads or hull frames. These *Abteilungen* were numbered with Roman numerals from stern to bow, thus Abt. I was the aftermost hull section while Abt. IX and X were under the forward fire-control centre and bridge. Bulkheads or *Spanten* were numbered in Arabic numerals also from stern to bow.

The ship had five main decks, bottom to top: lower platform deck, upper platform deck, armoured deck, battery deck and the main deck with the superstructure and guns. On the main deck between turrets A and D there were compartments for the sick bay, torpedo and artillery maintenance, the aircraft hangar, galleys for seamen and officers and the officers' mess. Accommodation for officers and seamen was located on the battery deck and the armoured deck. The armoured deck provided protection for the magazines and propulsion systems. The 80-mm thick belt armour covering the sides of the ship had a height of 3.8 metres and went 1.7 metres below the waterline. The main turrets had 70–160 mm armour, the conning tower 50–150 mm, and the bulkheads 20 mm. The main deck had 12–30 mm while the armoured deck had 20–50 mm. Like most other contemporary cruisers, *Blücher* was vulnerable to shells hitting from above. Steering was controlled by a single rudder and the ship had three shafts, each with a three-bladed propeller.

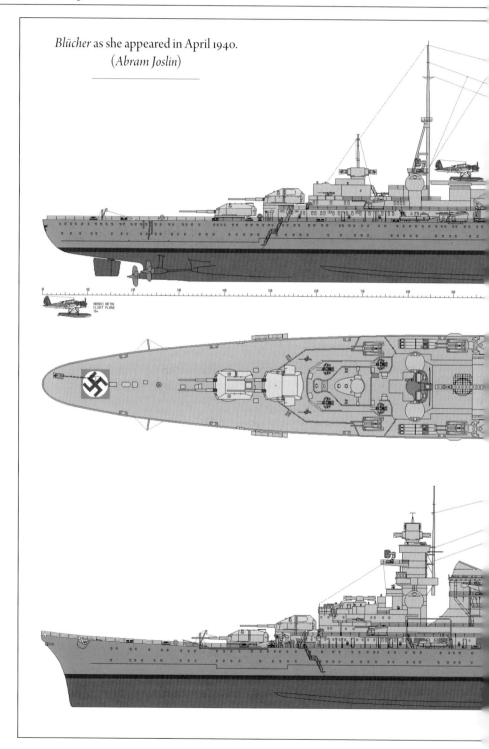

Blücher as she appeared in April 1940.
(*Abram Joslin*)

ARADO AR 196
FLOAT PLANE
11m

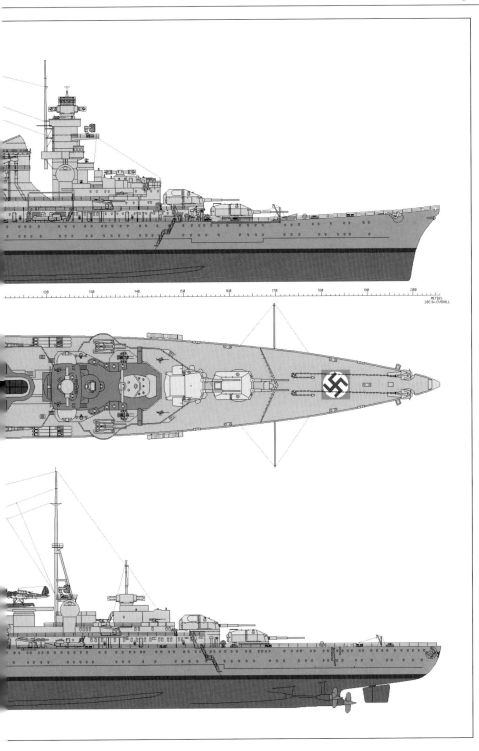

120   130   140   150   160   170   180   190   200

METERS
205.9m OVERALL

Engines, turbines, boilers and electrical generator compartments were distributed from sections II to IX, also numbered from stern to bow, thus K1 Kesselraum 1 was *Blücher*'s after boiler room, T2/3 Turbinenräume 2 and 3 were the forward engine rooms alongside each other. There were twelve oil-fired boilers aboard the ship, arranged in three boiler rooms in sections VI, VII and VIII. The Wagner was a high-pressure, hot steam, water-tube boiler with natural water circulation and two Saacke burners to each boiler. The burners were under Askania automatic control. The introduction of the high-pressure steam boilers was intended to reduce weight and need for space, lower the fuel consumption and increase manoeuvrability by faster power adjustments. The advanced boilers and the hydraulically operated regulator were complicated, however, and problems arose with the new systems from inadequate testing before the war. Further complication was the expansion of personnel and a large turnover of qualified men after the war began. Three sets of Blohm & Voss geared turbines in separate housings were contained in two turbine rooms. The turbines driving the outer shafts were together in the forward turbine-room in section V while the centre shaft was connected to the turbine in the after turbine-room in section III. Turbines and boilers were grouped together, but there were some who were critical of the chosen solution. If the boiler and turbine rooms had been arranged on the unit system, with turbines and boilers in each of the three hull sections, the propulsion system would have been less vulnerable.

Blücher was equipped with three electricity plants with four diesel generators and six turbogenerators each. Total electrical output was 2,900 kW. Electrical plant 1 and turbine 1 were in section III. Electrical plant 2 was in section IV. Turbines 2 and 3 were in section V. Electrical plant 3 was in section IX. At low speed, *Blücher* was unpredictably affected by wind and currents and with rudder hard over at high speed, the ships of this class heeled up to 14 degrees and lost up to 50 per cent speed. *Blücher* carried three bow anchors and one stern anchor. There were six boats aboard the ship and two cranes. The damage control organisation had three fire-fighting pumps, ten electrically driven pumps and a leak/bilge pump at its disposal. All pumps could be reversed to flood the magazines.

Upon completion, *Blücher* began what should have been intensive trials and working up in the Baltic. Harsh winter conditions with abundant sea-ice and extensive modifications, however, meant that she had only spent some twenty days at sea when it was decided to deploy her to Oslo. Neither the torpedo batteries nor the 20.3-cm guns had been fired live during the exercises. The young crew had been grouped together while she was still in the yard and they knew each other well, but few had experience from other ships – far less from war. The officers were largely inexperienced and only a handful had been in battle. Emergency training, damage control and action-stations drills were deficient or at best incomplete. Manuals were under implementation, except for those of the engine room, which were still being drafted. Nevertheless, SKL saw no particular risk in assigning the new cruiser to this presumably simple task and *Blücher*'s first and only captain, the 47-year-old Kapitän zur Zee Heinrich Woldag, was ordered to head for the Baltic with *Emden* soon as both ships were ready.

At the next level down, the second-in-command was Fregattenkapitän Erich Heymann. First Artillery Officer was Korvettenkapitän Kurt-Eduard Engelmann. Below deck, the Senior Engineering Officer, Fregattenkapitän Karl Thannemann ruled supreme.[7]

Key Officers on *Blücher* in April 1940		
Kommandant	Captain	KptzS Heinrich Woldag
I. Offizier	First officer	FKpt Erich Heymann
I. Artillerieoffizier	First gunnery officer	KKpt Kurt-Eduard Engelmann
II. Artillerieoffizier	Second gunnery officer	KKpt Hans-Erik Pochhammer
III. Artillerieoffizier	Third gunnery officer	KptLt Georg Hagene
FlaMWOffz.	AA gunnery officer	OblnzS Heinrich Wilhelm Schürdt
Art.-technischer Offizier	Artillery officer	OblnzS Friedrich Markworth
Leitender Ingenieur	Chief engineer	FKpt (Ing) Karl Thannemann
E-Ingenieur	Chief electrical engineer	KKpt (Ing) Helmut Karbe
Leckwehroffizier	Damage control officer	KKpt (Ing) Jürgen Engelhardt-Bergeshof
Navigationsoffizier	Navigation officer	KKpt Hugo Förster
Verwaltungsoffizier	Admin officer	KKpt Ramm
Rollenoffizier	Division officer	KKpt Werner Czygan
Bordnachrichtenoffizier	Intelligence officer	KptLt Walter Pommerehne
Adjutant	Adjutants	KKpt Kurt Zöpfel OblnzS Walter Freyberg-Eisenberg-Almendingen
I. Schiffsarzt	Senior doctor	Dr. Med. Bruno Kort

KptzS = Kapitän zur See; FKpt = Fregattenkapitän; KKpt = Korvettenkapitän; KptLt = Kapitänleutnant; OblnzS = Oberleutnant zur See

Chapter 2
The Price of Neutrality

A Hundred Incidents

In her memoirs, US Minister to Norway in 1940, Florence Harriman wrote:

> Hindsight we all seem to have. But it is fantastic that none of the things which happened in the week preceding the fatal daybreak of April 9th awakened us to danger. A hundred incidents should have prepared us. Instead, we were transfixed, still watching the war in Finland.[1]

The news of the German attack on Poland on 1 September 1939 was received with anxious apprehension in Norway. The empathy with Poland and anger with Germany was virtually unanimous, but so was the feeling that this was not Norway's war. During the afternoon of 1 September, the Norwegian government issued a declaration of neutrality and mobilised the Navy and part of the Coast Artillery. When Britain and France declared war on Germany two days later, the neutrality was extended to cover that conflict as well. With a firm belief that a proclamation of neutrality would suffice, the Norwegian government continued with business-as-usual as much as possible, adapting to the belligerents' demands and interests, believing that comprehensive neutrality regulations and a rudimentary coastal defence was sufficient to preserve Norway as a sovereign, independent state while Europe was at war. Great Britain was, as in the First War, seen as the guarantor for the country's freedom. Britain's Royal Navy ruled supreme in the North Sea and was best served by a neutral Norway, it was believed in Oslo. Germany could not and would not challenge the British naval hegemony. Neutrality was for all practical purposes seen as a political issue handled by the government. The military was the tool that upheld the neutrality, but the politicians did not initiate a dialogue with the military leaders to make sure that they understood the abilities and limitations of the country's military forces and the time and funds it would take to mobilise the defences if the crisis escalated.

A Labour government had taken office in 1935. The concept of war was repulsive to the Norwegian Prime Minister Johan Nygaardsvold and, for him, it was fundamental that Norway should be neutral. As long as he was Prime

Norway's Prime Minister Johan Nygaardsvold. He focussed on economic
and social progress for the large majority of the population and though he was
not entirely successful in his party's maxim 'all people at work', Norway was a
good society for most of its inhabitants by 1939. He was affectionately known
as 'Gubben' or The Old Man.

Minister, his country would not take part in any war. If the unthinkable
happened, though, he was equally insistent that Norway should not end up
on the 'wrong side' of the conflict. To side with Hitler's Germany was not an
option.

International issues were mostly handled by Foreign Minister Halvdan
Koht who took it upon himself to steer Norway outside the conflict. Koht was
a complex individual. He had been professor of history at the University of
Oslo and his level of learning was immense. He strongly believed that the
rights and duties of neutral states were laid down in established principles and
precedents of international law and saw no need for alternatives. A pacifist

Minister of Foreign Affairs Halvdan Koht.

by his own definition, Koht considered the best defence for a nation to be 'informed and sober politics' rather than armed forces and he believed neutrality, once declared, could be maintained without substantial armed forces.

Only if political means failed should the armed forces be alerted and prepared to fight. This relied on a 'Prescient Foreign Office', being able to decide if and when the international situation required military attention. The problem was that neither Koht nor many other members of the government or the Storting had much experience or competence in military matters.[2] Neither Koht nor any other member of the government, made any serious efforts to understand the state of the Norwegian defences and what an appropriate preparedness would mean in operational terms. Rather than developing a long-term programme, the government, with the support of the majority of the Storting, believed that extraordinary grants to the armed forces would put things right. Years of political neglect could not be restored overnight, however, and a constructive development would have required an efficient coordination between the services that the Ministry of Defence was unable to secure. When danger approached, it was in reality too late to take control of a complicated situation. In addition, significant parts of the limited Norwegian military resources were transferred to northern Norway for fear of Soviet intrusions. Perhaps worst of all, the politicians in Oslo did not comprehend that long neglect of the armed forces had created discontent among the officer corps and that many of them, certainly the younger ones with eagerness and initiative, had returned to civilian life.[3]

Koht's distaste for Nazism was indisputable, but it was paralleled by a rejection of imperialism in general. He later wrote:

In September 1939, the most challenging and difficult time of my life started. The seven months [before the German invasion] was every hour filled by a restless struggle to keep the country out of the war and secure its freedom. I was on duty day and night, weekdays and weekends – like on a tightrope between the belligerents. There is no doubt that the relationship with Britain – and therefore France – was the most difficult during this period and wore hard on my nerves. Politically, ideologically, nationally and personally my affinity, as well as that of the nation, rested with the Allies. Still, the British had a demanding attitude that was difficult to accept and they continuously forced their wishes onto us instead of negotiating affably.[4]

In London it was recognised that Norway might be important for Germany as a source of vital supplies. To prevent this and tie the country as closely as possible to the Allies with the smallest of means, Cecil Dormer, British Minister to Norway, was instructed to assure Koht formally and in confidence that Britain would give Norway support against potential German aggression and consider 'a German attack on Norway as tantamount to an attack on this country'. This he did on 11 September 1939.[5] Koht later wrote that the assurance pleased him and, as it was given to him in strict confidence, made him consider it a trustworthy commitment. As he 'did not wish to tie [Norway] closer to Britain than it already was', he replied curtly that he did not believe Germany would attack Norway as there was little to gain from that. Dormer reported to London that Koht made few remarks, but it probably 'had a good effect'. On the 22nd, the British Minister was back, though. He confirmed that Britain would respect the declared Norwegian neutrality, but this time added that this would only apply as long as Germany did the same. Again, Koht did not respond much, but later wrote that this visit caused him concern as it made British respect for Norwegian sovereignty depend on London's interpretation of third-party action, not Norway's own handling of affairs.

On 22 December, Koht told the Foreign Affairs Committee that he believed Britain and France would very much like to drive Norway out of its neutrality and into the war. He realised, correctly, that circles in London saw a direct interest in undermining Norwegian neutrality and provoking retaliatory German actions, which would force Norway into the war on the Allied side. He mistakenly believed, though, that Berlin would find the reasons for maintaining Norwegian neutrality more compelling than those for military action and not rise to the Allied lure. On 6 April, Koht revealed his thinking to the Storting:

Norway has time and again in various forms, but always with the same basic idea, announced to all the world that Norwegian policy is to defend the country from being drawn into war. We have nothing to gain from entering the war. We can't imagine going to war for another purpose than defending our independence and liberty […] A neutral state must observe the same rights and privileges versus all belligerents […] For this, we have international regulations and agreements […] providing security and justice at all times.[6]

Koht believed firmly in logic and judiciousness. In all his rationality, however, he failed to grasp that the leaderships in London, Paris and Berlin had a logic of their own. That the belligerents would be prepared to cross international boundaries and ignore declarations of neutrality if they believed it served a greater purpose, appears to have been inconceivable to him. Even after Austria, Czechoslovakia and Poland had been overrun, Koht still believed Hitler would decide that Germany was best served in the long run by a neutral Norway. For personal and political reasons, Koht declined several invitations to go to Berlin. He never travelled to London either, but later alleged this to be coincidental and largely due to lack of a good opportunity. That the politicians in London were offended by his apparent lack of distinction between the aggressive German warfare and what they considered defensive measures, did not occur to Koht. 'My impression was that both the Germans and the Allies were uncertain of me. I think this was to the benefit of my country,' he wrote. One may wonder.[7]

In December 1939, Oberst Birger Ljungberg was appointed Defence Minister. He was, according to himself, 'a conservative and not part of the labour movement at all'.[8] The choice of a professional military man was well received in the Storting, where it was believed the government would now be guided in the right direction. Welcoming his new minister to the government, though, Nygaardsvold bluntly advised him to 'concentrate on the administration of the defence [as] the political side would be handled by the other ministers'. Most likely, Nygaardsvold and Koht believed that the already mobilised forces were adequate to handle the neutrality issues and that the defence minister was taking care of military matters in a satisfactory manner. Between 1 September 1939, and 8 April 1940, however, there were no meetings between the government and the military leaders to discuss the political and military situation and there is no evidence to suggest that the Ministry of Defence sought to improve the situation. Only rarely did any of the ministers, beyond Ljungberg, meet the military leaders.[9] After the war, Ljungberg left few comments relating to the events of 1940 but in 1947 he wrote:

In the autumn of 1938, just after Munich, I came to London as Norwegian representative to the Non-intervention Commission for Spain and could

A handful of the most modern ships of the RNN in the autumn of 1939. The minelayer
Olav Tryggvason in the middle, flanked by the destroyers *Sleipner, Æger* and *Gyller* to
the left and one of the *Trygg*-class torpedo boats to the right.

see how poorly Great Britain was prepared for the coming war. They were
working hard [to change this], but we foreigners understood only too
well thatEngland would have to think of itself first. For Norway, this was
decisive. I considered it highly unlikely that England in the near future
should be able to give Norway – or others – effective help in case of an
attack.[10]

Ljungberg joined the government on 27 December 1939. He did his best
to put the Norwegian defence forces into some kind of shape, suitable for the
Neutrality Watch, but discovered quickly that, even though the government
provided liberal emergency grants, there was very little military equipment
available for purchase. The belligerents had little to sell and the armament
industries of other neutrals like Sweden and Switzerland were tied down
by long-term contracts. Later Ljungberg defended his lack of resolve
and initiatives in the few months he served by arguing that the Germans
would have come anyway and with their superior army and air force would
have laid Norway in total ruins had the resistance been stronger. 'We did
what we could with the means we had,' he said, adding 'and we did what

we considered best for our country. We had to follow the line that would mean least harm for the country. I doubt that it could have gone better, quite contrary I think it could have gone much worse.'[11] A statement not universally accepted then or now.

Neutrality

The Navy was seen as the key defender of a vigilant but passive neutrality, focusing on escort and patrol duties, but prepared to handle 'occasional violations'. This would not always be easy and the officers of ships and forts had to be prepared to respond to non-compliance with regulations by use of force. The air units of the Army and Navy were mobilised in support as were a few Army units and a limited part of the Coast Artillery. No minefields were laid, and the manning of the forts was kept low.

The Norwegian Naval Defence Force (Sjøforsvaret) consisted in 1940 of the navy proper (Marinen) as well as the Coast Artillery (Kystartilleriet) and the Naval Air Arm (Marinens Flyvevåben). The C-in-C, Admiral Henry Diesen, was titled Commanding Admiral – Kommanderende Admiral – and his HQ and staff were in Oslo. Below him, the coast was divided into three Sea Defence Districts (SDD), in turn sub-divided into Sea Defence Sectors (SDS). Each District was led by a Sea Defence Commander, based in Horten, Bergen and Tromsø respectively. The commanders of the coastal forts were subordinated to the relevant Sea Defence Commanders as were the aircraft of the Naval Air Arm.

The Royal Norwegian Navy (RNN) of 1939 was not a significant instrument of deterrence. Once a symbol of the Norwegian quest for independence at the beginning of the twentieth century, general disarmament and political developments during the thirties had reduced the once impressive naval force to an aging reserve fleet. By the end of September 1939, all ships fit for commissioning were in service, including two coastal defence ships. They had been well looked after while in reserve and most were found to be in acceptable condition.

By 8 April 1940, 113 vessels were in commission with the RNN. There were fifty-one chartered guardships and eight auxiliaries none of which were expected to engage in combat. Among the fifty-four warships, seventeen were of pre-1900 vintage. Seventeen torpedo boats were deployed along the coast, battle-ready but not organised for combat; seven small destroyers acted as escort vessels and supported the Neutrality Watch. The two coastal defence ships and six B-class submarines were the only vessels that could be considered anything like a strategic reserve.

Some 5,200 naval officers and men were in service aboard or ashore. Of these, 3,565 were seamen and 237 reserve officers, drafted for the neutrality period. The rest were professional officers and NCOs from the pre-war Navy. Some NCOs were given temporary commissions and sent to command guardships, leaving holes in the ranks and disrupting well-exercised routines and relationships aboard the more modern vessels. In addition, staff officers were drafted for onshore duties and coast-watch posts, air bases and communication centres were manned.[12]

Admiral Diesen considered the Navy more important than the Coast Artillery for the Neutrality Watch and the latter was given low priority during the mobilisation. The forts would have a role should an invasion be attempted and there would presumably be time enough to mobilise and prepare them, should the situation escalate. Stationary guns were of little use for escort purposes and since both parties appeared to intend to respect Norwegian neutrality,

Commanding Admiral Henry Diesen.

aggressive intrusions in force were not anticipated. Fewer than 3,000 officers and ratings were drafted to the Coast Artillery, around one third of the full roll. There was a general shortage of younger officers, in particular sergeants and sub-lieutenants, which meant a strict prioritisation of which guns and batteries to man. Test firing of the larger guns with full-charge ammunition was usually not allowed and neither guns nor men were prepared for extended firing, all the more so as the technical personnel needed for sustained live firing were limited. With an unfortunate short-sightedness, all the youngest and most recently trained ratings were drafted first. Thus, by the spring of 1940, a good number of the gunners had finished their tours and were being replaced by older men, trained up to twenty years earlier, or youngsters totally new to military life. At some forts, the crew had only been at their guns for a few days when the alarm sounded in the small hours of 9 April. No minefields were laid as it was believed these would disrupt and endanger civilian traffic.[13]

Foreign merchant ships from all nations, neutral as well as belligerent, could according to the neutrality regulations, sail legally inside Norwegian territorial waters. They should normally, however, stay inside the Leads – the fairway between the islands and the mainland – or between the baseline and the three-mile limit. The baseline was normally drawn between the outermost islands and skerries. Anything three miles beyond this was considered to be in international waters. Any stopping or anchoring in territorial waters should be approved in advance as should entering the inner waterways of the Leads. Radio could not be used by foreign vessels and guns for self-defence should be stowed away below deck or made inoperable as long as the ships were inside Norwegian waters. Since the Napoleonic Wars, Norway had unilaterally declared a four-mile territorial zone, opposed by most other European countries. To avoid undue problems, the Norwegian authorities chose to back down and enforce only the three nautical mile limit for the duration of the war. It remained a challenge, however, that some fjord mouths were wider than three miles, creating a difficulty over how to define the territorial limit between the nearest points of land.

Foreign naval vessels had access to Norwegian waters for no more than 24 hours of so-called innocent passage, when not part of any ongoing military operation.

Restricted areas, known as *krigshavn* areas, were defined near fortifications and key harbours such as the Oslofjord and the Leads around Kristiansand, Bergen, Trondheim and Vardø. Inside these, merchant ships could only travel by permission during daylight, while foreign warships were banned from entering altogether. To control ships not conforming to the regulations inside a *krigshavn*, the Coast Artillery and the Navy had clear instruction to use all available force, after due warning, in other words fire a warning shot and then fire for effect. Outside the *krigshavn* areas the instruction was to use force only when ordered by the Commanding Admiral or if being attacked.[14]

One episode in particular, the so-called *Berlin* affair from World War 1, had an impact on how the protection of Norwegian neutrality was handled then and in 1939/40. *Berlin* was a 17,300-ton auxiliary cruiser, with a crew of 450 men. On 16 November 1914 she appeared inside Trondheim harbour having passed into the *krigshavn* without being detected by any of the naval vessels in the fjord. The darkened ship had passed all defence lines during some convenient snow-showers, without being stopped and searched. In order to remain in Norwegian waters beyond the permitted 24 hours, the captain reported he had engine damage, and agreed to comply with the requirement of disarming his ship.

The unauthorised appearance of a warship inside Trondheim *krigshavn* was an embarrassment for the RNN, all the more so as before trespassing, *Berlin* had laid mines in British waters (which had in fact sunk the battleship *Audacious*). Following the *Berlin* affair, the Navy and the Coast Artillery made efforts to improve their ability to raise the alarm if unauthorised entering of Norwegian territorial waters should occur. More guardships were requisitioned and deployed in layered zones and these were backed with onshore observation posts. Improved warning systems were installed and the threshold for sounding an alarm lowered. Finally, the wording of the regulations that unknown intruders should, after due warning, be met with determination was underlined. These measures had an impact during the rest of the WW1 neutrality period and would still apply in 1940, especially among those officers who had served in 1914–18.[15]

Chapter 3

'Winston is Back'[1]

Control of the Approaches

In the late thirties, about 10 per cent of Britain's imports came from Scandinavia, mostly food – bacon, butter, eggs and fish – or important raw materials – iron ore, ferro-alloys, timber, wood-pulp and paper. Should these supplies be cut off, the country would suffer, in particular from the loss of iron ore, timber and butter. Exports *to* Scandinavia made up about 10 per cent of the total British export trade, mainly coal, cotton, wool, machinery and chemicals, but it was not considered problematic if this should come to a halt. The direst concern in London over Scandinavia was that the countries might not actively join the blockade of Germany. British knowledge of Norwegian politics and culture was limited and the fact that the Norwegian government was socialist added to the concern. Even so, the sympathies of the country's government and people would, according to the British Minister to Oslo, Cecil Dormer, 'favour the British cause, to a greater extent perhaps than in any other neutral country'.

One of the few who showed an interest in Norway, was the First Lord of the Admiralty (Britain's Navy Minister), Winston Churchill, appointed on 3 September 1939 after a long spell without a government job. Why this was so is slightly puzzling as before the outbreak of war he apparently had the same disregard for the country as most other British politicians or military leaders. Shortly after his appointment, he started to refer to the Norwegian coastline being of 'immense strategic significance' and severing the German iron ore import from Scandinavia, particularly the portion that went through Narvik, as paramount. Soon after his arrival at the Admiralty, staff members who had considered alternative British naval strategies in a new war, pointed to Norway's significance based on experiences from the First War. Churchill initially had his eyes on the Baltic, but the First Sea Lord (the professional head of the Royal Navy) Admiral Dudley Pound reasoned against sending ships into such confined waters, arguing that sending destroyers into Norwegian territorial waters to lay minefields, supported by the Home Fleet, was a much better option. This would infringe Norwegian neutrality, though, and Churchill was at first against 'any drastic operations like landing forces or stationing ships in Norwegian waters' but accepted that the Admiralty could assess the option of blocking the Leads to German naval and merchant traffic by laying minefields 'at some lonely spots on the coast, as far north as convenient'. It is quite possible that the First Lord's interest in Norwegian territorial waters, simply grew from the lack of alternatives. The thing that mattered most to Churchill was that Norway stood firm on the Allied side in the fight against Nazi Germany and that Great Britain could take advantage of what Norway could contribute in terms of its merchant fleet.[2]

First Lord of the Admiralty Winston Churchill and First Sea Lord Admiral of the Fleet Dudley Pound, his closest associate.

At the outbreak of World War 2, Britain had the largest merchant fleet in the world, even if its share of the world's tonnage had gone down from 43 per cent in 1914 to just over 26 per cent in 1939. To sustain another war, the British Empire would have to charter a large number of ships from other countries, including Norway. The Norwegian merchant fleet was the world's fourth largest, almost five million gross register tons (grt), of which 20 per cent were large, modern motor tankers. Controlling these ships and keeping them out of German use would be essential. Hence, on 5 September 1939, the Foreign Office instructed Cecil Dormer to contact Foreign Minister Koht to secure a trade and shipping agreement with the Norwegians.[3] Negotiations were hard, but by 8 April 1940 2.45 million tons of Norwegian shipping sailed under British charter, of which 1.65 million were tankers. The next day, when the Germans attacked, the situation changed completely, and further agreements secured the use of most of the Norwegian fleet for the Allies.[4]

Iron Ore

On 19 September, Churchill for the first time drew the attention of the War Cabinet to the issue of Swedish iron ore exports to Germany. He fully supported the recently initiated negotiations for chartering of the Norwegian merchant fleet, but at the same time urged that diplomatic pressure be applied to halt German ore traffic inside the Norwegian Leads. Failing this, Churchill said, he would be compelled to propose more drastic measures such as the laying of mines inside Norwegian territorial waters to drive the ore vessels outside the three-mile limit into international waters where they could be intercepted. The Cabinet accepted the importance of the ore imports for Germany but would give no support to actions beyond diplomatic means to try and sever them. First of all, practically no German ore ships had left Narvik since the outbreak of war. Secondly, the Chiefs of Staff Committee (CoS) had two weeks earlier stated in a note to the War Cabinet that Germany, in view of Norway's economic importance to it, was unlikely to violate Norwegian neutrality, except if provoked by an Allied intervention or an interference with the iron ore supplies. Last but not least, there was fear of negative reactions from the USA and other neutral countries if Britain were to instigate actions that violated any part of Scandinavian neutrality.[5]

By mid-November, the Admiralty had developed plans for how and where the Royal Navy could control the approaches to Narvik to divert as much of the iron ore as possible to the UK. On 30 November, Churchill brought to the War Cabinet a report he had received a few days earlier from the Ministry of Economic Warfare (MEW), concluding that 'stoppage of Swedish export of iron ore to Germany would [...] end the war in a few months' – a conclusion based on the sustained severing of *all* Swedish ore exports to Germany, not only through Narvik. Churchill asserted that during the coming winter the Baltic would be closed by ice and the export confined to the Norwegian Leads and even small minefields would force the ore ships into international waters where the Royal Navy could intercept those bound for Germany. The Chief of the Imperial General Staff (the head of the Army), General Edmund Ironside, agreed that the Swedish iron ore was a significant strategic objective and there were advantages in taking the war to Scandinavia, 'seizing the initiative from Hitler'. Laying mines would only annoy the Norwegians, though, at little gain, he held, and instead he advocated a sustained operation to take control of the entire Lapland area with well-equipped troops and careful planning. Germany would certainly be provoked, but not able to react before May, when the ice broke in the Baltic and Gulf of Bothnia, giving ample time to establish a defence. All the more so, Ironside said, as in 'such a remote and forbidding country a very small force could hold up a large one'. Not quite convinced either way, the War Cabinet 'invited the CoS to prepare an appreciation of the military factors involved [...] to stop the import of iron ore to Germany by the sea route from Narvik, either by stationing a naval force in the Vest Fjord or by laying a minefield on the Norwegian coast'. At

Narvik with the railway, harbour and ore loading facilities was considered
to have a strategic importance out of all proportion to its size.

the same time, MEW was asked to consider the effect this might have on
the Germany economy. Both reports should also address potential counter-
measures Germany might take by military or economic means.[6]

From 1935 to 1939, overall German iron ore imports rose from 14 to nearly
22 million tons, of which the high-grade Swedish ore accounted for around 9
million tons.[7] Mined in the Kiruna–Gällivare district of Lapland, just
north of the Arctic Circle, the ore was exported through Luleå in the Gulf
of Bothnia or Narvik in Norway. Purpose-built railway lines connected the
mines with both ports. In the winter, when the Gulf of Bothnia froze and
Luleå became icebound, normally from late November to mid/late-April,
the export went solely through Narvik. Of the 6.5 million tons of Swedish
ore shipped through Narvik during the winter of 1938/39, some 4.5 million
tons went to Germany in addition to some 1.2 million tons of Norwegian ore,
mainly from Kirkenes. After the outbreak of war, the export to Germany sank
fast while that to Britain increased comparably. During the first seven months
of 1939, 763,000 tons went to Germany, versus 798,000 tons to Britain. No
ore ships were sent from Germany to Narvik between 3 September and 25
October 1939. In early November, the imports to Germany restarted, but by
then British offtake dominated.

On 18 December, the last ore-transport of the year left Luleå and from
then on, until the ice broke in the Gulf again, German purchases of Swedish
iron ore would be stockpiled or go via Narvik. The export facilities in Narvik

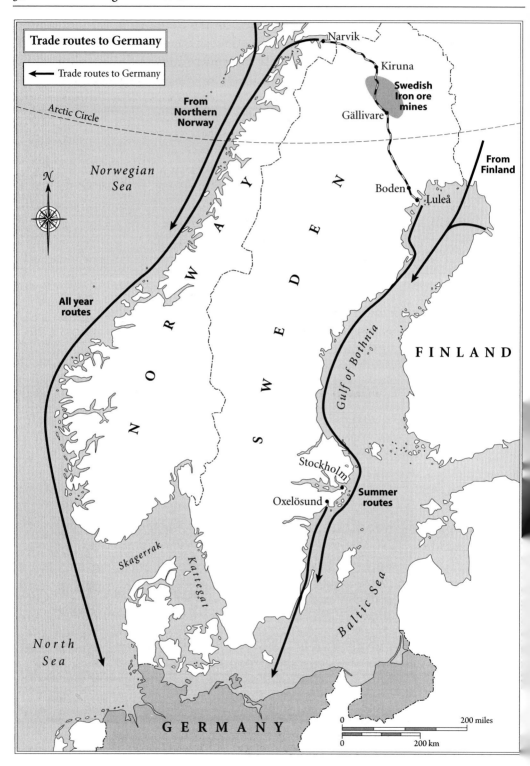

Trade routes to Germany

← Trade routes to Germany

Narvik

Kiruna

Swedish Iron ore mines

Gällivare

Arctic Circle

From Northern Norway

From Finland

Norwegian Sea

N

Boden

Luleå

All year routes

Gulf of Bothnia

FINLAND

Stockholm

Oxelösund

Summer routes

Skagerrak

Kattegat

Baltic Sea

North Sea

GERMANY

N O R W A Y

S W E D E N

0   200 miles

0   200 km

were thus opportune, but not indispensable for the Germans. Severing the traffic through Narvik without halting that through Luleå would at best have limited consequences – and only during the winter. This was clearly spelled out by the MEW report in early December to the War Cabinet where it was concluded that 'the principal argument therefore put forward by the First Lord in favour of action in Norwegian waters [is] invalid'. Later, in February, the War Cabinet was made aware through a report from the Ministry of Shipping that the dependence of Britain on the Narvik ore was 'more serious' than previously realised. In late March the Norwegian Minister to the UK Erik Colban presented a memorandum to the British Foreign Office where it was pointed out that of the 600,000 tons of iron ore waiting to be loaded in Narvik harbour, 400,000 were destined for Britain and only 200,000 for Germany. Shutting down Narvik harbour would therefore be negative for Great Britain but have hardly any influence on German imports as they would simply be routed through Luleå and the Baltic which was about to become ice-free. This information was confirmed by Swedish sources, adding that 'non-cooperation' at the railways delayed the German iron ore traffic while pressure on the Norwegian Pilot Association for a boycott was beginning to take effect, forcing German ships out of the Leads and into open waters.[8]

Iron Ore Shipments from Narvik, August 1939–March 1940 (tons)

	To Germany	To Britain	Others
August 1939	492,091	152,822	50,000
September	70,418	20,893	66,800
October	16,286	117,363	100,515
November	75,383	59,408	113,786
December	96,948	76,022	38,363
January 1940	281,740	148,291	105,318
February	99,391	131,855	58,794
March	113,957	212,960	55,000
Total Sept–March	754,123	766,792	538,576

These are the official Norwegian numbers presented to Halifax by Colban in March 1940 as documented in FO 371/24821. Other sources, have slightly different figures, but are of a similar order of magnitude

Between 7 and 13 December 1939, the Greek freighter *Garoufalia* and the two British freighters *Deptford* and *Thomas Walton* were sunk off the Norwegian coast. Investigations by the Norwegian Navy could not conclude with absolute certainty whether *Thomas Walton* had been inside the three-mile limit, but *Garoufalia* and *Deptford* most likely had. The culprit in all three cases was the German submarine *U 38* under the command of Kapitän-leutnant Heinrich Liebe. Seizing the moment, Churchill submitted a new memorandum to the War Cabinet on the 16th, arguing that

> The effectual stoppage of the Norwegian ore supplies to Germany ranks as a major offensive operation of war [...] If Germany can be cut from all Swedish ore supplies from now onwards till the end of 1940 a blow will have been struck at her war-making capacity equal to a first-class victory in the field or from the air, and without any serious sacrifice of life [...] British control of the Norwegian coast-line is a strategic objective of first-class importance.[9]

On 27 December, the War Cabinet discussed the Scandinavian issue again, now with firm conclusions from the Admiralty that the three merchant ships had been torpedoed inside Norwegian territory. Norwegian authorities, though not directly to blame, had been unable to prevent this, and steps to stop the German traffic from Narvik down the Norwegian coast were advised. This time the War Cabinet concurred. Before any operations were started, however, Oslo and Stockholm should be informed that they could count on Allied help should they undertake to assist Finland, followed by a notice to Norway that Britain was planning to send warships to intercept the German traffic. Meanwhile, the CoS were instructed to finish their report on the military implications of severing the iron ore from Sweden to Germany, while the War Office should continue preparing 'to send a force to Narvik'.[10]

Winter War

At dawn on 30 November 1939 more than 450,000 Soviet troops moved into Finland after the government in Helsinki had refused to cede territory for new Russian bases north-west of Leningrad. Led by Field Marshal Carl Gustav Mannerheim, the Finnish soldiers, contrary to all expectations, put up a spirited resistance making full use of the terrain and the coldest winter of the century up to that point. The Russians suffered grievously and the 'Winter War' ground to a halt.

Internal pressure in France made the Daladier government almost desperate for diversionary measures away from the feared horrors of a new Western Front and in mid-December, the French delegation to the Allied Supreme War Council proposed to send a *Corps d'expédition* via Norway and Sweden to help Finland. Officially that is – but unofficially to take control of the Swedish ore deposits including the export facilities in Narvik and Luleå on the way. French Prime Minister Édouard Daladier argued that

The railway from the ore-fields in Swedish Lappland to the coast at Narvik passes through a spectacular landscape. This train-set contains empty waggons going back to Kiruna for a new load.

depriving Germany of the ore might lead to a swift victory while failing to act might prolong the war by several years. There is, however, little doubt that the underlying objective of the proposal was to provoke a German attack on Scandinavia, far from French soil.

The French proposal was discussed in the British War Cabinet and Churchill enthusiastically reiterated the proposed naval intervention as a limited alternative. British Foreign Secretary Lord Halifax, rather less excited, felt the consequences of actions in Norwegian waters were unpredictable. Severing the iron ore from Narvik alone was of limited importance, he argued, without also stopping the supplies from Luleå. Prime Minister Neville Chamberlain concluded there were two distinct projects for Scandinavia, the 'smaller scheme', halting the traffic from Narvik, through mines or naval action, and the 'larger project', securing the ore-fields proper and blocking the supply of all Swedish ore to Germany. The latter, which the French had proposed, would require 'the good will of both Norway and Sweden', and diplomatic pressure was the most he was prepared to apply at the moment. No firm decisions were made at the meeting, but the CoS were again asked to consider the military implications of a policy aimed at stopping the export of Swedish iron ore to Germany.[11]

The 4,034-ton British ore-carrier *Deptford*, sunk on 13 December 1939 inside Norwegian waters by the German *U 38*. Thirty-four seamen died.

The Swedish and Norwegian ministers in London were called to the Foreign Office on 27 December and given *aide-memoires* informing them that Britain and France contemplated giving assistance to Finland in its fight for independence. How this could be done in the most efficient manner was being assessed. The two countries were requested meanwhile to assist Finland themselves and be ready to 'afford all necessary facilities for help from other sources'. The Allies would in return be willing to discuss protection against the consequences of such permission. The Norwegian answer came over the New Year: Norway would be pleased to assist in any aid to Finland, including transit of non-military material. Any persons going to Finland would have to do so as civilians. The note concluded that 'the Norwegian Government was grateful for the offer of an assurance for the preservation of the integrity and independence of Norway' but saw no need at present to have this assurance 'more precisely defined'. The Swedish answer was similar.[12]

On 31 December, the CoS reported to the War Cabinet that, provided it was ascertained that Germany would be adversely affected by an interruption of the Lapland ore supply, sending an expeditionary force to Scandinavia could be worthwhile as long as the security of France was not compromised. It would, however, represent a 'fundamental change' in British policy which needed to be understood and accepted. The significance of the Swedish iron ore for the long-term German ability to wage war was obvious, according to the CoS, and severing the supply through Narvik would almost certainly provoke a response from Berlin. What kind of response was unclear, but besides direct action in Sweden a likely retaliation could be to seize bases in southern Norway, probably between Kristiansand and Stavanger. A move on Oslo was considered unlikely, as this would be a much larger operation most likely to be met with Norwegian opposition. German actions north of Stavanger were considered improbable as an invasion fleet would be met by the Royal Navy and the range of most Luftwaffe aircraft would prevent effective support from home bases. Churchill was not convinced the Germans would react in force at all and urged immediate action to 'see what happened', adding that British naval forces were standing by, ready to respond. Chamberlain wished to gauge the Norwegian reactions more precisely and the delivery of a second, stronger memorandum to the Norwegian government was agreed. Meanwhile, the CoS should consider the consequences of a German occupation of southern Norway and how these could be avoided, including by pre-emptive occupation of Stavanger, Bergen and Trondheim.[13]

On Saturday 6 January, Halifax called Minister Colban to his office again, presenting him with a memorandum expressing the dire concern of His Majesty's Government over the 'recent flagrant violations of Norwegian territorial waters' by German U-boats, making the Leads a theatre of war. The British government, Halifax said, would soon be obliged to take appropriate actions to prevent German use of Norwegian waters, if necessary by operating inside the territorial limits themselves.

'Colban's report from the meeting with Halifax shocked me and I really felt the war looming' Koht wrote. 'Not for a second did I doubt that the Germans would see this as a provocation and turn their war machine against Norway.' In meetings with his government colleagues, he stated that, whatever happened, it was vital Norway was not brought into the war on the German side. He cautioned his colleagues, though, that such consideration in itself compromised their neutrality and should not become known outside the government. The reply from Oslo to London eventually took the form of an emphatic letter from King Haakon to King George VI, delivered by Colban on the 9th. The King's letter, no doubt endorsed by the government, underlined his 'great surprise and consternation' over the plans to make Norwegian territorial waters a location for British naval action and appealed to the British King to prevent such steps, which inevitably would bring Norway into the war, endangering its existence as a sovereign state. Embarrassed by this approach and fearing Norwegian reactions might harm the larger project, Chamberlain and Halifax decided to stand down and curb any operations against the Narvik traffic for the time being. As the Swedish reactions were also very negative, the War Cabinet accepted this on the 12th. The CoS were nevertheless asked to consider the possibility of capturing the Kiruna–Gällivare ore fields in the face of Norwegian and Swedish opposition.[14] No indication of the decision to stand down should be given to the Scandinavian governments, but Laurence Collier of the Foreign Office remarked sourly to Colban a few days later: 'You have won – so far.'[15]

Scandinavia was not off the agenda of the War Cabinet for long. The concept of the 'larger project' was pursued consistently by the military and by the second half of January, it had grown to three parallel, complementary operation plans; Operation *Avonmouth* would ensure control of the ore fields in Lapland while Operation *Stratford* was to intervene in west Norway and Operation *Plymouth* in southern and central Sweden. Four to five divisions, including French and Polish units would be deployed to Narvik–Lapland–Luleå while five additional battalions would occupy Trondheim and Bergen.

In all, some 100,000 British and 50,000 French/Polish troops with naval and air support would be deployed under overall British command. Of these, two or three brigades were all that, according to the plans, would end up in Finland. There they should stay near the railway to avoid getting too close to the Russians or being cut off by a likely German intervention when the Gulf of Bothnia unfroze. The ports of Narvik, Trondheim and Bergen all had rail links eastwards and had to be secured permanently to maintain supplies and transport of weapons, ammunition, and men. The front line would go from somewhere south of Bergen, via Oslo to Stockholm. South of this, German air-strikes would likely be fierce, and counter-invasions would have to be expected. Stavanger would be temporarily occupied, but if German landings threatened the airport or port, both would be destroyed, and the Allied forces withdrawn towards Bergen.

In early February, the French Ambassador to London, Charles Corbin, asked Halifax for the policy in Scandinavia and Finland to be discussed in the next meeting of the Supreme War Council. The meeting was convened in Paris on 5 February and Chamberlain advocated the large project, combining assistance to Finland with control of the Lapland ore fields. Daladier was happy to comply and, on this day, almost two weeks before the *Altmark* incident, the Council agreed to set up an Anglo-French expeditionary force – to be ready by 20 March – allegedly to help Finland but first and foremost to secure the Swedish iron ore, gain strategic control over the Norwegian coast and hopefully divert substantial German forces from the Western Front. To overcome their unwillingness, it was decided to exert 'vigorous moral pressure' on Norway and Sweden while Finland would be asked to issue an official appeal for help to add moral pressure. The Germans would respond, but this would take time, and meanwhile any attack in the West would be postponed – it was assumed. The main objective of the British planners was the Norwegian west coast and the Swedish iron ore, not Finland. Paris had more genuine concerns for Finland, but this was strongly underlined by the desire to engage the German armed forces anywhere but on French soil.[16]

Norwegian volunteers gathering in Oslo before heading for Finland in January 1940, some bringing their own skis and rucksacks. Around 900 Norwegians went to Finland, but few of them would see combat at the front.

Altmark

In February 1940, the German naval tanker and supply ship *Altmark* entered Norwegian territorial waters. *Altmark* had assisted the German Navy raider *Admiral Graf Spee* on its mission in the South Atlantic the previous autumn. The wreck of the raider lay broken on a sandbank off Montevideo, but *Altmark* with 300 seamen captured in the South Atlantic, had managed to evade the British and French patrols looking for it and now planned to use Norwegian waters for the last leg of the journey home. The captain claimed *Altmark* was a state-owned ship entitled to refuse inspections, but still demanded the right of free passage of a regular merchant vessel. Inspecting officers of the RNN were not allowed below deck but concluded beyond doubt that there were prisoners on board. Still, Commanding Admiral Diesen, supported by the Foreign Office, decided to let *Altmark* through. The Germans got as far as past Stavanger. Shortly before midnight on 16 February 1940, Captain Philip Vian, on Churchill's orders, took the destroyer *Cossack* into Norwegian territorial waters at Jøssingfjord. In spite of protests from Norwegian naval vessels, *Altmark* was boarded, and the prisoners were liberated. During the skirmish, eight Germans were killed.[17]

This was at the height of the Phoney War and the incident created headlines all over the world. In Norway, feelings were harsh. The otherwise British-friendly Stortingspresident Carl Hambro considered what had happened in Jøssingfjord as 'the most flagrant violation of the territory of a neutral state'.[18]

In London, Minister Colban handed a protest note from the Norwegian government to Halifax over what was seen as a serious violation of Norwegian territorial waters. Halifax was somewhat embarrassed and answered that he did not deny that it had technically been an infringement of Norwegian neutrality, but it followed as a consequence of the Norwegian failure to free the British seamen held in captivity on board the ship.[19]

Relations between the UK and Norway were at a historic low. Churchill's position, on the other hand, had risen sharply. British newspaper headlines were massive, with radio and magazines full of interviews and commentaries. Captain Vian had represented the Royal Navy with grand flair, resolute, tactically superior and with a dismissive attitude to laws and regulations – and it was Churchill who had given the orders. At the War Cabinet on 18 February, he grabbed the occasion and submitted a written proposal to stop all German shipping in Norwegian waters. Halting the iron ore traffic to Germany would be key to Allied victory, he brazenly added. No voices were raised against the proposal and a few days later the Admiralty was instructed to start preparing plans for mining the Norwegian Leads.

The question was whether Norway should be given another chance to 'effectively stop the German misuse of Norwegian territorial waters', or the time had come to take matters into Britain's own hands.[20]

Consultations for further use of Norwegian tonnage were ongoing as were negotiations for a trade agreement and Halifax wished to ensure that, whatever other actions were found necessary, both negotiations continued according to plan. Hence, at the Cabinet meeting on the 21st, he proposed that the potential minelaying would have to be seen in a larger context and not rushed into. In his opinion, the Norwegian government should be informed that London could not accept the current practice of allowing German use of the Leads. It had to be terminated immediately, or the British government would have to consider action. To underline the seriousness of the situation, Halifax added that he had been informed by the Finnish Minister to London, Georg Gripenberg, that large quantities of supplies were being sent from Germany to Murmansk through Norwegian waters, for Russian use in Finland, though this seems unlikely and cannot be substantiated. On the contrary, significant amounts of British and French war material, including aircraft, went to Finland using Norwegian ports, airfields and railways, without being mentioned at all. Chamberlain, cautious as always, agreed that a note to the Norwegian government could be prepared, but it should not be sent until the matter was better clarified. It was essential to retain freedom of action and keep all possibilities open.[21]

At the next Cabinet meeting, on the 23rd, Halifax presented a draft message to Norway. He had to admit that it had been difficult to find a good moral justification for the Royal Navy to establish a base in Norwegian waters. The *Altmark* case was clear enough, but even if the sinkings in December were inside territorial waters, the Admiralty was unable to provide any firm evidence of further German misuse of Norwegian territorial waters. Therefore, the main argument of the memorandum was that, as Germany had adopted an aggressive line in the naval war, Britain could not be constrained by international rules of war in its attempt to survive. This, a number of Cabinet members argued, would be difficult to accept for other neutrals, especially Italy and the United States. The situation could easily backfire, with no gain versus Germany. After a lengthy discussion, it was concluded that further action inside Norwegian territorial waters was not desirable at that time. Churchill objected but could not present weighty arguments and was overruled.[22]

Hence, things settled down. Both the Norwegian and British governments preferred not to disrupt the shipping and war trade agreements that had been negotiated during the autumn. An official note from Halifax to Koht on 15 March was kept in a subdued, factual tone, covering all relevant aspects of the case as seen from London's side. The arguments were the same as before but significantly muted. The note ended with a desire to accept that in this matter there was no right or wrong, but different perceptions, and leave it there. A Norwegian response arrived in London on 7 or 8 April and was being translated in the Legation when the Germans invaded on the 9th. This, according to Colban, was 'quite friendly in tone' but apparently never delivered.[23]

Two essential issues can be read between the lines of the official British documents from this period. First, the almost desperate search for justification shows the impromptu nature of the action in Jøssingfjord. Churchill seized a chance that offered itself without either planning or contemplation. Second, there was a dawning understanding that the incident and the controversy afterwards showed that Norway, after all, was on the Allied side. This may have led British planners to take it for granted that there would not be much resistance if the Allies were to find it necessary to land in Norway as part of the war against Germany. On the other hand, as the German planners came to similar conclusions, there is little doubt that the events in Jøssingfjord triggered processes that were the basis of the invasion on 9 April.

Altmark heading for the mouth of Jøssingfjord, pursued by British destroyers.

The Swedish envoy to London Björn Prytz made some observations in a letter to the Swedish Foreign Minister Christian Günther on 6 April. Ironically the letter was received in Stockholm on the morning of the 9th.

> Since the beginning of the war, it has become obvious to the neutrals that the question of observing international rules and regulations by the belligerents will deteriorate [...] During the last months, one has observed, through the *Altmark* case and the iron ore issue, how the British Foreign Office, and not least Lord Halifax personally, has adopted a way of thinking that justifies the view that the Allies must be ready ruthlessly to violate 'technical' obstacles. Protests from neutrals come not so much from a concern over the legal issues as from fear of the consequences such violations might create. As there is a growing belief that the Allies to a large extent are fighting the war on behalf of smaller states, this becomes increasingly acceptable.[24]

Urgent Request

On 10 February, the Russians broke through the Finnish defences on the Karelian Isthmus after a lengthy artillery bombardment. The Finns

The Norwegian torpedo boats *Kjell* and *Skarv* positioning themselves between
Altmark inside the fjord and the much larger British destroyer *Ivanhoe* just outside.

continued defending their territory with desperation but could not hope
to resist for long. To try to avoid disaster, Mannerheim advised his government to opt for peace while the Kremlin still believed an Allied intervention
was an option.[25] Meanwhile, the French pushed for the British to implement
the plans from January. Seen from Paris, sending an expeditionary force
to Finland via Norway and Sweden was an attractive proposition. German
forces facing the Maginot Line would almost certainly be pulled away and if
the flow of iron ore to the German armaments industry could be cut, there
might be no German attack on the Western Front in the near future. The
British would bear the greatest burden of the expedition and contributing a
few thousand Alpine troops and Foreign Legionnaires to Scandinavia would
not disturb French defences much. Admiral Gabriel Auphan, at the time
a member of the French naval staff, later wrote: 'It is cynical to have to say
it, but no one really thought we would be able to stop the Soviet army and
save Finland. The idea was to use the excuse this gave to secure the Swedish
ore fields and prevent the export of ore to Germany.' The French politician
Paul Reynaud made similar comments, but more diplomatic, in his memoirs.

British Prime Minister Neville Chamberlain.

International condemnation for violating Norwegian and Swedish neutrality was a low price to pay if it could prevent a German attack on France. The Norwegians had received the warnings they needed in January, argued Prime Minister Daladier, and pushed for a swift implementation.[26]

Having voted to hold back on direct naval actions inside Norwegian territorial waters a week earlier, the British War Cabinet nonetheless gave in and accepted the French proposal on 1 March. It was agreed to send a note to Oslo and Stockholm requesting cooperation and acceptance of transferring an auxiliary force to Finland via Narvik and Kiruna–Gällivare, based on a Finnish request for help. The following day, 2 March, the notes were delivered by the British and French envoys in Oslo and Stockholm and within two days both governments had firmly rejected the proposals. The Allied military leaders hardly registered the rejections and planning continued. During the first week of March, Général Sylvestre-Gérard Audet and his Corps Expéditionnaire were standing by in France and most things were also ready in Britain. Major-General Pierse Mackesy, commander of 49th Division, was confirmed as overall land commander and Admiral Edward Evans as commander of the naval force.[27]

On 11 March, the British War Cabinet confirmed its acceptance of the French plan to land troops in Norway without consent. Assistance to Finland was still given as the underlying objective, but the port of Narvik, the railway and the Swedish ore fields should be firmly secured on the way. Norwegian reactions to the landings were uncertain and force should only be used in self-defence. British soldiers were only to fire back 'as an ultimate measure of self-defence should their forces be in jeopardy' and limited losses against minor Norwegian opposition could be accepted. How to recognise 'minor opposition' was not elaborated.[28]

The British decision-making process at this stage became imprecise and ambiguous. The likelihood of Allied troops reaching Finland was small and the whole adventure could end up as an invasion of Norway and possibly Sweden with significant losses on both sides. If the expeditionary force had to halt, or even worse, was chased back, failure would be total. If successful, it could quickly evolve into a quagmire of commitments, resulting in critical resources having to be drained from other fronts. Chamberlain, Halifax and even Churchill realised they were about to let loose a tiger they might not be able to control and in the afternoon of 12 March, the War Cabinet decided, on Churchill's request, that only the landings in Narvik, Operation *Avonmouth*,

British Foreign Secretary Edward Wood, Viscount Halifax, in 1940.

should be carried out at first to secure the railway and advance to the Swedish border as quickly as possible. Based on how this progressed, a decision would be made to enter Lapland or not and whether to land reinforcements in Trondheim. Only after this had been completed would the landings in Bergen and Stavanger be assessed and whether the troops in northern Sweden should proceed into Finland at all. In other words, the entire military planning was set aside by the political leadership in London. The loading of the first part of the expeditionary corps, with destination Narvik, began in British ports in the early morning of 13 March. Dormer was instructed to be prepared to deliver a 'formal and urgent request' to the Norwegian government for the passage of 'a force of Allied troops across Norwegian territory to Finland' as soon as the first soldiers were confirmed onshore.[29]

The Finnish government decided that the Allied offer for large-scale support was unrealistic and authorised its negotiators in Moscow to sign an armistice on 12 March, to become effective the following day. Around midday on the 13th, the news of the ceasefire broke. Churchill, supported by Ironside, argued that the primary goal of the expedition, the Lapland ore fields, remained and insisted that the landings at Narvik should still go ahead, but was overruled by an obviously relieved Chamberlain who issued orders to suspend the expedition during the afternoon. In the War Cabinet the next day, the expedition was officially cancelled, and orders given to disembark the troops. The majority of the *Avonmouth* forces were diverted to France. Ships were sent on other missions or back to their bases and staff officers cleared the desks. Only 10–12,000 British, French and Polish troops were kept on standby in Scotland should anything happen in Norway from the German side, which required rapid action.[30]

In France, bitterness over a missed opportunity to divert German aggression prevailed and within a few days, Daladier resigned, and Paul Reynaud took over. The first meeting of the Supreme War Council with Reynaud as French Prime Minister was held in London on 28 March. French suggestions that operations should be carried out against German ships in Norwegian waters, as well as in the Baltic, were swiftly dismissed by the British. The discussions were in part heated and ended with a compromise according to which the French should lay mines in the Rhine to disrupt German domestic traffic, while the British should lay minefields in Norwegian territorial waters to disrupt ore traffic. The following day, Chamberlain informed the war Cabinet that they had once again decided to submit diplomatic warnings to Norway and Sweden, upholding the Allies' right to stop the German iron ore traffic and send such help to Finland 'as they deemed appropriate'. That the Allies had already decided to act would not be included in the note. Minelaying in the Rhine, Operation *Royal Marine*, would commence on 4 April followed by mining in Norwegian waters, Operation *Wilfred*, on the 5th. In addition, the French and British general staffs were instructed to make plans for the interruption of the German ore traffic from Luleå as soon as the Gulf of Bothnia became ice free.[31]

The justification for the violation of Norwegian and Swedish neutrality was as before to stop German abuse of Norwegian territory but the underlying desire was to stop resources from Scandinavia reaching Germany. A German response would justify an allied intervention. The basic plan was along the lines of what had been intended earlier in March, but this time the available forces were significantly reduced, Finland was no longer an objective and whether some of the forces would cross into Sweden at all would be decided later. The minelaying, Operation *Wilfred*, should interrupt

The Winter War 1939–1940

Norwegian Sea

Petsamo
Murmansk

Narvik
Kiruna
Salla
Gällivare
Rovaniemi

Planned Allied Expedition

Boden
Kemi
Luleå

Russian Axis of attack

Suomussalmi

Trondheim
Östersund

F I N L A N D

N O R W A Y

S W E D E N

Lake Ladoga

Viipuri

Bergen

Turku Helsinki
Åland

Oslo

Leningrad

Stockholm

Hanko

Stavanger

Tallinn

ESTONIA

RUSSIA

LATVIA
Riga

DENMARK

Baltic Sea

LITHUANIA

Copenhagen
Memel
Kaunas

Königsberg

Danzig

East Prussia

Hamburg

G E R M A N Y

0   200 miles
0   200 km

the iron ore traffic out of Narvik and give the Royal Navy new opportunities. *Plan R4*, as the landing operation was called, would be activated when the Germans took the bait and 'set foot on Norwegian soil, or there was clear evidence they intend to do so' – although what evidence of German action was needed was not specified. Landings at Narvik alone made little sense to the CoS and part of the plans from two weeks earlier were put forward again while efforts were initiated to try to re-assemble as much as possible of the dispersed *Stratford* and *Avonmouth* forces. Troops for southern Sweden were no longer available and *Plymouth* was abandoned for good. The CoS concluded that 'All preparations should be made for the dispatch of at least one British battalion at the same time as the laying of the minefield, to be followed by the remainder of the force at the earliest possible date.' Within parts of the military, it appears *Plan R4* was expected to go ahead without waiting for the Germans. Churchill told the War Cabinet on the 29th that it was necessary 'to continue in a state of readiness to dispatch a light force to Narvik and possibly ... Stavanger' but added he 'personally doubted whether the Germans would land a force in Scandinavia.' Most likely he deliberately kept the issue low-key so as not to raise objections and postpone the minelaying once more. Ironside held that 'the projected operation in Scandinavia [has] a different political background from that [...] in early March when similar operations were contemplated.' Apprehensively, he added: 'From this beginning, we cannot foresee what may develop' and advised to 'have in hand a reserve, pending German reactions', including plans for 'the withdrawal of two to three divisions from France'. The mines would be laid without Norwegian consent and when the landings were tied to the German response to this, the political safety valve, which had been a prerequisite for the War Cabinet so far, was lost. Less than two weeks after they had been saved by the Finnish capitulation, Chamberlain and Halifax had lost control of events again. This time, they would not regain it.[32]

Chapter 4

Threat from the North

Silken Glove

There were no German plans whatsoever for an attack on Scandinavia at the outbreak of the war in September 1939. As long as unrestricted use of neutral sea lanes secured the supply of Swedish iron ore and other critical raw materials from the north, such as minerals, timber products and fish, any strategic benefits gained from capturing bases on Norway's west coast were subordinate. 'Nobody in Germany – at least not in the Navy – worried about Norway in the first weeks of the war', wrote Großadmiral Raeder.[1] The German envoy to Norway Heinrich Sahm (who died in October 1939) told Foreign Minister Koht that Germany wished to maintain a good relationship between the two countries and would fully respect Norwegian neutrality, provided an unquestionable objectivity was maintained and no violations from any side were accepted. Inside the silken glove, however, was the usual iron fist. Should repeated violations of neutrality be allowed to occur, the German government would be compelled to attend to the matter itself and protect the interests of the *Reich* in a manner appropriate for the situation.[2] Koht answered unperturbed that the regulations were well described in the Neutrality Act which he took for granted would be respected by the belligerents. Two days later, Sahm was back, accompanied by Ulrich von Hassel, a special envoy from the Foreign Office in Berlin. Prime Minister Nygaardsvold was also present at the meeting and the four men agreed to maintain normal bilateral relations as much as possible within the regulations of the Neutrality Act.[3] On 6 October, Hitler said in a speech to the Reichstag:

> Germany has never had any conflicts of interest or even points of contro-
> versy with the northern states. Neither has she any today. Sweden and
> Norway have both been offered non-aggression pacts by Germany
> and have both refused them solely because they do not feel themselves
> threatened in any way.[4]

The rationale for Hitler to change this position and unleash his dogs of war on Norway and Denmark six months later developed during the winter as a result of a series of successive, intertwined incidents, concern over

Hitler attending a naval parade at the Laboe memorial outside Kiel in June 1936. Raeder is to his right, minister for war, Generalfeldmarschall von Blomberg to his left.

disturbances to supply, internal hierarchical controversies and German fear of being outflanked – as well as Allied aspirations to establish an alternative front in Scandinavia, then or later. Hitler interpreted the world around him in his own way and when he perceived the Norwegian government failing to defend their neutrality in the face of British impertinence, the consequences became unpredictable. In the War Diary of SKL, there are three marked phases. Before mid-October 1939, Norway is barely mentioned at all. For some weeks following, the country appears in connection with various strategic studies and around New Year there are occasional references to *Studie Nord*. From late February, however, there is barely a day without mention of Norway and Operation *Weserübung*. Norway had definitely gained Hitler's attention.[5]

Extended Operational Basis

After the outbreak of war, Großadmiral Raeder, C-in-C of the Kriegsmarine, occasionally brought up the expansion of his service's involvement with Scandinavia. His motives for this were many and complex. On one hand, he wished to threaten British supply lines, on the other, he sought opportunities for his Navy to excel in the war, which had commenced much earlier than he had been told to plan for. In a comment to the SKL on 29 November, Raeder said that due to the Luftwaffe failing to increase its efforts to support the Kriegsmarine, it would be up to the Navy to conduct the war against

Britain on its own.[6] The Army and the Air Force would be in the lead as long as the focus of the war was on the Western Front or on a long-term eastward expansion. It would be essential for Raeder to create initiatives in which the Navy could play a central role and not be left behind by the other services in the allocation of resources. At Nuremberg and in his later memoirs, Raeder defended himself against the accusations of initiating a war of aggression. He claimed that he had preferred a political development, if one could be found, and that German intelligence had such detailed knowledge of the Allied plans for invading Norway that the German invasion was purely preventive. This is also the general tone in the memoirs of other senior German naval officers after the war – undoubtedly a convenient explanation after 1945. Available documents, however, indicate that the reality was more complex and that the decision process that ended up with German ships and soldiers in Norwegian waters in April 1940 developed through a number of interacting, coinciding events and presumptions.[7]

In Berlin, these developments commenced on 2 October, when, one month after the outbreak of conflict, the OKW realised it was time to develop a realistic long-term strategy for what had now become a full-blown war. The Kriegsmarine was asked for its opinion on three options: (1) a land offensive in the West, (2) a defensive war on land and at sea or (3) a siege of Britain keeping the land war as limited as possible. The following day Raeder directed the SKL to produce the answer. It was clear that the Luftwaffe would be prioritised in the second and third cases, whereas the Army would receive precedence and eventual fame from the first. In the planned attack on the Western Front the Navy would only have a minor role to play – 'Fall Gelb ist für die Kriegsmarine nur eine Nebenfrage'. A siege of Britain – 'Belagerung Englands' – would be the only scenario that would give the Kriegsmarine a significant part to play and priority of resources. It was clear, though, that a compelling set of arguments would be needed to convince Hitler and the OKW of the strategic necessity to pursue such a development of the war. The SKL Chief of Staff Admiral Otto Schniewind, learned from the Army Chief of Staff General der Artillerie Franz Halder that it would be over-optimistic to expect naval bases along the Channel coast, even if the campaign in the West should be successful and France conquered. Bases in western or northern Norway were even less likely. Difficult terrain, limited infrastructure and overstretched supply lines made a campaign in that country problematic. Above all, though, Germany might end up at war with Sweden should such an operation be initiated, and Halder could see no strategic reason whatsoever why such an adventure should be risked. An offensive up Jutland towards Skagen in Denmark could be easier and might be given some consideration at a later stage. Contacts with the Luftwaffe staff in early October to try to

Raeder in Wilhelmshaven in March 1940 with Konteradmiral Friedrich-Wilhelm Fleischer, Coastal Commander of Ostfriesland. Most likely Operation *Weserübung* was among the items discussed.

sound out their line of thinking gave similar negative results. Suitable aircraft to assist in an effective blockade of the British Isles would not be available in sufficient numbers until the end of 1940 at the earliest, and until such times a blockade in the North Sea region would be at best a secondary task for the Luftwaffe. The attention of Hitler and OKW was at this stage clearly on the Western Front. The Nordic countries were neutral, and this served Germany well as long as the neutrality was unbiased or even better, pro-German.[8]

This was dire news for the Navy, and in a series of memoranda and reports during the autumn, Raeder started highlighting the importance of securing German imports of iron ore, pyrites, nickel and other raw materials from Scandinavia, while at the same time denying these and other commodities to Britain. The concept of an extension of the operational basis towards the north is mentioned in the War Diary of the SKL for the first time on 3 October. Such an extension, it is held, would improve the strategic and tactical position of the German Navy significantly and make a British blockade very difficult.

Encouraged, Raeder instructed SKL to assess which places in Norway would give the best conditions for bases, how they could be acquired, and not least how they could be defended after an occupation. There was at this stage no mention of the ore traffic or any other commercial issues. Raeder later claimed that he trusted diplomatic pressure on the Norwegian government might be enough to secure the bases without aggression, but it is hard to accept that the *Großadmiral* really believed he could have them without the use of military force. A full-scale occupation of Norway seems not to have been part of his scenarios, though. With a limited surface fleet, where anything resembling a capital ship could be counted on one hand, and no carriers, the full value of bases in western Norway lay far into the future. U-boats would have to take the major burden of a blockade of Britain, but that would require industrial priority for the Navy, and it is quite possible that Norway at this stage was put forward as a long-term scenario for no other reason than this. On 9 October, Befehlshaber der Unterseeboote, Konteradmiral Karl Dönitz, submitted a memorandum to Raeder in which Narvik and Trondheim were held up as the preferable sites for U-boat bases in Norway. Both places were outside the Bergen–Shetland Narrows, both were railheads, ice-free year-round and had good, defensible port facilities. Narvik was the less favoured of the two having its railway connection through Sweden and being very far from home and from the Atlantic sealanes. Trondheim on the other hand was ideal – except that it might be vulnerable to British air attacks.[9]

On the same day, 9 October, the SKL delivered the required strategic considerations to OKW in a comprehensive memorandum. The conclusion was a clear recommendation to maintain the status quo. A strictly neutral Norway was by far the best choice, considering the Kriegsmarine's strength now and for the foreseeable future, as long as there was no direct threat of British actions. Only the U-boats would benefit from bases in Norway, and only if such bases were able to supply and service the boats fully, which was unrealistic, considering the existing infrastructure and transport facilities. Furthermore, such remote bases would be vulnerable to British attacks and the Royal Navy would still be waiting in the Faeroes–Iceland Gap and the Denmark Strait before the U-boats reached the main Atlantic trade routes. On that very same day, 9 October, *Führer* Directive No. 6 was issued in which Hitler reaffirmed his intentions to open an offensive in the West as the next step, relegating the Kriegsmarine to a supporting role. Norway was not mentioned at all.[10] Raeder wrote to Admiral Kurt Assmann, the official German naval historian:

> During the weeks preceding the report of October 1939, I was in correspondence with Admiral Carls, who in a detailed letter to me pointed out

the importance of an occupation of the Norwegian coast by Germany. I passed this letter on to C/SKL for their information and prepared some notes based on this letter for my report to the Führer [...] my opinion was identical with that of Admiral Carls, while, at that time, SKL was more dubious about the matter. In these notes, I stressed the disadvantages, which an occupation of Norway by the British would have for us; control of the approaches to the Baltic, outflanking of our naval operations and of our air attacks on Britain, pressure on Sweden. I also stressed the advantages for us of the occupation of the Norwegian coast; outlet to the North Atlantic, no possibility of a British mine barrier, as in the year 1917–1918. Naturally, at the time, only the coast and bases were considered, including Narvik.[11]

In the afternoon of 10 October 1939, Raeder met Hitler to give a general overview of the situation at sea and discuss plans for an increase in U-boat production. During the discussions, Raeder told the *Führer* that in his view as well as that of the SKL, an unlimited, ruthless blockade of Britain would be the only way to continue the war successfully. Hitler did not disagree, and Raeder continued, stating that a priority of resources and raw material for the Kriegsmarine would be absolutely necessary for such a development. Towards the end of the meeting, Raeder, responding to a question from Hitler, answered that bases on the Belgian coast would be of limited benefit to the U-boats in enforcing a blockade of Britain. Instead, the Admiral advocated Norway and Trondheim as a constructive alternative, despite the unenthusiastic attitude of his staff. According to his memoirs, Raeder backed up his arguments by pointing to the fact that Admiral Wilhelm Canaris, head of the Abwehr, the OKW intelligence service, in person had informed him in late September that, according to his sources, Britain was considering occupying bases in southern Norway. Should Britain possess such bases, Raeder stressed, the whole strategic situation in the north would change, seriously disrupting the possibilities for German naval and air operations against Britain while facilitating British attacks on Germany. Raeder said he considered this information particularly important and reliable as Canaris had relayed it to him in person, which the Abwehr chief only did on rare occasions. In his memoirs, Raeder described his role in this meeting as merely giving a passive warning of the consequences of British bases in Norway, not quite as aggressive as the minutes may indicate. Whatever took place, Hitler was preoccupied with the offensive in the West at this stage and not prepared to let Norway become an issue of priority. Nevertheless, he asked the admiral to leave behind the hand-notes he had brought for him to consider later. As far as available documents imply, this was the first time aggression against Norway was discussed in the German High Command.[12]

On 23 November, Hitler addressed his senior commanders in a lengthy speech on the progress of the war so far and his plans. Norway was not mentioned at all. His attention was in the west for the moment, but ultimately in the east. The Scandinavian states had declared neutrality, and if this remained sustainable, it would be in Germany's interest to maintain the situation.[13]

In December 1939, during an informal meeting between the Swedish Naval Attaché in Berlin, Kommendörkapten Anders Forshell, and Raeder's Chief of Staff, Fregattenkapitän Erich Schulte-Mönting, the latter spoke freely of his impressions from the inner German naval circles. Above all, he said, Hitler wanted peace with Britain and cooperation with the Nordic countries through 'affirmative neutrality'. If, however, Germany's interests were to be seriously threatened the response would be ruthless. Germany's military resources were superior, and Hitler would not shy away from using them if necessary. His ambition was a 'United States of Europe' under German leadership, in accord with Great Britain. The Nordic countries were inside the German sphere of economic interest, according to Schulte-Mönting, but there were no territorial interests – provided other countries, Russia and Britain in particular, left them alone.[14]

Thus, three months into the war, there were no concrete German plans for a military attack on Norway, Sweden or Denmark. Raeder tried again in a meeting with Hitler on 8 December, this time arguing that the British were using Norwegian neutrality for their own trade traffic. Intelligence reports also started to indicate that the revived German iron ore traffic through Narvik had become an important Allied preoccupation. Hitler was apparently not very interested this time either, but his attention would soon be swayed northwards.[15]

Monologue

On 10 December 1939 a train rolled into Berlin. On board was the Norwegian National Socialist leader Vidkun Quisling who came to update himself on political issues and to try to activate German support for his micro party Nasjonal Samling (NS). Instead, he was to become entangled in an improvised play, the consequences of which were out of all proportion. Before his visit to Berlin, Quisling played no real role in Norwegian politics, except in his own mind. He was at best background noise and his followers were few. The key person at that moment was Quisling's man in Germany, Albert Hagelin. On the morning after his arrival, Quisling was taken by Hagelin to see Reichsleiter Alfred Rosenberg, head of the Nazi Party's internal Foreign Policy Office and Propaganda Section – Außenpolitische Amt der NSDAP, not to be confused with the traditional Foreign Office. Hagelin was also a

Vidkun Abraham Jønsson Quisling. Quisling's party Nasjonal Samling, the National Unification Party, was founded in 1933. The party programme was largely based on 'return to law, order, justice and tradition'. Contrary to his own expectations, the elections in 1933 and 1936 were disastrous and NS was never even close to entering Parliament. Before the war, the party virtually collapsed and following a series of withdrawals and exclusions was reduced to a small core of followers, faithful to Quisling in person.

friend of Fregattenkapitän Erich Schulte-Mönting, and in the afternoon, with Rosenberg's blessing, Quisling was brought to the naval headquarters at Tirpitzufer. Here, Schulte-Mönting introduced the Norwegians to Raeder. Quisling presented himself (correctly) as an ex-major who had served in the Norwegian General Staff and as Defence Minister. Raeder, who probably had not even heard of the man before, was impressed and gave him his attention. All the more so as Hagelin (falsely) managed to pass an impression of Quisling being the leader of a significant political party with strong military and ministerial connections. At the *Führer*-conference on the 12th, Raeder recounted his conversation with the Norwegian, referring to Quisling as well connected and 'making a reliable impression'. He recounted Quisling's statements that public opinion in Norway was increasingly hostile to Germany, with growing British influence. A British landing in Norway, which Quisling held as very likely, would create serious problems for Germany's use of the Leads and the Kriegsmarine's ability to maintain an effective merchant war against England, Raeder added. Cautioning that the Norwegian might be playing a political game of his own, he nevertheless recommended Hitler to meet him and form his own opinion. If the *Führer* was left with a positive impression, he added, the OKW should be tasked with working out provisional plans for an occupation of Norway, peacefully or by force. Hitler consulted Rosenberg, who recommended Quisling highly, and invited the Norwegian to the Reichskanzlei on 13 December.[16]

Quisling came accompanied by Hagelin and Rosenberg's subordinate Amtsleiter Hans-Wilhelm Scheidt, head of the Nordic Office. Neither Raeder nor Rosenberg attended. Scheidt was supposedly a specialist on Norway and he had visited

Amtsleiter Hans-Wilhelm Scheidt, head of the Nazi Party's Nordic Office.

Oslo several times. He was hastily called to Berlin when Quisling turned up, evidencing the improvised nature of the events. Scheidt later wrote that Hitler listened 'calmly and attentively' to Quisling who spoke a slow, halting German in a pensive manner. Hagelin frequently had to translate or clarify what Quisling had tried to express in his poor German.

The general Norwegian attitude, Quisling said, had been firmly pro-British for a long time. In his opinion, it was obvious that Britain did not intend to respect Norwegian neutrality. Stortingspresident Hambro was of Jewish ancestry and Quisling asserted he had close connections to the British Secretary of State for War Leslie Hore-Belisha, of a Jewish family.[17] These two, he claimed, were conspiring to bring Norway into the war on the Allied side and secure British bases in Norway. Indeed, there was evidence the Norwegian government had already secretly agreed to Allied occupation of parts of southern Norway, from which Germany's northern flank could be threatened. Concluding, Quisling asserted that his party, the NS, had a large and growing group of followers, many of whom were in key positions in the civil administration and the armed forces. Although not the case, he alleged that with the support of these, he would be prepared to intervene to avert Hambro's plans and after having seized power, 'invite German troops to take possession of key positions along the coast'.

Hitler then delivered a twenty-minute monologue underlining that Germany had no plans for an intervention in Norway as long as its neutrality was properly enforced. He had always been a friend of Britain, he held, and was bitter about the declaration of war over Poland. He now hoped to press the British to their knees through a blockade rather than full-scale war. A British occupation of Norway, however, would be totally unacceptable and, according to Scheidt, Hitler made it clear that any sign of that would be met with appropriate means. It would be preferable to use the troops elsewhere, but 'should the danger of a British violation of Norwegian neutrality ever become acute [...] he would land in Norway with six, eight, twelve divisions, and even more if necessary'. Quisling wrote that upon mentioning the eventuality of a violation of Norwegian neutrality, Hitler worked himself into a frenzy.

When Quisling had left, Generalmajor Jodl at OKW was instructed to start a low-key investigation with the smallest of staffs of how Norway could be occupied should it become necessary. During the following days, several meetings were held regarding Norway. Quisling, Hagelin and Scheidt participated in some of them and apparently received repeated promises of support. Unprecedentedly, Quisling was invited back to the Reichskanzlei on the 18th. This time, Hitler was virtually the only one to speak. He re-stated his preference for a neutral Norway but repeated that unless the neutrality was strictly enforced, he would be required to take measures to secure German interests. British landings in Norway were unacceptable and would have to be pre-empted. Finally, Hitler underlined the confidentiality of their meetings but indicated that Quisling would be consulted should a pre-emptive intervention become necessary. There was no mention of any plans for a coup.

Contrary to Quisling's claims, an alliance between Norway and Britain was never even close to reality, in spite of British chartering of Norwegian merchant ships and the signing of a War Trade Agreement in March. Quisling's skewed description of the situation in Norway was at best a product of his imagination, but his assessment of the alleged political situation in Norway made an impression in the Reichskanzlei. Hitler was already frustrated by the growing anti-German sentiment in Scandinavia, and the Norwegian's tale of a Jewish-influenced, Anglo-Norwegian alliance, conspiring for offensive operations, made sense to him – far from reality, but with the right ingredients. Used by internal German forces looking after their own interests, Quisling had authenticated previous warnings of Allied intentions in Scandinavia and events were about to take a new direction. Rosenberg noted in his diary that Raeder afterwards talked of Quisling as a 'handshake from fate' ('*ein Wink der Schicksals*').[18]

Neither the German Legation in Oslo nor the Foreign Office in Berlin had been involved in Quisling's visit and when Foreign Minister Joachim Ribbentrop learned that he had met Hitler, he became rather disturbed. The new German Minister in Oslo, Curt Bräuer, confirmed that Quisling had exaggerated his leverage in Norway and vastly overstated the number of his followers and their political and military influence. Bräuer agreed that

Quisling's sympathies were national-socialistic and pro-German enough, but his politics could not be taken seriously. In his opinion, openly siding with Quisling and his party would at best be a waste of resources and could very well harm German interests. 'Nasjonal Samling has no influence in this country and will probably never have one,' he concluded, adding there were no indications that Quisling had support among Norwegian officers. As far as could be judged by the Legation, the officers were loyal to the government, which was really making an effort to maintain its neutrality. The OKW frowned at the thought of an operation that would depend on support from Norwegian confidants – not to mention the problem of maintaining security. 'Quisling has no one behind him,' Halder remarked laconically in his diary. Hitler listened for once and it was decided that even if Scheidt went to Oslo to keep an eye on events, he should hold the Norwegian at arm's length and, above all, not

The German Minister to Norway in 1940, Curt Bräuer. Unlike the German leadership in Berlin, he really tried to understand the intentions of the Norwegian government and respect their wish to remain neutral.

involve him in any planning. Scheidt used the word '*integer*' in his notes which translates to 'untouched', indicating he might become useful *after* a potential invasion. Whether these were Scheidt's thoughts or Hitler's is not obvious. Quisling took all he had been promised at face value and went home trusting that plans were being developed in Germany that would eventually put him in power in Norway. He never acknowledged the consequences of his visit to Berlin, however, later claiming he had only had 'political discussions'. Some 200,000 Reichsmarks were sent to NS from Berlin as a gift and used to renew the party offices and re-establish the party newspaper. A request for military training for some NS men was deferred, though. Quisling would have no further involvement in the ensuing preparations for the invasion of Norway. It is doubtful if he realised that he had been side-lined, and that neither he nor his coup figured in the German plans. As in most phases of his life, he stood alone in his treachery and nobody except Hagelin was fully involved.[19]

Studie Nord

At the Reichskanzlei things matured over Christmas, and after attending a *Führer*-Conference on 1 January, General der Artillerie Halder wrote:

> It is in our interest that Norway remains neutral. We must be prepared to change our view on this, however, should England threaten Norway's neutrality. The *Führer* has instructed Jodl to have a report made on the issue.[20]

The plan for an intervention in Scandinavia was still no more than a contingency. Focus remained firmly in the West, but wheels had been set in motion. As a first step, the Swedish legation in Berlin was discreetly informed by a high-ranking officer at the OKW that should the Allied help to Finland include soldiers, 'whether singly or in groups, in civilian clothes or in uniform', it would be taken as hostile towards Germany and might well result in certain parts of Sweden being occupied.[21]

The initial, basic sketch of the plan, *Studie Nord*, was completed by OKW during the second week of January. The Luftwaffe and Army staffs were preoccupied with the attack on France and showed little interest when asked to comment. Raeder on the other hand ordered the SKL to assess *Studie Nord* in detail and prepare constructive feedback. This they did, concluding on the 19th that continued Norwegian neutrality remained the preferred option. British interference with this could not be tolerated, though, and pre-emptive plans would have to be developed – just in case. Hitler agreed and on 27 January he instructed OKW to set up a special staff – Sonderstab *Weserübung* – to progress the development of such plans. Keitel should oversee the exercise and Kapitän zur See Theodor Krancke, captain of the *Panzerschiff Admiral Scheer* (soon to be reclassified as a heavy cruiser), which was about to dock in Wilhelmshaven for a lengthy overhaul, was ordered to Berlin and given the task of leading the project. Hitler ordered Krancke to develop Operation *Weserübung* based on an updated version of SKL's comments to *Studie Nord* in such a way that it could be 'integrated with the overall conduct of the war'. Knowledge of the concept was to be restricted and the interest in Norway should not be known outside OKW. Two basic principles quickly emerged when the Sonderstab began work on 5 February. Firstly, an occupation of bases in southern Norway alone was pointless. Trondheim, Narvik and possibly Tromsø would have to be occupied as well to secure the sea lanes. Secondly, occupation of at least parts of Denmark would be necessary to secure sustainable connections to Norway across the Skagerrak, prevent Allied access to the Baltic and acquire air bases to facilitate anti-shipping operations and reconnaissance in the North Sea.[22]

A rough sketch of plans was developed over the coming two weeks. For *Weserübung Nord,* the invasion of Norway, six divisions would be made available, one of them a mountain division. On the invasion day, regimental-strength landings would take place from warships at Narvik, Trondheim, Bergen and Kristiansand while the telegraph stations at Egersund and Arendal operating the undersea international cables were assigned a company each. The equivalent of two regiments would head for Oslo, plus support units. Parts of the Oslo force would secure the naval base at Horten en route. Fornebu airport outside Oslo and Sola airport outside Stavanger were to be captured in airlift operations spearheaded by paratroopers. *Weserübung Süd,* the invasion of Denmark, would primarily secure the air and sea bridge between Germany and Norway. The main objectives of *Weserübung Süd* were Copenhagen and the airfield at Aalborg in northern Jutland, the latter to be captured by paratroopers followed by an airlifted battalion. Mechanised units would cross the border in the south and push north on the Jutland peninsula, while smaller warships and requisitioned civilian vessels would land troops on the west coast and the islands.[23]

Taking Control

When told in the morning of 17 February of the events involving the boarding of *Altmark* in Jøssingfjord, Hitler became furious. 'No opposition, no British losses!' he shouted.[24] The Royal Navy had humiliated Germany and the Norwegians had been unable – or unwilling – to defend their neutrality against the British intruders. Rosenberg wrote: 'Downright foolish of Churchill. This confirms Quisling was right. I saw the Führer today and [...] there is nothing left of his determination to preserve Nordic neutrality.' Raeder was summoned to the Chancellery and told by an angry Hitler that as Norway was no longer able to maintain its neutrality, the time had come to take control of events rather than just prepare for an eventuality. Planning of the still sketchy Operation *Weserübung* was to be intensified immediately. Raeder, uncomfortable with the sudden hurry, advised caution. In another meeting with Hitler a few days later, he argued that maintaining Norwegian neutrality remained the best solution. A German intervention would inevitably result in the ore traffic being threatened by the Royal Navy and protecting the 1,400-mile coastline would be challenging, requiring U-boats, aircraft and surface vessels not readily available. On the other hand, British bases in Norway would be totally unacceptable, all the more so as this, in

Raeder's opinion, would put pressure on Sweden and also threaten the ore traffic through the Baltic. Hitler agreed; Norway must not fall into British hands. Germany would have to act, whatever the cost.

Jodl suggested giving responsibility for the planning to one of the corps commanders with experience from Poland and an established staff. The *Führer* agreed, and the 55-year-old General der Infanterie Nikolaus von Falkenhorst, commander of XXI Army Corps, was called from his quarters on the Rhine to Berlin on 21 February. Falkenhorst had been a staff officer during the brief German intervention on the White side in Finland in 1918 and was one of the very few German generals with some experience in overseas operations. In the Reichskanzlei Hitler at first invited him to speak of his experiences in Finland. After listening for a while, the *Führer* took him to a large table covered with maps and told the general that a similar expedition was being considered as a pre-emptive strike to forestall British intervention in Norway. Enemy bases in Norway would change the whole strategic situation, Hitler said, and it would be vital to secure the northern flank prior to opening the campaign in the West. Britain was already preparing landings in Norway and had, according to reliable sources, reached an agreement with the Norwegian government to this effect. The recent *Altmark* episode demonstrated beyond all doubt what was going on. A small staff had considered the question of Norway for some time, but now the time had come to take the issue seriously. Stressing the need for absolute security, Hitler invited Falkenhorst to leave for a while, think through how he would occupy Norway and come back in the afternoon. Somewhat shaken, Falkenhorst realised his career was at stake. He went into a bookshop, bought a Baedeker tourist guide and sat down to find out how to conquer a country he barely knew the whereabouts of a few hours earlier. At 17:00 he was back with some ideas and sketches. These were to Hitler's liking and, adding that in addition to pre-empting a British intrusion, occupation of Norway was necessary to give the Navy operational freedom and secure the supply of iron ore from Scandinavia, Falkenhorst was ordered to gathered trusted members of his staff and start the work immediately. Jodl noted in his diary that Falkenhorst 'accepted with enthusiasm'.[25]

Generaloberst Walter Brauchitsch, C-in-C of the German Army, was less enthusiastic. He called Falkenhorst to his office and told him frankly that he disapproved of Hitler's decision and saw the whole operation as 'unnecessary'. Besides, he had not been consulted and the *Führer* was 'doing all of this only with the advice of Raeder'. It probably did not improve Brauchitsch's opinion of the operation that Falkenhorst was to report directly to OKW and not to him – an unprecedented break with principles. Halder, the Army Chief of Staff, also expressed discontent with the operation and the fact that OKH was largely kept out of the planning. According to Falkenhorst, Hitler had

Eight German seamen were killed during the British action against *Altmark* in Jøssingfjord. Six coffins are prepared on deck for burial on 19 February. One died later in hospital, and one was missing.

Funeral of the dead from *Altmark*. The uniformed man speaking is Curt Bräuer, the German Minister to Norway. Behind him to the right with the goatee-beard is *Altmark*'s captain Heinrich Dau. Quite a few of the local population turned up too, accompanied by a large German press corps. Hitler was furious.

him report to OKW to secure cooperation with the other arms and 'avoid problems with the Luftwaffe'.[26]

Falkenhorst and his staff took up work in some secluded back-offices of the OKW building on Bendlerstrasse in Berlin on Monday 26 February. His key associates would be his Chief of Staff, Oberst Erich Buschenhagen, and his Operations Officer (Ia), Oberstleutnant Hartwig Pohlmann. The Krancke group had produced a workable outline plan for the invasion which was now detailed and elaborated. Initially, only some fifteen officers were directly involved. Kapitän Krancke remained a member of the group, representing the Kriegsmarine, although Raeder and his closest staff remained deeply involved in the development of the plans for *Weserübung*. Generaladmiral Hermann Boehm, the former Fleet Commander, was appointed to become Admiral Norwegen on 7 March. He was not part of the *Weserübung* team but would work closely with Krancke and secure communication and co-ordination between the team and the Navy. Oberst Robert Knauss from the Luftwaffe and Major Karl Strecker from the Abwehr handled liaison with their respective services. Oberst Walter Warlimont, Deputy Chief of the Operations Office, would secure a close connection to OKW – though he was not involved in the details of the planning. It was repeatedly stressed by OKW and the *Weserübung* team that secrecy was paramount, and that information was only to be provided on a strict need-to-know basis. Neither Quisling nor any other Norwegian was ever involved with the planners at Bendlerstrasse at any time during the preparations.[27]

In late February, less than two weeks after *Altmark*, German Naval Attaché Korvettenkapitän Richard Schreiber and Air Attaché Hauptmann Eberhart Spiller were called from their posting in Oslo to Berlin and asked to give their view to the planners of the general situation in Norway and the attitudes of the military and civilian administration. In particular they were asked to present their opinion on what opposition the Norwegians would put up against an invasion, German or Allied. They both replied that resistance against Allied intruders would be symbolic at best, as the *Altmark* episode had demonstrated. How a German invader would be met was more doubtful, but also in this case they apparently both assumed that opposition would be limited.

It is unlikely that the two were given full details of Operation *Weserübung*, but they returned to Norway with instructions to report as much as they could find on the Norwegian armed forces, fortifications, airfields and harbours. Neither could travel freely in Norway, and the information they provided was mostly taken from public sources and largely limited to the Oslo area, adding little to the information provided by the professional intelligence officers of the Abwehr office at the Legation.[28]

German knowledge of Norwegian infrastructure, administration and armed forces was meagre and outdated. An invasion of that country had been so inconceivable that methodical intelligence had been neglected. Maps were scarce and it was often necessary to rely on travel guides and tourist brochures. In addition, a discreet search was initiated for merchant seamen, businessmen and artists who had been to Norway. The Legation in Oslo had sent a fair amount of military information over the past years, but most of this had simply been filed. When dug out of the archives it was found to be unsystematic and outdated. An intense programme of intelligence gathering was initiated under Major Erich Pruck, sent to Oslo to work with Berthold

The 55-year-old General der Infanterie Nikolaus von Falkenhorst (1885–1968), commander of XXI Army Corps, was chosen to lead Operation *Weserübung*.

Benecke already with the Abwehr in Norway. Germans who lived in Norway were contacted via the so-called Ausland Organisation of the Nazi Party (NSDAP/AO), but they probably did not contribute much, as few responded positively. Scheidt came to Oslo during December and Hagelin in January. Both started to produce a series of intelligence reports, but these were largely analytical and lacked detail, as neither of them were military men.

On the day of the invasion, the German commanders would still have a surprising amount of information available to them even so, giving credit to the efforts of the German intelligence. The problem was that there were significant gaps, and no way of knowing what was missing or downright wrong, while some signals contradicted each other. Intelligence updates issued in late March for example, incorrectly reported that the base for the Norwegian submarines was on Jeløya on the east side of the fjord, across from Horten (*see* Chapter 11). On 23 March, a signal from naval attaché Schreiber said that a remote-controlled minefield existed at Drøbak Narrows even though its exact location could not be confirmed; ten days later, however, in early April, another signal from the attaché concluded that the mines were not yet laid after all.[29]

In the afternoon of 29 February, Falkenhorst and his staff met the *Führer*. The first concepts of *Weserübung* were presented. Around 8,850 men would be on board warships in the first wave of the attack, followed by an additional 3,900 men, 742 horses and 950 vehicles by transport ship and 3,500 men by air during the first invasion day. About 25,000 men were supposed to follow by ship and air during the first week, and during May around 100,000 men were supposed to secure German domination in Norway. Clearly satisfied, Hitler approved the scheme with a couple of minor changes. Before he left, he asked OKW to be updated every other day through meetings with Keitel. A sense of urgency rushed through the OKW. Hitler had made up his mind and everything changed. Before *Altmark*, Krancke and his men did not think they were working on a project that would be implemented. Afterwards, there was no doubt. On the next day, 1 March, the first directive for *Weserübung* was issued in nine copies. One to Falkenhorst, one to each of the C-in-Cs of the services and five for various parts of OKW.[30]

> The development of the situation in Scandinavia requires that all preparations are made for parts of the Armed Forces to occupy Denmark and Norway (Operation *Weserübung*). Through this, British assaults on Scandinavia and the Baltic will be prevented, our ore supplies from Sweden safeguarded and the Air Force and Navy's basis for the war with England extended [...] The forces to be used for Operation *Weserübung* shall be kept as small as possible [...] and compensated for by bold actions and surprise. An effort is to be made to give the operation a peaceful character to provide protection of the neutrality of the Nordic states.[31]

The rest of the four-page document gave the framework for the operation and its overall command structure. 'The *Führer* is pushing the preparations for Operation *Weserübung* forward,' Jodl noted in his diary 'Ships must be fitted out, troops must be ready.' He proposed to Hitler to develop *Weserübung* independently of Operation *Gelb*, the campaign in the West and this was accepted, even if the two operations had to be synchronised. As a starting point, it was agreed that *Gelb* should be implemented three days after the attack in the north. The Army High Command protested repeatedly against diverting forces to what they considered a secondary operation in the north. Protests were futile, though, and the same day the directive was issued, Jodl noted laconically in his diary that 'The Army agrees [to Operation *Weserübung*]' while Halder added 'Full speed ahead for *Weserübung*' in his diary, a few days later. It was no longer a question *if* Norway should be attacked, but *how* and *when*.[32]

The SKL discussed Operation *Weserübung* on 2 March and concluded in the War Diary:

> SKL is well aware of the challenges of implementing *Weserübung*, involving as it does the entire Navy. The issue is now no longer purely military but has grown into a fundamental question of politics and war industry. It is no longer solely a case of improving Germany's strategic position and gaining isolated military advantages [...] but is now a matter of the Wehrmacht adapting swiftly to political circumstances and necessities. The SKL is therefore of the opinion that demands on the Wehrmacht from the political leadership must be fulfilled through use of all available means. The timing of *Weserübung* is still unknown, but current developments indicate it may commence soon if the weather is fitting. In this situation the Navy is resolved to set aside all doubts and to sweep aside any difficulties through commitment of all forces.[33]

Adding over the next couple of days:

> The Führer has ordered all preparations for *Weserübung* to be completed as quickly as possible. Plans for the operation are to be completed by 10 March, so that from this date [...] the operation can be initiated at four days' notice [...]. British interference in the Russo-Finnish conflict will only be a pretext for obtaining the true strategic goals of landing in Norway: the severing of German iron ore imports from Norway and Sweden through occupation of the north Norwegian ports and the Swedish mining area [...] All other operations are cancelled, effective immediately, and submarines ready to depart shall be held back for now [...] After *Weserübung* [...] the strategic situation for the Navy will be somewhat better, but [can] only be partly utilised in practice, due to lack of naval resources.[34]

In an unsigned report to SKL dated 5 March, it is stated that the Norwegian government had given in to French and British pressure and accepted transit of Allied troops as well as the establishment of naval bases. It was part of the agreement that the Norwegian government should deny the existence of the treaty and protest against any intrusions, as they had done during the *Altmark* episode.[35] On 6 March Halder noted in his diary that it had now been confirmed that the Allies had requested free transit of troops to Finland through Sweden and Norway, adding that 'The Führer will act.' In a review with Hitler on the 9th, Raeder argued that, based on the information he had, he Allies had decided to send aid to Finland and would occupy Norway and Sweden along the way. Operation *Weserübung* was now 'compellingly necessary' – and it was urgent. Raeder added that, though risky, he was convinced the operation would succeed if momentum and surprise could be maintained. An important basis for the firm conviction in Berlin that Allied action was being planned was a letter sent by Oberst Konrad Sundlo, the Norwegian commander in Narvik, to Quisling. In the letter, Sundlo said that the assistant French naval attaché, Lieutenant de Vaisseau Kermarrec, had visited him, accompanied by the British consul Gibbs, resident in Narvik. The Frenchman, who was probably unaware that Sundlo was a member of Quisling's NS party, was rather loose-tongued and told the Norwegian officer that there were Allied plans for an action against ports in western Norway from Stavanger to Narvik and possibly Kirkenes. The plans included motorised units as well as artillery and the Frenchman was particularly interested in water depths, port facilities and defences as well as the rail line to Sweden, including the height of the tunnels and strength of bridges. Quisling's associate Hagelin carried the letter to Berlin, handing copies to Rosenberg and the Navy, claiming that Kermarrec had made similar visits to several other western and northern ports. The SKL concluded that there was no doubt that the Allies would act against Norway and Sweden. The only uncertainty was when. The Norwegians would object to any request for form's sake, but once the Anglo-French forces landed, there would be no more than diplomatic protests.[36]

In the following days, the number of intercepted radio messages to and from British ships increased, not least to and from submarines in the North Sea and Skagerrak. An extensive report from the intelligence department in SKL on the 10th, summarising all information they had about British and French interest in Scandinavia since long before *Altmark*, concluded that something was undoubtedly going on. Ice conditions in the Kattegat and parts of the Baltic were still such, however, that no German preventive action was possible, and no troops or transport ships were anywhere near ready to be sent to Norway. A minor crisis ensued among the planners, but the news of the Winter War ceasefire on the 13th put the work back on track. On the 15th, intercepted British signals confirmed that the Finnish–Soviet armistice had thwarted the Allied plans – this time. OKW saw no reason to change anything and Falkenhorst was told that the work should continue as fast as possible to be prepared for immediate action, while always maintaining secrecy. The danger of the Allies moving first to occupy key locations in Norway still existed. Hitler believed that Scandinavia would remain an area of unrest and insisted that preparations for *Weserübung* should continue unabated.[37]

In a meeting with Hitler on the 26th, Raeder explained how close the enemy had come to landing in Norway. Sooner or later, though, he said, the British and French would find a new excuse, or provoke one themselves, and it was essential that *Weserübung* was carried out – for preventive reasons.

Earlier in the day, Raeder added, he had been visited by Hagelin, who this time told him that the C-in-C of the Norwegian Navy, admiral Henry Diesen, believed that Great Britain would take control of Norwegian territorial waters within the foreseeable future, either directly or through an arranged provocation. In addition to severing the iron ore transport, Diesen held, London wanted to use the airports at Stavanger and Kristiansand as bases for future air attacks on Germany and prevent the Luftwaffe from using the same against Britain. There was disagreement within the Norwegian government about whether this should be accepted or not, but there would be no active military opposition in any case. Quisling was ready to try to avoid such a development, Hagelin had said, but needed German backing. Based on this, Raeder advised that *Weserübung* should be planned during the next new moon period and no later than 15 April. After that, the nights became too short to cover the crossing. Hitler agreed and a preliminary date for *Weserübung* was set between the 8th and the 10th. All efforts should be made to be ready by then and all security measures should be intensified to keep the operation secret.[38]

Two days later, on the 28th, a note from SKL to the leading naval commanders held that the Norwegian Admiral Staff, according to sources in Norway, considered a British offer 'to take over the protection of neutral territorial waters' imminent. The note also held that the Norwegian government was uncertain how to react to such a development. The conclusion, according to SKL, was that *Weserübung* could be triggered at any time and participants at all levels would have to remain prepared and vigilant.[39]

Oslo is Norway's capital with a major port and airfield, located at the centre of the national road and rail system. In 1940 it would be at the end of the safest and most easily defended sea route from Germany to Norway, vital to bring in the troops and supplies needed to occupy the country by sea or air. Secondly, Oslo was (and is) the seat of the King, government, Parliament, ministries, departments and most other political functions. Taking Oslo by surprise in a swift military operation would most likely secure Norwegian cooperation in an orderly occupation. The tactical problem was how to achieve surprise, given the long and challenging approach up Oslofjord and the uncertain prospects of a weather-dependent air assault.

The first detailed sketches for occupying and controlling Oslo, came from the *Weserübung* staff on 9 March. At the time, the heavy cruiser *Lützow*, the light cruiser *Königsberg* and a mixed group of torpedo boats and R-boats were assigned to the task. The knowledge of what they were to expect in terms of Norwegian defences was remarkably incomplete. Guns at Rauøy and Bolærne in outer Oslofjord were expected, but what type of guns and how many were not known. Horten with the main naval base was considered an important target and 300 men should be landed there to take care of the yard and an expected battery of modern 15-cm guns, which did not exist. At 'Dröback' the guns of Oscarsborg and the batteries on the mainland were correctly placed on the adjoining map, but there were no indications of the torpedo battery at Oscarsborg or any minefield in the fjord. In the adjoining text, the plan was for the cruisers to go through the Narrows at dawn and land soldiers north of the Narrows by use of the R-boats. As soon as possible, *Lützow* should continue towards Oslo, while *Königsberg* remained to give fire support should it become necessary. Shortly after this order was issued, *Königsberg* was crossed out by pencil and replaced with *Emden*; no resistance was obviously expected and *Königsberg* had been transferred to Group III for Bergen.[40] Should the outer Oslofjord be closed for some reason and the ships unable to move up the fjord, the troops should be landed at Sandefjord and Larvik on the western side or Fredrikstad on the eastern side of the fjord. From there, they could move to Oslo by road or rail. In case they could enter parts of the fjord but not be able to pass the Narrows at Oscarsborg, Horten and Son were pointed out as alternative landing sites.[41] Five days later, a second memorandum detailed the tasks of 163rd Infantry Division:

- Take control of Oslo, the fortresses along the fjord and the airfields at Fornebu and Kjeller.
- By daylight on the invasion day have complete control of the city but cause as little disturbance as possible to public transport, commerce and the people in general.
- Prevent mobilisation of the Norwegian Army by controlling the civil administration and all relevant departmental functions.
- Through occupation of the capital give credence to the demands of the Führer versus the Norwegian government.
- Secure Oslo harbour as the main port for German supplies and reinforcements.
- Until Falkenhorst and his staff arrived on *Wesertag* +1, the commander of 163. ID [163rd Infantry Division] is to be in command of the occupied areas.

A final note from OKW on 2 April stressed that Hitler had given firm orders that the kings of Denmark and Norway, Christian and Haakon, should not be allowed to escape from their respective countries under any circumstances. Immediately following the landing, they should be apprehended by armed units assisted by the German ministers in the two capitals to ensure the monarchs were under control.[42]

'To succeed with this operation' wrote Raeder to his group-commanders 'will be a decisive step in the continuation of the war with Britain'.

Chapter 5
Let Slip the Dogs of War[1]
1–6 April 1940

The Boldest Operation

During March, intelligence accumulated in Berlin that implied consistent Allied pressure on the Norwegian government to allow transit of troops to Finland and the establishment of bases in Norway. There would be protests, said the reports, but only nominal and no opposition would be offered. One report for instance, arriving via Scheidt, was that a person close to both King Haakon and Admiral Diesen considered a British intervention imminent. Another source reported with certainty that the British had requested right-of-passage through Narvik and permission to establish a naval base in Kristiansand for Baltic operations. Further reports alleged that Allied officers were surveying Norwegian ports with tacit Norwegian acceptance. These reports, though in fact largely inaccurate, came to Berlin through different channels, apparently confirming each other. Virtually all, however, originated in the same environment in Oslo and were filtered through Scheidt's group at the Legation, painting a one-sided picture of Allied threats and Norwegian compliance. Other reports of increased British intelligence activity in Norway, troop-ship concentrations in Scotland, French alpine troops embarking on ships in the Channel ports, strengthening of the British Home Fleet by withdrawing cruisers from the Northern Patrol, were taken as evidence that the assumptions were correct. There was little doubt in Berlin that an Allied operation was under development against Norway to sever the iron ore traffic and establish bases. Minister Bräuer, who saw things differently and more realistically, advised Berlin to support Norwegian neutrality rather than break it but was ignored. *Weserübung* was formally approved by Hitler on the afternoon of 1 April after a five-hour, detailed review of the operation in the Reichskanzlei. Falkenhorst and all senior Navy, Army and Luftwaffe commanders involved in the operation were present and according to Falkenhorst Hitler talked to each one of the officers. 'He cross-examined every man, who had to explain very precisely the nature of his task. He even discussed with the ship commanders whether they would land their men on the right or on the left side of a given objective. He left nothing to chance; it was his idea, it was his plan, it was his war,' Falkenhorst later wrote.[2]

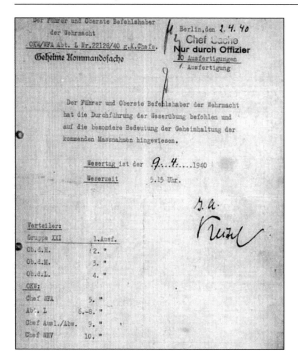

The document signed by Keitel telling key officers of Army Group XXI, the armed forces and OKW that Hitler had decided to invade Norway and Denmark on 9 April. The note was issued in ten copies only. This is copy no. 1, which went to Falkenhorst and his staff.

Satisfied with what he heard, the *Führer* ended the meeting with a commanding appeal, underlining the importance of the operation to prevent Britain cutting Germany's supply of raw materials from the north. Germany could not accept Britain's self-imposed role of overseeing Scandinavia and now the time had come to do something about it.[3]

The following day, 2 April, Hitler asked for assurances from Raeder, Göring, Keitel and Falkenhorst that all preparations were completed and neither ice nor weather could stop them. This they gave. Hitler then asked Oberst Buschenhagen, Chief of Staff for Group XXI, as the XXI Corps had been renamed, what was the latest possible date to cancel the operation. The baffled Buschenhagen, who had worked day and night for five weeks, had not given this much thought, but after some deliberations answered *Wesertag* minus five. The operation could be cancelled or postponed without risk up to five days before the designated day of the invasion. After that, the number of involved personnel with knowledge of what was happening would rise sharply.[4] Hitler gave the answer some consideration and decided the invasion should commence at 05:15, German time, on 9 April. The first supply ships would be at sea within less than forty-eight hours. Falkenhorst did not fully agree with his Chief of Staff, and later told his *Führer* that all ships could be called back, at an increasing risk of being exposed, until 15:00 on the 6th, *Wesertag* minus three.[5]

Virtually the entire Kriegsmarine would be directly involved, and all other naval operations were suspended, including U-boat sorties into the Atlantic and preparations for the offensive in the West. It is quite telling that Stavanger, which was on the initial list of invasion ports, was taken out and replaced by an air-lifted attack while Åndalsnes, between Bergen and

Trondheim, was taken out of the original list of invasion ports altogether. Both changes were made to avoid depleting the number of ships being sent to the ports considered strategically most important. There simply were not enough operational ships to cover them all.[6]

At 19:17 on 2 April a laconic signal was sent from the *SKL* to Marine-gruppenkommando West (Naval Group Command West) in Wilhelmshaven and Marinegruppenkommando Ost (Naval Group Command East) in Kiel, C-in-C U-boats and C-in-C Fleet: '*Wesertag ist der 9. April*' – *Weser*-day, the start of Operation *Weserübung* had been set to 9 April.[7] A note was made in the SKL War Diary:

> With the order from the *Führer* […] *Weserübung* has been initiated, com-mencing one of the boldest operations in the history of modern warfare. Its implementation has become necessary in order to defend vital German interests and supply of raw materials, which the enemy is attempting to sever […] The outcome of the venture will to a large degree depend on the quality and the readiness of the naval forces as well as the determination of the individual officers in command. The landing operation will predominantly take place in an area where Britain rather than England has naval supremacy. Surprising the enemy […] is important for success, and will depend on the extent to which, in the coming days, secrecy can be maintained.

And on 5 April:

> The at times limited operational options of the German sea and air forces will improve significantly through an occupation of southern Norway. Germany now has the capacity to implement such an incursion swiftly. The basis for the operation will obviously be the loss of Norwegian neutrality to England and the total inability of the Norwegians to resist.[8]

Commander of Marinegruppenkommando Ost, Admiral Carls wrote in his War Diary on 6 April that:

> The significance of this operation is not only to secure the ore supplies and sever British trade with Norway, but to include the whole of Scandinavia in the German power-sphere […] The British have to a large extent influenced the timing of the operation. A massive attempt from their side to forestall our seizing of the Norwegian harbours is to be expected […] The risks to the deployed units of the Navy are well known to the SKL as well as to the *Führer*; [Raeder] has seen to that, in the same way as all group commanders have been made aware that the success of this operation, contrary to conventional operational considerations, is based on secrecy,

Transport ships of 1. Seetransportstaffel ready for departure in Stettin.

surprise, lack of Norwegian opposition and ruthless use of force to overcome all difficulties.[9]

The multiple reasoning behind Operation *Weserübung* is apparent. Quisling set the scenario of a British intervention in Norway firmly on the agenda of OKW in December 1939 and the decision to launch the operation matured over time, advocated by Raeder and Rosenberg and ignited for real by the *Altmark* incident. Gradually the question changed from *if* it should be initiated to *when*. Whether German intentions were aggressive, or defensive has been argued at length since 1940. In fact, they were both, or rather a complicated, multi-dimensional combination of several aspects, some of which had aggressive and strategic rationale, some defensive and tactical, intended to secure German control of supplies and forestall allied intentions. Berlin had no direct knowledge of the plans for Operation *Wilfred*, but the Abwehr intelligence organisation duly registered the build-up of an expeditionary force for Finland. In addition, the French and British press reported freely on plans for Scandinavia and both Churchill and Reynaud were rather talkative about their intentions.[10]

The greatest weakness of *Weserübung*, besides the lack of cooperation between the services, was the absence of alternative political and military plans. There was no in-depth assessment of the assumption that the Norwegians would not defend themselves. Neither was there any fallback if the occupation did not evolve as swiftly and efficiently as planned – other than application of brute force. The political and administrative aspects of the invasion and subsequent occupation were nowhere near as well considered as the military, largely because few outside OKW had any knowledge of the operation. Division commanders, staff officers and other leaders were informed individually at the latest possible moment – and with details only of the part of the operation they were to be involved in. The Foreign Office was most likely aware that an operation was being deliberated through Ribbentrop's connections with the Reichskanzlei but was officially notified only through a memorandum from Keitel on 2 April with instructions for the German Ministers in Oslo and Copenhagen. Thus, they had little time to prepare, far less influence the issue. This would benefit security but was detrimental to any joint policy or preparations prior to the operation.[11]

A draft note on the administration of the occupied areas was issued by Oberst Warlimont in late February and appears to have been accepted without much discussion. A key element in the note was to secure military control of Norway with minimal disturbance of the existing civil administration.

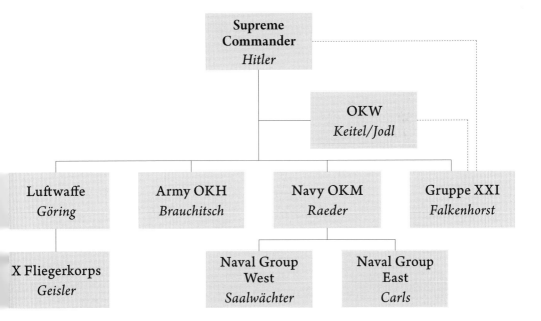

Command lines were confusing at best in Germany in 1940. There were no clear distinctions between military and civilian administration. In the case of *Weserübung*, Falkenhorst reported directly to Hitler, partly through OKW, but his communication with Raeder, Brauchitsch and Göring varied and was at times challenging.

Hitler believed King Haakon could be persuaded to legalise the occupation following a convincing show of force and it was considered particularly important that he remained in Oslo. Government, civil administration and police should continue as undisturbed as possible, provided there was collaboration. Uncooperative individuals should be removed immediately while political parties and the Storting should be ignored and eliminated as soon as possible. Radio broadcasts were to be taken over by German personnel, while press loyal to the new regime could remain. The people should be won over through propaganda. During the operation and the ensuing take-over, all communication with the Norwegian government and other politicians should be through Minister Bräuer. Falkenhorst and his men should focus on the military tasks of the occupation and suppress any activity directed against German interests. When Raeder queried the political development in Norway following the occupation, Falkenhorst and Keitel reassured him that Hitler would handle that and they, as soldiers, need not worry. Shortly after, it was confirmed in a memorandum from OKW that necessary measures to deal with Norwegian political, administrative or commercial bodies would be taken care of by the *Führer* in due course. Falkenhorst assured Raeder it would be feasible to collaborate with Foreign Minister Koht, a statement Raeder later referred to as 'politically naïve'.[12]

In a memorandum issued on the 27th, signed by Buschenhagen, it was stated that although there seemed to be an increased vigilance in the Norwegian defences, with some reinforcements being deployed, there were no signs of mobilisation.

> In spite of several reports from reliable sources, there is no clear picture of how a permission to open fire will be handled by the Norwegian armed forces. As was seen in the *Altmark* case, the Navy and Air Force appear to have received orders not to open fire on superior forces to avoid unnecessary losses. The Anti-Aircraft Artillery has orders to open fire only on aircraft that are clearly offensive [...] Lately, however, it appears that the decision to open fire has been shifted to the discretion of the local commander. Two confidential sources have told the naval attaché that they believe this also applies to the Coast Artillery, which the attaché has no information to disbelieve.[13]

There was no recognition among the German planners of the difference between Norwegian territorial waters in general and what the Norwegians defined as *krigshavn* (*see* Chapter 2) The instructions issued by Marine-gruppenkommando Ost on 9 March to all participants in the occupation of Denmark and eastern Norway stated:

Entering Norwegian territorial waters, ships shall fly British flags. German naval ensigns shall be hoisted at the latest when the troops start landing or when it is decided to open fire […] A peaceful occupation is to be pursued, but in case of resistance all available means shall be employed immediately. Own ships shall avoid combat before *Weserzeit*.[14]

This order was based on the information the *Weserübung* staff had, that the Norwegians would not open fire on a British force being landed more or less openly. A week later, the order was partly countered by an additional order that it was paramount to enter the target harbours and start the offloading of the troops at the set time. As it was necessary to enter Norwegian territorial waters beforehand to be at the ports by *Weserzeit* it would be critical that all troops were kept below deck so that the ships could claim to be suffering an emergency and refer to the 24-hour rule if challenged on their way in, rather than to pretend they were British. In the afternoon of the 8th the order was abandoned altogether, and no British flags were used during *Weserübung*, though there were a few places where ships tried to disguise their identity when signalling to guardships during the entry phase.[15]

Utmost Secrecy

On the afternoon of 3 April, Minister Colban in London sent a telegram to the Foreign Office in Oslo passing on the information that Philip Noel-Baker, a Labour MP, had led him to understand that the British government was preparing an operation against the iron ore traffic inside Norwegian waters. Foreign Minister Koht later wrote that the telegram from Colban worried him much more than any of the information that came from Berlin and this message, which was copied to Nygaardsvold and Ljungberg, would certainly focus the attention of the Norwegian government and military in the days to come.[16]

On the same day, 3 April, the head of Abwehr Group I, Oberst Hans Piekenbrock, met in utmost secrecy with Vidkun Quisling in room 343 at the Hotel d'Angleterre in Copenhagen. Quisling had asked for the meeting to take place in Stockholm, but this was rejected by the German side and he travelled to Copenhagen. Hagelin, who had facilitated the meeting, was at the hotel, but it is unclear if he attended the meeting. Questioning Quisling on the status of the Norwegian defences and their willingness to fight, a disappointed Piekenbrock received the impression that the taciturn Norwegian had limited knowledge and was largely out of touch with reality. There were two things the Norwegian was certain of, though: there was no minefield in the Oslofjord, and the coastal forts would not open fire without explicit orders from the government. Many senior officers, Quisling claimed, were members or sympathisers of his NS party and would only offer token resistance once it was clear the intruders were German. Piekenbrock did not reveal anything about *Weserübung*, but Quisling must have sensed that something was going on. All the more so as two weeks earlier, around 22 March, Major Walter de Laporte of the Abwehr had contacted him clandestinely in Oslo, asking to what extent the Norwegians would oppose an Allied invasion. The SKL noted in their diary that there was little news of relevance to the Navy in Piekenbrock's report. Jodl made a similar note in his diary but added that the meeting had created an increased unease in OKW that the defences in Norway might have been alerted. During his trial after the war, Quisling denied any recollection of the meeting, claiming he only met Frits Clausen, the leader of the Danish National Socialist Workers Party. There is no doubt, however, that he met Piekenbrock.[17]

The next day, 4 April, a much better source of information came to Berlin. The head of the Abwehr, Admiral Canaris, had unexpectedly shown up at the Legation in Oslo on 31 March, disguised as 'Oberregierungsrat Fuchs', partly to relieve unease between the Navy and Abwehr personnel at the Legation, partly to inform his staff what was happening and to get a last-minute update in person. Pruck, the head of intelligence-gathering related to *Weserübung* in Norway, was in Narvik and could not get back in time. It seems therefore that Canaris focussed on the personnel issues and did not discuss *Weserübung* with anybody. Sensing he had missed something important when he got back to Oslo, Pruck took the Lufthansa morning flight to Berlin on the 4th – on his own initiative. Canaris was at first upset that he had come and afraid his man might not get back in time, but mellowed when he realised that the Abwehr, through Pruck, could present vital information. Hence, Pruck was told of the imminent invasion and ordered to brief key officers before heading back to Oslo as fast as he could. First, Pruck met Oberst Buschenhagen and Oberstleutnant Pohlmann of Falkenhorst's staff. The two men were mainly interested in whether the Norwegians would fight or not and Pruck answered that in his opinion, based on extensive discussions with officers and politicians, they would. Their tactics would be to establish a defence with smaller units, using the terrain, pending mobilisation of the main forces and Allied help. A perturbed Pohlmann claimed this contradicted other sources, but Pruck was firm: the Norwegians would defend their neutrality – also against the Allies, but with far less vigour and stamina. In particular there were reasons, in Pruck's opinion, to fear the guns and torpedoes of the coastal forts. Though old, they had a considerable sting, and he was certain they would be used. The conversation ended with Pohlmann telling Pruck he would come to Oslo on the afternoon of the 8th, ahead of the invasion forces. Pruck promised him all possible help and wished both men good luck.

Admiral Wilhelm Canaris (*front left*), Norway, 1940. He visited the country at least twice that year and this rare photo was taken on his second visit, after the occupation.

He then hastened to meet Generalmajor Edouard Dietl who was to lead the troops landing at Narvik. Having been to that city only a few days earlier, Pruck was a unique source of information for the general, adding details to the map of Narvik and its defences. Having completed his round of briefings, Pruck headed for Tempelhof airport to take the Lufthansa flight back to Oslo, while it was still in operation.[18] A memorandum from Minister Bräuer in Oslo confirmed Pruck's interpretation of the Norwegian will to resist, as he reported Foreign Minister Koht having told him that the neutrality forces had received strict orders to open fire on any foreign ship or aircraft that appeared to penetrate Norwegian waters or airspace illegally.[19]

'*Weserübung* is being implemented according to plan,' General Jodl wrote in his diary on 5 April.[20]

Growing Tension

On the morning of Friday 5th, the main story of the Norwegian newspapers was the attack on the passenger ship *Mira* with 107 people on board. The ship had joined British convoy ON24 on its way from the UK to Norway. These convoys had sailed regularly between Great Britain and western Norway after the outbreak of the war and more and more ships joined them for protection – although the massing of ships also made them tempting targets for German aircraft and submarines. According to the reports made available to the press, the *Mira* had been attacked eight times by German aircraft. There had been no direct hits, but some bombs had fallen very close to the ship, terrifying for those on board. Two passengers had been wounded. The episode was a grim reminder of the danger to the Norwegian fleet in international waters from the ravages of war. Foreign Minister Koht would have to prepare a Norwegian reaction to the incident, among all the other issues he had to deal with.[21]

For most Norwegians, a quiet weekend lay ahead. Heavy snowfall in the south had slowed the country down more than on a normal Friday afternoon and the weather forecast was not particularly good. For Koht, there would be no rest at all. The British and French Embassies had jointly asked him to receive their respective Ministers that same evening. Arriving around 19:00, the British Minister Cecil Dormer and the French Minister Comte de Dampierre handed Koht a joint memorandum from their governments.[22] It was a harsh note, claiming that events over the last few months had shown that the Norwegian government was under pressure from Berlin and unable to act independently. Britain and France could no longer accept the continuous flow of resources and raw materials to Germany from the Scandinavian countries. Five points followed. The first four were of general character. The last held that the Allied governments were waging war on behalf of the smaller, neutral states and could not accept any advantages for Germany whatsoever. There was no reference to iron ore or any specific demands, but the note concluded that the Allies considered it within their rights ...

> to take such measures as they may think necessary to hinder or prevent Germany from obtaining from those countries, resources or facilities which for the prosecution of the war would be to her advantage or the disadvantage of the Allies [...] The shipping of Norway, Sweden and other neutral countries is attacked and destroyed almost daily by German submarines, mines and aircraft, in defiance of international law and with deliberate disregard for the loss of life involved. The Allies will certainly never follow this example of inhumanity and violence, and when the successful prosecution of the war requires them to take special measures, the Norwegian Government will realise why they do so [...] and the Allied Governments feel confident that this fact will be duly appreciated in Norway.[23]

Koht was stunned. He had little doubt that this was a warning of imminent naval intervention in Norwegian waters, most likely provoking a

German response. Most of the content of the note was uncalled for he told the Ministers angrily, particularly allegations that Norway was commercially and politically under German control, and he found the language 'disdainful, unworthy of His Majesty's Government'. Distressed by the note himself and by Koht's reaction, Dormer timidly defended his government by claiming the words were directed towards Germany more than Norway. Koht did not think so. The Allies had given themselves *carte blanche* to proceed at will in Norwegian waters and from this point on, Koht was preoccupied with the threat of an Allied aggression. Mounting evidence of a parallel threat developing on the German side was dismissed as out of sequence.[24]

After seeing the Allied ambassadors off, Koht left his office to dine at the US Legation. It does not seem that he even considered informing the Prime Minister or the other members of the government of the Allied note, far less the Foreign Affairs Committee. Koht arrived late and excused himself to Mrs Harriman, saying that the day 'had been the most nerve-racking of his official life'. He did not go into any detail, but the American envoy noticed that 'his face was drawn, [indicating] that the day truly had been more tense than usual'.[25]

On that same evening, the German Minister Bräuer entertained a large number of Norwegian politicians, civil servants and officers at an official reception in the German Legation. More than 200 guests were present, including Commanding General Laake and several officers of the General Staff, ministers, officials and journalists. Some of the invitees, including Koht, did not turn up. Nobody knew why they were there, but after a rich supply of snacks and drinks, the surprise was revealed: there was a film to be shown! Titled *Feuertaufe* or 'Baptism of Fire', the reel had come from Berlin that same day with orders for it to be shown as soon as possible to a selected audience. To everybody's embarrassment it turned out to be a propaganda film from the conquest of Poland, covering the bombing of Warsaw in particular. Accompanied by Wagner's music it showed in ghastly detail what happened to the Polish capital – thanks to the intervention of the Poles' British and French friends, according to the commentator. The concluding scene was a map of Britain going up in flames. After the show there was a long silence before quiet conversations began on anything but what they had just seen. Most of the guests excused themselves and left as soon as they could. It had been a tactless demonstration of power, and few believed it had been unintentional.[26]

Next morning, Saturday 6 April, Koht gave an account to the Storting of the political situation. There was great public interest in the meeting and the open galleries were crowded. For over an hour the Foreign Minister elaborated the international situation. A large part of his account focussed on the Norwegian merchant fleet. Since the start of the war, he said, 54 ships

Foreign Minister Koht giving a reassuring account to the Storting on 6 April.

had been sunk and 392 Norwegian seamen had been killed. He referred to the attack on the *Mira* but concluded that the Norwegian will to remain neutral had not faltered and, surprisingly, added that none of the belligerents had attempted to drive Norway away from this policy. He ended his speech by stating that 'employing all available resources to defend Norway's national independence is a duty to our country and to the future'. Nobody in the Storting disagreed and no formal debate followed. Koht mentioned neither the warnings from Berlin (see below) nor the Allied note or any of the other threats received during the week. Later he wrote that he believed it would have been inappropriate to reveal what had been given to him in confidence as he did not wish to frighten the public. Unknown to Koht, though, several European papers reported the contents of the Allied note that morning and the news was in the Norwegian newspapers by lunchtime.[27]

After the orientation, Koht at last told other government members of the note he had received the night before but made it clear that he would handle this alone, as usual, and there was no need for the others to worry. Minister of Finance Oscar Torp did worry and insisted the Neutrality Watch should be strengthened around Oslofjord immediately. Nygaardsvold asked him to discuss the matter with Ljungberg to see what could be done. Eventually nothing was. Unbelievably, neither Koht nor Ljungberg brought up the reports from Berlin and Copenhagen and when Hambro, Stortingspresident and chairman of the Foreign Affairs Committee, called Koht in the afternoon to ask what was going on and why he had not been informed of the Allied notes, he was curtly assured that everything was under control and the Foreign Office would handle matters. Nygaardsvold and Hambro suggested a meeting would be appropriate. Koht saw no need to rush things and agreed to meet on the following Tuesday, 9 April.[28] Nobody in the government or the Storting had any notion that Operations *Weserübung* and *Wilfred* were both already under way. The almost universal lack of ability to understand and interpret the signals that came to Oslo, Copenhagen, London and Paris and realise what was about to happen is one of the great enigmas of Operation *Weserübung*.

At Tirpitzufer in Berlin, the officer on duty over the weekend entered in the SKL War Diary during the evening of the 6th that Koht had told the Norwegian Storting earlier that day that his objective was 'sustained Norwegian neutrality'.

> [There is] growing tension in most countries over the development of the Norway issue [but] there is no evidence that the Allies have recognised Germany's strategic intentions. At least, they do not grasp the dimensions of the operation. The measures of the enemy indicate [...] that he himself is very close to initiating his own actions in Norwegian waters. As he is undoubtedly aware of German preparations of some kind and will anticipate immediate German reactions, we must expect him to be well prepared to defend his own forces. How far in its preparations the enemy is, or if this operation has already been initiated, is not known. The SKL is, however, of the opinion that the launch of *Weserübung* is now highly urgent. 9 April appears to be the last possible date for the operation.[29]

How right he was – and how wrong. Operation *Wilfred* was indeed under way. Reynaud went home after the meeting on the 28th to discuss the novel plans with his Comité de Guerre. The committee supported minelaying in Norwegian waters but, to his surprise, rejected any laying of mines in the Rhine. Frustrated over what he considered French manipulation, Chamberlain told Ambassador Corbin 'No mines, no Narvik' and considered both operations postponed.[30] In the Cabinet meeting on 3 April, however, Churchill argued strongly that no matter how the French government dealt with sending mines down the Rhine, the minelaying in Norwegian waters had to be carried out as planned. All the preparations had been made, and it would be very difficult, both security-wise and operationally, to keep the forces on standby. He therefore suggested that Operation *Wilfred* should be held back for a couple of days while he travelled to Paris to persuade the French to accept mining the Rhine. The warnings should be submitted on 5 April and the mines planned to be laid on the 8th. Churchill failed in France, but on his return, he managed to persuade Chamberlain that it was right to lay mines in Norwegian waters anyway. *Wilfred*, Churchill claimed, would most likely provoke German counter-reactions, allowing Allied forces to enter Norway and Sweden and intercept the ore traffic with a clear conscience. Allied troops were ready in British ports and could be sent towards Norway 'the moment the Germans set foot on Norwegian soil, or there is clear evidence that they intend to do so' and the opportunity was too good to miss.[31] The fact that the Germans were already heading for Norway, including Narvik, was not realised by the War Cabinet, the Admiralty or the CoS, despite several warnings.

The minelayer *Teviotbank* put to sea from Scapa Flow on the morning of 5 April, before the warning note was delivered in Oslo. Escorted by four destroyers she was heading for Stadandet south of Ålesund to lay the southernmost of the *Wilfred* minefields. Another minefield would be laid in the approaches to Vestfjord north of Bodø, while a third area off Bud between

Mines for Operation *Wilfred* are loaded onto British destroyer *Ivanhoe* at the naval base at Immingham.

Molde and Kristiansund would be declared dangerous, without any mines actually being laid. Confrontations with Norwegian naval forces were to be avoided, but if the mines were swept, they should be re-laid as soon as possible. Later that same day, Vice-Admiral William 'Jock' Whitworth set out from Scapa Flow aboard the battlecruiser *Renown*, screened by four destroyers. On the morning of the 6th, the 20th Destroyer Flotilla fell in with its four mine-laying destroyers *Esk*, *Ivanhoe*, *Icarus* and *Impulsive* (Force WV), carrying sixty mines each for the Vestfjord minefield, escorted by *Hardy*, *Hunter*, *Havock* and *Hotspur* of the 2nd Destroyer Flotilla under the command of Captain (D)2, Bernard Warburton-Lee. In view of the potential situation that might arise from swift German reaction to the minelaying, it is difficult to understand why the Admiralty did not order the rest of the Home Fleet to sea as well. From a central position north of the Bergen–Shetland Narrows, both minelaying operations could have been covered against German reactions without exposing the ships to the Luftwaffe.[32]

Weighing Anchor

In the operational orders for the occupation of Norway, issued by Falkenhorst on 5 March in twelve copies to his key officers, it is stated clearly that

> … military–political strength used against Norway, shall be kept at a minimum. To compensate, the relatively weak forces must be deployed cunningly and with utmost secrecy to achieve maximum effect. An effort shall be made to give the occupation a peaceful character with the aim of providing armed protection of Norwegian neutrality. The Norwegian government will be informed correspondingly at the start of the occupation to ascertain they forsake any form of armed resistance and will cooperate loyally from the start […] any resistance offered despite this shall be met with a firm military response.[33]

It was expected that a rapid occupation of key political and military objectives followed by 'firm, soldierly behaviour' would shock the Norwegian people and their armed forces into submission. If not, bombing from aircraft or bombardment from the warships bringing the soldiers in, should be a sufficient deterrent. A meeting on the 26th, however, between Falkenhorst's staff, OKW and the main regional commanders confirmed that:

> The operation will start by landing the troops, not as previously discussed, through diplomatic negotiations. At *Weser*-time each regional commander will have the authority to open fire if very short negotiations do not succeed. If so, all available means shall be employed, including deception and ruses. The objectives must be met under any circumstances.[34]

A number of support ships were to enter the invasion ports shortly after the invasion fleet and be ready to unload once the harbours were secured. The warships that should carry most of the troops had limited storage facilities and slower transports would arrive at their destinations following a detailed timetable, on the invasion day or in the following days, some in groups, others alone. The transport ships of the Ausfuhrstaffel (literally 'Export Group') and the tankers of the Tankerstaffel would be disguised as civilian merchantmen and travel ahead of the invasion fleet to the more distant invasion ports of Trondheim and Narvik as well as Bergen and Stavanger. The ships would bring heavy weapons, fuel and supplies vital for sustaining the operations of the initial assault groups. Of these ships, few would survive the invasion. The transport ships were a constant source of worry for the SKL. Security was not properly maintained during their loading, and once at sea any incident they might become involved in could potentially compromise the operation. Originally, the ships were to carry equipment and provisions with a minimum of troops on board. During the last few days before departure, though, to the surprise of the Navy, a large number of soldiers arrived to be transported to the invasion ports on orders from Group XXI.

Having a long way to go, the German transport ships *Rauenfels*, *Bärenfels* and *Alster*, destined for Narvik, departed Brunsbüttel at 02:00 on 3 April. In the afternoon, the tanker *Kattegat* followed. Over the next several days, the freighters *Main*, *São Paolo*, *Levante* and the tanker *Skagerrak* left for Trondheim; followed by *Roda* for Stavanger. Other vessels sailed from Lübeck and Stettin heading for the southern *Weserübung* ports, packed with almost 4,000 men, 742 horses, 950 vehicles and other heavy military equipment. Officially these ships were to take supplies to East Prussia, which had been isolated by floods, but out of sight from land they turned west for the Danish Belts and the Norwegian coast. SKL was extremely unhappy about the transport ships being ahead of the warships. They believed the risk of exposing the operation to both the British and the Norwegians was heightened exponentially by so many ships carrying soldiers and equipment being at sea. Their repeated protests were brushed away by the planning team, though. The ships were an integral part of the plan, and the men and supplies were needed in the landing ports on the invasion day.[35]

At 20:30 on the 6th, a signal from Dönitz to all U-boats contained the codeword *Hartmut*, indicating sealed envelopes with orders written on water-soluble paper should be opened. The envelopes contained detailed orders for all boats to move into new locations along the Norwegian coast, taking care not to reveal their positions. Allied warships and troop transports could still be attacked, but Norwegian or Danish ships should be left alone. Following the confirmation of Operation *Weserübung* on the 2nd, a total of thirty-two

Loading of German transport ships in Stettin. The narrow boxes
with arched roofs and rolled-up tarpaulins are to transport horses.

U-boats were at sea; fourteen Type VII and Type IX boats from Stad and
northwards and eighteen Type II boats in the Skagerrak and the North Sea.[36]

The naval ships taking soldiers to the Norwegian ports of Narvik
(Group I), and Trondheim (Group II), assembled in Wesermünde and Cuxhaven respectively, during the first week of April.[37] Group I consisted of ten
destroyers loaded with *Gebirgsjäger* (mountain troops) of the 3. Gebirgs-
division. Group II had four destroyers and the cruiser *Admiral Hipper*,
Blücher's sister ship, also loaded with mountain troops. The battleships
Scharnhorst and *Gneisenau* would act as cover for Groups I and II and carried
no troops. Kapitän zur See Hellmuth Heye, captain of *Hipper* was in charge
of Group II, the warships for Trondheim. During the afternoon of 6 April,
the embarkation of soldiers in Cuxhaven commenced under the supervision
of *Hipper*'s First Officer Korvettenkapitän Wegener. The troop trains were
shunted into the closed-off Amerika-Kai and the soldiers started to climb the
gangways: 1,700 men in all, 900 to *Hipper* and 200 to each destroyer. Heye,
who considered the threat a fire in his cruiser would pose as high, was very
careful that all explosives, ammunition, fuel and other dangerous items were
stored below deck. Extra space was made in the magazines by storing as much
as possible of the ammunition for the ship's guns in ready lockers. Explosives
that could not be kept below the armoured deck were spread throughout
the ship in small crates and boxes to minimise the risk from incoming fire.
The troops were confined below deck with orders to remain there until they

were well out into the North Sea. Engine rooms and turrets would be out of bounds at all times. No smoking would be allowed outside or in the doorways after dark. On Heye's insistence, every soldier, few of whom had ever been aboard a ship before, was issued with a personal lifebelt. When ready, *Hipper* and the destroyers cast off and crossed the Bight towards the Schillig-Reede off Wilhelmshaven to join Group I. Few people on board knew what was happening and where the ships were heading.[38]

Scharnhorst and *Gneisenau* weighed anchor from Wilhelmshaven shortly after midnight on the night of 6/7 April. The SKL considered the risk of alerting the Allies to *Weserübung* by sending the battleships to sea worth taking. Should they be sighted, it might even be that the Admiralty would anticipate an Atlantic breakout and concentrate British forces between Iceland and Shetland, an advantage for the ships following behind. Reaching Lightship F at 03:00 on the 7th, the battleships were joined by *Hipper* and her destroyers for Trondheim as well as the ten destroyers for Narvik. The most powerful fleet the German Navy had mustered in over twenty years headed northwards at 22 knots.[39]

Transport ships leaving Stettin in the afternoon of 6 April, heading for Kristiansand. Photo is taken from *Kreta* with *Westsee*, *August Leonhardt* and *Wiegand* following. After a delay *Kreta* arrived on the 13th. The other three arrived as planned on the 9th.

Forewarnings

Intelligence consists of four elements, acquisition, analysis, interpretation and distribution. If one is missing or weak, the others become meaningless. Identification of relevant information from 'noise' in a flow of often contradictory signals can be demanding, as even the significant signals are often ambiguous and can, more often than not, justify several rational interpretations. Thus, the psychological concept of cognitive priming or confirmation bias must be accounted for, where the appreciation of new information is influenced by the receiver's expectations and beliefs. That which confirms an existing point of view is far more readily accepted than that pointing in an unfamiliar direction. This was certainly true for the Norwegian government of 1940. There were individuals or groups with access to all available intelligence material tasked with assessing threats to the country's neutrality. The ministers had to do this themselves, in addition to their many other tasks, without professional military analysis and management systems. Koht in particular believed himself to be the best man to interpret and understand the incoming information and decide how to act upon it – or not, in most cases without seeking a second opinion. Except for a handful of civil servants and one senior under-secretary, he had no group of analysts to try to help him see the larger picture and he never took any initiatives to have incoming reports systematically verified or cross-checked. The so-called Foreign Office Committee with representatives from the political parties of the Storting, meant to be an arena for sharing information and discussing consequences was largely kept inactive in this period. The threat from Germany was recognised by the military, but as the analysis of strategic intelligence rested with the Foreign Office, the Ministry of Defence and the Army and Navy staffs lacked the necessary political perspective on their part of the intelligence. Tactical intelligence was not recognised as a concept and certainly not the need for such information to be gathered, shared and systematically assessed between the political and military administrations. Defence Minister Ljungberg did not systematically forward the assessments given to him by the military staffs to the government; nor did the military themselves forward all information they possessed to their minister.[40]

As with most tasks in the Norwegian military, intelligence was handled separately by the services. The Admiral Staff had an intelligence office led by kaptein Erik Steen and the General Staff a similar unit led by oberstløytnant Harald Wrede-Holm. Both offices were understaffed but worked together in an informal manner and shared most of the information they received. Interactive communication between military intelligence and the government was non-existent, however – even after September 1939 – and no

Kaptein Erik Anker Steen, head of the intelligence
office at the Norwegian Admiral Staff.

systematic assessment of the incoming information in a political context existed. Information was forwarded to the Ministries of Defence and Foreign Affairs 'when of interest'. Similarly, information came to the intelligence offices from the ministries, but rarely with any comments or analysis.

Between the military intelligence offices of the Nordic countries an unofficial and informal cooperation, largely unknown to the politicians, existed on a personal level between individual officers. The Foreign Ministers were made aware of the contact, and were apparently content with keeping it at a functional level. The only written agreement that can be found regarding this is a loose 'plan' between the intelligence departments of the Swedish Defence Staff and the Norwegian Admiral Staff to keep each other 'informed of foreign warships in the vicinity of each other's coasts', signed by the respective department heads Steen and Kommendörkapten Sven Linder of the Swedish Defence Staff's intelligence department, in March 1939, before the outbreak of war. The scope of the intelligence cooperation between Sweden, Norway and Denmark was widened as the situation became tense to include 'all German military matters' but remained informal. According to Swedish sources, the Danes had particularly good insight into what went on in Germany, whereas the Norwegians seemed more concerned with allied aggression during the winter of 1939/40.[41]

In the early part of the war, British intelligence was no less fragmented than in Norway. Coordinated acquisition of intelligence from reliable sources was rare and the exchange of analysis and interpretations almost non-existent. Hence, the disregard of the mounting evidence that Germany was preparing to invade Norway and Denmark is almost a textbook example of lack of coordination and inability to conceive that the opponent could actually do something else than perceived. The German readiness to face British supremacy at sea, landing troops around the coast from Oslo to Narvik, ran counter to all predictions made to the British government by its military advisers. On 28 December, two weeks after Quisling set the wheels in motion in Berlin, the British War Office sent a summary note to the Foreign Office indicating signs of possible German plans for Scandinavia, picked up by the Secret Intelligence Service (SIS). Two weeks later, on 8 January, the War Cabinet received a memorandum from the Foreign Office, concluding from compiled intelligence, that Germany was contemplating invading southern Scandinavia, but nobody pursued the issue.[42]

On 17 March, the British military attaché in Stockholm, Lieutenant-Colonel Reginald Sutton-Pratt, reported to London that he had heard from Swedish officers that visiting German officers had told them that Norway 'would be taken care of, soon'. A week later, on 26 March, this was followed by a message from the Embassy in Stockholm regarding increased concentrations of aircraft and ships in northern Germany and the Baltic, which was now rapidly becoming ice-free. It added that a senior naval officer in the Ministry of Defence had disclosed that 'Swedish Staff believe Germans are concentrating aircraft and shipping for operation which Swedish intelligence consider might consist of seizure of Norwegian aerodromes and ports. Pretext being disclosure of Allied plans of occupation of Norwegian territory, thus compelling German intervention.' Handwritten on the front-page of this report is: 'I wish I could believe this story. German intervention in Scandinavia is what we want!' – signed by Laurence Collier of the Foreign Office.[43]

Several reports followed in the coming days confirming nervousness in Germany over Allied intentions in Scandinavia. On 28 March, the Deputy Chief of Naval Staff, Rear-Admiral Tom Phillips summed up the information in a memorandum to Churchill and Admiral Pound. He concluded that Germany seemed to be getting ready for some kind of operation against southern Scandinavia in the near future. It was not clear, however, whether the operation was an independent German measure, or would be launched as a response to Allied action against Norway. As a precaution, Phillips advised, the Army and Navy should be put on standby and ready to improvise a counter-reaction should the Germans strike first. It appears, however, that the two naval leaders were preoccupied with their own forthcoming mining operation and did not believe that the Germans would act until provoked. The memo was obviously read, but no actions advised, neither to the War Cabinet nor to the CoS.[44]

On 31 March, the British Naval Attaché in Oslo Hector Boyes called the Norwegian Navy Chief of Staff Elias Corneliussen, asking about rumours of German preparations in the Baltic. Corneliussen admitted he had received reports to this effect but was not concerned as he believed the activity was related to Allied assistance to Finland, in which Norway was not involved.[45]

For a number of reasons, including earlier warnings of German naval operations against Norway that never materialised, Koht had limited faith in the Norwegian representatives in Berlin. Minister Arne Scheel, an elderly diplomat of the old school, was of the opinion that in order to be as neutral as possible he should attend all functions he was invited to. Koht, however, believed he should stay away from official Nazi Party events. Furthermore, in March, Scheel sent a rather concerned letter to the Foreign Office in Oslo claiming that Norway had come to the foreground of German attention due to threats to the iron ore transport through Narvik. He recommended Norwegian neutrality be 'upheld as strongly as our utmost abilities permit' – words Koht partly interpreted as reflecting the German point of view and partly as a criticism of him and his policy. Koht and Scheel were thus not on friendly terms. They had to respect each other and communicate but there was an unfortunate lack of confidence between the two which would have grim consequences. To make matters worse, the Vice-Consul of the Legation, Ulrich Stang, had developed Nazi sympathies during his assignment. Neither Koht nor Scheel was happy with this and they had discussed having him removed. Stang was still in Berlin in April 1940.[46]

The Swedish naval attaché in Berlin, Anders Forshell and Raeder's chief of staff Erich Schulte-Mönting met frequently, discussing various issues. On the evening of 28 March, Schulte-Mönting told Forshell over dinner that political and military developments in the north were 'highly disturbing'. There was concern in the German leadership that Britain might venture into Norwegian waters and establish bases, particularly in the Narvik area from where they would certainly advance on Kiruna. As he had explained in December, Schulte-Mönting held that this would not be acceptable and various countermeasures were being considered. A pre-emptive strike was far better than a belated reaction he argued, the challenge being where to strike and when. What Schulte-Mönting knew of *Weserübung* is unclear, but it is unlikely that he had detailed knowledge of the plans at this stage. Forshell had since early February expected this development and, based on pieces of information he had gathered from Schulte-Mönting and others, he was convinced Germany was developing plans for an attack on Denmark and Norway, while Sweden most likely would be left alone.[47]

On 31 March, the Swedish Foreign Office received another note from Berlin saying that reliable sources had told the Embassy that troops, horses, vehicles and equipment had been embarked in 15–20 large ships in Stettin and Swinemünde. The troops might be intended for a preventive seizure of key areas in Sweden to secure the supply of iron ore. Supplementary information over the next few days confirmed the embarkation, but shifted the potential target to southern Norway and Narvik and held it would probably

Kommendörkapten Anders Forshell (*left*), Swedish Naval Attaché in Berlin, and his Danish colleague, Kommandørkaptajn Frits Hammer Kjølsen. Both were central in bringing the warning of the German intentions to Stockholm, Copenhagen and Oslo.

not be initiated without direct Allied provocation. The Swedish envoy to Berlin, Arvid Richert, expressed concern. Something was going on. The embarkation took place behind guarded fences, but bars and restaurants in the Stettin docks had been invaded by many new naval personnel, unfamiliar to the regulars. Most likely the Germans anticipated an Allied intervention in Scandinavia but they might be ready to act on their own.[48]

The Nordic envoys Richert and Scheel exchanged information at times, though their relationship was formal, rather than friendly. In a letter written on 1 April, Scheel reported to Oslo that Richert had told him the Reichskanzlei was concerned regarding imminent British actions to block the German ore transport through Narvik and ended the letter with a summary of the information Richert had provided regarding troops embarking on ships in Baltic ports. The letter arrived in Oslo on the 3rd but neither Koht nor Nygaardsvold saw any reason for concern from its content. When the two envoys met again a few days later, German disinformation had confirmed that the troops and equipment were intended for East Prussia, where flooding had caused an emergency, and both agreed there was no reason for alarm.[49]

In a new meeting with Schulte-Mönting on 2 April, Forshell brought up the loading of troops in Stettin. Schulte-Mönting brushed it away; nothing was happening in Stettin and there were no German threats towards Sweden. Still, Forshell concluded next day in a report to the Chiefs of Staff and

Foreign Office in Stockholm that he found reason to believe that Germany was planning a preventive intervention in Norway. Germany would not accept any change of status quo in Scandinavia and British air bases in southern Norway would be particularly intolerable. The report was copied to the Swedish envoys in Oslo and Copenhagen on the 4th but its content appears not to have been forwarded to the government or military authorities of the two countries.[50]

Oberst Hans Oster was one of Canaris's closest associates in the Abwehr. He was a convinced anti-Nazi and when learning of the plans for *Weserübung*, it appears he saw an opportunity to cause a military defeat large enough to provide the occasion for a coup against Hitler. It has not been possible to ascertain whether Canaris endorsed Oster's actions, but the two men had a close personal and professional relationship, and it is unlikely Canaris was completely unaware of what Oster was about to initiate. Oster asked an old friend, the Dutch Military Attaché in Berlin Gijsbertus Sas, to see him on the afternoon of 3 April. The details of what exactly Oster told Sas are lost to history, but Sas later insisted Oster said that imminent German operations would be directed simultaneously at Denmark and Norway and the offensive in the West would follow shortly after. Whether this was the case and subsequent distortions were made inadvertently when forwarding the information or remembered differently by those becoming involved, we shall never know. Oster was treading a fine line. Most likely, his goal was a political change in Germany, and he may deliberately have tainted the information to protect himself and to avoid unnecessary loss of German lives. Or perhaps he tried to make what he was doing less treasonous in his own eyes by not revealing the plans correctly. In any case, Oster confirmed to Sas next morning that the operation was set and encouraged his friend to forward the information to the embassies of the countries involved.[51]

During the morning of the 4th, Sas contacted Swedish Naval Attaché Forshell, informing him of the information he had received from Oster. According to Forshell's notes, Sas told him that Denmark would be occupied the next week, followed by an attack on Norway while Sweden would be left alone. An attack on Holland and Belgium, would follow shortly after Norway. Forshell who was already conscious of German plans against Norway from his conversations with Schulte-Mönting, realised the seriousness of the information given to him by the Dutchman. He briefly informed Minister Richert and hurried across to the Danish Embassy, asking to meet Kommandørkaptajn Frits Hammer Kjølsen. The stunned Danish Naval Attaché who had been in Copenhagen four days earlier forwarding rumours of a German attack on Narvik to prevent a British blockade of Swedish iron ore imports, listened with growing unease to Forshell telling him his country would be the subject of German aggression within a week, as part of an attack on Norway. Troopships were ready in the Baltic and soldiers were embarking at that very moment. Unaware that Forshell had already been to the Danish Embassy, Major Sas came shortly after to share the information from Oster, asserting it came from reliable sources inside the OKW. Sas later stated that he told Kjølsen both Denmark and southern Norway would be invaded simultaneously on the morning of 9 April. Kjølsen, however, categorically denied having been given any dates for the invasion other than 'next week', claiming the accounts of Sas and Forshell were 'near identical'.[52]

The Norwegian legation in Berlin was one of the few without a military attaché and Vice-consul Stang was therefore Sas's natural level of contact. Sas was aware of Stang's friendly relations with a number of high-ranking German officials, however, and chose to bump into him at the Hotel Adlon where he would most likely have his lunch. Sas later claimed he had emphasised in a few brief sentences that both Denmark and Norway would be attacked simultaneously on 9 April. Stang, however, denied this, alleging that Norway had not been mentioned at all and that he had forwarded exactly what he had been told. Based on what Sas told Forshell and Kjølsen, it is hard to believe he did not mention Norway to Stang.[53]

Kommandørkaptajn Kjølsen passed the information from Forshell and Sas to his Minister, Herluf Zahle, who then called the Norwegian Legation asking to be received in the afternoon to discuss matters of utmost political consequence. Unknown to Kjølsen his telephone was tapped and his calls to Zahle and the Norwegian Legation were intercepted by German intelligence. The information ended up in the OKW and eventually in the SKL on the 7th, where it was concluded that the Danish Naval Attaché somehow had obtained information on the forthcoming Operation *Weserübung*.[54]

At the Norwegian Legation, Kjølsen told Minister Scheel of the information he had received. Understandably, the old diplomat was very upset to learn of the serious threats to his country. Later in the evening, Stang, who had not been present at the meeting, came to the Danish Embassy to discuss matters. Kjølsen and Under-secretary Steensen-Leth presented all the information they had to Stang. He responded that he was informed of German plans without elaborating, but claimed, to the surprise of the Danes, that the attack would not be directed north, but towards Holland and France. After the meeting with Stang, Zahle signed a note to the Foreign Office in Copenhagen written by Kjølsen and had it couriered home on the afternoon flight. Next day Kjølsen submitted a supplementary note, stating that he believed Major Sas's information to be reliable.[55]

What discussion took place between Stang and Scheel in the Norwegian Legation during this day is not known. It appears, though, that Stang's view prevailed as next morning, the 5th, a telegram was received in Oslo informing the Foreign Office that the Legation 'had been informed from an attaché at one of the neutral embassies – in strict confidence – of German plans to invade Holland in the near future'. Denmark was also threatened as Germany might be seeking bases on Jutland's west coast. Norway was not mentioned at all. The Legation forwarded the information with care, it was underlined, as it could not be verified even if the attaché who had forwarded it was usually reliable and well informed. The telegram was composed by Stang and signed by Scheel in spite of the somewhat different information he had received from Kjølsen. It must have occurred to Scheel that the message could be misleading as some hours later, a second telegram followed adding that information from Danish diplomats indicated places on the Norwegian south coast might be threatened as well.[56]

In Oslo, Koht rated both telegrams as rumour and took little notice of either. The telegrams received were copied to Ljungberg, but not to any other member of the government. No initiatives were taken by the Foreign Office or the Ministry of Defence to discuss the information in the government or with the other Nordic foreign offices. The telegrams were forwarded to the Admiral Staff and the General Staff during the day, but no actions were taken by either body.[57]

Contrary to Scheel, Swedish Minister Richert found the information from Sas highly disturbing, even if Sweden was not directly threatened. He asked Forshell for a meeting on the evening of the 4th. Kjølsen was also invited to this meeting in which a memorandum to the Swedish Foreign Office, detailing the information received by Kjølsen and Forshell, was compiled. This and a similar memorandum from Forshell to the Swedish Naval Intelligence Staff were couriered to Stockholm on the first available flight. The Swedish government, Foreign Office and Military Intelligence were thus informed of Operation *Weserübung* on the morning of 5 April. Richert added that information from other sources indicated that Hitler appeared to have made 'some important decision' on 2 April and persons in the German Foreign Office appeared 'nervous and pre-occupied'. Forshell in his short military style summarised that Denmark would be occupied next week, whereafter Norway would come under attack at several locations from Oslofjord to Bergen. No aggression was intended towards Sweden. Reports of mountain troops in northern Germany confirmed in his opinion that Norway was on the list of targets. Unknown to the Danes, a discreet message from the German Ministry of Propaganda had come to the Swedish Legation in Berlin late on the 4th that Sweden would not be threatened by Germany in the near future. Richert concluded in a brief telegram to the Foreign Office in Stockholm on the 7th that, in his opinion, 'Far-reaching actions towards

Denmark and Norway are to be expected shortly; most likely within days.'[58] The following day he explained that the information behind the telegram came from reliable sources and that he believed them to be accurate. Decisions had been taken and actions initiated based on a German wish to secure the ore supply from Sweden. Sweden was not threatened at this stage, according to Richert. Hence, the Swedish political and military leadership had solid information on what was about to happen, but no documents have been found suggesting that the information was forwarded from Stockholm to Oslo in any form. Why is difficult to understand today. Both Richert and Forshell concluded that the operation was imminent as all the foreign military attachés in Berlin had been invited on a tour of the Western Front, starting on the evening of Sunday 7 April. Forshell had decided not to attend this tour, with his Minister's approval, as he believed it was a pretext to have the attachés out of the way.[59]

In Copenhagen, the Danish Foreign Ministry finally took the reports from Berlin seriously. On Friday the 5th, around 11:40, the Norwegian envoy to Denmark August Esmarch telephoned Under-secretary Jens Bull at the Foreign Office in Oslo. He had been called to the Danish Foreign Office earlier in the morning, he said, as had the Swedish envoy, Carl Hamilton. Both had been queried on their respective countries' reactions to the recent information from Berlin of a German offensive against the Low Countries, western Denmark and southern Norway. Esmarch had no knowledge of this and made the call to Bull requesting advice on what to tell the Danes. Being careful on the open telephone line and assuming Oslo had received the information referred to, he just forwarded the request without going into the background he had been given by the Danes other than mentioning the danger of a German attack on Denmark and southern Norway. 'Copenhagen was nervous' according to Esmarch and wanted to know as soon as possible the considerations from Oslo. Bull did not question Esmarch in any detail, apparently as he assumed Koht would know what this was all about. When learning of the telephone conversation with Esmarch, Koht dismissed the issue as the same rumours Scheel had mentioned and took no action to ascertain what the Danish request referred to. Bull returned a call to Esmarch just before 14:00 informing him that Oslo would do nothing based on rumours – and he could say so to the Danish Foreign Office. No information of Esmarch's request for a Norwegian reaction went outside the inner circles of the Foreign Office. Esmarch on his side reported back to the Danes that Oslo did not give the report any significance at all. Swedish Minister Hamilton had a similar answer. Satisfied, the Danish Foreign Office forwarded a summary of the information to the British Embassy and did little else. During the 8th, a letter arrived in Oslo from Copenhagen, explaining the background for the telephone call on the 5th, but this seems not to have been registered by anybody outside the staff at the Foreign Office.[60]

During the evening of the 5th, Överste Carlos Adlercreutz, head of intelligence at the Swedish Defence Staff, called his Norwegian counterpart at the General Staff in Oslo, oberstløytnant Wrede-Holm, informing him, off the record, that Sweden had reliable information from Berlin of an imminent German attack on Denmark followed by a similar attack on Norway. Shortly after, an almost identical message arrived from the Danish General Staff. Reports of these communications were sent to the Commanding General, the Admiral Staff and the Ministry of Defence. Ljungberg later said he had 'no positive recollection of the issue' and neither could he remember having seen any of Sheel's letters. The information was not disseminated and nobody in the Foreign Office or the government appears to have to have been informed – or taken notice if they were. Likewise, neither the operational commanders nor their intelligence officers were informed of the comparable information coming from the legations to the Foreign Office.[61]

Meanwhile, the Norwegian journalist Theo Findahl, stationed in Berlin for the Norwegian newspaper *Aftenposten*, somehow got hold of the rumours about an imminent attack on southern Norway. He was subject to strong restrictions but managed to submit an article to Oslo during the weekend. Unfortunately, Findahl stated the number of German soldiers to be landed in Norway to be in the order of '1.5 million'. The editor, while preparing a dramatic front page for Monday's edition, contacted the office of the Commanding Admiral in the evening for comments, speaking to kaptein Håkon Willoch, the duty intelligence officer in the Admiral Staff. Willoch referred the inquiry to the Commanding Admiral who found the story of 1.5 million men 'too fantastic'. To his dismay, the editor received a call from the Foreign Office shortly after with instructions to halt the publication of the report.[62]

In the afternoon of Sunday 7th, yet another telegram from Scheel in Berlin arrived at the Foreign Office in Oslo. It stated that according to reliable sources, 15–20 large ships loaded with troops and equipment had left Stettin and Swinemünde in the early hours of 5 April, heading north and west. An unknown destination should be reached on the 11th. Ulrich Stang later told the Commission of Inquiry that this new information came from Kjølsen, adding that the reference to a westerly course should have indicated to Oslo that Norway was at risk.[63] The cypher secretary on duty, Gudrun Martius, considered the message serious enough to call Koht at home as no senior member of the political staff was present in the office. After the telegram was read to him, Koht reassured Martius that the ships were not heading for a destination in Norway, but 'into the Atlantic'. How Koht knew this, and what a large fleet of German transport ships loaded with troops was hoping to achieve there, was not discussed. A copy of the report was couriered to the Admiralty and General Staff that evening, but no further measures were taken, as Koht had given no instructions. The next day, a copy of the signal was sent to the Ministry of Defence, but it is unclear if it reached Ljungberg. It appears the mention of the 11th, which was several days away, to a large extent affected Koht's dismissal of Norway as the target. Martius was confused after the conversation with Koht but could only conclude that as the Foreign Minister took the telegram so calmly, he had other information that put the situation in a different light.

A copy of the signal reached kaptein Willoch at the intelligence office around 22:00, via the Ministry of Defence. He called the Commanding Admiral and, quoting it, asked if he should initiate any measures, for example alert the districts and prepare for mines to be laid. Diesen answered no and assured the surprised Willoch that he himself would make sure those who needed to know would be informed. Willoch's frustration was considerable, all the more so as he never heard back on the issue. According to Steen, the Commanding Admiral and his chief of staff agreed that the troopships were most likely related to an attack on Holland.[64]

Thus, the information from Oster and Sas arrived in Oslo by circuitous routes. It was backed up by other sources, but these were blurred, and the details did not quite match. The main message was clear enough: a German attack on Norway was under development. Nevertheless, neither Koht nor Ljungberg considered the signals to indicate serious danger and no one took any action to have the information verified. Prime Minister Nygaardsvold and the rest of the government never received an overview of all information available, and no initiatives were taken to discuss the situation with the military commanders or their staffs. Neither was any contact made with the other Nordic governments to hear their views on the development. Indeed, the initiative from Copenhagen to do just that was dismissed. There are independent accounts of Koht having commented on the reports from Germany something like 'either the rumours are false, in which case there is no cause for alarm, or they are correct, in which case we will not have any useful answers if we ask'. That might be, but no attempts were made to compile the signals and assess them jointly either. Why this was so, is less obvious. Arguably, the telegrams to Oslo were less precise than those received in Stockholm and Copenhagen, partly due to the omissions and distortion of the original message by Stang, but this cannot explain it all. Perhaps it was personal issues that made the warnings from Scheel and Stang less believable? Perhaps it was cognitive priming? Whatever the reasons, the information lost its significance somewhere between Berlin and Oslo, remaining one of the great enigmas of April 1940.[65]

Chapter 6
No Way Back
7 April

Control of Oslo

For the British, the western coast of Norway was key. Because of Britain's focus on the North Sea, the Norwegian interior was of limited interest, except the railway connections towards Sweden. The country east of the airport at Kristiansand, including the capital Oslo, rarely figured in any of the Allied plans. During the planning for Operations *Stratford* and *Avonmouth*, the CoS held that if the Germans were to choose to try their hand at Oslo, it would certainly be through landings on either side of the fjord, far south, as it would be too risky to send warships up the narrow Oslofjord. German landings north of Stavanger were not considered at all.[1]

Seen from Berlin, the picture looked very different. The British supremacy in the North Sea was well recognised, and during *Weserübung* the German warships and transports would have to sneak in, deliver the troops and get out of harm's way before the Royal Navy could react. Losses were bound

to occur. Any British counter-landings would certainly be in the west and German troops to combat these as well as reinforcements and supplies to their troops landed on the west coast on the 9th would have to come via Oslo and then by road or rail. Taking control of the capital as soon as possible was therefore imperative for military as well as for political reasons. The invasion was intended to be peaceful, if not friendly, and the ideal situation would be that the Norwegian king and government accepted reality, put their hands in their pockets and continued as before, accepting German administrative command and control of the country's defences. This could only happen if Oslo was taken in a swift coup-like action at the beginning of the operation to thwart resistance and avoid an armed Norwegian response. Closing the Skagerrak by extensive mine barrages to prevent the Royal Navy attacking the supply route was also considered essential to secure safe communication with the Homeland.[2]

The warships sent to the western ports would be followed closely by an initial group of supply ships, but it was not expected that further transports could reach these ports, once the Royal Navy had been alerted. The initial group of transports, 15 ships carrying troops, horses, vehicles and 6,000 tons of supplies, designated 1. Staffel, would go to Oslo, Kristiansand, Stavanger and Bergen. The remaining 23 transport ships, separated into two groups, 2. and 3. Staffel, would go to Oslo only. After completing the first trip, most ships would return to Germany and then begin a shuttle service from Germany to Oslo and other ports in the east, until sufficient forces and supplies had been

brought in, securing Oslo and for three columns to advance overland towards the western invasion ports.[3]

It had been the intention since before *Weserübung* came on the agenda, to send the heavy cruiser *Lützow* into the Atlantic at this time, threatening supply convoys to Great Britain. At first, however, she was drawn into the planning for Norway as flagship of Group V heading towards Oslo. After a while, many in SKL found this a waste of a good opportunity and during the first half of March, more and more voices argued for taking the

The heavy cruiser *Lützow* carried six 28-cm guns.

Blücher during trials in the Baltic. The foredeck was 'wet' even in moderate seas.

opportunity of the turmoil that would inevitably be raised by *Weserübung* to let the heavy cruiser slip through the British lines and into the Atlantic. On 23 March, this was approved in principle and Kapitän zur See August Thiele received orders to prepare his ship accordingly. SKL saw no problems replacing her with the brand-new cruiser *Blücher* as the lead ship for Oslo. The orders confirming the change were issued by SKL on the 28th.[4]

The original plan was to have *Blücher* ready for battle, *Gefechtsbereit*, on 3 May, following final testing and work-up in the Baltic. This date was now brought forward by a full month. The focus for the ship's officers suddenly changed from making her fully battle-ready to acquainting the crew with the ship, organising watches and making sure NCOs and seamen knew their quarters and stations and who was reporting to whom. Written instructions were few and far between and exercises involving damage-control virtually non-existent. Ten or twelve inflatable Marcks rescue floats, each with room for 15–40 men, arrived just before sailing, after much pressure from Kapitän Woldag, together with lifebelts for the crew. Some 700 men with action stations below deck were issued with inflatable jackets. The rest were told they had to manage in an emergency with baggy kapok lifebelts that were tied to the railings of the upper deck and superstructure to save time and space. When she left the yard, *Blücher*'s magazines contained practice ammunition of all calibres. From lack of time due to the haste of the preparations and to avoid compromising security, it was decided not to offload this, but merely stow as much live ammunition as there was room for on top, resulting in full magazines and storage rooms. On 7 April the ship's officers reported to OKM that: 'Cruiser *Blücher* is ready for simple tasks. Main artillery has not been fired, no action stations exercises, no engine emergency trials, and no damage control exercises have been performed.' Chief Engineer, Fregatten-

Kapitän zur See Heinrich Woldag (*left*) was a gunnery specialist who had served in battleships during the Great War. In the inter-war years he served on the old *Schleswig-Holstein* and held various posts ashore, including commanding the artillery school, before his promotion to *Kapitän* and appointment to the still outfitting *Blücher* in October 1937. He was small in stature – and well-liked by his crews. His friends called him *Dakkel*, a slang-word for a type of dog. *Blücher*'s First Officer, Fregattenkapitän Erich Heymann (*right*) had also been to sea during WW1.

The light cruiser *Emden.* Three of her eight 15-cm guns can be seen here.

kapitän Karl Thannemann later wrote that in April, the engines were 'ready for war' (*gefechtsklar*), except for a few issues considered minor at the time, such as cramped conditions in the damage-control centre, poor emergency lighting in some rooms, leaking pumps and sensitive boiler-pipes.[5]

Weserübung naval command was split between Marinegruppenkommando West in Wilhelmshaven and Marinegruppenkommando Ost in Kiel. Head of Group West Generaladmiral Alfred Saalwächter was on leave but returned on 6 April while Admiral Rolf Carls, who had handled both commands in his absence, returned to Group East in Kiel. During the transfer of Group V to Oslo, Konteradmiral Oskar Kummetz would be in charge, reporting to Carls in Kiel.[6] Kummetz embarked on *Blücher* with his staff on the afternoon of the 5th in Kiel after which the cruiser headed into the Baltic in the company of the light cruiser *Emden*. *Blücher*'s junior adjutant Oberleutnant zur See Walter Freiherr von Freyberg-Eisenberg-Almendingen – usually known as Oberleutnant Freyberg – was made available to the Admiral and served as his flag lieutenant for the operation. Only Kummetz and Kapitän Woldag and their senior staff officers knew what was going on. The rest of the crews were told they were preparing for another exercise.

On docking in Swinemünde in the morning of the 6th, preparations were immediately initiated with the staff of 163. ID for the embarkation of troops. The majority of the soldiers who came on board *Blücher*, were from II./IR 307 (2nd Battalion, 307th Infantry Regiment). In addition, there were personnel from Group XXI, 163. ID and an advance party of Falkenhorst's staff, as well as technicians, propaganda personnel, war-correspondents, and others: in all 822 men (*see* Appendix C). Kapitän zur See Werner Lange of *Emden* was asked to come on board *Blücher* and learned of the attack on Oslo and his ship's role in that for the first time. He also learned that *Emden* would have some 600 soldiers on board during the transit to Norway. The embarkation of the soldiers began as darkness fell. On *Blücher*, most of their equipment was stored on deck while the men made themselves comfortable in the confined, unfamiliar environment below. Few of them received any information on what to do in an emergency. The many practice shells taking up the storage space in the magazines meant that heavy weapons, ammunition and other equipment brought on board by the soldiers, some 30 tons of it, had to be stowed wherever there was room, partly unprotected in corridors or directly on deck, partly in the torpedo workshop and the aircraft hangar. When *Blücher* left Kiel on the 8th she had the following live ammunition on board:

- 20.3-cm: 1,280 rounds
- 10.5-cm: 4,800 rounds
- 3.7-cm Flak: 4,000 rounds
- 2-cm Flak: 16,000 rounds
- Torpedoes: 20[7]

Lack of time as well as fear of compromising security prevented bringing on board additional lifejackets for the Army personnel. Amidst the general hurry and confusion of the brand-new ship, there was time only for a very hasty safety demonstration for the soldiers. One of the officers who came on board was Rittmeister Paul Goerz. He was a reserve officer now drafted from his position as Director at the Blaupunkt factories to the *Weserübung* staff where he was to be responsible for supplies coming in for the German forces via Oslo after the first landings. One of the first things he checked on entering *Blücher* in Swinemünde was safety equipment. It was not easy to find, and when he asked, he was told to his surprise that there was nothing extra for the soldiers.[8]

In late March, *Lützow* lay fully stored and fuelled in Wilhelmshaven waiting for Operation *Weserübung* to commence when Hitler intervened again. On a request from Group XXI through OKW, he decided *Lützow* should accompany Group II to Trondheim. There, she should land some 400 mountain troops before heading for the Atlantic, covered by the battleships *Scharnhorst* and *Gneisenau*. Neither the SKL nor Thiele was happy about the detour to Trondheim which meant departure at a fixed date, not when the forecast predicted ideal weather for a breakout. The Fleet Commander Vizeadmiral Günther Lütjens was alarmed as well, as *Lützow*'s cruising speed was 21 knots, and her emergency speed would barely exceed 24 knots. If challenged by superior British ships, Lütjens would have to decide whether to leave her behind or stand by. Neither officer could do anything but accept the decision, though, and Thiele took *Lützow* from Cuxhaven to Wilhelms-haven on the 5th to embark the *Jäger* and their equipment. Next morning, he tried once more to convince Group Commander West that having *Lützow* as part of Group II for Trondheim was a bad idea but got the same answer as before: orders are orders.[9]

At 15:00 on the 6th, however, only a few hours before departure, Group West was informed that cracks had been discovered in the base of *Lützow*'s auxiliary motor no. 1. The cracks could be temporarily welded but maximum speed was reduced to 23 knots. An Atlantic breakout was out of the question without dockyard repairs, as was a passage through the Bergen–Shetland Narrows, and at 17:00 on the 6th, Raeder re-assigned *Lützow* to Group V where she would be less exposed. To catch up, Thiele had to depart as soon as possible and in the small hours of the 7th, after a hurried embarkation of 400 *Gebirgsjäger* of IV./GjR 138 and some fifty Luftwaffe ground-crew in addition to 23 tons of ammunition and equipment, *Lützow* cast off, heading for Kiel through the Kaiser Wilhelm Canal.[10]

Blücher and *Emden* left Swinemünde accompanied by the torpedo boats *Möwe*, *Albatros* and *Kondor* at 05:30 on the 7th. First, they steered east, but when out of sight from land, they turned west heading for Kiel. During the day, *Blücher*'s main guns were fired for the first and, as it turned out, last time with live ammunition: one round for each gun. Further exercises were held all over the ship, particularly focusing on battle drill and damage control. The two Arado Ar-196 aircraft on board were also launched from the catapult and hoisted back aboard again. The Army soldiers were, under protest, kept below deck practising disembarkation drills. After the test, one of the two Arado 196 aircraft was stored in the hangar, un-fuelled, while the second aircraft

Blücher in Swinemünde on 6 April.

remained on the catapult, partly fuelled. Four 50-kg aircraft bombs were stored in the hangar. It has not been recorded that anybody voiced concern over this. Shortly before 21:00, the group dropped anchor in Strander Bucht off Kiel alongside *Lützow*, which earlier in the day had come through the canal from Wilhelmshaven. All soldiers had been unceremoniously sent below deck and were only allowed up again in small groups wearing Navy garments borrowed from the seamen. Most of the men still believed they were involved in an exercise and found the masquerade quite funny – all the more so as very few of the *Landser* had been on board a ship before and found the situation quite confusing. Questions from the officers over emergency exercises and lifebelt drill were dismissed by the accommodation personnel as 'unnecessary'.[11] Waiting for departure time, Kummetz invited captains, navigation officers and Army commanders aboard *Blücher* to inform them of the real nature of the operation and discuss the last details with Generalmajor Erwin Engelbrecht, commander of 163. ID. Engelbrecht would be in charge once the troops landed in Oslo and would be acting C-in-C until Falkenhorst arrived. For most of the officers this was the first they learned of their mission. During the night, some heavy weapons and equipment not going to Oslo were transferred to the torpedo boats that were to take them to their assigned targets along the fjord.[12]

Eight small motor-minesweepers or R-boats (*Räumboote*) of the 1. Räumbootsflottille were also assigned to Group V. These boats *R 17, R 18, R 19, R 20,*

Torpedo boats *Möwe* and *Albatros*, tied up next to sister ship *Greif.*

R 21, R 22, R 23 and R 24 were nimble and versatile, used for a multitude of tasks in sheltered waters including minesweeping, landing of troops, escort and anti-submarine work. They were armed with two 20-mm automatic guns and depth charges. Kapitänleutnant Gustav Forstmann was in charge of the flotilla. In a meeting with Kummetz and the other commanders in Kiel Bay on the morning of the 7th it was decided that the best plan would be for the boats to make the crossing from Kiel to Oslofjord independently, going through Storebælt in the evening of the 7th. Together with the R-boats, the two converted whale-catchers *Rau VII* and *Rau VIII* should also head for Oslofjord as auxiliary vessels (*see* Appendix C).[13]

The R-boats and *Emden* were to remain in Oslo as long as needed to add to the general defence of the harbour and take over escort of the transport ships in the inner reaches of the fjord. In addition, it was expected that captured Norwegian ships would augment the Kriegsmarine's fleet in Norway. There were nine Germans ships in the port of Oslo in early April, but these were all civilian vessels carrying coal or other cargo and were not included in the initial planning of *Weserübung*.[14]

The *Weserübung* forces used code-names for all cities, ports and harbours in Norway and Denmark relevant for the invasion. Horten was *Hameln*, Rauøy was *Remagen*, Bolærne was *Bautzen*, Oslo was *Oldenburg* and so on. For *Blücher* and her group, the contemporary German documents use both *Gruppe V* and *Gruppe Oldenburg*. Consequently, both Group V and Group *Oldenburg* are used in this text.

The majority of the soldiers on board the ships, except *Lützow*, came from the 1st and 2nd Battalions of IR 307. In addition, but there were staff personnel from Group XXI and 163. ID as well as naval gunners, communication personnel, pioneers, war correspondents, miscellaneous Navy and Coast Artillery personnel and ground crew for the Luftwaffe units to be stationed at Oslo-Fornebu. In total there were almost 2,200 men. In addition, two battalions

Captain Henry Denham, RN, observing *Blücher* and the other heavy ships of Grouppe Oldenburg heading for Kiel on 7 April.

and the staff of IR 324 plus one pioneer company would come by air via Fornebu. The rest of 163. ID would land in Oslo by transport ship in the days following (*see* Appendix C).

The British Naval Attaché in Copenhagen, Captain Henry Denham, picked up rumours of German minesweepers off the Danish coast and on the morning of Sunday 7th he drove south to Gedser to investigate. To his immense excitement he observed large warships on the horizon and having seen them again off Rødby on a westerly course, rushed back to Copenhagen to report. Based on other recent reports, Denham was in no doubt that these ships were part of an action towards Norway, probably Narvik, and added this to his telegram to the Admiralty. Some months later in London, Denham met his friend Captain Ralph Edwards

> … who had been Duty Captain at the Admiralty on the evening of 7th April when my telegram, reporting enemy ships and their probable Norwegian destination, had been received. He told me he had taken it straight across to Winston Churchill who, after studying the contents,

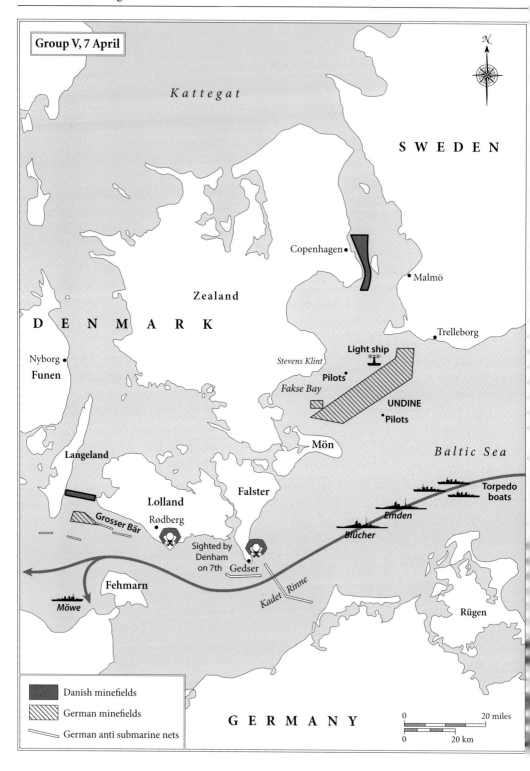

Group V, 7 April

Kattegat

SWEDEN

Copenhagen •
• Malmö

Zealand

DENMARK

• Trelleborg

Nyborg •

Funen

Light ship

Stevens Klint

Pilots •

Fakse Bay

UNDINE

• Pilots

Mön

Baltic Sea

Langeland

Torpedo
boats

Falster

Lolland

Grosser Bär

Rødberg

Emden

Blücher

Sighted by
Denham
on 7th   Gedser

Fehmarn

Kadet Rinne

Rügen

Möwe

Danish minefields

German minefields

German anti submarine nets

GERMANY

0   20 miles
0   20 km

had merely remarked 'I don't think so.' Months later when the two men happened to be together at sea, crossing to a Washington conference, Churchill, recognising Edwards and remembering their earlier meeting about my telegram, generously admitted his error of judgement.[15]

The last entry of the Admiralty War Diary on the 7th, at 23:58, notes the Naval Attaché in Copenhagen having reported personally sighting the cruiser *Blücher* and other German warships south of Gedser on a westerly course at 14:00 and again at 17:00. The report was dismissed, however, with the comment 'evidently doing exercise with ship out of sight'.[16]

A few hours later, all *Weserübung* ships would be at sea and there would be no way back. 'No disturbing news,' General Jodl wrote in his diary.[17]

Heading North

Dawn on Sunday 7 April found the ships of Group I and II in calm seas between the Danish Jutland peninsula and the German *Westwall* minefield. During the afternoon, a deep area of low pressure moved in from the Atlantic as predicted by the German meteorologists and the fine weather gave way to low clouds and rain showers. Visibility was reduced to less than a mile and the sea state started to worsen with a mounting gale from the south-southwest. Towards midnight the wind reached force 8 or 9 and a heavy swell from aft developed. Just before midnight, the ships passed the latitude of Bergen. The wind increased further and some of the destroyers lost touch with the flagship.[18]

Back in Wilhelmshaven, Group III for Bergen, a mixed group of light cruisers *Köln* and *Königsberg*, training ships and torpedo boats, departed some 24 hours behind Groups I and II, before dawn on the 8th, and Group IV with the light cruiser *Karlsruhe* and torpedo boats for Kristiansand and Arendal also left Wesermünde. The last of the groups to leave for Norway was Group VI, four minesweepers carrying 150 soldiers to secure Egersund, near Stavanger. Groups X and XI, heading for Denmark followed (*see* map on page 136, and Appendix C). Meanwhile, Falkenhorst and his staff moved from Berlin to Hamburg. The Hotel Esplanade had been emptied of guests and during the 7th was turned into a temporary headquarters for *Weserübung*, including the command group of Fliegerkorps X who would control all air support during the operation. To uphold security, the area was closed off and armed guards kept all unwanted persons out.[19]

The first report of German warships at sea reached Whitehall at 06:37 on the 7th when it was logged that an aircraft had sighted a large, unidentified ship heading north at 15–20 knots off Heligoland the night before. At 08:48 a reconnaissance aircraft reported a cruiser and two destroyers steering northwards west of southern Denmark. The report reached the C-in-C Home Fleet at 11:20 and thirty minutes later was confirmed by a new report stating that the force probably consisted of a *Nürnberg*-class cruiser with six destroyers. A group of Blenheims of 107 Squadron were sent off to attack them but achieved nothing. After the attack, the lead aircraft sent a brief report but used an incorrect wavelength and the signal was never received.[20] Only after the aircraft had landed shortly before 17:00, did it emerge that a large German fleet was at sea. By then, another report had come in of three destroyers sighted off Horns Reef heading south, apparently back towards Germany. To further blur the picture, a signal was sent from the Admiralty at midday:

> Recent reports suggest a German expedition is being prepared. Hitler is reported from Copenhagen to have ordered unostentatious movement of one division in ten ships by night to land at Narvik with simultaneous occupation of Jutland. Sweden to be left alone. Moderates said to be opposing the plan. Date given for arrival at Narvik was 8th April. All these reports are of doubtful value and may well be only a further move in the war of nerves.[21]

The wording of the signal was that of the Deputy Chief of Naval Staff, Rear-Admiral Tom Phillips – despite him having warned Churchill and Pound a week earlier that the Germans appeared to be planning an operation of their own. Admiral Charles Forbes, C-in-C Home Fleet, later remarked that in light of subsequent events, the last paragraph was unfortunate. First Sea Lord Admiral Dudley Pound was out of his office for most of Sunday the 7th. Admiral Pound did not modify any of the actions taken or signals sent when he came to Whitehall around 20:00 that evening, so it must be assumed he endorsed what had been done. Nor did he seek an update of the situation or verify the state of affairs with the other services or CoS. Neither did Churchill initiate any modifications or initiatives when he came by later. The difficult weather was a challenge for the British pilots. A Sunderland from 204 Squadron nonetheless discovered *Hipper* and Group II at 14:30 (BrT) and reported to the Home Fleet. Unfortunately, the force was on a westerly course when sighted, waiting for the right moment to turn east towards Trondheim. The message therefore seemed to confirm that the Germans were heading for the Atlantic, not Norway. It was incomprehensible to the Admiralty that Germany would try anything like invading western Norway – far less Narvik – across the North Sea. Such an operation would, it was believed, require ship concentrations well beyond the capacity of the Kriegsmarine. According to the diary of Captain Ralph Edwards, Director of Operations (Home), 'The Old Man [Pound] was away fishing for salmon and arrived back rather late in the evening dead beat.

DCNS [Phillips] was tired and the First Lord well dined. The result was they all failed to come to any useful decision.'[22]

Only at 17:27 was the Home Fleet alerted to the fact that German heavy ships were at sea and it was 20:50 before the battleships *Rodney*, *Repulse* and *Valiant* left Scapa Flow with the cruisers *Sheffield* and *Penelope* and ten destroyers in company. During the evening, further groups of cruisers and destroyers also set out. The carrier *Furious* was in the Clyde for a refit and it would be another 24 hours before an acceptable number of aircraft had been landed on for her to follow. At 22:51, the minelayer *Teviotbank* heading for Stadlandet to lay the southernmost of the *Wilfred* minefields was recalled and her destroyer escort instructed to re-join the Home Fleet after refuelling. During the night the Home Fleet steered north at 20 knots and at dawn on the 8th,

Generalmajor Erwin Engelbrecht, commander of 163. ID. He is wearing the Knight's Cross around his neck, and the photo was probably taken on 9 May 1940 in celebration of the award that day.

60° North was passed, between Shetland and Bergen. By then the German fleet was some 200 miles further north-east, off Trondheim. Admiral Forbes was preparing to intercept an Atlantic break-out, leaving the North Sea and the Norwegian coast uncovered.[23]

Admiral Whitworth arrived off Vestfjord on the evening of the 7th and the minelaying destroyers and their escorts were detached according to plan at 19:00. They headed for Landegode north of Bodø, while *Renown* and one destroyer waited some 30 miles off Skomvær Lighthouse. The minelayers reached the designated area without incident and by 05:26 on Monday the 8th, 234 mines had been laid, as planned, inside Norwegian waters.[24]

During the first months of 1940, most home-based British submarines operated in the North Sea and Heligoland Bight: 2nd Submarine Flotilla out of Rosyth, 3rd Submarine Flotilla out of Harwich and 6th Submarine Flotilla out of Blyth.[25] Vice-Admiral (Submarines) Max Horton was one of the few British naval commanders convinced that Allied minelaying off the coast of Norway would bring immediate German counter-measures. During late March he therefore started concentrating his boats along the Norwegian coast, including east of Skagen into the Skagerrak. Horton summoned his flotilla captains to a meeting at the submarine headquarters at Northways on 1 April and gave orders for all available boats to be at sea by dawn on the 5th, covering the exits from the German Bight, Kattegat and Skagerrak as well as likely German landing points in southern Norway. German warships could be attacked but otherwise the boats should conceal their presence as much as possible. Merchant ships should be left alone – unless German warships and transports were encountered together, in which case it would be most important to attack the transports. At the time of the conference, *Triton* and *Swordfish* were off Skagen and *Trident* off Arendal. During the next few days, *Sealion, Sunfish, Unity* and the Polish *Orzeł* took to sea to join them. On the evening of the 4th, after Operation *Wilfred* had been postponed to the 8th, Horton moved some of the boats deeper into the sea lanes; *Orzeł* east of Lindesnes, *Trident* off Larvik, *Sunfish, Triton* and *Sealion* into the northern Kattegat to cover the exits from the Danish Belts.[26] Lieutenant-Commander Bryant of *Sealion* found the new orders challenging, as he wrote on the 7th:

> Some 25 merchant vessels were sighted during the day, mostly northbound. Some were suspicious, but none that I could say definitely were German transports [...] One small ship marked Estonia had a funnel corresponding to that of Saaberk Co of Hamburg. Five ships had no flags or markings, three being greyish. It was not possible to surface and investigate them so no action was taken. I was much concerned that I might be letting enemy ships by owing to taking no action. On the other hand, orders received conveyed the impression that it was essential not to compromise my position. The definition of a 'transport' was not clear in my mind.[27]

In his memoirs he added:

> As we crept south, another trouble beset us. The melting snow had freshened the water of the Baltic and Kattegat. We pumped out more and more ballast water and still we got 'heavier'. We were ballasted for salt ocean water; our destination had been too secret to enable us to have some of the lead ballast removed from the boxes in our keel before starting. Presently we had only just sufficient ballast water in our auxiliary tanks to give control. We had to pump out our fresh water, leaving only just enough to drink. The order went round: *No washing, not even the hands.*[28]

By midday on 7 April, receiving information that a German fleet was at sea, Horton was convinced a German intervention was developing and ordered all remaining boats to sea with the utmost despatch, bringing the number of submarines at sea up to twenty, including two French boats. The next day, he discussed his dispositions with the Admiralty and to his surprise, received instructions to withdraw the boats from Norway and re-deploy them to a line in the North Sea, south of Stavanger, intercepting German naval forces heading home after a sortie into the Norwegian Sea. Before these instructions could be put into force, however, reports were received from Oslo that the German *Rio de Janeiro* had been sunk east of Kristiansand and that German soldiers were being rescued. Horton took this to mean he had been right all the time and made only minor adjustments to his prior dispositions. Horton's measures were so effective that some fifteen German transports and supply ships would be sunk or severely damaged between 8 and 29 April, in addition to half a dozen warships (*see* Chapters 8, 14 and 15). Due to improved signal discipline, German sigint had problems tracking the British submarines and a crisis arose in the OKW and among the *Weserübung* staff. The moving of troops and supplies to southern and western Norway had to be reorganised, diverting significant naval and air resources from other tasks to anti-submarine patrols in the Skagerrak.[29]

Chapter 7

Towards Oslo

8 April

Danish Waters

At 03:00 on the morning of the 8th, Group V weighed anchor and headed north towards the Danish Belts in darkness. *Blücher* was in the van; *Lützow*, *Emden*, *Kondor* and *Albatros* followed. At 05:30, *Möwe* also fell in after having spent the night at anchor further offshore.

The R-boats of 1. Räumbootsflottille under the command of Kapitän-leutnant Gustav Forstmann would sail independently accompanied by *Rau VII* and *Rau VIII* and meet up with the larger ships at the entrance to Oslofjord.[1]

There are three passages through the Danish Belts from the Baltic to the Kattegat and Skagerrak: to the east, the Sound (Øresund), past Copenhagen and along the Swedish coast between Helsingborg and Helsingør; in the west the Little Belt (Lillebælt) makes a passage along the Jutland peninsula

Rau VIII. These boats were converted whale-catchers.
Sturdily built, they were well suited for inshore work.

R 18 and *R 19*. The R-boats (*Räumboote*) were small 115-ton motor minesweepers intended to operate in coastal waters but also used for many other roles. They were nimble and fast and armed with two or more 20-mm cannon and depth charges. Many of them had Voith-Schneider propulsion rather than regular propellers and could reach a top speed of over 20 knots. Crew was normally 30–34 men.

between Middelfart and Fredricia. The main passage is the Great Belt (Storebælt) between the islands of Funen and Zealand. The southern part of this, between Lolland and the German island of Fehmarn is known as Fehmarn Belt. Øresund and Lillebælt had navigational challenges and were prone to ice during winter. In addition, they were both heavily covered by minefields. Hence, the only practical way into the Skagerrak from Kiel was the central route through Storebælt. This route was also covered by a minefield, but there was a safe gap marked by buoys through this, well known to the German Navy. The harsh winter meant there had been abundant sea ice in southern Scandinavia earlier in 1940, but by around 1 April most of the regular sea lanes were ice-free. All three passages are defined as international waters through a treaty of 1857 even though they are within what are normally considered Danish waters. Denmark could not hamper free travel, but Group V and all other ships passing through the Belts would be observed by the Danish Navy and Copenhagen duly informed.

During World War 1, on German request, Denmark closed Storebælt and Lillebælt with mines to keep the belligerents out. After September 1939, Germany again requested the Danes to lay mines, but asked them this time to keep the international fairways open. The Danish Navy obliged, and the Germans placed supplementary fields south of the Danish ones giving themselves the means to close the belts completely, should they consider that necessary. In Storebælt, the international passage was closed by some 180 mines between Lolland and Langeland, except for a well-marked passage through the centre. This could be closed by laying additional mines, should circumstances require. The ice conditions during the winter had led the mines to be disarmed, but in early April, they were being re-activated. The

1. R-Boat Flotilla, 7 and 8 April

Danish Navy kept the Storebælt passage free from drifting mines and had pilots available for ships that needed help as well as a torpedo boat guarding the entrances of the passage. The Lillebælt and Øresund passages were not guaranteed ice-free during the 6th and OKM and SKL agreed that all naval forces, including those heading for Copenhagen, should go north through the Storebælt as planned.[2]

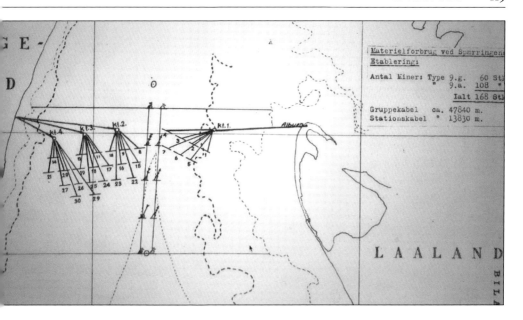

The Danish minefield closing the southern entrance to Storebælt. It contained 168 mines in all, and the safe channel between the anchored mines was marked by buoys. If considered necessary, these could be removed, and the channel mined.

Some officers questioned the wisdom of sending warships through the Danish Belts on their way to Norway as they would inevitably be sighted and reported to both the Norwegians and the British intelligence services. It was quickly determined, however, that sending all the invasion forces to the North Sea ports and having all the ships loaded there would not be possible. Group V would have to depart from the Baltic ports and go through the Belts. It would be necessary, though, to keep all soldiers below deck while the ships were in sight from land and give the impression of a routine naval mission.[3]

On 26 and 27 March, German minesweepers checked their own minefield in Storebælt, allowing *Altmark* to sail safely through. The German pilot service resumed the practice of having a vessel standing by about 3 miles north of the barrier on 4 April. On the same day, four trawlers were sent through Storebælt to verify that everything was in order. On the 5th and 6th, respectively, 27 and 16 German ships sailed through the barrier northwards while the number of German aircraft over the Belts increased significantly. On the 8th more than 20 were registered by the Danish. To be on the safe side, nine German minesweepers were sent through Storebælt on the 7th to make sure the entire passage was free of all ice and safe for Group V. The minesweepers reported the passage clear and ice-free with lightships at both ends in the correct positions.[4]

Danish submarines.

Recognised Sea Picture

What in naval terminology is known as a recognised sea picture or RSP is the listing of all vessels within a particular area, each being identified as friendly, neutral or hostile, and containing additional information such as type of vessel, mission, and so on. The information may be drawn from several different sources, including reports from own naval vessels, coast-watch posts, lightships, harbour authorities, and intercepted signal traffic. In 1939, a signal centre had been organised by the Danish Navy, next to the naval staff in Copenhagen. Hence, most basic elements for a recognised sea picture were available and working and during the morning of 8 April, the extent of the German sea and air activity became obvious to the Danes. Surprise was no longer possible, but confusion is an effective camouflage too. Nevertheless, Group V was a conspicuous naval force with large naval vessels different from everything else at sea in the Kattegat or Skagerrak on this day. On the 7th, 9 minesweepers, 8 R-boats and 16 German merchant ships were registered as

Opposite, top to bottom, Blücher, Lützow *and* Emden.
These photos are included here, despite their mixed quality, as uniquely they were taken as Group V passed through Danish waters on 8 April.

passing through the Danish minefield at Storebælt. On the 8th 4 large naval vessels were reported, along with 4 torpedo boats, 10 minesweepers and around 50 trawlers or other vessels likely in military service. The ships were heading north with a purpose, and there was no doubt that a major operation was under way.

At 04:45 Danish time, on the 8th the Coast Watch Post at Keldsnor Lighthouse reported to Naval Command in Copenhagen, Søværnskommandoen, that *Gneisenau, Emden, Leipzig* and three torpedo boats or destroyers were heading for the mine barrage. The identification was later changed to a *Gneisenau* class, a *Deutschland* class, a *Köln* class cruiser and three *Albatros* class torpedo boats. At the same time, it was reported to the Danish Naval Ministry that up to 100 armed German trawlers and R-boats were operating in the Anholt–Læsø area of the Kattegat. Eight submarines were also reported off Læsø with two support vessels. The submarine report was later corrected to eight R-boats and two trawlers, and the number of other vessels reduced to 46, some having been counted twice by a misunderstanding. There was nevertheless no doubt that something untoward was going on. Most of the vessels had passed the minefield in Storebælt on the night of 7/8 April or earlier.[5]

At 11:00, the Danish naval command was informed by the Foreign Office that, according to telephone tapping, it would not be long before the Germans would take action as a result of the British minelaying in Norwegian waters. At noon, reports came of German troops in Rendsburg moving north towards the Danish border. Nevertheless, the Danish naval C-in-C Viceadmiral Hjalmar Rechnitzer believed the German ship movements were directed at Norwegian fjords or harbours and was not overly concerned. He later wrote

> The German naval movements in Danish waters [on 8 April] were perceived by the Danish Naval Command as being the start of the expected German occupation of one or more fjords or ports on the southern coast of Norway around or east of Lindesnes, from which, by extensive mining of the Skagerrak, there could be at least some possibility of maintaining contact with the homeland.[6]

Rechnitzer was of the opinion that Germany was best served by Denmark remaining neutral. For him, a German attack on Denmark was not worthwhile as long as the Danes maintained their neutrality. British aggression on Danish territory was unlikely and there was therefore no reason for a German occupation of Denmark. The two countries were not at war. Quite the contrary: there was a still valid non-aggression pact between the two countries – in principle. That the Germans had intensified air activity over Storebælt and the Skagerrak significantly as well as minesweeping outside

the Danish three-mile limit was duly registered by the Danish Navy, but just added to the enigma of what was astir. At lunchtime, the trawlers of 7. Vorpostenflottille heading north to take up positions at the mouth of Oslofjord and prevent British submarines coming in after Group *Oldenburg*, sighted a submarine near the island of Hjelm north of the Belts. This was most likely one of the Danish boats, but the trawlers had no time to hunt it down, leaving one vessel to keep the boat submerged, while the others hastened north.[7] Rechnitzer believed that his contacts at the highest levels of the German Navy, and Großadmiral Raeder whom he had met, were to be trusted and would notify him in a real emergency. A sharpening of naval readiness could provoke the Germans, he feared, and Danish naval contingency plans were not implemented on 8 April. Nor was any alarm given, except calling back the crew of the coast defence ship *Niels Juel*, who had just been given leave.[8]

Around 15:00 the German naval attaché in Copenhagen delivered a protest to the Danish high command over a Danish lightship's extensive reporting of observations of German naval forces by radio. This was against international agreements, he held, and should stop. Within an hour a signal was issued, and the reporting stopped. The rest of the day, reports of German ships in or near Danish waters only came to Søværnskommandoen from the Navy's own ships and observation posts.[9]

War Stations

As agreed, 1st R-boat Flotilla accompanied by *Rau VII* and *Rau VIII* left Kiel heading for Storebælt on the afternoon of the 7th. They passed the minefield during the evening without any problems. There was no ice in the Kattegat and Forstmann chose to follow the Danish coast northwards. Having passed Læsø on the eastern side, the boats anchored up just north of the island, outside Danish territorial waters, for a rest and to discuss with the captains of *Rau VII* and *Rau VIII* how best to make the crossing of the open Skagerrak. The weather remained good with a south-westerly wind and a moderate swell, but the boats were small and fragile and entering such open waters was not routine. After about two-and-a-half hours, they continued the journey, zigzagging and keeping a strengthened lookout for any submarines. Several aircraft were sighted overhead, but otherwise the passage was problem free. Two of the aircraft were recognised as 'civilian Norwegian', one of them probably the mail-plane from Copenhagen via Torslanda airfield at Gothenburg to Oslo. Naval MF11 floatplanes from the base at Karljohans-vern-Horten had for some time flown daily reconnaissance missions over outer Oslofjord past Færder into the Skagerrak up to 30 miles offshore, about one third of the distance to Skagen (the Skaw in English). On the 8th, the aircraft reported a few freighters and fishing boats, but no warships. By 21:30 German time, Forstmann could see the first Norwegian lighthouses and slowed down to remain unobserved.[10]

Blücher with Group *Oldenburg* reached the southern entrance of Storebælt at 05:00 on the 8th, and passed the Danish naval vessels respons-ible for monitoring the minefield and the approach.[11] The weather was

The Norwegian built MF11 floatplanes were robust and well suited for reconnaissance over Norwegian territorial waters. They could carry two 50-kg bombs and up to three machine guns. In this photo, they are flying over Karljohansvern with the naval airbase to the left and the naval yard to the right.

fine with a light southerly breeze and the sun was climbing into a nearly blue sky as the ships entered the Langelandsbælt approaching the Danish mine barrage. Shortly before 06:00, German minesweepers confirmed the Storebælt passage was free and Group V passed through without any incidents. By 08:00 *Blücher* and her consorts were beyond the Halsskov Rev lightship and continued north at 18 knots between the Danish islands of Funen and Zealand. Entering more open waters at 11:15, the torpedo boats fanned out as submarine protection for the cruisers, which took up a zigzag course in line astern formation. Overhead, aircraft arrived for escort. A so-called *Kriegswache* or war alert was set aboard the ships of Group V, not full Action Stations, but guns, communications and engines were adequately manned to handle an emergency while some parts of the crew were allowed to rest. On board *Blücher* it was the first time this had happened in earnest. As long as they were inside the belts, the *Landser* were confined below deck in hiding from any observers, but after passing the Schultz's Grund lightship around 11:40, they were allowed up if they could find some Navy

Blücher and the other ships in Group V kept a meticulous lookout
to avoid submarines, aircraft and other surface vessels.

clothing to cover their Army uniforms. Off-duty crewmen were gathered
on the after-deck and informed by Kapitän Woldag of their mission. There
was widespread excitement about going into action, but some puzzlement
over why it was considered necessary to occupy Norway.[12]

Once they were safely through Storebælt the *Kriegswache* was reduced
and only manned for anti-submarine and anti-air defence to allow more of
the crews to rest. The ships continued north with the cruisers in line astern
and the torpedo boats searching for submarines ahead and on either side. The
task force deviated from the normal deep-water route by steering west and
north of Anholt before going east of Læsø. The German ships' War Diaries
are curiously quiet about their route, but the Danish reports are clear that the
German heavy ships went west of Anholt. Here, the water is very shallow, in
places no more than 12–14 metres (40–45 feet), considerably less exposed to
enemy submarines. Denmark was not at war with Germany on 8 April and
Danish torpedo boats and submarines that knew these waters well, posed no
threat prior to *Weser*-time.[13]

In the afternoon, a signal reached Kummetz from Group Command in Kiel, stating that recent intelligence indicated there were no mines in the Drøbak Narrows after all. Other reports told of British naval forces including submarines in the North Sea and Skagerrak but not dangerously close. Nevertheless, the number of lookouts was increased with special instructions to watch for anything that looked like a periscope. Tension rose markedly, particularly among the young, inexperienced crew on board the flagship. The first submarine alarm at 12:45 was a fishing boat and just after 13:00, a fishing buoy was riddled by machine-gun fire from *Blücher*, after being mistaken for a periscope. The gunners and the fire-controllers were nervous and the medium guns of the two leading cruisers, including *Blücher*'s 10.5- and *Lützow*'s 15-cm weapons, opened fire. Submarine alerts were sounded over the tannoys, but it seems that nobody remembered to tell the soldiers below deck what the alarm meant. Many were scared, not least as the alarms made the seamen run about, man their guns, and close the hatches, trapping the soldiers below deck. Later this uncertainty was part of the basis for the criticism that arose from the Army towards the Kriegsmarine.[14]

Some of the crew nevertheless took a few moments to smile for the photographer.

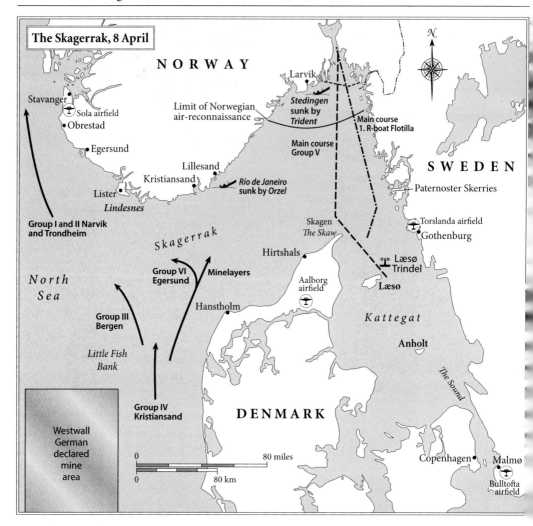

At 14:17, a signal from the German ship *Kreta* was picked up (see page 145). She had been fired at by an enemy submarine near the western entry to Oslofjord and though she got away, tension rose. Messages from the radio room that a Danish Radio news broadcast from Kalundborg had reported heavy German naval units in Danish waters, heading north, did nothing to ease the tension. Around 17:00, an order from Kummetz was passed down the line via *Lützow*. Opening fire was only permitted on Kummetz's direct order – *Feuererlaubnis nur auf Befehl Kommandant* – and that would only be given if the Norwegians fired first, with live ammunition. Warning shots would be disregarded. Searchlights should be met with counter-lights but no gunfire. To pass time, the signal staff assisted by the interpreters started preparing various false messages meant to confuse the Norwegians if they were challenged. On

German Army officers on the deck of *Blücher* in borrowed Navy coats.
Left to right: Leutnant Carl Otto Tewaag, Rittmesister Paul Goerz and
Major Horst von Necker, all from the advance party of Falkenhorst's staff.

board *Blücher*, there was a small group of interpreters who had been given a crash update in their Norwegian over the last couple of weeks and a unit of Propaganda-Staffel Norwegen that was to take control of information and public opinion after landing. Most of these men had some kind of connection to Norway, through family, studies or extensive travelling.[15]

Torpedoes Astern

Passing Læsø, Group V left the last of the Danish naval vessels in the Kattegat, the coast defence ship *Peder Skram* and the torpedo boats *Hvalen* and *Laxen*, astern. A third torpedo boat *Dragen* was on patrol beyond the Skaw but there is no known report of it observing the German ships.[16] By late afternoon the deep swell of the Skagerrak could be felt by the ships of Group V. They passed Skagens Rev lightship at 19:00, and the Danish Navy noted that the force was on a north-westerly course. This was the last time the group was observed by the Danes, and it was not noticed that the ships later turned towards

The British submarine HMS *Triton*. On station north-east of Skagen on the 8th.

north-northeast. As darkness approached, full *Kriegswache* was implemented aboard all ships. A signal from Kummetz to Lange instructed him to prepare to disembark three officers and 60 men as support for Korvettenkapitän Otto Karlowa who was to take up the position as Harbour Commander – *Hafenkommandant* – in Oslo as soon as they had arrived.[17]

Suddenly, at 19:05, *Albatros* on the starboard side of the cruisers, hoisted a signal and flashed a warning. Submarine contact! This time it was real. Torpedo tracks were sighted, apparently aiming for *Lützow*, but she was already turning to starboard as part of a routine zigzag manoeuvre, and they all passed harmlessly ahead. The torpedo boats hunted the submarine for a while, but only *Albatros* stayed with the contact, dropping half a dozen depth charges while the group resumed a north-northeasterly course into the Skagerrak.

The torpedoes had been fired from the British submarine *Triton*. She had been on patrol in the area east of Skagen for a week, without much happening, when four large trawlers appeared at dawn on the 8th. Lieutenant-Commander Edward Fowle Pizey suspected they were German and pulled slowly southwards to be out of harm's way. At 16:50 British time, the hydrophone operator reported several heavy ships approaching from the south-east. In the periscope, Pizey identified the first ship to be a *Gneisenau* class vessel (actually *Blücher*) the second as *Nürnberg* or *Leipzig* (actually *Lützow*) and the third correctly as *Emden*. Group V was travelling fast, and he had little time to position his submarine without getting too close to the trawlers. Rather than miss the opportunity, Pizey chose to fire at *Lützow*, the second ship in the line, chancing a long shot. Just as he was about to fire, though, at 17:55 British time (18:55 German time), *Blücher* zigzagged, coming into a more favourable position. Pizey decided she was the more important target and fired all ten torpedoes from 7,000 metres. *Blücher* was travelling faster than he had estimated, however, and all torpedoes missed astern, coming close to *Lützow*. *Albatros* came down the tracks but never found *Triton* and eventually followed the rest of the ships. Pizey put his mast aerial up, sending a brief sighting signal at 18:25 before an aircraft appeared and made him go deep. This signal was not received in Britain. At 19:45 however, Pizey was able to surface and send:

> One German battleship of *Gneisenau* class with one heavy cruiser escorted by *Emden* and destroyers have passed Skaw westward 18:00. Speed 20 knots.[18]

At 20:31, a second report, this time from *Sunfish* 20 miles north of Skagen read, 'One *Blücher*-class, two cruisers, one destroyer observed at 18:12, steering north and zigzagging.' *Sunfish* was too far away to close in for an attack, but Horton was thrilled. He ordered *Trident* and *Orzeł* to proceed with utmost despatch to a position off Larvik, where he personally believed the group was heading as the port had railway connections to the capital and no defences. Luckily for Group *Oldenburg*, this cleared the entrance to Oslofjord for them. Not even Horton could imagine that the Germans would be sufficiently unconventional to risk sending large warships up the fjord against the hostile fortresses there.[19]

By nightfall, all German naval ships involved in *Weserübung* were either on their way to Norway or somewhere off Denmark, heading for their designated positions, ready to strike at *Weser*-time.

Chapter 8
A Day of Highest Tension
8 April

Off Western Norway

The Norwegian guardship *Syrian* was patrolling the landward side of Vestfjord at dawn on 8 April. As light grew, the British minelaying destroyers were observed and kaptein Bjarne Kaaveland sent a preliminary radio signal to SDD3 in Tromsø while heading for the lead destroyer to find out what was going on. Having been informed that they were laying mines and delivered a protest, which had no effect, Kaaveland sent a second, more detailed signal to Tromsø, including coordinates. This was promptly forwarded to the Admiral Staff in Oslo. While reading the signal, the Duty Officer at the Admiral Staff, kaptein Willoch, was told that the British and French naval attachés were in the building, requesting an urgent meeting with him. Captain Hector Boyes and his French colleague Capitaine de Frégate Albert d'Arzur wished Willoch a good morning and handed him a copy of a comprehensive memorandum, adding that at that very moment the original was being presented to the Foreign Office by their respective Ministers, Dormer and de Dampierre. The memorandum, which Boyes insisted required immediate attention, argued at length how the deliberate increase in German violations of Norwegian neutrality and the Norwegian inability to prevent this, forced the Allied governments to take measures believed necessary. With reference to the memorandum of 5 April, of which Willoch had no knowledge, it had been decided to deny Germany the use of stretches of Norwegian territorial waters and three minefields had been laid the same morning – off Stadlandet, off Bud and off Landegode at the mouth of Vestfjord. The co-ordinates of the minefields were given, and it was added that British warships would patrol the fields for 48 hours to prevent ships entering the danger zones. The news of the British minefields was immediately forwarded to Commanding Admiral Diesen who had hurried to his office.[1]

The first German knowledge of the British minelaying was a signal picked up at 07:35 from the British radio station at Cleethorpes, announcing the three danger areas. Politically, this development could not have come at a better time for the Germans, perfectly underlining the need for a 'rescue operation' in Norway. The minefields would not affect the landing operations, but they might disturb the supply and tanker traffic to the northernmost bridgeheads. SKL believed the British warning might very well be a bluff, but during a telephone conference with Admiral Saalwächter, it was agreed that no chances should be taken, and the danger areas would be avoided, if necessary, by going outside the Leads.[2]

Some 100 miles west of Trondheim, the ships of Group I and II started re-assembling after having been partly scattered through the stormy night. During this, some of the ships ran into the British destroyer *Glowworm*, which had lost a man overboard on 6 April and while searching for him had lost contact with the battlecruiser *Renown*, whose escort she originally was part of. *Hipper* was ordered to take care of the enemy destroyer and the encounter that followed is legendary. Unfortunately, it ended with *Glowworm* being sunk – the only British surface ship to gain certain contact with the German invasion fleet on the 8th. A few brief distress signals sent before she went down confused the British, and *Repulse* and *Penelope* with destroyers were detached northwards from the Home Fleet while *Renown* was ordered south, away from the minelaying force. Nothing

Dawn of 8 April. Mines are laid from the destroyer *Ivanhoe* inside Norwegian territorial waters off the island of Landegode, north of Bodø.

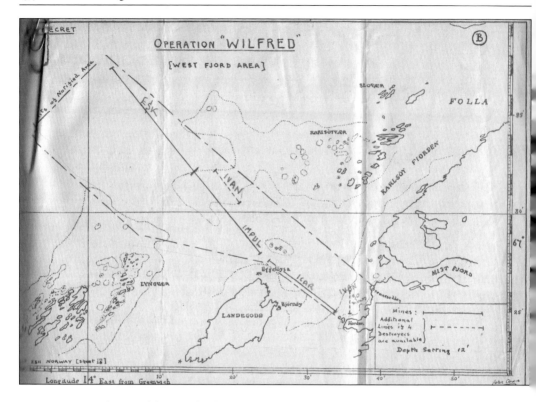

British map of the minefield at Landegode. The larger, dashed area is the 'danger area' declared by the British through the coordinates announced and given to the Norwegian Navy. Inside this, however, the four destroyers laid only five lines of mines.

more was heard from *Glowworm* and *Renown* turned north again, shortly after midday, to meet up with the minelaying destroyers, some 20 miles south-west of Skomvær Lighthouse. The destroyers had just been ordered by the Admiralty to leave the mines to the Norwegians and fall in with the battlecruiser. Having dealt with *Glowworm*, *Hipper* and her four destroyers, that were going no further than Trondheim, steered west to wait until it was time to turn landwards. *Scharnhorst*, *Gneisenau* and the ten destroyers for Narvik continued north. The wind had turned to the north-west and reached full storm force. At 21:00 Group I reached the latitude of Bodø and the destroyers were detached into Vestfjord while *Gneisenau* and *Scharnhorst* turned into the Norwegian Sea. Further south, the other German groups continued towards their destinations, unknown to the British, who were preparing their own plans.[3]

The troops for the Narvik part of Plan *R4* were assembled on the Clyde and instructed to commence embarkation of the transport ships on the morning of the 8th. The 2nd and 18th Cruiser Squadrons were earmarked as strike forces, but there was no carrier available to support the operation. The main force, a British brigade and other units, supported by French troops would land at Narvik. The first units would leave during the 8th escorted by cruisers. One British battalion would land in Trondheim and two battalions each in Bergen and Stavanger. The troops for Bergen and Stavanger had already embarked on other cruisers in Rosyth on the 7th and were ready to go to sea. It was assumed these forces – in all some 18,000 men – would be able to forestall potential German reactions until reinforced, even if they were short of AA defences. Through a series of misinterpretations, the Admiralty decided, however, to reposition the naval forces west of Norway to intercept what seemed to be a major German naval threat to the Allied shipping routes in the Atlantic. The intended minelaying off mid-Norway was cancelled and the cruisers at Rosyth and in the Clyde were ordered to unload all troops and sail forthwith. It was too late. By nightfall, the weather was worse than ever, and the British admirals had lost their tactical opportunity. The decision to abandon Plan R4 and disembark the troops intended for western Norway was, according to General Ian Jacobs, Assistant Military Secretary to the War Cabinet, made by Churchill without consulting the Chiefs of Staff or the Cabinet. The orders came by phone from the First Sea Lord to the Clyde and Rosyth around 11:30, confirmed by signal shortly after. During the Cabinet

HMS *Hyperion* at Hustadvika guarding the fake minefield. No mines had actually been laid here, only waterfilled oil drums, giving the illusion of minelaying to passing fishing vessels.

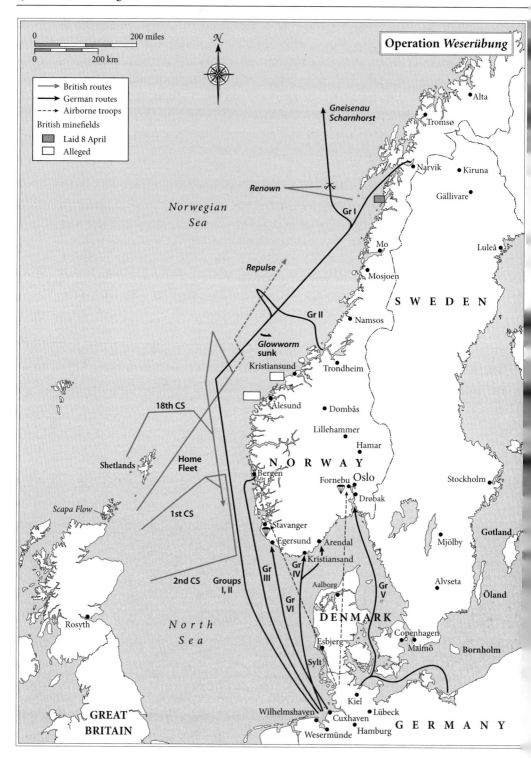

Operation *Weserübung*

0 | 200 miles
0 | 200 km

British routes
German routes
Airborne troops
British minefields
Laid 8 April
Alleged

N

Gneisenau
Scharnhorst

Alta

Tromsø

Renown

Narvik
Kiruna

Gällivare

Gr I

Norwegian
Sea

Mo

Luleå

Repulse

Mosjoen

S W E D E N

Gr II

Namsos

Glowworm
sunk

Kristiansund
Trondheim

Ålesund
Dombås

18th CS

Lillehammer

Hamar

N O R W A Y

Shetlands

Home
Fleet

Bergen
Fornebu   Oslo

Stockholm

Drøbak

Scapa Flow

1st CS

Stavanger

Egersund

Gotland

Arendal

Mjölby

Kristiansand

2nd CS   Groups
I, II

Gr
III

Gr
IV

Alvseta

Aalborg

Gr
V

Öland

Gr
VI

Rosyth

North
Sea

D E N M A R K

Esbjerg

Copenhagen

Malmö

Bornholm

Sylt

Kiel
Lübeck

GREAT
BRITAIN

Wilhelmshaven   Cuxhaven

G E R M A N Y

Wesermünde   Hamburg

meeting the same morning, Chamberlain asked where the *R4* cruisers were and when they would be able to put the troops ashore. To everybody's surprise, Churchill answered that the soldiers had disembarked, and the cruisers were about to join the fleet, after which there was no further discussion. Plan *R4* was intended as an answer to a German invasion provoked by the minelaying. That the Germans came of their own accord should only have made things better. Churchill and the Admiralty focussed on the naval situation, which they misjudged, and lost the strategic overview.[4]

No Ordinary Merchant Vessel

On Monday 8 April, Norway woke up to a new reality. The newspapers had large headlines about minefields at Stad, Hustadvika and Vestfjord. About halfway down the pages were less conspicuous articles reporting German cruisers, destroyers and minesweepers heading north through Danish waters. It was also announced that the Norwegian steamer *Navarra* had been 'torpedoed without warning' two days earlier west of the Orkneys with

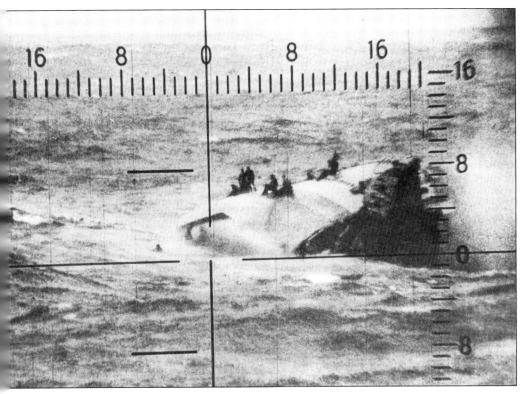

Glowworm capsized and sinking after the encounter with *Hipper*. A few survivors can be seen, clinging to the hull. The photo was taken through one of *Hipper*'s gunsights.

Left & above: Survivors from *Glowworm* being rescued by *Hipper, Blücher's* sister ship.
Forty men were pulled out of the water from a crew of 149. At least two later died.

12 dead and 14 rescued. Few realised what was happening, but most felt fear, uncertainty and frustration. There would inevitably be German reactions to the minelaying and unless the crisis could be countered quickly, there might be actions of war inside Norwegian territorial waters.

While the crew of *Glowworm* were fighting for their lives in the stormy sea off mid-Norway, the Polish submarine *Orzel* of the 2nd Submarine Flotilla was cruising at periscope depth in the Skagerrak.[5] The weather was much calmer here and Lieutenant-Commander Jan Grudzinski had no problems observing the merchantman approaching his submarine off Lillesand at 09:45. She carried no flag, but on closing in he could read the name *Rio de Janeiro* on her bows and, a bit later, the home port of Hamburg could be discerned aft, even if it had been sloppily painted over.[6]

Unknown to the Polish captain, *Rio de Janeiro* was one of the transports assigned to Group III, heading for Bergen, having left Stettin at 03:00 on the morning of the 6th. Originally a 5,261-ton liner carrying cargo and passengers between Europe and Latin America, *Rio de Janeiro* was now loaded with military equipment including four 10.5-cm guns, six 20-mm

The Polish submarine *Orzel*. After escaping the Baltic for Britain in September 1939, *Orzel* was assigned to the 2nd Submarine Flotilla at Rosyth, with the pennant 85A. Once her torpedo tubes had been adapted for British torpedoes, the Admiralty cleared *Orzel* for independent patrols in the North Sea and off the coast of Norway in mid-January 1940. The first patrols were uneventful and no German ships were sighted.

AA guns, 73 horses, 71 vehicles and 292 tons of provisions in her spacious hull. In addition, there were 320 passengers, most of them in uniform: 107 soldiers came from I./IR 159 and 56 pioneers came from 169th Pioneer Battalion; the rest were Luftwaffe men from 13th and 33rd AA Regiments and administrative personnel. The crew consisted of 50 men. At the time of departure very few of the crew or soldiers knew their destination.[7]

In spite of orders to the contrary, Grudzinski brought *Orzel* to the surface at 11:00 and hoisted flags signifying 'Stop engines.' Kapitän Rudolf Voigt obeyed but, apart from slowing down, nothing happened aboard the vessel and nobody came on deck, except the regular lookouts. A new signal 'Send boat with Master and ship's papers,' followed by a few bursts from the submarine's Lewis gun, resulted in the flag 'Message read and understood' being hoisted. A boat was lowered from *Rio de Janeiro*, but it stayed close to the liner with apparently no intention of coming over. Something was weird with this vessel. All the more so as *Orzel*'s radio operator reported a coded radio signal being sent. After about fifteen minutes with nothing happening, Grudzinski hoisted yet another signal to abandon ship as he was about to fire a torpedo. Still, there was no reaction other than another 'Understood' flag being hoisted. No lifeboats were made ready or even swung out.

While the bow of the submarine was swung towards the German and the torpedoes prepared, the Norwegian coaster *Lindebø* and the fishing vessel *Jenny* chanced to pass nearby. Grudzinski considered them to be out of harm's way and at 11:45 gave the orders for one torpedo to be fired. According to *Orzel*'s logbook, the German was '1.8 miles outside neutral waters' at the time. The range was 300–400 metres, and the torpedo hit amidships on the starboard side. Apparently, it did not explode, at least not as it should have, but still made a large hole in the hull of *Rio de Janeiro*. Steam and smoke poured out, she started to list and suddenly her deck came alive with men in field grey uniforms, falling or jumping into the sea. Lifebelts and pieces of wood were thrown over the side as more men followed into the water. No one seemed to try to lower the lifeboats, though the boat already in the water started picking up some of the swimmers. While Grudzinski observed the bustle in his binoculars, an aircraft was reported approaching from landward and he gave the order to dive.[8]

At 11:15, Kristiansand SDS received a signal from Justøy Coast Watch Post that they could see the tower of a submarine on a westerly course just outside the territorial limit and a merchant

Lieutenant-Commander Jan Grudzinski of the Polish submarine *Orzel*. In April 1940 Lieutenant-Commander Keith d'Ombrain Nott was on board as liaison officer, with Yeoman of Signals Walter Green and Petty Officer Telegraphist Leslie William Jones.

ship, which appeared to be stopped next to it. The nationalities of both vessels were unknown. An MF11 reconnaissance aircraft was ordered up, arriving just as the torpedo struck. The crew could see chaotic conditions on board with people running through flames and smoke, tumbling into the sea and trying to reach a few nearby floats. Several dead men were floating face down and horses were also in the water, adding to the horror. Two small Norwegian vessels appeared to be picking up survivors. The submarine, which had dived as the aircraft arrived, was nowhere to be seen and the MF11 headed back towards Kristiansand to report.

Grudzinski, who had taken *Orzel* around to the other side under water, fired a second torpedo from periscope depth. It struck at 12:15, exploded as it should, and the transport broke in two. *Lindebø* had splinters flying over her deck from the explosion and several of the just rescued seamen were killed or wounded. The hull of *Rio de Janeiro* rolled over and sank minutes later, leaving hundreds of men to fight for their lives in the freezing water. *Lindebø* and *Jenny* rescued many, as did the small fishing boat *Agder II* that hurried towards the explosion. The destroyer *Odin*, which had been sent to investigate, arrived at 12:45, but by then there were as many dead as there were survivors to pull out of the freezing water. Soon the surface was scattered with lifeless bodies. Eventually some 150 men were rescued by various Norwegian vessels while around 180 perished (19 crew and about 160 soldiers) plus all

Rio de Janeiro in Stettin, just prior to departure.

the horses. Grudzinski took *Orzeł* away from the carnage and eventually surfaced to send a report. In the following days, *Orzeł* brushed repeatedly with German aircraft and anti-submarine patrols. She was depth-charged on several occasions before returning to Rosyth on the 18th.[9]

Odin headed for Kristiansand with 17 wounded and 18 dead under a tarpaulin on the deck, flying her flag at half-mast. Most of the others ended up in Lillesand. In all 133 survivors and 10 dead were brought ashore here. The dead were taken to the chapel at the local cemetery. The less severely injured were treated by three local doctors in the harbour area while the seriously wounded were sent to the hospital in Arendal. The Germans were wet and miserable and obviously shaken by their ordeal. Police Officer Nils Onsrud arrived at the quay in Lillesand to take charge of the operation and have the men taken care of. He became very concerned when he discovered how many they were and that virtually all the survivors wore uniform. Some even had weapons. What was obviously an officer tried to maintain some order and shouted '*Wehrmacht hier! Marine hier!*'[10] These were no ordinary seamen! Onsrud started questioning them but there were no clear answers. An officer, presenting himself as Leutnant Hermann Voss, maintained that *Rio de Janeiro* had been a regular merchantman loaded with general provisions. Then doctor Peter Jamvold, attending the wounded, came over and told Onsrud one of the soldiers had woken from unconsciousness and asked if they were in Bergen yet. When the doctor asked what they were to do there, the soldier had answered that they were heading for Bergen to assist the Norwegian Army against an allied invasion – at the government's request. Onsrud realised he had stumbled onto something of great importance. He cordoned off the harbour area as best he could and organised dry clothes, food and cigarettes to keep the Germans busy, while he went looking for a telephone. His call to Kristiansand SDS came through at 14:30, but to Onsrud's astonishment, the naval officer he spoke to doubted his observations, and saw no need to initiate any actions other than the ongoing rescue operation. Angered, Onsrud called Undersecretary of State Eivind Rognlien at the Lord Chancellor's Office in Oslo. Rognlien believed him and called both the General Staff and the

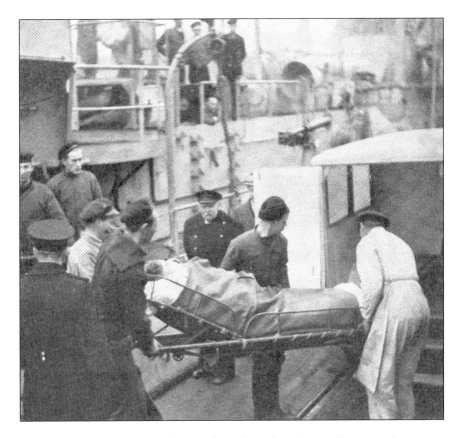

Survivors from *Rio de Janeiro* being brought ashore in Kristiansand and rushed to hospital.

Admiral Staff to inform them. He was very surprised, though, to learn that the Admiral Staff already knew about the Germans in uniform claiming they were heading for Bergen, having received the same information on *Odin's* return to Kristiansand. They did not consider the matter serious, compared to the British mines. The Minister of Defence had been informed but had taken no action. Rognlien could only call back and ask Onsrud to do the best he could. Norwegian soldiers eventually arrived in Lillesand at 20:30, to disarm the German soldiers and keep them under control until he knew what to do with them.[11]

The reports from Lillesand and Kristiansand were forwarded to the Ministry of Defence and the Foreign Office around 18:30 and referred by Defence Minister Ljungberg to the Storting shortly after 20:00. Nobody reacted and no precautions were taken. Grudzinski's report never reached the Admiralty. They only heard of the sinking of *Rio de Janeiro* through Reuters around 20:30 and apparently thought little of it.[12]

Meanwhile, further east, off Svenner lighthouse, *Trident* intercepted the 8,036-ton tanker *Stedingen* intended for Stavanger-Sola airfield with 8,000 tons of aviation fuel. Lieutenant-Commander Alan Seale wrote:

> A large tanker, laden, with no National marks or name on her side was sighted steaming west outside territorial waters. This vessel appeared most suspicious and was thought to be a German Auxiliary. I decided to investigate and at 12:15 surfaced on her port quarter and fired a blank shot. She turned to starboard for territorial waters and increased speed. I then fired two rounds of SAP which fell just short in line with bridge. This caused her to stop engines. I closed on her quarter with 'Do not transmit' flying and made by lamp 'Abandon ship, I shall torpedo you in five minutes.'[13]

Stedingen was a civilian tanker and carried the name *Posidonia* for a while before being re-named when requisitioned by the Kriegsmarine as a support tanker (*Stützpunkttanker*) in January 1940. The telegraphist used *Stedingen* in the SOS. When stopped by *Trident*, the name *Posidonia* had been painted over, although it was still discernible aft. The crew shut down the engines, opened the seacocks and took to the lifeboats. When they cast off, the tanker had been hit twice, but none of the crew were hurt. *Trident* intercepted the boats and the German Master, Schäfer, was detained and taken on board the submarine. *Stedingen* was sinking slowly, and Seale finished her off with a torpedo before heading away. The rest of the crew, some fifty men, continued towards land and the lifeboats were eventually towed into Stavern by a pilot vessel. Løytnant Roald Thommessen flew down from Horten to find out what was going on, but the first officer ordered the crew to say nothing when interrogated, arguing they were under military command. The only information he gave was that they were in ballast, which was false, and that the name of the ship was *Posidonia*, which was also false. The crew were eventually sent by bus and train to Oslo to be taken care of by the Legation.[14]

Shortly after, *Kreta*, one of the transport ships for Kristiansand, was fired at by *Trident*, but she escaped into Norwegian waters near Færder, and Seale prudently let her go. Inside Norwegian territory, *Kreta* was stopped by the guardship *Skudd II*. Questioned what was going on, the Master answered (falsely) that his ship was on her way to Narvik and that they were seeking shelter in Norwegian waters as they had been informed that a German tanker had been torpedoed by a British submarine further south. He was told to leave the *krigshavn* and follow the normal regulations for using Norwegian territory. *Kreta* turned south-west and *Skudd II* returned to her position west of Færder. For some time, *Weserübung* headquarters in Hamburg believed that *Kreta* had also been sunk, but this was corrected during the night of 8/9 April.[15]

Intelligence

The dominating headline in the morning news in Norway on 8 April was the British minelaying off the coast, being widely reported in the newspapers and by radio. These minefields, of which only the one at Landegode was actually laid, would monopolise the attention of the Norwegian politicians and naval commanders and to a large extent take it away from the approaching German *Weserübung* vessels.

Alerted by a telephone call from the Admiral Staff, Commanding Admiral Diesen arrived in his office just before 06:00 and Defence Minister Ljungberg in his some time after 08:00. Meanwhile, Diesen was on the telephone with several of his subordinates around the country as well as Foreign Minister Koht. Diesen asked for a meeting with Ljungberg to discuss what to do with the mines and the British ships guarding them. Chief of Staff Corneliussen was also present in the meeting, which started around 09:00. The discussion had moved towards whether the Norwegian Navy should lay its own mines in outer Oslofjord when the Minster was called to a government meeting. Ljungberg had ruled that minelaying required a decision from the government, and Diesen expected he would bring up the question in the meeting he was heading for, but he did not, and nobody heard back from the minister on the issue later in the day. Still, Diesen ordered Corneliussen to make sure preparations were initiated so that minefields *could* be laid at short notice should the government have time to make appropriate decisions.

Diesen was intriguingly passive during this day – despite access to ample intelligence to create a comprehensive picture of the threats developing. Oberst Hans Hammerstad, C-in-C of the Coast Artillery, was asked to attend a brief meeting with Diesen during the morning, after the 9 o'clock meeting. To his surprise, he was only instructed to be prepared to draft further men to the forts – if orders were issued. There are probably two main reasons for Diesen's reserve: his strong belief that the Royal Navy ruled supreme in the North Sea and his unfaltering loyalty to the government. When neither Ljungberg nor Koht nor Nygaardsvold issued instructions to change mode from neutrality to war, he was not the man to rock the boat. Just before 10:00 Diesen was called to the Foreign Office to meet a group of MPs and explain to them what was happening. Before joining the meeting, he gave instructions to the SDDs for 'Increased Preparedness', but it was left to each local commander to interpret what this meant. Information that arrived at the Admiral Staff during the day from Denmark and Sweden of German ships moving north did not worry the Commanding Admiral unduly. 'I did not consider Norway to be their target,' he later wrote.[16]

Another reason for Diesen's restraint could be that around Christmas he had raised the alert level, based on reports of German ships moving north through the Belts, and been reprimanded by Koht for creating anxiety. The slap on the wrist had upset Diesen and he admitted after the war that he was not very eager to have this happen again. Chief of Staff Corneliussen also referred to this incident as an explanation of why the Admiral Staff hesitated to order a full alert early on the 8th. Instead, except where local commanders exercised their own initiative, the focus of the Admiral Staff remained on the British mines most of this day.[17]

Even though he considered torpedoes from submarines or fixed coastal batteries more effective than mines, since his appointment as Commanding Admiral in 1938, Diesen had argued for the responsibility of laying mines to be given to him as part of the revised neutrality act. This the government flatly refused, and the issue was left as was. There would be ample warnings in case of a crisis it was believed, and the government wanted responsibility for such a drastic measure that would considerably affect civilian traffic to remain in political hands.[18]

The Navy and Army intelligence staffs were also focussed on the British minelaying, but during the morning other signals started to come in. Around 10:00, the Norwegian Admiral Staff's duty intelligence officer received a call from Kommendörkapten Sven Linder of the Swedish Defence Staff's intelligence department. He conveyed to the Norwegians for the first time that 'Gneisenau, Blücher and Emden, accompanied by numerous smaller units,' had passed through Storebælt that morning. Even if the identification of the ships was partly wrong and he could give no destination, the information was disturbing. Shortly after, at 10:30, a similar call was received from the naval intelligence office's regular contact in Denmark, Kommandørkaptajn

Fredrik Carl Pontoppidan, secretary to Viceadmiral Rechnitzer. He confirmed that '46 German R-boats, 38 armed trawlers' had passed Østre Flak lightship during the night and morning and spread out into the Kattegat, but were not yet north of Skagen. In addition, Pontoppidan said, *Gneisenau*, *Leipzig* and *Emden* had passed Langeland on a northerly course between 06:00 and 07:00, followed by three torpedo boats and six armed trawlers. In return, Pontoppidan was told about the British minelaying off the coast of Norway.[19]

None of the intelligence officers had any knowledge of Group *Oldenburg*, and though the identification of the larger ships was still incorrect this was the first information of Group V heading north. It was 10:43 in Denmark and Norway when the message was noted in the war diary of the Norwegian Admiral

Kommandørkaptajn Fredrik Carl Pontoppidan, secretary to Viceadmiral Rechnitzer and a regular Danish contact with the Norwegians for the exchange of naval intelligence.

Staff. *Weser*-time was 17½ hours away. At 13:30, the message was sent on to kontreadmiral Smith-Johannsen, commander of SDD1 in Horten, together with information that the Legation in Berlin reported German transport ships having left the Baltic, for an unknown destination.[20]

Around lunchtime, Överste Adlercreutz, head of intelligence in the Swedish General Staff in Stockholm telephoned his friend Wrede-Holm in Oslo about a strong German naval force heading north. Nobody in the Norwegian intelligence community doubted that something was stirring. Steen and Wrede-Holm shared the information they had with their superiors, but it is not clear if these reports reached the Ministry of Defence. Nothing more was heard from Stockholm and the Swedish air patrols apparently did not see much of interest, most likely as they did not venture beyond the Swedish three-mile limit.[21]

The German naval attaché in Oslo, Korvettenkapitän Richard Schreiber, was nervous on the 8th. He was one of the few in Norway who had prior knowledge of *Weserübung* and was undoubtedly aware that the next 24 hours would be decisive for his career – if not his life. To pass the time and perhaps get some last-minute information to forward he paid a visit to the Norwegian Admiral Staff – by chance shortly after one of the messages from Pontoppidan had been received. Steen gave him the latest on the British mines that should be swept as soon as possible, but also asked carefully about the German ships passing through Danish waters. What was going on? Schreiber answered that he had no information regarding their intentions, but assumed they were heading for the North Sea to protect the German coast. Germany feared, he said, that the many British ships at sea might make an attack on the Danish Belts. Perhaps a second battle of Jutland was on its way?[22] Steen later wrote that when the naval attaché left, Schreiber said: 'Goodbye, Captain, and thank you for your pleasant companionship.' When Steen, somewhat puzzled, asked if Schreiber was leaving Oslo, he replied: 'No, but I still say goodbye.'[23] Later in the afternoon, Schreiber reported a certain 'anxiety' in the Norwegian Admiral Staff and Ministry of Defence in a telegram to Berlin but ascribed that to the British minelaying.[24]

Soon after, the British naval attaché Captain Boyes also arrived; Diesen had not yet returned. While talking to Steen, Boyes said he had 'reason to believe that a British naval force was on its way to meet German naval forces that had taken to sea'. Boyes was totally wrong in his assumptions, but as his message was conveyed to Diesen and Corneliussen, it gave them, and the rest of the Norwegian Admiral Staff, the impression that London was aware of German movements and intentions and not least that the Royal Navy would handle any threat, wherever it was directed.[25]

At 13:30, signals from the Naval Intelligence Staff in Oslo to the Sea Defence Districts summed up the information they had so far regarding the minelaying and the German ships moving north. Shortly after, kontreadmiral Smith-Johannsen of SDD1 ordered the minelayers *Laugen*, *Glommen*, *Nor* and *Vidar* to start loading mines and prepare to close the entrance to Oslofjord between Bolærne and Rauøy.

The issue of mines in outer Oslofjord remains controversial to this day. After the war, Ljungberg claimed that, according to his recollection, he had told Diesen he had the authority to make the decision to lay the mines himself, if he found it necessary. Corneliussen maintained that he, through a personal phonecall, forwarded Diesen's order to prepare the mines to SDD1 at midday. Smith-Johannsen denied having received any such call, however, and stated he had given the orders on his own initiative based on receiving information of German ships moving north through the Kattegat. Wherever these orders originated and whichever way they filtered down, the minelayers of 1st Minelayer Division, assigned to SDD1, were ordered to head for the mine depot at Vestre Bolærne, take on board mines and arm them, ready to close the gap between Rauøy and Bolærne on further orders. The minefield was planned as three to four rows of contact mines, 8,000 metres long. It would take at least twelve hours for the vessels to load the mines, arm them and be at the site to start laying. Diesen maintained he had given orders to lay the mines before midnight, but it has not been possible to find any record of this.[26]

At 15:40, a signal from the Admiral Staff to SDD1 said (incorrectly) that a British force was heading into the Kattegat to counter the German ships and, at 18:20, orders came to SDD1 to bring in additional conscripts to man the secondary battery (four 12-cm guns) at Bolærne and one extra searchlight there and at Rauøy. Engineers and personnel necessary to lay the minefields at Oscarsborg should also be called, but it was underlined again that no mines should be laid anywhere until further orders arrived from the Ministry of Defence. Later in the day, the sinking of *Rio de Janeiro* and *Stedingen* made it clear that British submarines were on the prowl outside the territorial limit.[27]

The first reports of the demise of *Rio de Janeiro* and *Stedingen* came to the Admiral Staff just after lunch. At 16:16 further signals confirmed that some of the dead and survivors were being brought in at several places and all reports confirmed that soldiers in uniform had been on board the *Rio de Janeiro*. One report from Kristiansand at 17:35 said there were around 100 surviving German soldiers in Lillesand and that there had been horses and guns on board the ship when she went down. Some of the soldiers divulged that they had boarded the ship in a Baltic port on 5 April and were on their way to Bergen at the request of the Norwegian government. A summary of these reports was forwarded to Ljungberg, who was in the Storting at the time. The torpedo boat *Ravn* and the minesweeper *Hvas* were sent to follow up *Stedingen* of which little was known at this stage other than she appeared to have been torpedoed.

Kommandørkaptajn Pontoppidan phoned the Norwegian Admiral Staff twice more during the afternoon, at 15:35 and at 18:25. On both occasions he confirmed that German ships – warships and transports – were moving north through Storebælt and Kattegat and that there appeared to be troops on board some of the vessels. Information of the German ships passing through Danish waters was forwarded to Oscarsborg, without comment, at 22:50.[28]

Admiral Diesen and his staff believed that the Royal Navy had sea supremacy and that a naval battle was developing between the German and British naval forces in the Skagerrak. They underestimated the Germans' ability to achieve local superiority at sea by establishing air control combined with mine barrages, preventing British warships from operating effectively in the Skagerrak and Kattegat. British reports to the Norwegian Admiralty reinforced the impression that the Royal Navy would intervene against the German forces. The thinking of Diesen and Corneliussen was that the Germans had fallen into a trap. British supremacy at sea would be the decisive factor in Diesen's opinion. 'We trusted in England,' Diesen said after the war. He later explained to the Commission of Inquiry that although he 'considered the situation threatening, both from the Allied and the German side, neither he nor Corneliussen believed a German attack on Norway was imminent at nightfall on the 8th'. The information from the survivors of *Rio de Janeiro* that they were heading for Bergen was considered 'camouflage' and he judged that the German ships were heading for Denmark, Shetland, the Faeroes or Iceland. Diesen's attention, and that of Corneliussen, was taken by the British minelaying and both were kept busy attending drawn-out meetings in the Foreign Affairs Committee and the Storting. The British mines off the West Coast were what concerned the Norwegian naval leadership, not the danger from the south. Except for instructions during the afternoon to Oscarsborg and the forts further down the fjord to call additional personnel to lay mines if ordered and man batteries and searchlights at Rauøy-Bolærne efficiently, things remained as they were.[29]

Around 14:00, Minister Esmarch in Copenhagen forwarded to Oslo information he had received directly from the Danish General Staff of 'two German battlecruisers, one battleship, three torpedo boats and several smaller vessels' having passed through Storebælt. In addition, German troops were marching northwards (if still some distance away from the border) and the transport ships loading in the Baltic ports had departed. At about the same time, the Norwegian Legation in Berlin sent a brief signal to the Foreign Office, stating that the Danish Embassy had let them know several troop transports had been observed on a northerly course through the Belts. These signals were already in the Foreign Office and Ministry of Defence when the reports of German soldiers being rescued from *Rio de Janeiro* came in, but nobody apparently saw the connection.[30]

A Day of Meetings

Foreign Minister Koht was up as usual shortly after 06:15 on the 8th. While he was having his breakfast, a courier from the Foreign Office arrived with a copy of the Allied note. Koht telephoned Prime Minister Nygaardsvold at his home and suggested the government should meet as soon as possible. Nygaardsvold wanted to include the Foreign Affairs Committee in the meeting as well. Koht disagreed, but was overruled, and the meeting was set for 10:00. While finishing his breakfast and waiting for Nygaardsvold to confirm the meeting, Koht received a call from Commanding Admiral

Diesen. He feared that British ships guarding the minefield in the Vestfjord might attack German ore ships at Narvik and sought Koht's approval to give the Norwegian Coast Defence ships orders to oppose them should this happen. Koht agreed and when Nygaardsvold called back shortly after, he had no objections to Diesen's request either. It is notable that Diesen called Koht and not Ljungberg. Most likely, neither Koht nor Nygaardsvold really believed the British ships would attack Narvik – and if they did, they would certainly turn back if they were met by opposition – before anything serious developed. Prior to the meeting of the Committee on Foreign Affairs, Diesen and Corneliussen met Ljungberg, as described above, but besides discussing alternative ways of guarding and eventually sweeping the supposed British minefields no decisions on Norwegian minefields were made.[31]

At 10:00 the members of the government sat down with the Foreign Affairs Committee to discuss reactions to the minelaying. At first, Koht went through parts of the Allied note of Friday the 5th and that of the same morning. For most it was the first time they had heard of either. Admiral Diesen was called to the meeting and, while he pointed out where the minefields allegedly were, Koht was asked to come to the telephone to talk to Swedish Foreign Minister Günther in Stockholm. He returned with the information that there was no apparent action in Swedish waters. The rest

Prime Minister Nygaardsvold and some of his ministers studying the maps of the British minefields as printed on the front pages of the main newspapers.

Commanding Admiral Diesen and his chief-of-staff Corneliussen waiting to be called into the meeting with the government. This kept the two decision-makers away from what should have been their main task on this day: taking charge and considering how to react to what was happening in the Skagerrak and the North Sea.

of the meeting was spent discussing how to respond and how others would react, Germany in particular. A firm protest would have to be made to London and Paris, quickly, and the mines would have to be swept as soon as possible. The note said that British ships would guard the minefields for forty-eight hours, and the Norwegian Navy should be ready to move in once the British were out of the way. A bit later in the morning it was decided to send the two modern minesweepers *Otra* and *Rauma* to do the job, protected by a handful of torpedo boats and guardships.[32]

After this meeting, the ministers sat down with the Foreign Affairs Committee. There, there was widespread agreement that events must not lead to Norway entering the war against Britain – despite the anger over the minelaying. Hostilities with the Royal Navy would have to be avoided. Britain had been seen as the guarantor of Norwegian neutrality and now – for the second time this spring – that neutrality had been ruthlessly violated. Koht added: 'There have been several reports in the last couple of days from Germany regarding planned actions against Norway. These are reports without any official foundation and we cannot know what they are based on or how serious they are.' Koht later denied using the word 'official', but the stenographer asserted the minutes were correct. Either way, Foreign Minister Koht in this meeting, some eighteen hours before *Weser*-time, told his government colleagues that he doubted the validity of the warnings and saw no reason to act upon them. Mobilisation needed a decision, but none was taken. The meeting of the Foreign Affairs Committee lasted until 12:30. There were many participants, and most had something to say. Towards the end, Koht brought up Minister Esmarch's discussions with the Danish Ministry of Foreign Affairs and the reports of German ships heading north through the Belts but brushed lightly over both.[33]

At an improvised press conference around 12:55 in one of the corridors of the Storting, Koht briefed journalists on the situation, concluding that the Norwegian government could not accept mines being laid inside Norwegian territorial waters. After a short lunch, Koht met briefly with the assistant Swedish chargé d'affaires in Oslo, Carl Douglas. Curiously, Koht told Douglas that the government had initiated 'certain military security measures, notably the alerting of the coastal fortresses and the concentration of the Norwegian Navy at certain key points'.[34] It is not clear exactly what Koht was referring to and most naval officers would probably contest that this was happening. Perhaps Koht and other members of the government believed that such precautions were obvious and would be initiated by the Ministry of Defence. When Douglas left, Koht sat down to fine-tune the protest and plan what to say in the Storting later in the evening.

At 15:00, Koht was interrupted again, this time by an urgent telephone call from the Norwegian Legation in London. A few hours earlier, the Legation had been requested to send an envoy to the Admiralty regarding a matter of utmost importance. At the Admiralty, the Deputy Chief of Naval Staff, Rear-Admiral Phillips, had told Vice-Consul Ingvald Smith-Kielland that German naval forces had been sighted off the Norwegian coast heading north. 'It is strongly suspected that operations against Narvik are intended and that they could arrive at Narvik before midnight' had been Phillips's conclusion. A telegram detailing the warning would be sent from London as soon as possible. Koht acknowledged and went back to work. 'I was so absorbed that it needed a mental effort to gather my thoughts on what I had heard,' Koht later wrote. Narvik was so far north it was difficult to comprehend the significance of the information. But since the news came from the British Admiralty, Koht felt sure that whatever was going on, the Royal Navy would take care of it. Besides, there were Norwegian naval ships in Narvik and significant Army units, which would handle things, he believed, if necessary. The information was eventually forwarded to the Ministry of Defence, the armed forces in the north and the Sea Defence Districts – without any discernible urgency.[35]

The Storting assembled at 17:15. Both service Commanders and their Chiefs of Staff were asked by Ljungberg to watch from the public gallery and thus taken out of contact with their staffs for over three hours that evening. The meeting attracted significant interest among the public, and there were long queues outside the Storting of people who wanted to sit in the gallery. Koht, visibly tired and distressed, opened by referring to parts of the Allied note of the 5th, the note regarding the minelaying and the Norwegian protest, which had by now been forwarded to the French and British Embassies in Oslo. There could be no justification, Koht said, for the Allies to 'bring the war to Norwegian territory' and the mines laid that morning were a severe intrusion. Several of the representatives expressed concern and frustration over the minelaying but cautioned that this must not lead to Norway going to war with Britain. Some of the speakers advised that the time had come to increase the preparedness of the Navy and the coastal forts, including laying Norway's own minefields. Nobody suggested a mobilisation. At 18:00 the meeting was closed to the public, but the discussions continued over what to do. To many it looked that neutrality might fail, and that Norway would have to choose sides. When, towards the end of the meeting, Ljungberg reported the sinking of the *Rio de Janeiro* and the subsequent rescue of several hundred German soldiers in uniform, the news was hardly discussed at all. Ljungberg later told the Commission of Inquiry that he assumed the German ships were heading somewhere else, or were part of a force responding to Allied provocations. Stortingspresident Hambro, who was to act very decisively once he understood what was going on, later wrote that the reports of the uniformed survivors from *Rio de Janeiro* claiming they were heading for Bergen were taken as confirmation that German soldiers would believe anything they were told by their officers. Few of those present in the Storting that evening really believed Norway was hours away from being at war.[36]

At 18:00, the telegram from the Norwegian Legation in London arrived at the Foreign Office, confirming the warning given by Rear-Admiral Phillips. It read:

> German naval forces were sighted in the North Sea yesterday accompanied by, it is believed, a merchantman, possibly a troop transport. This morning, the vanguard was observed off the Norwegian coast heading north. It is with certainty assumed their intention is to operate against Narvik and that they will arrive there before midnight. Admiral Phillips added the Germans might arrive at Narvik as soon as 10 p.m.[37]

After decyphering, the telegram was copied to the Admiral Staff where it arrived at 19:05. It is unclear if Koht or Ljungberg read the telegram. It is certain that none of the other members of the government including

Nygaardsvold saw it – or even heard of it. When the Storting eventually concluded its proceedings close to 21:00, most of the MPs were worried, but of the opinion that there was no imminent danger. Berlin would be provoked, but it was expected that the Germans, as before, would wait and see how the Norwegians handled the situation before they reacted. Nygaardsvold, Koht and Ljungberg all tried to close the meeting several times so they could return to their offices.[38]

The government convened at 21:00. By now, they were all tired, in particular Koht and Nygaardsvold, and the meeting was brief. No minutes have been preserved and details of what was said or agreed have been difficult to ascertain. Going through the relevant documents available today, it becomes clear that the government believed that Commanding Admiral Diesen and Commanding General Laake had a joint responsibility 'to take the initiative in instigating the actions necessary to maintain a satisfactory military preparedness at all times'. The two C-in-Cs on the other hand believed that mobilisation required a political decision and while they could suggest such an action to the defence minister, he would have to bring it to the government for a decision. With hindsight, that this critical issue had not been clarified remains a major mistake, for which the government must take responsibility. The issue of mobilisation was certainly on the agenda, but Ljungberg later insisted no concrete decisions were taken during the meeting, contrary to the accounts of several other ministers. Whatever was discussed or decided, nothing was set going that evening and no written orders were issued. According to Prime Minister Nygaardsvold, the meeting decided to lay the defensive minefields in Oslofjord. Trygve Lie later stated that this was the case, but none of the other ministers left with such an understanding and Admiral Diesen never received any orders. What *was* decided in the meeting was to sweep the British mines as soon as possible and not later than the morning of the 10th unless the British started the removal themselves. Ljungberg had already dismissed the General Staff for the night and made no attempt to contact anybody there or in the Admiral Staff after the government meeting adjourned at 21:40.[39] At 21:30, a request for permission to shut down the lighthouses was sent to the Commanding Admiral from SDD1 and shortly after approved.[40]

The situation at this stage, therefore, was that while the decision-makers were in the Storting or other meetings, several disturbing reports had arrived at the intelligence offices of the Navy and Army from various sources. Most of the signals were forwarded to the Foreign Office, the Ministry of Defence and the Admiral and General Staffs according to standing procedures, but apparently not with any comments as to their significance. The most important warnings that with hindsight should have triggered a response in Oslo, as well as Copenhagen and London, were:

- The information from Berlin on the 5th that rumour had it that Denmark would be occupied as well as harbours on the Norwegian south-coast.
- The information from Berlin on the 7th that 15 to 20 large ships loaded with troops and equipment had left Stettin and Swinemünde, heading for unknown destinations to be reached on 11 April.
- Signals from Sweden and Denmark on the 8th regarding German ships moving north through Danish waters.
- The sinking of *Rio de Janeiro* and *Stedingen*.
- The report from the British Admiralty of German ships heading for Narvik.

Why Ljungberg hesitated to mobilise, despite the clear and present danger has never been explained. His inability to appreciate the situation probably played a role as did diffidence in bringing drastic measures to the government and his awkward relationship with the senior officers of the General Staff. The ultimate accountability for the lack of clarity as to what was actually decided in the meeting, who was responsible and when the decision should be executed, rests with Prime Minister Nygaardsvold who went home to spend some time with his family before going to bed, exhausted after a long day. Koht was also tired when he left his office in the evening to join a lady friend for supper. Expecting a quiet night, he did not even leave a phone number where he could be reached.[41] Koht admitted in his memoirs that he misinterpreted the situation that evening. His and many others' attention was focussed on the threat from the Allies, and he saw the signals from Berlin as indications of the coming of the long-expected German offensive in the West. 'No-one can regret this miscalculation more bitterly than me', he wrote, adding:

> Something must have failed in my brain that evening. I was unable to make the right combinations and could not see the fragments of information I had received in a proper context. Perhaps I was too tired. The truth is I could not give the government a complete and correct overview. I did not have it myself, which is why the subsequent events would come as such a shock to me.[42]

Nightfall

It was a cold night in Norway, windy, gusting to storm, with frequent snow squalls in the north and dense fog in the south. Many families remained huddled around their fireplaces or the stoves in their kitchens throughout the evening. The day had been dramatic with extra newspaper editions and news broadcasts. The last bulletin on the radio was at 22:00 and few missed it. In restaurants and cafés, those who had not already gone home asked for the radios to be turned on. Concert halls and cinemas were empty; nobody wanted to go places where they could not talk. Few believed there was a direct threat against Norway, but many expected clashes between German and British naval forces during the following days leading to violations of Norwegian territory involving the Navy and endangering civilian ships. Newspapers and news agencies established a duty roster, preparing for the morning editions. Towards midnight, everything was quiet in Oslo and few lights remained burning. At the British Legation, Minister Dormer had an early night and slept well.

Vidkun Quisling had played no role whatsoever in the German preparations for *Weserübung* after his return from Berlin just before Christmas. None of the military planners wanted anything to do with him and he himself had been ill most of the winter and out of the public eye in Norway for several months. From the middle of January, Quisling first had a kidney disease, then sinusitis and finally needed surgery for a jaw problem. He was only back on his feet in mid-March, still not fully restored. Still, Quisling must have guessed from his contacts with de Laporte and Piekenbrock that something was about to happen even if he had no concrete knowledge of what or when. Late in the evening of 8 April, NS secretary Harald Knudsen persuaded Quisling to leave his home and check in at the Hotel Continental in central Oslo, as they feared for his safety. The minelaying could indicate the British were on their way and if the Germans came first, as the sinking of *Rio de Janeiro* might indicate, 'those who felt guilty [for the inability to protect Norway's neutrality], might wish to eliminate him', Knudsen later wrote. Quisling alleged at his trial in 1945 that, 'upon hearing the news of the German transport sunk with horses and vehicles aboard', he believed the Germans were on their way to Norway as well and agreed to go into hiding 'to avoid being detained'. Knudsen booked a single room in his own name and smuggled Quisling up through the back stairs. The two men settled in for the night; Quisling in the bed, Knudsen on the couch.[43]

Among the passengers on the train from Copenhagen via Sweden arriving in Oslo on the morning of 8 April, was Oberstleutnant Hartwig Pohlmann, Operations Officer (Ia) in Falkenhorst's staff. Pohlmann travelled under his real name, but he was in civilian clothes and passed through immigration on a brand-new diplomatic passport giving his title as *Ministerialrat* (advisor) from the Ministry of the Interior. His luggage, handled by a secretary, was protected by diplomatic immunity and thus not searched. Had it been, it would have created a major diplomatic crisis as it not only contained Pohlmann's uniform, including his sidearm, but also several incriminating maps and sealed envelopes for the German Minister in Oslo. Pohlmann was met at the station by the Abwehr man Erich Pruck and given a tour of the city to familiarise himself. Later, from his hotel room, Pohlmann called the German Air Attaché in Oslo, Hauptmann Spiller, instructing him to meet at Fornebu airfield next morning to receive the German forces, expected to land around 07:45. Excited, Spiller, who had been called to the telephone from entertaining a handful of Norwegian officers in his home, confirmed he would be there but added that the fighters at Fornebu had been put on alert. Pohlmann was not impressed. A handful of small Norwegian fighter aircraft would mean little against the German squadrons arriving next morning.[44]

Having concluded the talk with Spiller, Pohlmann prepared for dinner with Minister Bräuer at the German Legation. Bräuer had been sidelined from the start of the planning and it was only that evening that he learned fully what was about to happen. Among the staff at the Legation, only the attachés Spiller and Schreiber and the Abwehr men Erich Pruck and Berthold Benecke had prior knowledge of Operation *Weserübung*. 'Rarely have I seen a man more surprised than [Bräuer] when I told him of the events to come and his designated role in them,' Pohlmann later wrote. Bräuer had been told by Benecke a few days earlier that something was being planned but not in any detail. Now he was given two envelopes. The first contained a letter from his superior, Foreign Minister Ribbentrop, outlining his intended role vis-à-vis the Norwegian authorities. The second was a lengthy ultimatum to the Norwegian government, demanding surrender. This was to be hand-delivered to Foreign Minister Koht at 04:20 next morning – precisely. This would be a few minutes after the German landing operations had started but, the Germans hoped, while confusion still reigned. Bräuer was not to request the meeting or make any prearrangement before 04:00, so as not to raise any suspicion, and he was not to reveal the nature of the meeting when insisting upon being received. If Koht was not to be found, the memorandum should be presented to Prime Minister Nygaardsvold or the Deputy Foreign Minister. From midnight, Bräuer would be the 'Authorised Representative of the Reich', *Der Bevollmächtigte des Deutschen Reiches bei der norwegischen Regierung*, the highest civilian German authority in Norway and the only political contact between Berlin and Oslo. His objectives were clear: making Nygaardsvold and his government co-operate and ensuring King Haakon remained in Oslo under German control. Major German warships would be in the harbour with their guns trained on the city to underline the demands, Pohlmann said, and troops would be made available if necessary. Norwegian reactions should be reported to Berlin as soon as possible, using the radio at the Legation or the public telephone line via Sweden, using simple code words. These codes reveal which answers Berlin expected: four referred to situations in which the Norwegian government accepted

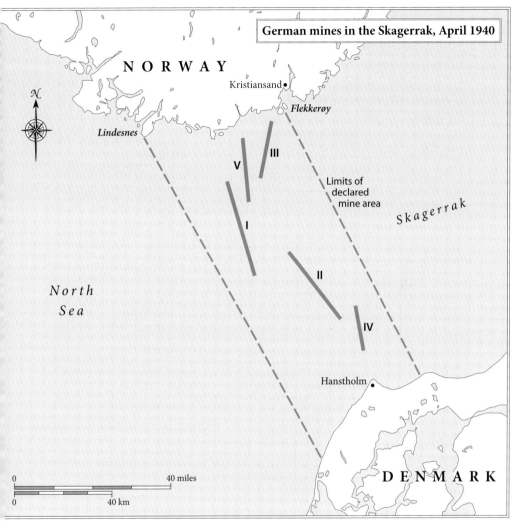

German mines in the Skagerrak, April 1940

the terms, withheld orders to fire, negotiated or offered symbolic protests. Only one referred to resistance being offered. The Norwegian government was not expected to stand up in defiance against the mighty Wehrmacht. Bräuer later maintained that he was stunned by the news of what was about to happen, but after talking to Pohlmann, the two men agreed that the Norwegian government would likely comply with the German demands and allow the German forces to land – provided the ultimatum was backed up by warships in the harbour, before any widespread fighting had commenced.[45]

Naval Attaché Schreiber had been in Berlin a couple of times during the winter, presenting his views on Norway in general and naval matters in particular to Raeder and the SKL. On one occasion in February, just after the *Altmark* episode, the *Großadmiral* had told him that a German attack on Norway might be initiated unless the country showed a significant improvement in the handling of Allied violations of Norwegian neutrality. On his last visit to Berlin in March, Schreiber repeated what he had said before: the Norwegians would not oppose a German occupation when it was made clear they came as friends. Falkenhorst later wrote that Schreiber was well informed about the social life in Oslo, but as he could not travel around as he wished, he had little to add of real value to the planners of *Weserübung*.[46]

On the 5th, Schreiber had been told by a coded telegram from Berlin that *Wesertag* would be 9 April and that he, at 05:00, should be ready to receive Generalmajor Engelbrecht in Oslo harbour. Before that, he should reconnoitre places where large warships could dock and offload troops that could take the city quickly under control. This he had done.

On the evening of the 8th, the Abwehr officer Leutnant Hermann Kempf boarded the German freighter *Widar* at anchor in Oslo harbour off Bygdøy. Schreiber had briefed him in the morning and, at Pruck's suggestion, ordered him to board *Widar* to supervise her radio transmissions until Group V arrived. *Widar* had arrived in Oslo harbour on the 7th. She was a regular merchantman loaded with coal but, like several other German freighters, equipped with a high-powered radio with codebooks and special orders in a locked cabinet. The captain knew nothing of *Weserübung* but was instructed by Kempf to observe closely all traffic at sea and in the air and report to the Abwehrstelle in Hamburg. As soon as the warships arrived early the next morning, Kempf was to board *Lützow* and make sure she docked where she could have the fortress of Akershus under observation. Akershus Fortress was a relic from older days, centrally located in Oslo Harbour. In 1940, it was used as an administrative HQ and base for the Army but had no defensive value.[47]

A last call from Kommandørkaptajn Pontoppidan in Denmark came in some time between 22:30 and 23:10. The Danish officer told the Norwegian Admiral Staff that the three large warships that had been reported earlier had been observed from Skagen at a range of 12 nm on a westerly course at 19:00. The smaller ships seen in their company earlier, had not been observed on this occasion. Together with the report from London that German naval forces were off the Norwegian coast, probably heading for Narvik, a new dimension to the picture seemed to emerge. The Norwegians informed Pontoppidan of the communication from London and he noted in his diary that he sensed a 'certain nervousness' from his Norwegian colleague.[48]

As part of *Weserübung*, a mine barrage was laid in the approach to the Skagerrak between Kristiansand in Norway and Hanstholm in Denmark, known by the Germans as Skagerrak Sperre or Skagerrak Warngebiet.

The intention of the barrage was to prevent Allied naval forces entering the eastern Skagerrak to keep them away from the supply lines between Germany and Norway. The first mines were laid on the night of 8/9 April. The minelayers *Preußen* and *Königin Luise* laid Barrage II with 325 mines just before midnight while *Roland* and *Cobra* laid 384 mines in Barrage I just after. Four minesweepers protected the operation.[49] The two lines overlapped and closed the entry to the inner Skagerrak. In the coming weeks, further barrages were completed and by 24 April, five lines (I–V) with a total of 1,642 mines had been laid. They were all regular EMC-type anchored horn-mines with 250-kg explosive charges. The main passage of the barrage was close to the coasts on either side, usually guarded by armed trawlers supported by mobile artillery on land.[50]

During 9 April, after the first landings had taken place in Denmark, warnings of the minefields were issued by radio as an announcement of a restricted area bound to the west by a line between Lindesnes and Lodbjerg, and to the east by a line from Flekkerøy to north of Hanstholm. The warning came too late for two Swedish fishing vessels, the 48-ton *Ines* and the 47-ton *Dagny* both vanished, with their crews of six men each, the following morning leaving only wreckage and debris after explosions were heard by other boats in the area. A third boat, *Knippla*, had two mines tangled in her net but managed to cut the wires before the horns hit her hull.[51] East of the declared area, the Germans established sea control in the Skagerrak and Kattegat on 8 April with aircraft and escort vessels. The ultimate intention, full sea supremacy, was not achieved due to the presence of British submarines.

In Wilhelmshaven, Admiral Saalwächter sat down to summarise the situation around midnight. He was optimistic that the British minelaying gave Germany the right to 'meet this act of violence with similar measures'. On the negative side, it probably meant that parts of the British fleet would be at sea. It was not yet clear if the Admiralty realised the German objectives or if they were reacting to what they believed to be an Atlantic breakout. Saalwächter feared that the sinking of *Rio de Janeiro* had given the German intentions away but reckoned that even if this should be the case, it was too late for London to initiate effective counter-measures against the invasion forces. Nothing could stop the German warships at this stage. The SKL arrived at the same conclusion; 'Operation *Weserübung* has left the stage of secrecy and camouflage [...] The element of surprise has been lost and we must expect resistance at all points.'[52] However, Falkenhorst became worried when he was informed of the sinking of *Rio de Janeiro*. 'It was a critical moment that could have jeopardised the whole operation,' he later wrote.[53]

'The 8th was a day of highest tension,' Jodl wrote in his diary.[54]

Chapter 9

The Guns of Oscarsborg

Defence of the Capital

Commander of the 1st Sea Defence District (SDD1), kontreadmiral Johannes Smith-Johannsen at Karljohansvern naval base in Horten was responsible for the defence of the south-east coast of Norway, from the Swedish Border to Egersund, including the fjord leading up to Oslo (*see* Appendix B). There is no doubt that the Oslofjord was his priority but, except for three obsolete submarines, only minesweepers, minelayers and guardships, all with limited combat value, were in this area. The available torpedo boats were deployed along the southern coast, outside Oslofjord.

The defence of Norway's capital rested with the fortresses in the fjord – the first line at Rauøy and Bolærne at the mouth of the fjord, the second line at Oscarsborg at the head of the Drøbak Narrows. Beyond a few 7.5-cm anti-aircraft guns and some machine guns, there were no defences in Horten or at the naval base of Karljohansvern except the guns of any naval ships that happened to be present at the time. The fjord towards Drammen had no defence at all in 1940. The fort at Svelvik was no longer operational, and the German missed an opportunity for easy access there.[1]

By the end of the nineteenth century, a number of fortresses existed along the coast of south Norway, defending the main coastal cities. When built, they were state-of-the-art, but development of guns, naval vessels and armour was never ending and during the first part of the twentieth century guns were replaced and ramparts and emplacements rebuilt literally on a continuous basis. By 1940, though, most of the forts were obsolete due to the lack of AA guns and overhead cover. Even so, the guns were well maintained and among the most potent weapons of the Norwegian defences – if adequately manned. Fire-control and range-finding systems had been modernised, so the accuracy of the guns was fair if a trained crew handled them.

The command bunkers of the artillery batteries were equipped with orographs (a type of surveying device) used here for measuring the range to the target. This was conveyed by telephone or by signal to each gun in real time and the gun crews set the range accordingly. Though the equipment was basic, almost primitive, it was nevertheless accurate and functional in 1940, provided there was sufficient daylight, or the target was illuminated by

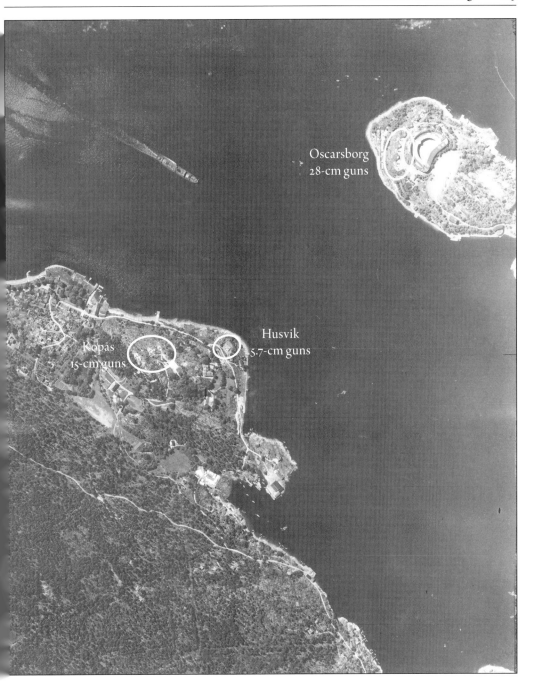

Oscarsborg
28-cm guns

Husvik
5.7-cm guns

Kopås
15-cm guns

The Drøbak Narrows. This aerial photo shows how narrow the passage is.
Oscarsborg fortress is the horseshoe-shaped building on the island.
The Kopås and the Husvik artillery batteries are on the mainland.

The three 28-cm guns at Oscarsborg totally dominated the approaches to Oslo.
The guns had been acquired from the German Krupp factories in the early 1890s
and were state-of-the-art when installed in open but shielded mountings.
The ship in this image is in roughly the same position (though heading in the
opposite direction) as the vessel shown in the aerial photo on the previous page.

searchlights. The target was followed horizontally by the trainer at each gun
using a telescope sight. Hence, the bearing to the target was the easy part of
the targeting even when the target was moving at high speed. The time factor
was crucial. Attacking vessels would only operate for a limited time in the fire
sectors of the guns. Early warning was essential, and the commanders had to
be determined to open fire at first sight.

The Norwegian armed forces of 1940 had a small proportion of professional
officers. The majority of the officers, as well as the other ranks, were conscripts. In the earlier interwar years, the soldiers of the Coast Artillery
served for 60 days initially and were not given any subsequent training. By
1938, the service time had increased to 84 days. After the outbreak of war
in 1939, the soldiers were drafted for three months at a time. Those coming
in in September were thus released in December and a new rotation took
place during March. In the Navy, the service time for drafted seamen was 6
months.[2]

Oscarsborg Fortress

Oscarsborg was built on the island of Søndre Kaholmen in the Drøbak Narrows around 1850 as a defence against enemy ships entering Oslo harbour. In the 1870s, an underwater wall, a so-called *jeté*, was built on the west side of the fjord to compel larger ships to pass the fortress on its east side. Here a remote-controlled cable-minefield was prepared, to be laid in the main channel in case of emergency. The southern part of the fortress was buried in ballast delivered from commercial shipping and the result was a robust tunnel system which could withstand bombing and bombardments in 1940.

In the early 1890s a new main battery (Hovedbatteriet) on Søndre Kaholmen was completed with three Krupp 28-cm L/40 Model 1889 guns, in addition to some older weapons. At the turn of the century a torpedo battery was built into the rocks of Nordre Kaholmen, north of the main battery. New batteries were built on the rocky island of Håøya behind Oscarsborg and at Kopås on the eastern mainland. Håøya had one battery of two Armstrong 12-cm K/43.9 Model 1897s, one battery of eight 12-cm K/36 Model 1891s and one battery of four 28-cm Whitworth Model 1892 howitzers. Supplementing these guns, a battery of three 15-cm Armstrong K/47.5 Model 1897s was set

The Kaholmene islands. To the right, south, is Søndre Kaholmen with Oscarsborg fortress and the 28-cm main battery. To the left is Nordre Kaholmen with the torpedo battery. Kopås is in the background with Drøbak town further south.

up at Kopås, on the east side of the fjord, north of the small town of Drøbak. Several smaller batteries with 5.7-cm guns were also constructed to protect the minefield and to combat small warships. Two of these guns were located at Husvik, below the Kopås battery, four on Nesset on the west side in front of the *jeté*, in addition to several guns at Søndre Kaholmen and Nordre Kaholmen.[3] During the interwar period, the guns at Kopås were reconstructed to permit firing at higher elevation and the shells received ballistic caps. These measures extended the range from 10,000 to 14,000 metres.[4]

All guns of the Oscarsborg fortress were in open concrete emplacements, with no overhead cover. The command posts on the other hand were fully covered. East of Drøbak there were defensive infantry positions to protect the fortresses from landward attack. To rationalise the use of resources and avoid too many idle conscripts, Oscarsborg was set up for minimum manning in quiet periods, only to be fully manned and prepared during a crisis. Hence, the fortress was fully mobilised in 1905, following the Norwegian declaration of independence from Sweden and partly mobilised in 1914–18 to maintain neutrality during World War 1.

The need for a defence line in outer Oslofjord was obvious, due to the threat against other towns along the fjord and the main naval base of Karljohansvern. During the 1930s, work on permanent fortifications and guns at Rauøy and Bolærne commenced. This led to Oscarsborg no longer being prioritised, receiving virtually no funding for modernisation in the interwar years.[5]

Oberst Birger Kristian Eriksen was born in 1875 in Flakstad in Lofoten. He joined the armed forces in 1893 after secondary school, was commissioned three years later and was promoted to *oberst* in 1931. After having served at several other coastal fortresses, he was appointed commander at Oscarsborg in 1933. At the time, the decay of the fortress was obvious, and Eriksen repeatedly requested funds to modernise and improve the installations. Especially after the outbreak of hostilities in September 1939, he argued that the strategic position of the main fort made it the key to the defence of the capital, but he was not heard, and little happened. The mainland batteries had no protection against air strikes and among the measures he applied for in vain was money to build air-raid shelters at Kopås. Søndre Kaholmen had several tunnels and reservoirs that could be used for shelter and the torpedo battery at Nordre Kaholmen was underground anyway, so here the needs were less.[6]

At the start of the neutrality period, Eriksen established a line of guardships at Filtvet, at the edge of the effective range of the main guns at Kaholmen. There was also a signal station and an orograph in this area to measure distance to target and give directions, both being regularly manned.

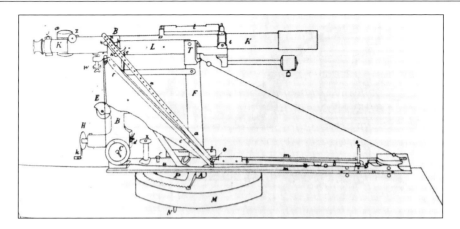

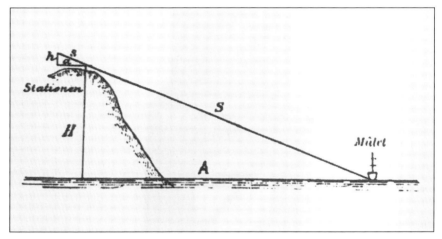

The Coast Artillery used orographs as rangefinders in 1940. The instrument (*shown at top*) measured the range to the target by the downward angle (*above*). The range, which was read at a ruler, was forwarded to the guns. The trainers at the guns aimed their sights at the target and the layers elevated the guns according to the range forwarded from the orograph. The orograph could also be used for indirect fire-control but this potential was not exploited in 1940. A map underneath the orograph would then be used to give both the range and bearing settings to the guns.

These stations would report vessels moving up the fjord and if necessary control the fire from the fortress. All ships were identified and the permission to pass verified. Ships could only pass during the hours of darkness if night travel permission had been given. At the mouth of the Narrows, control was handled by the signal station at Filtvet and one of the guardships, *Alpha* or *Furu*. In the Drøbak Narrows the auxiliary *Kranfartøy Nr. 2* and the signal station at Oscarsborg took over. For anti-aircraft defence, the fortress had two 40-mm L/60 Bofors guns at Seiersten east of Drøbak and a number of 7.92-mm Colt machine guns on Søndre Kaholmen, Kopås and Håøya. In addition, there were manned searchlights on the mainland between Drøbak harbour and Kopås.[7]

To strengthen the Coast Artillery in general a new group of recruits was drafted on 1 April 1940; 430 of these arrived at Oscarsborg the next day. The newcomers, organised as a battalion, were distributed with a battery (company equivalent) at Søndre-Kaholmen, another on Håøya and the rest in the Drøbak area. None of the recruits had taken part in basic weapons training by 8 April. To make room for the recruits, trained soldiers at the batteries at Kopås and Nesset on the mainland were sent home. The recruits were strictly speaking trainees and not a strengthening of the number of personnel at the fortress – quite the contrary. At the main battery at Søndre-Kaholmen there was also a change of command, and kaptein Magnus Sødem took over as battery commander of the main 28-cm guns on 1 April. One of the first orders he received from Eriksen was to send 10 gunners to the battery at Nesset, and 25 gunners to Kopås. On 7 April Sødem had 2 officers, 2 sergeants and 44 other ranks to man the battery and take care of all other tasks including guard duties, stores and administration. About 20 of the men had non-combatant status; most of the rest had been drafted about a month earlier. He was left with only enough men to man one 28-cm gun properly with 24 gunners. After first clearing the battery area and the guns of snow and remnants of the winter, Sødem had three new HE shells per gun brought up from the storage magazine to the traverses between the guns, from where they could very quickly be rolled on carts to the guns. This ammunition gave the guns a maximum range of 20,900 metres.

The guns at Kopås required ten men each to operate. In addition, the communications system and the orograph posts required crews with a minimum of training. The men sent over from the main battery were spread over two of the guns, but few, if any, of these had ever served on the Armstrong guns. Other trained forces in the area included the NCO training school at Husvik, close to Kopås. They could be activated as a trained unit. The mines for the Drøbak Narrows were stored in magazines on Bergholmen island, south-west of Håøya. They were rather old and would have taken days to prepare and lay, but were suitable for the Narrows. There were also batteries at Håøya, but these were buried in heavy snow and could not be used at short notice.[8]

The torpedo battery inside Nordre Kaholmen had a small but trained crew of 7 officers and 8 other ranks on duty. The battery consisted of an entry-tunnel and a large mountain-hall with three shafts containing one ready and one reloading launch-frame each, a storage room and maintenance facilities. The torpedoes were 45-cm (18-in) Whiteheads, Model Vd, with explosive

Gun no. 2 of the three 15-cm Armstrong guns at the Kopås battery on the mainland.
To the right is the ready-use ammunition magazine and the site of a former
rangefinder/orograph platform.

charges of 118 kg of TNT (known as trinol in Norway at the time). There were
nine of them available and they had been stored and maintained next to the
shafts since the outbreak of the war in 1939. The compressed air used to fire
them was constantly replenished. To launch the torpedoes, they were pushed
into the steel cradle and lowered into the shafts for underwater launch. Each
shaft could be reloaded independently once it was fired, a process which took
only a few minutes. The torpedoes could not be remotely controlled after
firing and were only suitable against ships passing in front of the openings.[9]

On the morning of 8 April 1940, Oscarsborg had no more than a skeleton
garrison. The fortress was not mobilised and manned as it should have been.
The main command centre at Håøya was not manned at all and Eriksen
had no second-in-command and no chief of staff. He was very alone in his
command and would, for all practical purposes, take most decisions unaided.
No additional mobilisation had been ordered, beyond the minimum manning
found necessary for the Neutrality Watch. At 19:30 a signal from the Admiral
Staff in Oslo arrived with instructions to make sure sufficient personnel were
available to lay the mine barrage – should it be ordered. At 22:50, information
that German capital ships and torpedo boats had passed through Danish

German soldiers having a good look at the torpedo-battery from a passing
transport ship at some point during the occupation. The shadow to the right of
centre is over the torpedo caves. Above this are the observations posts.
To the left is the quay and main gate of the fort.

waters during the day also arrived, without further comments. Six minutes
later at 22:56, a second signal arrived with details of the message from the
British Admiralty that German naval ships had been sighted in the North Sea
heading north, possibly for Narvik. Again, there were no comments with the
signal nor any orders for additional precautions.[10]

Outer Oslofjord Sea Defence Sector

During World War 1, a temporary, improvised line of defence was established
in the outer Oslofjord, collectively known as Ytre Oslofjord Sjøforsvarsavsnitt
or YOSA. Its main task was to block the entrance to the fjord completely,
protecting the capital Oslo and the other cities in the Oslo fjord, including
the main naval base and shipyard at Horten. The key elements of YOSA
were the forts at Rauøy and Bolærne. All forts and facilities had been under
modernisation since the mid-thirties, but the work was far from completed
by April 1940. The most modern weapons were 15-cm L/50 Model 1919 Bofors
guns, which had a range of 16,500 metres with HE shells, directed by Eriksen
orographs which could measure up to 20,000 metres. The C-in-C of YOSA,

kommandør Einar Tandberg-Hanssen, and his chief of staff kaptein Trond Stamsø, had their headquarters and communication office at Tønsberg. The southern boundary of YOSA, which also marked the boundary of the restricted area of Oslo *krigshavn*, was guarded by requisitioned whale boats, old torpedo boats, and minesweepers converted into guardships. Coast Watch Posts supplemented the monitoring from Vikertangen (Hvaler), Torbjørnskjær and Færder at the mouth of Oslofjord. Group centres for communication were established in Sarpsborg, Skien and Arendal. In all, there were 750 men at the various forts and posts of YOSA, 90 of them officers.[11]

C-in-C of the Outer Oslofjord Fortress was oberstløytnant Kristian Notland. He had his HQ with communication centre and intelligence staff, about 20 officers and 35 other ranks, at Håøy fort on the western side of the fjord. The two 21-cm guns

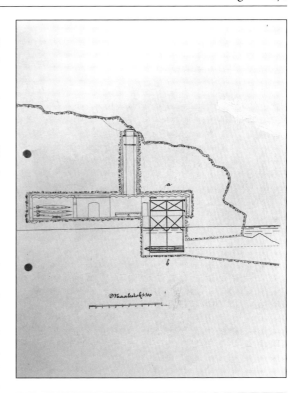

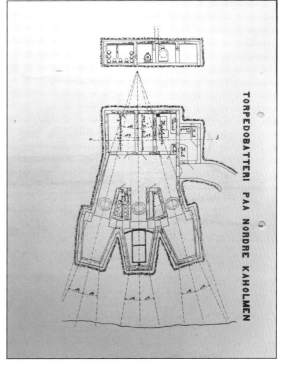

Top: Side-view of the Kaholmen torpedo battery and one of the observation towers and, *right*, the battery from above. The torpedo store and engine station were behind the main hall. The warheads were kept in the room to the left behind the launch positions.

German soldiers inspecting one of the Whitehead Vd torpedoes
during the summer of 1940, after the fort had been taken over.

at the fort were intended for defence of the entrance to Tønsberg town and
Melsomvik naval base; they could not fire into Oslofjord and were mainly
used for exercises and training. The battery of the new Måkerøy Fort had two
30.5-cm Bofors howitzers but was undermanned and for all practical purposes
not operational. A new fort was under construction at Torås but this had no
military value in April 1940.[12]

Commander at Rauøy Fort was major Hersleb Enger, the brother of
kaptein Vagn Enger at Kopås. The fort was largely manned by conscripts
who had arrived on 1 March supplemented by a smaller contingent arriving
on 5 April. Rauøy had two newly constructed 15-cm batteries, each with two
Bofors guns. There were three searchlights on the island, one 150-cm and two
110-cm. Only one of the 110-cm lights was manned. Missingen, the forward
signal station a few miles to the south, had an orograph, a mobile 110-cm
searchlight and communication equipment.[13] Both batteries were manned,
but neither officers nor men were properly trained on the new 15-cm Bofors
guns and intensive training was initiated. A corporal had to step in as gun
commander as he was more competent than his officer. On 7 April each
battery had 100 rounds of live HE ammunition brought up from the magazine
in addition to five inert shells for warning shots. The two 40-mm AA guns and
six Colt machine guns were also manned and ammunition brought forward.
Rauøy had no main shelter. The guns were exposed as the emplacements were

built on rather open high ground even if the ammunition magazines at each gun could protect soldiers for a limited time [14]

Major Fredrik Færden was commander at Bolærne in April 1940. The fort had one battery with three new 15-cm Bofors guns. Battery commander was kaptein Knut Telle. Bolærne also had a new contingent of soldiers arrive in early March, untrained on the new Bofors guns. The last newcomers, who appeared in early April, were spread equally on all the three guns – efficient for training but disruptive operationally. Two of the gun commanders were among the newcomers in April and had never seen this type of gun before. The fort also manned six 7.92-mm Colt machine guns organised into two troops, a signal station at Fulehuk, a 150-cm searchlight at Garnholmen and a 90-cm at Ramsholmen. Construction of a second main battery with four 12-cm guns had started during World War 1, had stopped in the twenties and was never completed. The construction of an artillery tunnel for these guns, with openings on one side for firing, was also halted. By then, two of the guns had positions inside the tunnel but two were still in open, uncovered emplacements. The tunnel was nevertheless suitable for shelter in case of air attack.[15]

Anti-aircraft defence was limited on both forts. It consisted of two 40-mm L/60 Bofors guns on Rauøy and twelve Colt machine guns, six on each island. The 40-mm L/60 was a modern gun that fired 120 shots per minute with an effective range of 1,500 metres against aircraft. The Colt machine guns were also newly acquired for the Coast Artillery in a considerable number but would for all practical purposes prove useless against modern aircraft.[16]

A minefield to close the entire Oslofjord was planned between Rauøy and Bolærne. The sites for the mines had been surveyed and 1,100 mines were stored in the tunnel depot at Vestre Bolærne so that the obstruction could be made effective as soon as possible – when decided. The minelayers of 1 Minelayer division – *Laugen, Glommen, Nor* and *Vidar* – under command of kaptein Ernst Schramm, had their station at Melsomvik where contacts and other equipment were kept and a forward station at Jarlsøy east of Tønsberg.[17]

Chapter 10

Trespassing

By 20:00 on 8 April darkness was falling in the Skagerrak. On the ships of Group *Oldenburg* approaching the funnel-shaped entrance to the long Oslofjord, the flags were hauled down as darkness fell. Total black-out was ordered, and all portholes shut, and deadlights locked down. There was a light south-westerly breeze and hardly any sea at all. Further north, however, a misty haze developed and near the mouth of the fjord, rain squalls and patches of fog reduced visibility. The distance between the larger ships was reduced to some 600 metres. *Blücher* remained in the lead with the others in line astern, maintaining contact through screened lanterns aft. All soldiers were below deck. Woldag switched off *Blücher*'s radar once Group V entered the fjord as the echoes generated by the surrounding mountains rendered it useless.[1]

In one of *Blücher*'s radio rooms Norwegian-speaking Sonderführer Willi Behrens listened in to Norwegian Radio's evening news at 22:00 Norwegian time (23:00 GeT). It included reports of the discussions in the Storting over the British minelaying, observations of German ships heading north through the Danish Belts and the sinking of *Rio de Janeiro*. Towards the end of the bulletin, the order for all lighthouses and radio beacons from Oslofjord to Trondheim to be shut down was repeated. Behrens, just out of OKW's interpreter school and assigned to the group with orders to take control of the Norwegian broadcasting service after the landing next morning, forwarded the information to his officers and was eventually called to the bridge to report to Kummetz and Engelbrecht in person.[2]

The same news bulletin was heard by *Lützow*'s radio operators and Thiele took it as a sure sign the Norwegians knew they were coming, all hope of surprise being lost. He sent a signal to the flagship, suggesting maximum speed to surprise the defenders at Drøbak before they had time to prepare. Kummetz, however, annoyed at the uninvited suggestion contradicting his orders, answered that they would pass the Narrows as planned. The admiral was of the opinion that even if the Norwegians knew they were coming, they would not open fire. Group V continued according to schedule.[3]

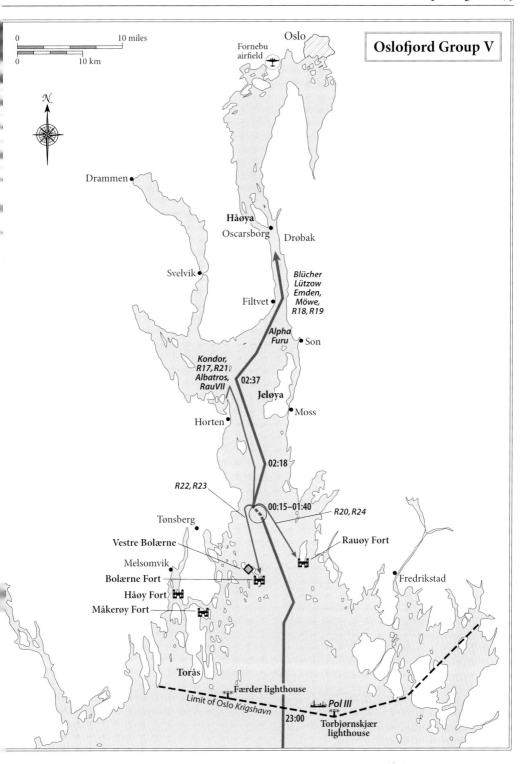

Oslofjord Group V

0 ————— 10 miles
0 ————— 10 km

N

Oslo

Fornebu
airfield

Drammen

Håøya
Oscarsborg   Drøbak

Svelvik   Blücher
                                     Lützow
                           Filtvet   Emden,
                                     Möwe,
                                     R18, R19

                         Alpha
                         Furu   Son

Kondor,
R17, R21
Albatros,   02:37
RauVII
                      Jeløya

Horten   Moss

                      02:18

R22, R23
                      00:15–01:40   R20, R24

Tønsberg

Vestre Bolærne   Rauøy Fort

Melsomvik
Bolærne Fort   Fredrikstad

Håøy Fort
Måkerøy Fort

Torås
               Færder lighthouse
        Limit of Oslo Krigshavn   Pol III
                      23:00
                               Torbjørnskjær
                               lighthouse

The torpedo boat *Albatros*. This photo was likely taken in the early 1930s
as she is flying the flag of the pre-Nazi German Republic. Except for the pennant
letters in the bow being painted over, she looked very much like this in 1940, too.

Shortly after, the lighthouses at Færder and Torbjørnskjær were sighted.
They were still burning despite the order that they should be extinguished.
Kummetz believed this confirmed his opinion. Within minutes, though, the
lighthouses were shut down one by one. From then on, there was no doubt
the Norwegians knew they might be coming. Thereafter the ships' exact
positions could only be ascertained from time to time when fixes could be
made on civilian lights or a few navigation marks that were visible or whose
lights had not been turned off. Depth soundings were also used to help
navigation and in a few places mountain tops visible against the sky could also
be identified. It was now midnight German time and 23:00 Norwegian time.
Kummetz, Engelbrecht and Generalmajor Wilhelm Süssmann (designated
head of Luftwaffe ground personnel) with their staffs joined Woldag on the
bridge of *Blücher*, which with the officers and seamen of the watch became
very crowded. To lessen the congestion, some of the petty officers and ratings
not needed for navigation and observation were ordered into the armoured
citadel. Passing between Færder and Torbjørnskjær in total darkness, the
German ships were inside Oslo *krigshavn*. They could meet Norwegian
warships at any time. And so they did. Almost immediately a small shadow
appeared to starboard, and *Albatros* was ordered to investigate.[4]

On the night of 8/9 April, four guardships were on station outside the
Rauøy–Bolærne line. *Pol III* was taking care of the central sector, crossing the
entrance to the fjord between the lighthouses at Færder and Torbjørnskjær.
Farm patrolled the eastern side between Torbjørnskjær and Tresteinen
lighthouse, while *Skudd II* was to the west between Færder and Svenner.
Further in, the minesweeper *Kjæk* patrolled between the lighthouses at

Fulehuk and Missingen, verifying that all ships passing into Oslo *krigshavn* had permission to do so.[5]

At 18:00, YOSA sent orders for 'Increased Preparedness' to all ships and forts, adding that live ammunition should be kept ready. No explanations were given as to what might happen. At 19:35 the signal 'Alert!' was issued, followed by a warning that the Norwegian submarines would leave their base at 04:00 next morning and head for designated positions in the outer fjord. Still no explanations were given.[6]

Pol III's commanding officer, kaptein Leif Welding-Olsen, had received the orders for 'Increased Preparedness' and 'Alert' from YOSA. The night was dark with swirling fog and rain and a south-westerly breeze. At 22:00 the broadcast order for the lighthouses to be switched off was heard. Something was definitely going on, even if nobody aboard the tiny ship knew what. Welding-Olsen ordered a sharp lookout before he turned in. The First Officer, overkanoner Hans Bergan, had the watch. At 22:50, the lighthouse at Færder was turned off, but the foghorn was started. Shortly after, at 23:00, *Pol III* made a routine turn off Torbjørnskjær and was heading back across the fjord on a course a little north of west. Two large, darkened ships

The 214-ton guardship *Pol III* had been built in 1926. With low freeboard, tall funnel, central wheelhouse and a nest for the lookout at the top of the foremast, *Pol III* looked like the whaleboat she was. After being requisitioned eight months earlier, she had some slight modifications, including an improved wheelhouse and bridge and the mounting of a 7.6-cm gun on the foredeck. The crew of fifteen on 8/9 April 1940 were largely conscripts, many of them whalers who had expected to spend the winter in the South Atlantic. Instead, they and their ship had been drafted for the Neutrality Watch.

Kaptein Leif Welding-Olsen – a 44-year-old reserve officer from Horten.

were sighted briefly, 300–400 metres away, steering north and Welding-Olsen was called to the bridge. He ordered full ahead on a following course and had the 76-mm gun manned.[7] At 23:06 engines were heard ahead. To the amazement of captain and crew, what appeared to be warships emerged from the mist. One immediately veered towards *Pol III*, turning on a searchlight while the other ships continued northwards. The approaching ship, *Albatros*, eventually turned off her lights and signalled 'Stop engines. Do not use radio.' *Albatros*'s radio operator had been warned to watch the 600-m band. He reported that the Norwegian was transmitting and was ordered to jam the signal. Before he could do so, the signal 'Foreign ships incoming at high speed' was received at the YOSA central in Tønsberg. It was 23:10.[8] The signal was immediately forwarded to SDS1 in Horten and from there to Naval Command in Oslo and Oscarsborg. A few minutes later, Færder Coast Watch Post reported seeing signal rockets and hearing gunshots from the entrance of the fjord. Something was amiss in Oslofjord.[9]

Pol III was hailed from *Albatros* again, restating the order to halt and cease all signalling. Kapitänleutnant Siegfried Strelow ordered a prize crew to prepare for transfer. The guardship was at maximum speed, however, and to Strelow's surprise, the Norwegian fired a warning shot. Shortly after, the two ships collided – most likely by accident in the murky darkness. *Pol III*'s reinforced bow opened a hole in *Albatros*'s port side, but damage-control crews made sure there was no serious leakage. Two Norwegian seamen jumped or were thrown onto the deck of *Albatros* and promptly detained.[10]

During the collision, the radio antenna of *Pol III* came loose, and no further radio signals were sent. Among the commotion, the radio operator climbed the mast to fix the antenna. Later *Albatros* turned around, as did *Pol III*, and as they glided along each other's sides, shouts were heard from the larger ship unmistakably in German. Welding-Olsen ordered one white and two red signal rockets to be fired, warning the other guardships in the fjord as well as the shore batteries. Strelow hailed his opponent and ordered all signalling to stop, or he would open fire. Welding-Olsen answered back in German, refusing to accept any orders and instead instructed the torpedo boat to surrender or leave Norwegian territory immediately – otherwise *he* would open fire.[11]

The signal rockets from *Pol III* were observed by *Farm*, the eastern guard-ship of the outer patrol-line, followed by gunfire and the use of searchlights. Kaptein Gustav Amundsen obeyed instructions and stayed away but sent the signal 'Unknown vessel near Færder fired two red rockets at 23:15' to the communication centre at Tønsberg, confirming the signal from *Pol III*. The alarm was sounded through the line of command of YOSA – Tandberg-Hanssen and Notland – and immediately forwarded to SDD1 in Horten. There it arrived at the same time as the telephone call from Færder Coast Watch Post reporting rockets and shots in the fjord. Both reports were forwarded to the Admiral Staff and to Oscarsborg within minutes. The Admiral Staff received the first signals of intruders in outer Oslofjord around 23:15, confirmed by several other signals in the next 20–30 minutes. Minister of Defence Ljungberg was immediately informed, as was King Haakon.[12]

Meanwhile, Strelow pulled *Albatros* some 200–300 metres away from *Pol III* to assess the situation. A repeated order to surrender and come alongside was not obeyed by the Norwegian and, after a short while, the German *Kapitänleutnant* turned the searchlights on the guardship again and, despite the orders from Admiral Kummetz, opened fire. Strelow later wrote that he believed the crew of *Pol III* were preparing to open fire on *Albatros* as the gun on the foredeck was manned and moving. It was later

Members of the crew of *Pol III* a few weeks before all hell broke loose.

found to be loaded with an inert or 'cold' shell for another warning shot, so Welding-Olsen was apparently not planning to open fire in earnest any time soon. Strelow, however, decided the possibility of a non-violent outcome had ended. Machine-gun fire raked the Norwegian deck and wheelhouse, as well as the mast where the radio operator was still trying to repair the antenna, and at least two 10.5-cm shells slammed into the guardship. Welding-Olsen was seriously wounded in both legs. *Pol III* did not return fire. The tackle for lowering the lifeboat was destroyed by the gunfire, but a small flat-bottomed barge was still intact. Welding-Olsen, bleeding heavily from his legs, was carried from the bridge and laid in the barge before it was lowered. He had lost a lot of blood and was very weak. Too many crowded the barge in the choppy sea, however, and it capsized. Most of the men climbed back onto *Pol III*, but Welding-Olsen did not manage to hold on for long. 'Don't worry about me, boys. I'm done anyway. Save yourselves,' he is said to have told the others as he drifted away.[13]

The crew of *Pol III* were taken aboard *Albatros*, which set the guardship on fire with HE shells and tracers before turning northwards up the fjord to re-join the fleet. The burning wreckage of *Pol III* drifted away, severely damaged. Leif Welding-Olsen was never seen again. The survivors were later transferred to *Emden* and taken to Oslo where they were released on the afternoon of the 10th.[14]

First Shots: 00:05–03:00, 9 April

The southern battery at Rauøy was commanded by kaptein Thomas Gullichsen and the two guns by sersjant Gotås and korporal Magnussen, respectively. When the alarm was sounded by the rockets from *Pol III*, the forts were alerted. Rauøy Fort reported ready at 23:28, Bolærne a few minutes later, and the searchlights started sweeping the fjord. At Rauøy they were not very efficient due to the mist and after a while the smaller ones were turned off and only the 150-cm was eventually used. Minutes later, the vague contours of two ships were sighted coming up the fjord at about 10 knots. The searchlight was turned in their direction, but mist, darkness and counter-illumination prevented identification. The range was reported by the orograph to be 5,600 metres. Time was short, the targets were already far into the fire-sector. Major Enger hesitated as he had no indication of the nationality of the ships. After a few seconds, however, he ordered the southern battery to fire a warning shot with an inert shell, aimed ahead of the lead ship and 200 metres short. This was fired at 23:32. As neither of the ships appeared to slow down and shone strong searchlights back at the fort, at 23:35 Enger gave Gullichsen the order to open up in earnest with HE shells against the leading, larger ship. Normal procedure would be to place salvos on either side of the target

The severely damaged and burnt-out wreck of *Pol III*. Following repairs and rebuild, she was renamed *Samoa* and assigned to Hafenschutzflottille Oslo as *NO 05*. Later, she was transferred to Tromsø. After the war, she was extensively rebuilt and served as a fishing vessel until 2011, when she was finally scrapped.

and adjust the range until the ship was straddled or hit, a process known as bracketing. Rapid firing would then commence. One of the guns encountered a mechanical problem, possibly induced by stress or lack of practice among the crew, and firing was delayed. It was quickly fixed, but the two guns did not fire simultaneously as was required. Only four rounds were fired before the ships vanished in the encroaching mist at 23:42 when range was down to 3,500 metres. This was too few to obtain an effective bracketing and the battery lost the opportunity for a hit. The northern battery was further up the island and did not open fire. The visibility decreased further.

Three unidentified ships were outlined in the searchlight beam from Bolærne and a warning shot was fired from an 8.4-cm field gun. Procedure was that this should be followed by an inert shell from the 15-cm battery before live fire commenced. None of this happened. Further ships were reported, and the searchlights were ordered to turn and start hunting for them. A mix-up between the orders to the searchlights and the guns resulted in the guns also being turned away from the already identified ships. Wavering and inexperience in the crowded command bunker added to the confusion and the battery commander, kaptein Telle, did not manage to sort out the misunderstanding in time before the fog set in, covering Bolærne until long after dawn. The lack of experienced men made it too complicated to operate

The crew of *Pol III* coming ashore from *Emden* in Oslo. They were taken
to Akershus Fortress. Having promised not to wage war against the Germans,
they were released later in the day, with money to buy a ticket home by train or bus.

searchlights and guns simultaneously and the result was only one blank shot
being fired from Bolærne. The counter-lights from the ships in the fjord were
also very disturbing, blinding officers and gunners alike.[15]

The result was that the ships of Group *Oldenburg* passed the effective kill
zone before any salvos could be fired from the guns of Rauøy or Bolærne.
Cumbersome procedures, technical issues and inexperienced gun crews
created major challenges for the outer defence line of Oslofjord. There was
no radar or star-shell ammunition for the Norwegian Coast Artillery in
1940 and the fog and darkness obscured the German vessels too quickly for
shooting to continue. The searchlights were ineffective in the fog and met by
counter-illumination from the ships. Had the minefields been laid, the result
might have been very different, but they were not, and the opportunity was
lost. No return fire was observed from the intruders, and they vanished in the
thickening fog about ten minutes after having been sighted for the first time.[16]

Both forts reported to YOSA who immediately forwarded the signals
to Oscarsborg and Horten. Enger in addition called Eriksen at Oscarsborg
personally just before midnight to inform him of what had happened. Enger
could not, however, ascertain that more than two warships had passed. At
23:50, SDD1 reported to the Admiral Staff: 'Rauøy and Bolærne have opened

fire.' Within half an hour, a signal came back with orders to start laying the mine-barrage between the islands. At this time, though, the mines were still being loaded at Vestre Bolærne, and those aboard the minelayers were not yet armed, so nothing could be done. The minesweepers *Laugen* and *Glommen* did not complete loading the mines until 03:15. *Nor* and *Vidar* were only ready at 04:30 and no mines were laid.[17]

The guardship *Kjæk* was patrolling south of the forts. At 23:15, the shadow of a large ship was observed, and løytnant Knut Kraft turned his ship towards it to investigate. To his surprise 'a large cruiser, followed by three smaller cruisers and several smaller vessels and submarines' appeared in the glare of his searchlights. Kraft immediately fired two red Very lights and later held he had been fired at from one of the cruisers. There is no German report confirming this. *Kjæk* did not carry a radio, and Kraft headed for the signal station at Fulehuk to report. The mist made this difficult, but eventually, after midnight, he managed to contact the station by Aldis lamp and reported 'four cruisers and several submarines entering the fjord' to be forwarded to YOSA. Apparently, Kraft mistook some of the R-boats for submarines and his report increased the confusion for a while. When *Albatros* passed a little later, he fired two more Very lights and signalled to Fulehuk that 'a destroyer' had been observed heading north.[18]

It is time now to review these events from the German point of view.

Shortly after midnight, German time, 23:00 Norwegian time, the First Officer of *Blücher*, Fregattenkapitän Erich Heymann climbed the ladder to the bridge to inform his captain that the ship was ready for battle – '*Klarschiff zum Gefecht*'. The ship was at action stations and the Army men below deck. The guns were ready, but not loaded. 30 rounds per 20.3-cm gun and 100 rounds per 10.5-cm gun were available and prepared for firing. Doors and hatches were clamped shut and all communication systems had been tested and found in order. Woldag acknowledged and told his First Officer to remain on the bridge, contrary to standing orders. 'At his express order, I remained on the bridge,' Heymann later wrote.[19] Normally the First Officer should have been aft at the damage control centre to avoid losing both senior officers in case something happened at the bridge. Why Woldag decided to keep Heymann on the bridge has never been explained. It is possible that the discussions between him and Kummetz had reached the point that Woldag wanted a senior witness if things should go wrong, which they certainly did. Or perhaps it was just that Woldag believed it would be easier for Heymann to oversee the offloading of troops near Horten from the bridge. Whatever the reason, Heymann did not inform the other damage-control officers and personnel spread around the ship that he would not be at his post in the centre managing any crisis from there as they had learned during exercises. Another

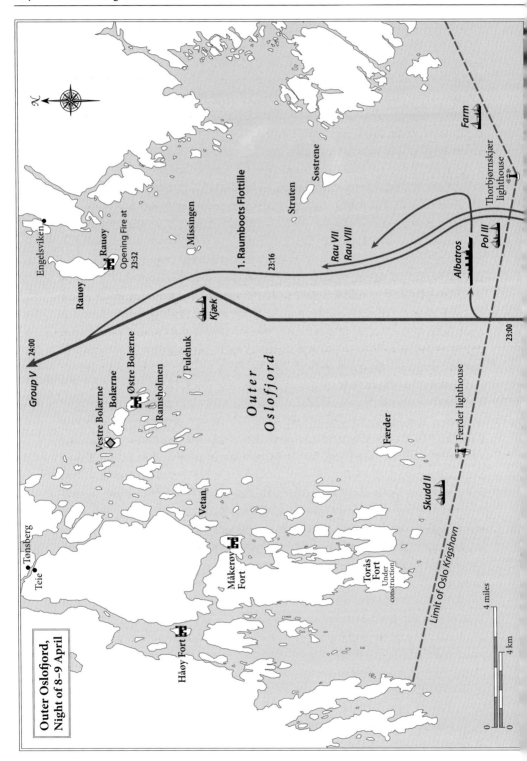

**Outer Oslofjord,
Night of 8–9 April**

Group V 24:00

Tønsberg

Teie

Håøy Fort

Engelsviken

Rauøy

Rauøy
Opening Fire at
23:32

Vestre Bolærne

Bolærne

Østre Bolærne

Ramsholmen

Fulehuk

Kjæk

Missingen

1. Raumboots Flottille

23:16

Struten

Sostrene

Rau VII
Rau VIII

Albatros

Pol III

Thorbjørnskjær
lighthouse

Farm

Mäkerøy
Fort

Vetan

Torås
Fort
Under
construction

*Outer
Oslofjord*

Færder

Skudd II

Færder lighthouse

Limit of Oslo Krigshavn

23:00

4 miles

4 km

anomaly was that 3rd Gunnery Officer Kapitänleutnant Georg Hagene, usually positioned at the aft fire-control ready to command the main battery from there if needed, was sent to the observation platform in the foretop with Senior Gunnery Officer Korvettenkapitän Kurt-Eduard Engelmann to coordinate simultaneous fire to port and starboard, if necessary. The 2nd Gunnery Officer Kapitänleutnant Hans-Erik Pochhammer was inside the main flak-control platform in the lower part of the foretop to control all anti-aircraft guns.[20]

In spite of advice from the Chief Engineer Fregattenkapitän Thannemann, Woldag had decided to steam with only some of the boilers fully fired. Thannemann had nevertheless, on his own initiative, lit three boilers in each row and reckoned that *Blücher* could achieve 31 knots, but would take some time to work up to this speed.[21]

The lighthouses had been seen and plotted before they were turned off and Group V could continue its course and speed as the contours of Rauøy and Østre Bolærne could be identified. On approaching the Rauøy–Bolærne line, Kummetz ordered *Blücher* and *Lützow* to train their guns on Rauøy to starboard while *Emden* and *Kondor* covered Bolærne to port. The distance between the forts at Rauøy and Bolærne is some 7,000 metres and the misty gloom in the fjord largely concealed the ships and forts from each other; increasingly so as the ships proceeded up the fjord. At least some of the torpedo boats added to the murk by producing artificial smoke for a while.

Around 23:25, searchlights from Rauøy illuminated *Blücher* and shortly after that the first warning shot sounded. Of the five rounds fired, only one was registered on board *Blücher*, and no splashes were seen at all. Lange noted in *Emden*'s war diary that 4–5 shots were heard from Rauøy and two from Bolærne, but as nothing fell disturbingly close, he saw no reason to send a signal to *Blücher*. Kummetz concluded that the single shot he heard was a warning that could be disregarded and decided not to fire back.[22]

Several of the accounts from the survivors mention the shots and many write that they were convinced 'the Norwegians would not accept a peaceful occupation of their country'. How much of this is hindsight we shall never know, and nobody on the bridge of *Blücher* seems to have spoken against Kummetz over his decision. Three of the shots from Rauøy were observed from *Lützow*. Thiele and his officers correctly identified them as from 15-cm guns and took this to mean that, as expected, the Norwegian defences were alerted and had received orders to fire. The feebleness of the fire puzzled them somewhat, though. No communication took place between the ships on the issue. For a while, *Lützow* was lit by the searchlights from Rauøy, but when she shone her own searchlights back, the light was moved to *Emden*, the next ship in the line. Even though several shots were heard, *Emden* observed only

Above & opposite: A 15-cm Bofors gun of the type which made up the main armament
at the forts at Rauøy and Eastern Bolærne, photographed during an exercise in 1937.
Senior officers of the Coast Artillery observe procedings.

one of the splashes from Rauøy. Lange later wrote that at the time he believed
the shots were symbolic, to show that Norway was prepared to defend its
coastline, but that the government understood that Britain was their enemy,
not Germany, and that the level of resistance would not escalate. Shortly
after, the searchlights went out, all shooting ceased, the fog thickened, and
darkness prevailed. Group V continued northwards, inside Oslo *krigshavn*.[23]

At 23:16 1. Räumbootsflottille approached the cruisers from astern. Nobody
on the forts or any of the Norwegian guardships had apparently noticed them
coming up the fjord and even though they were briefly illuminated by the
searchlights they were not seen. One of the splashes from Rauøy was seen from
the R-boats. *Rau VII* and *Rau VIII* had accompanied the R-boats across the
open sea but were left behind when they increased speed at Færder. Passing
between the outer forts the two whale-catchers were illuminated several times
by the searchlights, but each time left alone after a short while, probably as
they were not recognised as warships. The whale-catchers caught up with the
heavy ships shortly after midnight and followed the fleet northwards some 100
metres astern of *Emden* according to orders. Group *Oldenburg* was complete,
and all ships had come safely through the outer defences.[24]

At 00:15, Admiral Kummetz ordered the group to halt about half-way
between the forts and Horten. It was time to regroup. The fog was getting
worse, and visibility was at times down to 100 metres. Navigation was

challenging and space was needed. *Kondor* and *Möwe* circled towards the south, screening for submarines and prepared to take on any Norwegian guardships that might venture too close. Six of the R-boats drew alongside *Emden* to embark some 350 troops from I./IR 307 who were to seize Rauøy, Bolærne and Horten. *R 18* and *R 19* approached *Blücher* to embark the 150 men of 5./IR 307 (5. Kompanie – 5th Company – of IR 307) that should land at the Narrows if needed. The mountain troops on board *Lützow*, originally intended for Trondheim, stayed

where they were. With some confusion in the darkness, the transfer began. During the manoeuvres, *R 20* collided with *R 21*, but damage was slight, and the loading continued. After well over an hour, Kummetz became impatient: '*Mit Umschiffung beeilen*' – 'Hurry up with the transfer' – came the order from *Blücher*.

Eventually at 01:40, the work was complete, the R-boats pulled away and Group V continued up the fjord. *Blücher* was in the lead with *Lützow* some 600 metres astern and *Emden* following at the same distance again. *Möwe*, *R 18*, *R 19* and *Rau VII* made up the rear. *R 20* and *R 24* headed back towards Rauøy, *R 22* and *R 23* towards Bolærne. The landings there should take place at *Weser*-hour, 05:15 German time, by when the main force should have passed the Narrows, and be heading for Oslo at maximum speed. *Kondor, Albatros, R 17, R 21* and *Rau VIII* followed for a while longer, before being detached for Horten.[25]

Outside Oslofjord, the seven anti-submarine trawlers of 7. Vorpostenflottille took up position south of Færder as daylight approached. These were under the command of Kapitänleutnant Braune to prevent British or French submarines coming after Group *Oldenburg*. Later they were to protect the supply ships coming in with additional troops and equipment.[26]

For the naval staffs in Oslo and Horten the foreign intruders' ships had 'vanished' but there was no doubt that they remained inside Oslo *krigshavn*. The neutrality instructions called for all available measures to be used against intruding warships in the restricted areas and the Commanding Admiral saw no need to issue any further orders to the units in Oslofjord, Kristiansand, Bergen or Trondheim. Except for the order to SDD1 at 00:12 to start laying the mines between Rauøy and Bolærne and the order at 01:40 for the submarines at Teie submarine base (Tønsberg) to move to their patrol areas, no other direct operational orders were issued by the Commanding Admiral or higher naval authorities to any of the SDDs during the night of 8/9 April.[27]

Along the fjord, all lighthouses and navigation lights were extinguished, civilians near military installations were evacuated and communities ordered to turn off street lights, lights in public buildings and as many private lights as possible. At the naval base, kontreadmiral Smith-Johannsen had no information on the nationality of the intruders even if, based on the reports from earlier in the day, he believed they were German. As they had not returned fire at Rauøy, however, it could also be that they were part of the British fleet (wrongly) reported in the Kattegat. To find out, Smith-Johannsen decided to send the minesweeper *Otra* into the fjord. His Chief of Staff kaptein Gunnar Hovdenak suggested he should board *Otra* to see for himself, and this was agreed. *Otra* left Horten harbour at about 02:00 heading down the fjord; 12–15 minutes later, a darkened ship was sighted coming north, off Bastøy. When the searchlight was turned on, a strong counter-light was shone back, and the ship vanished in the haze before being identified. Kaptein Arne Dæhli gave chase. The ship was *Albatros*. After leaving *Pol III* behind, believing her sunk, Kapitänleutnant Strelow had navigated with some difficulty up the darkened Oslofjord before *Kondor* could be contacted on the radio-telephone to get a bearing. *Albatros* steered to join the force detached for Horten when intercepted by *Otra*. Approaching what was seen to be several ships, Dæhli closed to within a couple of hundred metres before turning on his searchlight. Counter lights were shone back once more, but not as promptly as the first time and not as blinding. 'Two destroyers and three minesweepers' were identified from *Otra* and radioed to SDD1 at 04:03.[28] A second signal at 04:10 confirmed that the ships were German; the first positive identification of the intruders for Smith-Johannsen. The signal was forwarded to the Commanding Admiral and to Oscarsborg, where it arrived after fire had been opened. Following at a distance, Hovdenak realised the German ships were heading for Horten and that *Otra* was cut off from its base. Engaging the four ships was unrealistic as *Otra* had only one 76-mm gun and two machine guns. Hence, he reported 'Enemy off Karljohansvern' at 04:25 and turned north heading for Filtvet to find a telephone to talk to the Admiral in person. On the way, in the increasing daylight, several ships were sighted, including *Lützow* and *Emden*.[29]

Chapter 11
Intruders
Entering the Narrows

Having completed transferring the soldiers to the R-boats, Group *Oldenburg* continued up the fjord. Navigation officer Korvettenkapitän Hugo Förster and his assistant Obersteuermann Rüdiger Perleberg gave advice and comments from the chartroom to Woldag who directed his cruiser up the fjord. The ships had drifted somewhat during the long transfer of the soldiers and Förster at first reported he was not entirely sure of their position but measuring the water depth gave a fair indication. He recommended a speed of 7 knots until he could make a few more-accurate observations in the misty darkness. All lighthouses and lights on both sides of the fjord were out, but after a while some lights from Horten could be seen. The small Mefjordbåen light and Gullholmen lighthouse at Jeløya on the starboard side were sighted and gave a good fix. Förster gave the all-clear for 15 knots.[1]

Several German documents mention *Festung Horten* – 'Fortress Horten' – and its guns. Even if these accounts accept that some of the batteries there were obsolete, they describe the naval base as controlling the fjord between Rauøy–Bolærne and Oscarsborg. In fact, the only guns at Horten, except for the armament on board the ships that were present, were anti-aircraft weapons. At Mellomøya, two 7.5-cm guns were manned as were two similar guns at Brårudåsen above the town. In addition, four Colt machine-gun posts with three guns each were spread around the harbour and Karljohansvern. All the rest of the guns that appeared on German intelligence maps were old relics, not manned. Tronvik torpedo station at Jeløya on the other side of the fjord was also considered as a threat but was in reality harmless. No shots were fired from any of the guns, partly as the crews had no orders to fire at anything but aircraft, partly because they saw no targets through the misty darkness. Hence, Group V passed Fortress Horten without being fired at, which may have led Kummetz and his senior officers to believe that, after the 'symbolic' fire from Rauøy–Bolærne there would be no further resistance.[2]

Once they passed Horten, the small island of Tofteholmen could be identified and later the contours of the Hurum peninsula could be distinguished, making the entry to the outer part of the Narrows easy to find.

Further up the Narrows, the light at Filtvet was burning, but shortly after having been identified, it was shut down and Förster, in response to a question from Kummetz, advised reducing speed to 7 knots to continue towards Drøbak. Kummetz wished to take no risks and, after a brief discussion with the navigators, decided it was best to approach the narrowest part off Drøbak just before first light, around 04:15–04:30. Then it should be possible to see the horizon despite the missing navigation lights. Time was running short. Group V would not be past the Narrows as planned, approaching Oslo in time for a show of force just after Bräuer had delivered his ultimatum. Kummetz most likely wanted to avoid losing even more time and likely took it for granted the Norwegians knew they were coming anyway. He later wrote:

> I decide not to put out anti-mine gear. Attitude of outer batteries indicates that Norwegian batteries are attempting to stop progress of Group by searchlights from guardships and warning shots. Questionable if serious resistance intended. Therefore keeping to my original plan to force the Dröbak Narrows. Have prepared Morse signal in Norwegian to deceive enemy but not yet used it as the situation does not appear to demand it.[3]

After the event, several of the officers, both on *Blücher* and the other ships, asserted that they had been sceptical about this decision. The pre-dawn light would give the Norwegian gunners an advantage as the ships would present silhouettes on the fjord while the batteries were still in shadow. Some reports say both Woldag and Engelbrecht argued against having *Blücher* in the van, but Kummetz had made up his mind. They would go through just before dawn and *Blücher* would lead. Group *Oldenburg* was behind schedule and there would be no more delays.[4]

Oscarsborg's first line of defence was at the mouth of the Narrows. There the signal station at Filtvet on the western side and Stjernåsen orograph station on the eastern side of the fjord were both manned on 8 April. The distance from Oscarsborg to Filtvet is about 10,000 metres and ships in this area would be inside Oscarsborg's arc of fire. In the fjord proper, the guardship *Furu* had the watch south of the two stations this night. At 23.30 Filtvet and Stjernåsen were both alerted from Oscarsborg by telephone and the signal was forwarded to *Furu* in the fjord by signal lamp. As tension rose during the night, a second guardship, *Alpha*, was ordered down from Drøbak to strengthen the patrol line.[5]

As Group *Oldenburg* approached, close to 04:00, it was dark and hazy and all lights along the fjord had finally been turned off. Both guardships shone their searchlights at the first approaching ship, identifying it as a large man o'war. *Alpha* was near enough to hear sighting reports shouted in German from the lookouts to the bridge on board the lead ship and kaptein Kristian

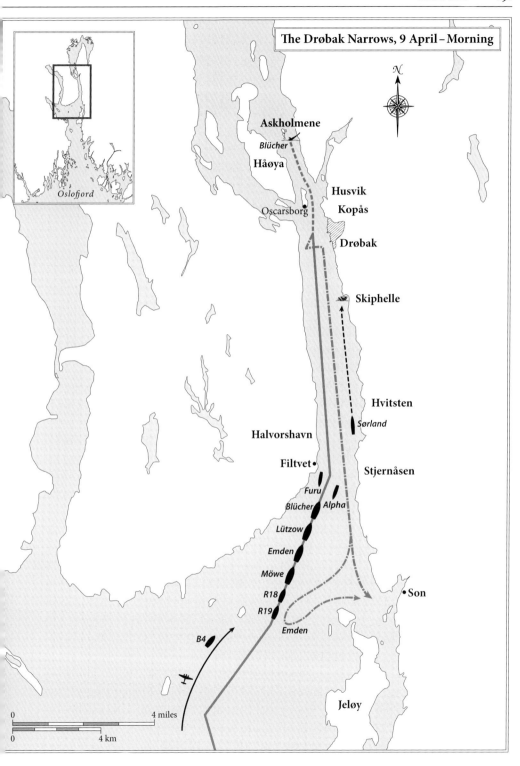

The Drøbak Narrows, 9 April – Morning

Oslofjord

Askholmene

Blücher

Håøya

Husvik

Oscarsborg

Kopås

Drøbak

Skiphelle

Hvitsten

Sørland

Halvorshavn

Filtvet

Stjernåsen

Furu

Blücher   Alpha

Lützow

Emden

Möwe

R18

R19

Emden

• Son

B4

Jeløy

0   4 miles

0   4 km

The guardship *Furu*, originally a tug.

Bøhmer headed for Filtvet to report to Oscarsborg. *Furu* was almost run down by *Lützow* and given shouted warnings in unmistakable German. No shots were fired. When all ships had passed, *Furu* also tied up at Filtvet to report. Neither of the two ships had radio, and communication with the signal station was by light or loudhailer. From Filtvet to Oscarsborg there was telephone communication.[6]

Aboard *Lützow*, the appearance of the guardships was further evidence for Thiele of Norwegian vigilance. He hoped the admiral would give the order for maximum speed; but no such order came. Thiele had been CO of fortresses on the Pomeranian coast of the Baltic for seven months in 1939 and knew the potential of land-based guns.[7]

According to the orders for Group V, *Sperrbrechers* should have proceeded ahead of the warships to verify that the inner waters of the fjord were clear. A *Sperrbrecher* or barrage-breaker was a former merchant ship given a reinforced hull, a 'cargo' of buoyant matériel and minimal crew, having the dubious mission of being sent into possible mine-laid waters ahead of more valuable vessels. The concept was that these ships should detonate any mines – in theory being able to endure the explosions. In his orders to the *Sperrbrechers*, issued on the 4th, Kummetz was clear: 'The *Sperrbrechers* shall bring Group *Oldenburg* through the Drøbak Narrows.' After describing the group and where to meet, – just after the offloading of the soldiers that were to take Horten, Rauøy and Bolærne – the order continued. 'The *Sperrbrechers*, camouflaged as merchantmen with navigation lights lit, shall enter Oslofjord in an unobtrusive manner. If challenged by coastal stations or guard vessels, an answer in English shall be given, providing relevant British ship-names. It is critically important that the operation is not compromised before *Weser*-time.' Kummetz concluded 'I intend to continue up the fjord behind the *Sperrbrechers* which shall advance in mid-fjord at 10 knots. If they encounter mines or are fired at, they should press on. If there is fog or the lighthouses are off, press on. If severely damaged, steer out of the way.' He added explicitly that, 'There is supposedly a mine-barrage in the Drøbak Narrows, electrically controlled from land,' but even with this information, it was still his intention to send the *Sperrbrechers* ahead at this stage. Ober-leutnant Freyberg later commented that the intelligence reports of a remote-controlled mine barrage at the Narrows came in after this order was given and claimed this was the reason for the change of plans. If the mines were remote-controlled, he says, the Norwegians would not detonate them when the *Sperrbrechers* were passing but wait for the more valuable naval ships. This does not match the copies of the orders that exist in the archives today and must, with several other obviously erroneous details in Freyberg's account, be disregarded. According to the account of Freyberg, two ships, *Sperrbrecher X* (ex-*Vigo*) and *Sperrbrecher XI* (ex-*Petropolis*), were assigned to Group V, to lead the warships through the Drøbak Narrows and find a safe way through any minefields that might be there. The master of *Sperrbrecher X*, Kapitän Richard von Stosch, had sailed to Oslo several times during his service in the merchant navy before the war and believed he could find the way – even if the lighthouses were shut down. For uncertain reasons, the *Sperrbrechers* never appeared and Kummetz changed his plans. The most puzzling aspect of this issue is that, according to their own war diaries, the two ships in question took 1. Räumbootsflottille through Storebælt on the afternoon of the 7th, leaving them at Samsø, and then spent the 8th guarding the northern entry to Storebælt and the minefield there, later being assigned to various tasks in Denmark. There is no mention of Norway or Oslofjord until 05:15 on the 9th when it is noted that the two countries 'have been occupied'.

In a document signed by the chief of staff of Marinegruppenkommando Ost, dated 28 March, it is concluded that it would be better to have the intelligence staff at the Legation in Oslo confirm there were no mines or, if there were, where the opening in the minefield was so that the ships of Group V could pass unhindered at high speed. The *Sperrbrechers* were extremely slow and would expose the warships to the guns of the fortress for an unnecessarily long time, should they open fire. It would be better to go straight in at high speed. If the legation could not provide the information, it was suggested that masters of merchant ships that had travelled the fjord lately were drafted to assist Group V. Hence it seems the concept of using *Sperrbrechers* was abandoned by the planners in Kiel a week before *Wesertag*.

Whether this was properly conveyed to Kummetz in time cannot be documented.[8]

A radio signal at midday on the 8th from Naval Attaché Schreiber at the Legation in Oslo and forwarded by Marinegruppenkommando Ost to *Blücher*, stated there were probably no mines at Drøbak after all. This could have been the reason for Kummetz's decision as he may have been so certain the Norwegians would not open fire that, rather than risk further delays, he would just press on and increase speed towards the capital as soon as they were through. Should the Norwegians open fire, he might have considered it best to have a ship in the van that could respond quickly and powerfully while going through at maximum speed. Hesitation was no option, turning back and not reaching Oslo inconceivable. Especially as Group *Oldenburg* was running late. The presence of the torpedo battery as well as the absence of the mine-barrage had been reported to Berlin by the Abwehr group at the Legation, but this signal appears to have been lost somewhere along the chain of command as it never reached *Blücher*. Falkenhorst later wrote:

> The concern over the passage of the Drøbak Narrows played a major role throughout the preparations. The responsibility for the problems encountered there must be placed fully on the leaders on board *Blücher* as they knew fully what to expect.[9]

It is notable that he uses 'problems' and not guns, mines or torpedoes. Hence, what the *Weserübung* management actually knew of the Narrows and when they obtained that knowledge is not made any clearer by Falkenhorst. Questioned during his interrogation in 1945 if he was aware of the torpedo battery at Oscarsborg, Falkenhorst answered:

> Yes, I knew of them. But I repeat once again that for me personally this was of limited interest. When you are on board a warship, the Navy has the full responsibility. The captain is in charge. We [the Army] were in the wings during this first act. Raeder and his subordinates are responsible for what happened to the ship [...] My knowledge of tactics at sea is limited.[10]

Again, what he does not say is perhaps most notable. The responsibility is put on Raeder and Woldag, Kummetz is not mentioned at all. Neither is his own responsibility in designing the operation and sending a fleet of large ships up Oslofjord, to say nothing of the concept of Group *Oldenburg* running the gauntlet while having the majority of the designated administrative and command personnel for Oslo on board. Kummetz was not aware of Eriksen's deliberations of course, but perhaps he should have realised that *Möwe* would have been large enough to provoke a reaction while small enough to turn away behind a smokescreen if attacked. And should *Möwe* become a loss, it would be of significantly less consequence than the flagship. Cynically, it would have been even better to risk *Emden*, which was of lesser naval value and had already disembarked a large part of her troops.[11]

Shall We Open Fire? – 23:15, 8 April–04:21, 9 April

Oberst Eriksen was usually reserved and not open to his subordinates. On 8 April, however, he must have felt the need for a partner and, as he had no second in command or adjutant, he discussed the situation on several occasions with his intelligence officer, kaptein Thorleif Unneberg. In the end, though, Eriksen was left to make his own decisions. He later stated that he had received no messages during the day 'that could indicate there would be an attack on Oslofjord'.

Shortly after 23:15 the first signal was received at Oscarsborg with information of foreign warships intruding, directly from the outer Oslofjord command centre. The exact time of the signal differs somewhat between the sources, but it probably arrived no earlier than 23:15 but before 23:30. At 23:55 admiral Smith-Johannsen called in person from Horten to tell Eriksen that Rauøy and Bolærne had opened fire and that an attack on Oscarsborg and Oslo could be expected. Already at this stage, Eriksen must have been clear in his mind that if foreign warships attempted to pass the Drøbak Narrows they should be stopped with all means available, whatever their nationality. They were inside the *krigshavn* and had received ample warnings from the outer forts. There was no need for more warning shots. Eriksen had been commander of the Agdenes Fortress after the *Berlin* affair in 1914 (*see* Chapter 2) and was aware of his predecessor's negligence in not stopping the auxiliary cruiser. This would not happen on his watch! The commander of the warships knew what risk he was taking and if he chose to continue, Oscarsborg would be ready.[12]

The guns at Oscarsborg, Kopås and Nesset and the torpedo battery were manned shortly after midnight. Meanwhile, Eriksen received reports of British naval movements that could be understood to mean that a British counter-attack might be under way in the Skagerrak. The intruders appeared to be coming up the fjord, however, and the police were alerted around midnight to initiate an evacuation of Drøbak town. In spite of the warning, however, a large number of civilians did not leave the town but instead assembled near the harbour to see what might be happening. Meanwhile, Oscarsborg was keeping track of ships on the fjord and orders were given to halt all vessels moving south.

The commander of the 28-cm battery, kaptein Magnus Sødem, had crossed the fjord at around 22:00 to discuss the situation with the officers at Kopås. His second-in-command, løytnant August Bonsak, knew where he was, and

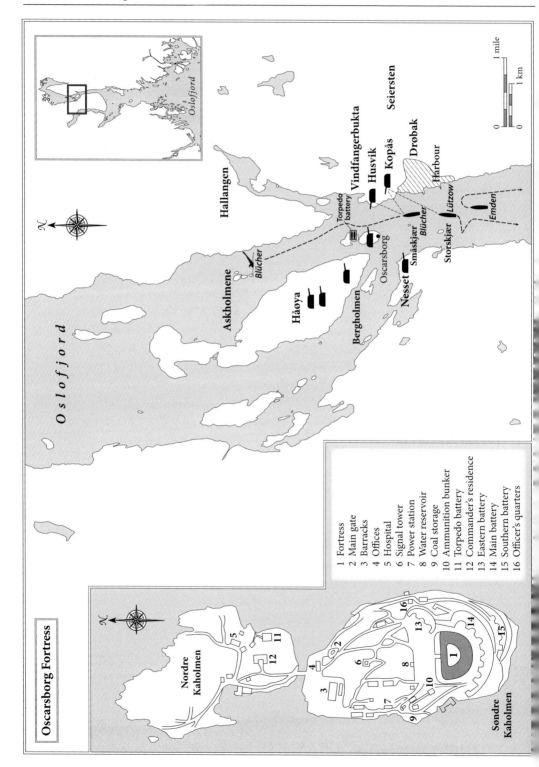

Oslofjord

Oslofjord

1 mile

1 km

Hallangen

Vindfangerbukta

Husvik

Kopås

Seiersten

Drøbak

Torpedo battery

Harbour

Lützow

Emden

Blücher

Askholmene

Oscarsborg

Blücher

Nesset

Småskjær

Storskjær

Håøya

Bergholmen

Oscarsborg Fortress

1 Fortress
2 Main gate
3 Barracks
4 Offices
5 Hospital
6 Signal tower
7 Power station
8 Water reservoir
9 Coal storage
10 Ammunition bunker
11 Torpedo battery
12 Commander's residence
13 Eastern battery
14 Main battery
15 Southern battery
16 Officer's quarters

Nordre Kaholmen

Sondre Kaholmen

a boat was ready to bring him back if needed. Sødem returned to Oscarsborg at 23:30 and was immediately told that orders had been given to man the battery. With less than a third of the full draft in place, manning the guns was a challenge. Handling the 28-cm shells and their separate charges required trained personnel and Sødem planned to concentrate his twenty-four men on one of the guns. On Sødem's arrival at the battery, however, Bonsak told him that Eriksen had already decided to rouse the men and send them to the battery. The gun crews were to be distributed between two of the guns while non-combat personnel were to report for ammunition and communication duties. Sødem had earlier ordered three shells with separate-loading charges for each gun to be brought from the magazine to the traverses between the guns. The shells were the new 255-kg projectiles with 32-kg TNT warheads. Only loading, aiming and firing of the guns remained. Sersjant Rækken and Sersjant Strøm were taking command at No.1 (west) and No.2 (centre) guns, respectively. Both reported ready at 00:30. Bonsak remained with the guns, while Sødem moved to the command bunker on the left side of the rampart where fenrik Høie operated the orograph and had a phone line to the guns.[13]

On the mainland, the Kopås battery could only count on the men who arrived earlier from the 28-cm battery at Oscarsborg. These were unfamiliar with the guns at Kopås, which they had never seen before. To reinforce the inexperienced crews and man as many of the guns as possible, kaptein Vagn Enger, the landside commander, asked for and was permitted to call on the NCO cadets of the nearby Coast Artillery NCO Training School under kaptein Klaus Nesse. Kaptein Enger had a week earlier been relieved as commander of the landside batteries by kaptein Peder Hjelvik, but due to the seriousness of the situation, Eriksen ordered Enger back in command by a phone call made by kaptein Unneberg at 23.15 on the 8th. The 52 NCO cadets and their officers made a valuable addition; 22 of them had been in training since the war started in Europe. Some were spread around where needed, but No. 1 15-cm gun at Kopås was manned entirely by NCO cadets.[14] The guns at Kopås were ready shortly after midnight.

The most important crewmen at the gun were the trainer (keeping the gun on the correct bearing with the sight) and the layer (for elevation). Both positions were taken by cadets at each gun. Commander of gun No. 1 was fenrik Lars Gjerberg from the NCO Training School. Gun No. 3 was commanded by sersjant Knutsen from the Neutrality Watch. Gun No. 2 was poorly organised when Enger inspected the battery and NCO cadet Jørgensen was ordered to take over, a job he performed well. Kaptein Enger and kaptein Nesse manned the command bunker together with Hjelvik. This bunker was also the site for the battery orograph. The ammunition had to be carried from the main magazine at the rear of the battery to ready-use magazines at each gun. The projectiles and the propellants for the guns were loaded separately, but the rate of fire would be high. Enger ordered up just 10 rounds of HE per gun. This would be easy to expend in two minutes, but he told Nesse that it would be sufficient.[15]

To add to the defence of the Narrows, the two guns of the 5.7-cm battery at Husvik were manned by men of the NCO Training School under løytnant Rolf Bertelsen. The battery was not a part of the Neutrality Watch and was regarded as an improvement of the defence. Bertelsen had the NCO cadets carry 50 rounds from the magazines to the ready-use stores close to the guns whereafter they manned the guns and the command bunker; they were ready at 02:30. There was no battery rangefinder at Husvik. Three searchlights were sited along the waterfront of Drøbak, two south of the church and one further north. On the evening of the 8th, the two southern ones were not operational due to maintenance and the auxiliary *Kranfartøy No.2*, moored in Drøbak harbour, was ordered to man its light instead, and to be ready. The third searchlight north of the harbour, which was in reserve, was ordered to be manned and stand by, but was not used.[16]

Løytnant Strand manned the three 5.7-cm guns at Nesset which could cover the *jeté* if anything would be attempted on the west side of the fortress.[17] Strand brought up 200 rounds per gun from the nearby magazine. In his area he also had two searchlights and at least one of them was manned as were the guns. Nesset reported all set a few minutes after Kopås.

At Horten, kaptein Gøsta Wendelbo of the 1st Air Wing decided to move his eight seaplanes to safety at Vindfangerbukta north of Kopås as they would be of no use during the night. The aircraft were not equipped for instrument flying and were to be taxied on the water due to the fog and low clouds. They left Karljohansvern between 02:00 and 03:30. The submarine *B4* was given similar orders as she was undergoing repairs and could not dive.[18]

At 01:32, a signal from Outer Oslofjord SDS arrived at Oscarsborg reporting that 'four large cruisers and submarines' had passed Bolærne, which had opened fire. Earlier reports had described only two warships entering the *krigshavn* and Eriksen made several telephone calls to major Færden at Bolærne to have the new number confirmed. Færden maintained that only two ships had been observed. The nationality of the intruders remained unknown, but it appeared they had not committed any hostile acts after they had passed. A 'destroyer' was reported passing as the two officers spoke at 01:50, but otherwise things appeared quiet in the south.[19]

Andreas Anderssen had been commander of the torpedo battery at Oscarsborg for a generation. In 1927, however, he retired from active service, moved to the reserve and settled as a senior pilot and businessman in Drøbak. In February 1940, the regular commander of the torpedo battery fell sick.

Oberst Eriksen asked the sixty-year-old kommandørkaptein Anderssen to return to take charge of the torpedo battery, the mine defences and the guardships operating between Filtvet and Drøbak. This he did after some persuasion and, despite there being new equipment and routines, the quiet, unassuming officer quickly settled into his old job. Like everything else on Oscarsborg, the battery was undermanned. Anderssen tried to make the best of a dire situation through a strict rotational system with long hours on watch. On the evening of the 8th overminør Albert Karlsen was in charge with four men. Anderssen had left Oscarsborg earlier in the evening, but when Eriksen called him at his home near

Kommandørkaptein Andreas Anderssen (1879–1945).

Drøbak at 23:15, he returned to the fortress as soon as possible. Within a short time, the entire torpedo complement was ready, comprising Anderssen, six officers and NCOs and eight soldiers, Eriksen ordered the first three torpedoes lifted into the frames, set to run for 600 metres at 32 knots at a depth of 3 metres. Despite having been produced some forty years earlier and test-fired numerous times, the torpedoes were in immaculate order and their 117-kg warheads were lethal. Once the first torpedoes were in place, the sights and firing mechanisms were tested and reloading procedures drilled.

The torpedo battery at Oscarsborg was literally built into the rock face of Nordre Kaholmen and could not be seen from the fjord. Anderssen was at the sights in the central tower inside the rock, three stories above where overminør Karlsen and his men were waiting to reload once the first torpedoes had left the underwater launching-shafts. Minør Sigurd Bexrud took position in the secondary observation tower to the south, ready to take over in case enemy fire should knock out the central tower. The torpedo battery was the only element of the fortress that was anywhere near ready for the intruders. The Germans were in for a nasty surprise.[20]

The Norwegian Navy operated small crane vessels (*kranfartøyer*) to lay controlled minefields in coastal waters. *Kranfartøy 2* was deployed at Oscarsborg as an auxiliary, laying mines, recovering torpedoes during exercises and controlling ships entering the Narrows. The crane on the foredeck could be lifted off its pivot and replaced by a 45-cm searchlight. In 1940 she was armed with a 3.7-cm gun. The crew of 16 men included the 62-year-old master, signalør Sophus Bakke, called back from retirement.

Things remained quiet at Oscarsborg and around 03:30, Eriksen decided to lower the alert level and ordered Sødem and Enger to let half of the men rest but be prepared to return to the guns at short notice. Minutes later, at 03:38, the situation changed completely. The signal station at Filtvet reported a large warship passing, two minutes later corrected to 'several ships not showing any lights. All men were called back to their stations again and Eriksen climbed the rampart between guns 2 and 3 to take the lead from there and have the best possible viewpoint. Neither of the two signals, entered by hand in the Oscarsborg signal-book contains the word 'German'. Kaptein Bøhmer of *Alpha* later held that his report to Filtvet clearly stated that the ships were German. This was confirmed by the commander at Filtvet, korporal Brinchmann, who wrote that *Alpha* had hailed that 'The fjord was full of German ships.' Bøhmer later claimed that Eriksen disregarded the word German because he did not accept that his informants could know this. Eriksen seemed to confirm this when he said he was not aware how close to the ships *Alpha* had been and thought that Filtvet could not have seen the ships well enough in the murky darkness to have identified them. In any case, the two incoming signals from Filtvet at 03:38 and at 03:40 left no doubt that large warships were approaching. At 04:02, this was confirmed from Stjernåsen: 'Three cruisers and two small ships passed the station at 03:58.'[21]

For Eriksen, the intrusion of foreign warships into Oslofjord was a breach of neutrality. He had no knowledge of any invasion far less that the lead ship was *Blücher*, even if he had a strong impression that the intruders were German. Sødem walked over to Eriksen and asked: 'Shall we open fire?' The answer was short and clear: 'Yes.' Anderssen asked for similar orders and received an equally clear answer at 03:58: 'The torpedo battery *shall* open fire.' Oberst Eriksen had made up his mind. He would defend Norway's neutrality according to his instructions.[22] He knew it would be his decision to open fire or not and he wanted to see for himself what they were up against. 'I considered it my duty to take full responsibility for opening fire from the main battery through personal observation,' he later wrote.[23] Eriksen knew it was unlikely that the guns would be able to fire more than once, so each shell had to be a hit. He found the ammunition was brought up and ready, but the guns were not loaded. This would normally be initiated by battery commander Sødem after he had received orders to open fire. Considering the time this would take with the largely untrained crews available, Eriksen ordered all three guns to be loaded forthwith.[24]

Minutes later, the tall shadow of the first ship appeared in the glare of the searchlight from *Kranfartøy Nr. 2*. Two more large ships and some smaller ones were sighted from Kopås and this was reported to Oscarsborg at 04:17. A minute later, *Kranfartøy Nr. 2* detailed: 'Five ships, one large in front, four following,' Signalør Sophus Bakke, on board the auxiliary, shone the light into the clouds above the lead ship pointing it down onto it at irregular intervals. After a while he reckoned the ship had been duly observed by both forts and shut down his searchlight. With some excitement the NCO cadets at the guns at Kopås first observed the shadows of three Norwegian aircraft, which they had not seen earlier, before several large ships appeared in the glare of the searchlight. In the command bunker at Kopås, they could see the approaching warships before Oscarsborg. The mist was thicker on the western side of the fjord than in the east. Kaptein Enger was in doubt, why did Oscarsborg not open fire? Should he open fire or not? Nesse, according to his own account, insisted he should. A large warship could be seen in the glare of the searchlight from below. There was no flag, and its identity was unknown. The man at the orograph shouted that he could see the waterline of the first ship and gave the range as 1,750 metres and closing, which was acknowledged from all guns. At the moment Oscarsborg opened fire, so would Kopås.[25]

At Søndre Kaholmen, fenrik Høie struggled with the orograph. He could not find the waterline in the dim light and gave the range as 1,800 metres. Sødem forwarded this, but Eriksen knew it to be incorrect and ordered the elevation to be set for 1,400 metres. He knew the range to the point where the ship would be when he intended to open fire, between Småskjær and Storskjær. There would be no need for warning shots. The intruders had had ample warnings further down the fjord and they knew what they were doing. Now they would have a fair chance of pulling back before reaching the torpedo batteries. Sersjant Rækken at No. 1 gun reported problems observing the target through his telescope and the trainer was instructed to aim the gun along the barrel, which would be adequate for such a large target at short range. When everything was reported ready, Eriksen checked his watch and gave the order to shoot. Sødem responded immediately. Seconds later, Enger gave the order to open fire from Kopås. It was 04:21.[26]

The Kill Zone: 04:00–04:31, 9 April

On the bridge of *Blücher*, the tension was immense. Instinctively everybody lowered their voice to a whisper. Dawn was approaching, but there was not enough light to distinguish any details ashore. The fog started to lift a little as the ships entered the Narrows proper, but the men on *Blücher*'s bridge and in the foretop had no idea what lay ahead. A little after 04:00 a searchlight was lit on the Drøbak side. From the German ships, it looked like a wall of light across the entire fjord. It was the 90-cm searchlight of *Kranfartøy Nr. 2*. It raked the cruiser from bow to stern and back; dazzling everybody on deck and then shone its beam up into the fog from where it was reflected onto the ship. Navigation Officer Förster took the searchlight to be a protest to the entry of the ships, but as only one assumed warning shot had been observed at Rauøy–Bolærne, he was somewhat relieved as he took the use of the search-light to mean there would be no armed resistance. Shortly after, a 'finger of

light' also appeared from the west side of the fjord. This was the searchlight at Nesset which was turned on for a short while before being turned off again. Nor-wegian accounts do not confirm this, but virtually all German sources mention that the fjord was 'closed' by two search-lights.[27]

Kummetz ordered Group *Oldenburg* to increase speed to 12 knots. Engel-brecht and his staff officers were still present on the crowded bridge of *Blücher*. What Woldag and Kummetz believed at this stage has not been recorded, but Woldag ordered a counter-light to be shone, just in case. Nothing could be seen on land. Between the reflections at the sea surface and the horizon on top of the hills around the fjord, everything was just a dark blur in the swirling fog, made

One of the 28-cm guns at Oscarsborg. They were time-consuming to aim and reload, not least because they used separate shells and charges. On 9 April 1940, 255-kg HE shells with 32-kg TNT warheads were used.

worse by the dispersed searchlight beam from *Kranfartøy Nr. 2.* Absurdly, at this time a tiny seaplane on its floats emerged just ahead of *Blücher*'s bow. It looked as if it would be run down, but turned to port and vanished into the shadows, just in time. The aircraft was F.308, one of the MF11s evacuated from Horten.[28]

Suddenly, a tongue of flame shot out from ahead to port, followed shortly after by a second similar stab a little more to the right. Oscarsborg had opened fire, and the improved HE shells would end Kummetz's expectations of a peaceful take-over of Oslo. Eriksen's guns were some 25 metres above sea level, slightly higher than the level of the bridge of *Blücher*, which was 18–20 metres above the waterline. Angled slightly upwards, the 250-kg shell passed right over the port side of the crowded open bridge, making everybody instinctively duck because of the pressure, before it exploded against the side of the foretop. Had not Eriksen aimed high, the entire command of Group *Oldenburg* would have been eradicated. Instead, the shell destroyed the base of the searchlight stand and blasted the main AA control position. Splinters rained down over the bridge and the shock of the blast hit most of the men hard, but nobody was seriously hurt. Most of the personnel in the small flak-control room, however, including Second Gunnery Officer Pochhammer, were killed. The Anti-Aircraft Officer Oberleutnant Schürdt was seriously wounded. The First and Third Gunnery Officers, who both were in the main fire-control higher up in the foretop, were shaken, but unhurt.[29]

The second shell, also HE, was aimed a little lower and slammed into the port side just aft of the funnel. The aircraft hangar was wrecked, both aircraft bursting into flames including the one on the catapult that was partly fuelled. The fireball that erupted was enormous and burning aviation fuel flowed along the deck and into the interior, rapidly spreading the fires. Most of the personnel waiting in the hangar to help fly off the Ar-196 aircraft were killed or severely wounded. The medical personnel were quickly working hard to help the wounded and save as many lives as possible. The civilian yard-workers still on board were ordered to assist.[30]

Moments after the main battery, Kopås and Husvik also opened fire from *Blücher*'s starboard side. Enger ordered an individual shot from gun no. 1, then no. 2 and at last no. 3. Surprisingly, he then repeated the process to be sure of the aim. Then, seeing that the guns were making damaging hits, he ordered rapid, independent fire. The guns at Kopås were placed higher than those at Oscarsborg and, at this short range, fired downwards. Due to the high kinetic energy of the shells and the delay setting in the fuzes most of the shells passed through the lower aft part of *Blucher*'s superstructure and exploded on the port side. Løytnant Bertelsen in charge of the Husvik battery ordered 'fire' immediately after the guns at Kaholmene opened up. He could

Signal from Oscarsborg to the Admiral Staff in Oslo at 04.25 reporting that the fort had fired on the intruders and that they had fired back.

see the 15-cm shells from Kopås hitting the side of the cruiser and the base of the superstructure and shouted to his gunners to aim a little higher at the bridge and the fire-control cupolas, later moving to the anti-aircraft guns along the starboard side. Some thirteen 15-cm shells were fired from Kopås and a further thirty 5.7-cm shells from Husvik during the few minutes of firing on *Blücher*. According to Enger virtually all shells fired at *Blücher* from both batteries were hits.[31]

Based on reports from the survivors, a reasonably accurate account of the hits from Kopås can be compiled. The first shell apparently hit low in the superstructure, close to the tower. Flak-control B was probably also damaged by this shell. Most of the following shells impacted in quick succession in sections IV to IX, below the 28-cm hits and above the armoured deck. The result was damage to all three port-side 10.5-cm guns in addition to destruction of Flak-control B. One or more hits were obtained in sections VIII and IX and the armoured deck was heavily bulged there. The area of the tower and behind was a good aiming-point for the gunners and due to the short distance, most shells went deep into the hull or perhaps through the decks before exploding on the port side. At least one shell from Kopås detonating in section V resulted in a hole in the armour plating above turbine 2/3 and electrical generator no. 2. In sections VI and VII an extensive blaze was started, soon merging with the fire from the second 28-cm hit just above, creating massive devastation.

Jointly, the hits from all three batteries turned 70–75 metres of the cruiser's superstructure and interior above the armoured deck into a scene of carnage. The hangar and the float plane on the catapult were totally engulfed and the torpedo workshop on the main deck exploded shortly after. Splinters, fragments and fire killed a large number of soldiers gathered in this area.[32]

Large parts of the central superstructure and the battery deck and armoured deck became an inferno as ammunition and explosives from the Army stores detonated, set off by burning aircraft fuel and explosions from the torpedo workshop. Efforts to contain the fires were futile. The heavy asbestos-filled smoke spread rapidly below decks, especially aft of section VI, and soon utter chaos reigned. Most of the electrical circuits failed. Lighting was restored in some places, but other areas remained dark and isolated. The men from all these positions were forced to evacuate their posts and those not wounded, were ordered to join the fire-fighting crews. Communication within the ship was crippled.[33]

Woldag was one of the first to recover from the blast of the shell passing close over the port bridge-wing and exploding 10 metres away. He immediately shouted '*Feuererlaubnis*' – 'Permission to fire' – and rang for full speed ahead. Orders to close all watertight doors and hoist the battle ensign followed. Below deck, the violent crash of the first hit was taken to be the cruiser's own guns opening fire. The second hit corrected that mistake. Lights went out in the boiler and engine rooms and heavy smoke made conditions almost unbearable. Open flames were coming out of the ducts below the fires in a fearsome spectacle. Emergency procedures were initiated, but these took time, though the speed of the cruiser increased slowly up to 12 knots. Woldag, Kummetz and most of the others moved into the armoured citadel.

One of the early hits on *Blücher* severed the rudder and engine telegraph cables from the bridge. As the rudder at that moment was trained to port due to a brief course change to passing Småskjær, Woldag had to order 'full astern' on the starboard screw via voice-pipe to avoid the ship running aground on Nordre Kaholmen. Emergency steering from the tiller-flat aft, on orders given by voice-pipe from the bridge, eventually restored some degree of control, but due to the time-lag between steering orders being given and executed, *Blücher* started to yaw, and speed dropped from the 12 knots briefly gained.[34]

At first, the fire from *Blücher* was erratic 'going in all directions'. After a while, though, the fire became more controlled and when the cruiser passed in front of Husvik, some of the German gunners could fire down onto the battery. To avoid casualties, Bertelsen ordered 'cease fire' and his gunners came running into the command bunker for cover. There were no casualties at Husvik or Kopås, except a few minor cuts from flying shrapnel.[35]

The gunners and fire-control stations received 'permission to fire' from the bridge but could not find any targets. Gunnery Officer Engelmann asked the bridge which targets he should engage but received no answer. Several of the directors had fallen out due to the hit in the foretop. Other directors could not identify targets and there was no coordinated use of the cruiser's own searchlights. All fire-control stations in the fore-part of the ship were out at this stage due to hits and casualties. Very little could be distinguished onshore, below the horizon. To starboard, the muzzle-flashes from the guns at Kopås and Husvik made their surroundings difficult to make out. No searchlights from any of the ships were used at this stage, probably as they would have made irresistible targets for any gun ashore.[36]

The 20.3-cm guns did not open fire. The forward turret *Anton* could not have fired anyway without traversing or elevating the barrels to avoid damaging the bow. In turret *Bruno*, the barrels were lowered so much that the indicators showed risk of damage to their own ship if fired without being traversed – but no orders came, and the 20.3-cm guns remained silent.

The medium and light anti-aircraft guns fired individually at anything remotely resembling a target – trees, houses, sheds, and telegraph poles. Streams of tracer stretched to the sides of the fjord in a spectacular but totally ineffective display. Søndre Kaholmen and Oscarsborg were indistinguishable from the towering Håøya behind to port even though Kaholmen was now only 300 metres away; virtually every shot fired to port went above Oscarsborg. One exception that can be seen today is a dent and hole from a 10.5-cm shell in one of the antiquated muzzle-loading guns displayed behind the ramparts of Oscarsborg proper. These guns were museum-pieces from the 1870s and had only ceremonial use in 1940. Not one Norwegian soldier or operational gun was hit during this phase except a few men lightly wounded by splinters from shells bursting in the trees. Some houses in Drøbak and Husvik were hit and five burned to the ground. Two local women, Anette Hansen and Olaug Nyhus, were killed.[37]

Korvettenkapitän Engelmann and Kapitänleutnant Hagene both had to leave the foretop fire-control in a hurry because of the smoke and the collapsing tower. Inside the foretop there were few casualties, except in the main AA control room, but the whole position filled with acrid smoke and had to be evacuated. The companion ladder was destroyed, and the wounded from the flak-station were evacuated in hammocks down the outside of the tower.

Torpedo Petty Officer Mechanikersmaat (T) Gutsche wrote:

> When the first shell hit, I was in charge of the starboard aft torpedo tubes. I saw large metal pieces and other debris fly from the foretop and the stack and took cover behind the tubes together with torpedo engineer Mechanikergefreiter Langkau. From there we saw the roof of the hangar being ripped off, splinters and metal fragments raining over the deck. Once things settled down, we manned the tubes again and reported by telephone to torpedo central that the training gear was out of order. We managed to fix it, but shortly after we had to leave the tubes again and take cover as the 10.5-cm gun started blazing away just over our heads [...] Langkau tried to contact the torpedo workshop but could not get past the hangar, which was all in flames. The Army ammunition stored there started to explode and a huge hole was torn in the deck.[38]

Oberfänrich (Ing) Hans-Joachim Löblich, lead engineer in boiler room 3, was shocked by the two first hits:

> The lights went out and everything was thrown about. Flames flashed into the room through the ventilator shafts and burning smoke hit our eyes. The air was filled with asbestos fragments. We tried to put on our gas masks, but the insides of the masks were covered in asbestos flakes and could not be used. No time to clean them! The emergency light came on but was not very efficient due to the thick smoke. I tried to read the manometers with my flashlight and get an impression of the damage [...] The engine telegraph was immediately set to 'Full Ahead' and the noise from the leaking pumps under increasing pressure was deafening.[39]

To save the ship from running aground, emergency manoeuvres were initiated by using the outer propellers but not long after, both outer engine-systems shut down as well, leaving *Blücher* unmanoeuvrable. The ship had a forward momentum though and she continued gliding up the fjord towards Askholmene, away from the guns.

At Oscarsborg, gun number three, the one nearest the command bunker, was also loaded. Kaptein Sødem briefly considered the possibility of ordering the crew of gun No. 2 to fire this one as well, but the 80-ton gun was pointing down the fjord and would have taken some time to train towards the large burning ship now passing to his left. From his report, it does not appear that he contemplated firing at any other ship further down the fjord, so his attention was probably all captured by *Blücher*. Within minutes she was too far past and out of the fire-zone of the guns at Søndre Kaholmen.[40]

In the observation-posts on Nordre Kaholmen above the torpedo battery kommandørkaptein Anderssen in the main bunker and minør Bexrud in the reserve position could both hear and feel the fire of the guns from Oscarsborg and they could see the guns at Kopås firing. In his time in the service, Anderssen had fired several hundred torpedoes during exercises, and he was recognised as one of the Navy's foremost experts on this weapon.

Just before 04:30, a large ship emerged into view, smoke streaming from multiple fires but some of its guns blazing away. After passing Husvik *Blücher* had continued firing to both sides. Løytnant Bertelsen observed several hits outside the torpedo battery at Nordre Kaholmen and then continuing upwards the rocky side of Håøya. Frightening for the people in the torpedo battery, but not dangerous.[41] *Blücher* was moving slower than anticipated and Anderssen calmly set the target speed to 7 knots; the range was only a few hundred metres, and it would be impossible to miss. The armour belt extended 1.7 metres below the waterline but the torpedoes were set to run at 3 metres. Shaft no. 1 was reported ready and in the darkness of the command bunker Anderssen fumbled for the firing-key. 'I had never thought I would fire my torpedoes in anger,' he later said. With the aim point a little aft of the main superstructure, he pressed the firing-key and to his immense relief heard the torpedo rumble away. The sights were re-adjusted to 6 knots and aligned on a new aim point a little further aft before the firing-key was pressed again. The third torpedo was reported ready, but before it could be fired an explosion shook the ship, followed shortly after by a second, and with professional pride Anderssen knew his torpedoes had worked as they should. Expecting further ships, he retained the third torpedo and ordered an immediate reload of the empty shafts. Anderssen had been told that five ships were coming and as he had nine torpedoes altogether, he had decided to 'give the four first ships two each and one for the last'. No further ships appeared, though, and when the communication centre reported that the other ships had turned back, the torpedoes were lifted out of the water and the firing mechanisms locked safe.

As the cruiser struggled out of the kill zone of the Norwegian batteries, two huge underwater explosions shocked *Blücher*'s crew, shifting the cruiser noticeably sideways. Glowing sparks were thrown out of the stack, followed by white steam.

The torpedoes hit close together on the port side. At least one hit in section V or VI, most likely both. This was probably the most damaging place the two torpedoes could hit, right by the central engine-room area. Turbine room no.2/3 in section V and boiler room no. 1 in section VI rapidly filled

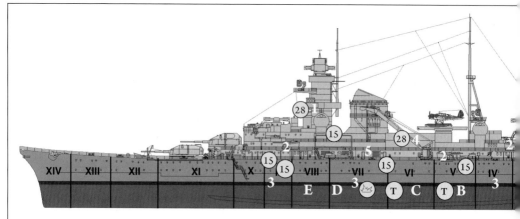

KEY

1	A/A Fire control centre (VIII)	**A**	Turbine room 1 (III)
2	10.5-cm guns (VIII/IX, V, III/IV)	**B**	Turbine rooms 2 and 3 (V)
3	10.5/3.7-cm magazines (IX, VII, IV)	**C**	Boiler room 1 (VI)
4	Hangar (VI)	**D**	Boiler room 2 (VII)
5	Torpedo workshop (VII)	**E**	Boiler room 3 (VIII)

with water. Most personnel in these rooms were killed instantly and the rest got out as fast as they could. Several bulkheads were opened to the sea and water poured into the ship. The damage-control parties could not cope. As the pumps ceased to work from lack of electrical power, the water continued into adjacent compartments through cracks and not-yet-sealed cable hatches.

A list of 8–10 degrees to port developed, adding to the confusion and uncertainty. Remaining communication was disrupted and most lights went out. Emergency lighting was turned on in some compartments, but a sense of panic started to spread below deck as few understood what was happening. Below deck, any thoughts that might have occurred to Thannemann and his more experienced officers of recoupling undamaged boilers and turbines were probably quickly abandoned due to the inexperienced crew. On the bridge, it was assumed that they had hit one or more of the mines of the barrier that apparently was there, after all. According to Heymann, it was only 'much later' that it was ascertained that *Blücher* had been hit by two torpedoes – '*Wie erst viel später festgestellt wird, hendelt es sich um zwei Torpedotreffer.*'[42]

By the time *Blücher* passed Husvik, six of the eight seaplanes heading for Vindfangerbukta from Horten had arrived. As already mentioned F.308 was overtaken but managed to stay in hiding during the fighting in the Narrows. At dawn, the pilot took off and flew to Vindfangerbukta, the last aircraft to arrive there. The other pilots and navigators had an experience they would

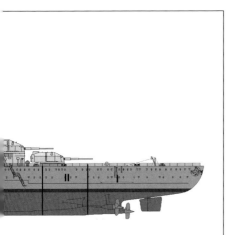

28   Hits from Oscarsborg 28-cm guns
5   Hits from Kopås 15-cm guns
      (initial impacts on starboard side)
      Torpedo hits
      10.5-cm magazine that exploded

Around forty shells and two torpedoes were fired at *Blücher* from Oscarsborg and Kopås. Exactly where they hit and what damage they caused is not possible to reconstruct from the available sources or the wreck today. Based on reports from survivors, however, a reasonably accurate assessment of the most important hits can be compiled. The illustration shows the hits from the 28-cm guns and the torpedoes and about half of the hits from the 15-cm battery at Kopås. The hits from the 5.7-cm guns at Husvik are not included.

never forget. Some of the shells from *Blücher* detonated on the mountainside behind them and shrapnel rained down over them and the planes. No one was injured, though, and the aircraft were still serviceable. F.84 took off from Vindfangerbukta as soon as there was a pause in the firing and flew over Group V, which sounded the alarm but did not open fire. The alarm went off again at around 05:00 when F.334 also took off, circling twice over Oscarsborg before heading off. This time the Germans opened fire, but the aircraft was not hit and disappeared in an easterly direction. F.306 also left shortly after, heading north. Four aircraft (F.304, F.308, F.338, F.202) could not leave due to ice problems and were captured by the Germans on 18 April. The torpedo aircraft F.86, which was last out of Horten, was too late and had to seek shelter near Hvitsten. Here it was discovered and sunk by *Rau VII* later in the day.[43]

Mêlée: 04:30–04:35, 9 April

Three to four minutes after the torpedoes hit, shortly after 04:30, *Blücher* finally cleared the kill zone of the Norwegian guns. She was by now gliding forward, slowing down from around 12 knots with a list of 10–12 degrees to port. The battle had lasted about ten minutes. 'Cease fire' was ordered from the bridge but many of the lighter flak guns kept firing into the night for some time. Nobody on the bridge at this stage, according to Heymann, had any understanding that the ship was mortally wounded and would not make it to Oslo.[44]

Chief Engineer Thannemann reported to the bridge that the torpedo hits had made a mess of *Blücher*'s propulsion systems and, as the list increased, things went from bad to worse. Slippery decks made everything dangerous and soon pipes started to crack, spraying deadly steam into the smoke-filled rooms. The rooms filled with water and had to be closed off as the men pulled back. There was limited hope of raising steam in the system any time soon. Watertight doors were closed where it was possible, but a few cable gates and shaft bushings were still open and the water poured through to neighbouring compartments. Below deck, an eerie silence spread as the engines shut down, fans and pumps stopped, and the lights went out. According to Heymann an enquiry from the bridge was answered by a report that at least one of the outer turbines could be restarted within an hour. Thannemann later categorically denied having authorised any such answer. Shortly after, all communication with the engine rooms was lost. Orders to evacuate the engine rooms were given – 'Raum verlassen.' With the engines out and most engine rooms abandoned by their crews, Thannemann went to concentrate on damage control on the armoured deck and around the guns and magazines. It was later estimated that some 3,000 m³ of water entered the hull in the first few minutes after the torpedo-strikes. Within a short time, this had increased to well over 4,000 m³, increasing further to almost 7,000 m³ as the list worsened. Together with water deliberately taken in to flood the magazines this started making the cruiser unstable.[45]

Apparently Woldag did not realise the perilous condition of his ship; he refused a suggestion to run her aground. In all likelihood, it would not have been possible anyway with the engines and steering out of action. Another proposal to offload some of the soldiers in an orderly manner and let them find their way to Oslo on their own was also rejected as was an alternative proposal to send the unit meant to secure Fornebu airfield ahead in the motorboats. Instead, Woldag decided to anchor where the ship was to avoid drifting uncontrollably in the fjord, a decision Kummetz approved. At this stage, the admiral appears to have been shocked beyond belief and rather meekly left command to Woldag. Korvettenkapitän Werner Czygan and Leutnant Hans Joachim Bertelsmann were sent forward with an anchor party. Due to the list, which by now was 15–18 degrees, the bow anchor would not drop, but eventually the starboard anchor rushed out, finding the bottom at 60 metres; 175 metres of chain was let out and the burning cruiser halted in the middle of the fjord, turning slowly with the current. All efforts would now be focused on tasks necessary to secure the ship and get her back into an operational state so she could continue towards Oslo. Above all, it appeared paramount to extinguish the fire amidships.[46]

Onshore, there was no damage to any of the batteries and Kopås and Husvik turned their attention to *Lützow*, some 600 metres behind the flagship. Kapitän Thiele saw the first two hits on *Blücher* from Oscarsborg and immediately ordered his ship to fire. *Lützow*'s gunnery officers could see little more than those on *Blücher*, however, and they were at a further disadvantage being further down the fjord with a limited sector of fire. The secondary guns opened up but had no clear targets either. Thiele realised something was wrong and reduced speed while trying to understand. Within a minute, however, *Lützow* received three 15-cm hits in quick succession. At the time, the officers on board believed they were hit by '24-cm shells from the battery at Fort Kaholm', but there is no doubt they were hit by 15-cm shells from the Kopås battery.[47]

The first shell hit on top of the central gun barrel of turret *Anton*, ripping off the crenel shutter, destroying the hydraulics and the cradle of the gun. The impact lifted the turret roof a few millimetres and splinters and fragments peppered the interior of the turret. Hydraulics and instruments were destroyed, fuzes popped, and the main turret motor was put out of action rendering the turret temporarily unserviceable. Four men were lightly wounded. The three barrels in the turret were uncoupled, so that the right-hand gun could be fired after five minutes; the left barrel was fully operational again after an hour-and-a-half. The central barrel remained unserviceable and was depressed to the lowest position.[48]

The second shell hit the hull on the port side, between the tower and the funnel, exploding on the armoured deck. It had a rather flat trajectory and penetrated the outer side of the hull, about two metres above the waterline, before exploding. The sick bay and operating theatre were wrecked, starting a serious fire that required hard work from the damage-control parties for half an hour to extinguish. Two Army men were killed and six more severely wounded while one of the doctors and some ratings were wounded, some seriously. The crew later counted 12–15 large holes in the bulkhead, a transverse frame was damaged, and the upper deck pierced in several places. The trim cell forward of the sick bay was penetrated by splinters about 20 cm below the waterline, possibly from a near-miss, and a minor leak ensued.[49]

The third 15-cm shell exploded near the base of the port crane. Splinters flew over a large area, killing four gunners and wounding several others. One of the two aircraft was damaged, searchlight cables were torn, the optics of the aft AA fire-control equipment destroyed, and a fire started amid the 8.8-cm flak ammunition. *Lützow* was also hit by ricochets and splinters from shells aimed at *Blücher*. In addition, machine-gun or light gun fire raked the decks and superstructure causing minor damage and forcing everybody in the open to seek shelter. This most likely came from *Blücher*.[50]

Thiele did not want to risk receiving the same treatment as *Blücher* and ordered 'Full astern' immediately after the first hit on turret *Anton*. Just before the blazing flagship vanished behind Oscarsborg, two huge explosions were seen. Thiele assumed these were from mines and that the passage to Oslo was closed for all practical purposes. *Emden* was reported approaching from astern and Thiele ordered 'Full ahead' again. As soon as the distance between the two ships had increased somewhat, he ordered the engines astern again, turning her stern to port behind Storskjær and continuing a clockwise turn, before lying still for a while. All light and medium guns on *Lützow*'s port side fired up the fjord even if targets remained elusive. Finally, Thiele ordered 'Full ahead' again and *Lützow* set off down the fjord while damage-control and fire parties were ordered into action. Smoke from the fire below decks continued to envelop the ship for a while but this was put

out within half an hour. The hole in the trim tank was small and quickly sealed. Turret *Anton* was operational again later, even if the centre gun was beyond repair for the moment and hung limply down at its lowest elevation. Otherwise, there was no serious damage to the cruiser. Six men were dead aboard *Lützow* and sixteen wounded, four of them seriously. One of the wounded men later died, bringing the total death toll up to seven.[51]

Emden did not open fire. There were no targets to be seen and the presence of *Lützow* and *Blücher* in front prevented any arbitrary firing. The explosions from the two torpedo hits on *Blücher* were clearly heard but taken to be from mines. A few shots appeared to be aimed at *Emden*, but there were no hits

and the shells landed harmlessly in the fjord. When *Lützow* turned, *Emden* did similarly towards the eastern shore and started down the fjord again. *Möwe* and the two R-boats took the van. While they were all turning, a shell landed close to *R 18*, but she was not damaged. Lange decided it would not be possible to land any soldiers at this stage to take care of the batteries from the landward side. At 04:35, a radio-telephone signal from *Blücher* confirmed that all engines were out, and she had severe problems.[52]

The situation was tense aboard the German vessels as they moved away from Oscarsborg. At least three Norwegian vessels were coming up the fjord this morning. Among them was the 107-ton Norwegian freighter *Sørland*, heading for Oslo with paper and foodstuffs. She ventured by misfortune straight into Group *Oldenburg* coming down the fjord. *öwe* challenged her with a signal lamp but, seeing that the approaching vessels were warships,

Blücher burning with a heavy list to port. Note the men gathering aft. Some are already in the water, clinging to rafts or trying to swim to safety.

Master Asbjørn Martinsen doused his navigation lights and turned *Sørland* towards the eastern shore. *Möwe* opened fire, followed by *R 18* and *R 19*, setting the wooden ship ablaze. Desperate, Martinsen grounded *Sørland* near Skiphelle where the burned-out wreck sank later in the morning. Two of his men, Ole Tornes and Hans Frisnes, died aboard. The rest of the crew of six swam to shore, deeply shocked.[53]

Abandon Ship: 04:35–06:30, 9 April

Aboard *Blücher*, saving the ship and the men took priority and Woldag ordered Heymann to leave the bridge and assess the situation. He found utter chaos. The leading damage-control officer, who was not aware that the First Officer had not been at his assigned station, gave a grim picture and admitted he was not in control of the situation. The centre parts of the main deck, armoured deck and superstructure were all a red-hot mass of flame. Explosive fires going through several decks raked the area of the aircraft

The last of the ship as seen from Askholmen. At least three boats are trying to rescue survivors, probably those of the Iversen family (*see* pages 227–30). There is burning oil on the surface of the water on the other side.

hangar, hindering movement between fore and aft. Below the forward port 10.5-cm gun, the ship's side was torn open with thick smoke and flames pouring out of the opening. At the site of the torpedo workshop, where much of the Army ammunition had been stored, there was now nothing but a large hole in the deck. Small arms ammunition and hand grenades were detonating continuously, and smoke canisters ignited by the many hits from the Kopås and Husvik batteries added to the inferno. Ill-trained fire-fighting parties struggled in vain to douse the fires, all the more so as splinters had riddled many of the hoses, more often than not making them useless. All over the ship, makeshift parties began to dump Navy and Army ammunition overboard. As the fires spread, some of the pumps stopped and in some sectors the hoses were not even to hand as they should have been. Flooding and wreckage blocked companionways and hatches, and communication with more and more sections of the ship was breaking down, hampering coordination. The number of dead and wounded increased by the minute and medical personnel worked hard to cope; most of the wounded were taken care of in makeshift dressing-stations set up beyond the reach of the flames and smoke, fore and aft. Some men managed to move into the blazing hangar, but most of these were killed when the four bombs stored there exploded. The fires spread increasingly out of control and as the pumps started to fail, even hand-held Minimax extinguishers were attempted – to no avail. Some of the ready-use ammunition from the ship's guns was hastily returned to the magazines below the armoured deck, some dumped in the fjord. Aft, the torpedoes in the starboard tubes were fired off as a precaution, two exploding against the eastern shore, the third grounding south of Drøbak. On the port side, it was only possible to remove the contact fuzes as the tubes could not be trained outboard. Forward, the port side tubes were gone, and the starboard ones could not be reached due to the flames and explosions.[54]

Shaken, Heymann returned to the bridge reporting to his captain that in spite of the purposeful efforts of the men, the fires were getting out of hand. Hearing this, Woldag ordered all gun-crews to be detailed to the fire-fighting parties as no danger from further attacks appeared imminent 'Alle Gefechtsstellen verlassen, am Feuerlöschen beteiligen.'[55] Priority was given to move as many as possible of the wounded to the less threatened areas fore and aft. The only undamaged boat was the starboard cutter. Kapitänleutnant Mihatsch was detailed to take command of this, once it was lowered, and take the seriously wounded ashore, accompanied by two medical officers and some lucky soldiers. Apparently one of the damaged boats was also lowered and used for some time. A limited number of men, mostly casualties, were rescued by the boats, but for most the way to safety was a 15- or 20-minute swim through the icy water.[56]

At Oscarsborg, Oberst Eriksen saw the rest of the intruders turning back after the first ship had passed out of sight, fiercely burning. The third gun had been loaded earlier and was ready but Eriksen saw no reason to fire a third shot. When the shadows of the other ships vanished in the fog, having turned around, Eriksen remarked to his officers that 'Well, we did not destroy many of them, but we certainly defended our neutrality.' He still found it hard to believe that the ships feebly approaching in line astern and not firing back with their heavy guns constituted an invasion. At 04:25 he sent a signal to the Admiral Staff in Oslo that he had opened fire on the intruders. At 04:43 he added the information that one cruiser was burning fiercely at Askholmene while the others had turned away.[57]

The Kopås battery continued firing until the ships were out of sight around 2,500 metres down the fjord at 04:40. No. 1 gun (manned by cadets) ran out of ammunition after firing the 10 shells that had initially been brought up from the magazine. Half of them were fired at *Blücher* and the rest at *Lützow*. Gun no. 2 had 1 or 2 rounds left, while gun no. 3 encountered temporary problems and stopped shooting after 3 or 4 shells so 21–23 rounds were fired in total presumably about 13 at *Blücher* and 8–10 at *Lützow* and possibly *Emden*. The Husvik battery had fired 30 shots, all or most of them at *Blücher*.

At 04:54, the Kopås Battery reported to Oscarsborg that the remaining ships had withdrawn to the south and that at least one of them was on fire, possibly sinking. The Narrows had been successfully defended and Eriksen allowed his men to stand down. They emerged from the batteries and shelters to discuss what had happened. The crews at Kopås started to carry new ammunition to their guns while two NCO cadets crossed to Oscarsborg in a rowing boat to get more firing tubes for the guns.

Dawn was approaching and the stricken cruiser could be seen to the north, burning fiercely. There were several explosions. She was obviously in trouble.[58]

Landing of infantry to the south was an obvious threat and Enger sent løytnant Bertelsen with a reconnaissance patrol towards Son and Moss in a couple of trucks. They came back around 12:30, reporting that the Germans had landed at Son, controlled the rail line at Såner station and were on the march in several directions. Enger sent a request to Oslo for more soldiers to avoid being overrun but otherwise his initiatives to establish a defence against a landward attack on the fort were limited. The fortress had no medical units, and the doctor in Drøbak was ordered by Eriksen to be ready to help. Later a medical unit was established in Vindfangerbukta.

At dawn, a fresh wind fuelled the fire, and the current turned *Blücher* around on the anchor, pointing the bow south-eastward. Smoke billowed forward across the bridge and fo'c'sle, worsening the conditions there

Blücher is gone. Only the heads of those swimming for their lives
and a few small floats or rowing boats can be seen.

significantly. With water rising and thick smoke filling the air, all boiler
and turbine rooms had been abandoned by around 05:00, the personnel
employed in the fire-fighting. As a routine precaution, flooding was started
in the forward magazines below turrets *Anton* and *Bruno* after the hits. It
quickly became clear, however, that there were no fires in the bow, and the
flooding valves of A magazine were closed, and the water pumped out again.
In B magazine, however, the after bulkhead started to get hot and flooding
continued. Later attempts to empty the room partly failed as the pumps
broke down from lack of electricity.[59]

The three main magazines for 10.5-cm and 3.7-cm ammunition were in the
centre of sections IV, VII and IX respectively. Of these, only the magazine in
section IX was sufficiently flooded. At 05:30 the magazine in section VII under
the armoured deck detonated in a massive explosion. The failing pumps could
not flood the magazine properly and no one could fight through the inferno to
neutralise the dangerous munitions. There was a perceptible jolt through the
ship and the list, which up to this point had been moderate, started to increase
significantly. The explosion ruptured the bulkheads between boiler rooms 1

and 2 (sections VI and VII) and the adjacent fuel tanks and the first flames from burning oil spread below deck as well as onto the sea. By now, Woldag must have realised that his ship could not be saved. Around 06:00 *Blücher*'s list reached 45 degrees and Woldag ordered the crew to prepare to abandon ship. As communication was largely down, the order for 'all-hands-on-deck' went by voice pipe or mouth from man to man.[60]

Confused and scared, the soldiers, who so far had remained below deck as previously instructed, streamed up from below – as best they could. Many found hatches and doors difficult to open. Very few had been told the evacuation procedures, far less been instructed to close the hatches again once they had passed through. Most were left open and smoke, fire and eventually water quickly spread. On deck, they were met by chaos and confusion but, according to most accounts, few orders or instructions. Dead or wounded seamen lay around, adding to the horror and bewilderment. The first who arrived on deck found lifejackets to wear and others were given them by seamen who considered themselves good swimmers. How many and how willingly the seamen gave their lifejackets away varies from account to account, but many undoubtedly did. Some of the Army officers later reported that seamen started abandoning ship well before any orders were given.[61]

When it was clear that *Blücher* would sink, attempts were made to extend or slip the anchor chain so the ship could drift closer to shore, but failed due to the list. The fires amidships eventually divided the ship in two with no communication. A few men risked climbing across on the slippery side of the ship outside the starboard railing, but few succeeded. Heymann ordered all men who could to assemble on the slanting foredeck. Around 06:00, Woldag gave a short address and called three cheers for the ship and the Fatherland after which Heymann called cheers for the captain and the admiral after which the order 'Abandon ship' was formally given by Woldag. According to Signalman Limbach, who was on the bridge, Woldag wanted to remain on the bridge, but was formally ordered by Kummetz to join him in leaving the ship. Heymann went into the water without a lifebelt shortly after the cheering – as did Kummetz, Woldag, Förster and Engelmann. Engelbrecht was given a lifebelt and a seaman rolled up his leather coat with his riding boots inside for him to use as an extra float and bring reasonably dry to shore. They all swam towards the mainland and were halfway to shore when the end came.[62]

Abandoning ship was not an obvious thing to do for the soldiers, despite the list and the fire amidships. Outside what was lit by the flames, it was still rather dark, the water was cold and there was limited rescue equipment

Both left: Survivors gathered on the mainland. Some are partly clothed and presumably miserably wet, others appear to be better off.

Survivors on one of the Askholmen islands. Obermaat Peter Schüller found a flag
and later he wrapped it round his body under his sweater to keep it safe when he was
detained by Norwegian soldiers. Schüller eventually brought the flag back to Germany
where it is now to be found in the Garrison Church in Wilhelmshaven.

to be found. Many of the soldiers were poor swimmers and the realisation
that there were insufficient lifebelts or boats to take them ashore created a
sense of hopelessness. Nevertheless, more and more men left the ship on
their own initiative. Most German reports praise the disciplined behaviour
of soldiers and seamen alike, but the Army reports almost uniformly lament
the absence of seamen and particularly naval officers to take command.
Norwegian eyewitnesses speak of men running back and forth on the listing
deck, shouting and crying for help. A few reports openly describe panic and
everyone-for-himself behaviour, while most have a more subtle account
where fear and confusion are seen only between the lines.[63]

Aft, Fregattenkapitän Thannemann, who could no longer communicate
with Woldag and Heymann in the forepart, took command when he emerged
on deck. Korvettenkapitän Czygan had moved to the quarterdeck after the
anchor handling and had already managed to get two dinghies afloat. When
the list of the cruiser reached 45 degrees, Thannemann gave orders to start

preparations for abandoning the ship. By then, however, many had already gone overboard with and without lifebelts. Undamaged Marcks rescue floats were thrown overboard as were hammocks, mattresses, crates, bundled gas-mask canisters and other buoyant material. The floats had arrived only a few days before departure, and few knew how to handle them properly. They took some minutes to inflate, and several soldiers drowned sliding off when trying to enter too early. One Army officer, Leutnant Tewaag, later told how he found a crate containing floats and had them inflated with the help of some soldiers reading aloud from the manual. Once in the water, the soldiers who managed to get on board, used their spades as paddles to row towards shore. Thannemann and a few soldiers were among the last to get into the water – after the ship had rolled past 90 degrees.[64]

Survivors at Askholmen. Major Horst von Necker, an intelligence officer from Falkenhorst's staff, took charge of the men on the island where he landed.

One of the Askholmen survivors seemingly getting little sympathy
from more fortunate comrades.

Blücher listed unrelentingly ever further to port and there was no hope of saving her any more. The battle ensign was where Signalman Gefreiter Heitmann had hoisted it on the after mast on orders from Czygan around 05:40. A huge war flag had been hoisted on the foremast earlier, just after the two first hits. When the ship fully capsized, the bow started sinking and the stern rose quickly, showing the three bronze propellers, before the whole hull slipped under around 06:25. Some men still clung to the rudder and shafts as she went, presumably non-swimmers. It was a little over two hours since oberst Eriksen had decided to open fire on the unknown warship. The time given for *Blücher*'s sinking varies between 06:19 and 06:32. Eriksen (1950) 06:19, Anderssen 06:21, Oscarsborg's log 06:22, Kummetz: 'about 06:23', the restored War Diary: 06:27, Goerz 06:28, Heymann 06:32.[65]

Snow Covered Rocks: 06:30–22:00, 9 April

Going into the icy water, swimming ashore one way or another, became the only way to safety for most when *Blücher* started to sink. The range from the stern to Askholmene was about 300 metres, from the bow to the mainland, some 400–500 metres and it was obvious to even the most optimistic that it would be a challenge beyond many. The air temperature was about 2 degrees Centigrade, the water temperature slightly warmer, but not much. Hypothermia would inevitably lead to exhaustion, cramps and heart failure. Once in the water, seamen and soldiers struggled for their lives in the icy fjord and individuals who could not swim and had not found or been given a floatation device quickly went under. Those who did not reach shore within 15 minutes or so were at peril from the freezing water. Others who managed to swim towards land died from exhaustion or heart attacks only metres from the beach. The currents were especially strong and difficult around Askholmene. As it sank, the burning superstructure made contact with the oil on the water and several intense fires were started killing the men who could not avoid it in a horrible manner. About ten minutes after the wreck disappeared, there was a violent underwater explosion. A huge burning bubble followed, from which a jet of flame ignited other oil spills, exterminating many of the last to get away.[66]

Those who managed to reach shore watched in shock as the cruiser capsized and slipped under, leaving nothing but wreckage and bobbing heads in the water. Fires were lit with pieces of driftwood and planking from boat-sheds and many gathered around, drying their clothes and warming up as best they could. The majority of the survivors, including many wounded, landed on the mainland at Digerud and Hallangen north of Drøbak. After a while, a headcount gave some 750 *Blücher* crewmen and around 200 soldiers, nearly all from the forepart of the ship, including Kummetz, Engelbrecht, Süssmann and Oberst Blohmeyer, commander of IR 307. They were all cold, exhausted and very miserable. Many were smeared in oil and quite a few had burns on their faces and hands from swimming through burning fuel. Others had frozen limbs from the icy water or walking barefoot in the snow. Some had no strength to drag themselves out of the sea and died literally metres from safety.

In the water, most of the men were alone, and each of the survivors had a dramatic story to tell. Korvettenkapitän Kurt Zöpfel, the ship's Admin Officer, went into the water from the bows and swam towards land holding on to a wash bowl:

Slowly, very slowly, the land came nearer and presented another problem. Big rocks and cliffs with sharp edges! How could we get ashore here? With my last, my very last, strength I managed to grab a rock and was helped up by a comrade already on shore [...] Slowly it dawned on me: 'You are safe!' What an indescribable feeling. But it did not last long. The cold crept unstoppably into us, legs arms and head, all started to tremble.[67]

Leutnant K. Johnsen of the Propaganda Unit wrote:

I got rid of my leather coat and uniform jacket and took off my boots. I kept my cap, however, as I had 50 cigarettes inside it and wanted to keep them dry. I slid on my bottom down the port side of the ship and tried to lower myself slowly into the water. Unfortunately, my head went under too and my cap with the precious cigarettes came off and drifted away [...] With six or seven other officers and countless soldiers I started swimming towards land. When *Blücher* went down, we were still some 50 metres away from the shore. I turned onto my back and saw some soldiers still clinging to the propellers – one of them lifting his arm in a German salute as he went down with the ship.[68]

Sonderführer Pinckernelle, another of the interpreters, wrote:

Without a lifebelt, I would not have been able to swim ashore as I had a minor heart issue and was not a particularly good swimmer. Halfway to shore, a man just ahead of me gave up and drowned. He had no lifebelt, and I was unable to help him. Many men cried for help close to shore. Those already on land yelled at us 'Keep Up! Keep Up!' and I believe that this encouragement saved the lives of some. Shortly after I had gone into the water a lieutenant from the air force swam up to me and asked if he could hold on to my life belt as he had overestimated his own strength in the cold water. He seemed to be a good swimmer, but nevertheless we made slow progress as we hampered each other. About 20–30 metres from shore, he let go, probably due to cramps. I tried to help him, but my own hands were useless from the cold, and I could not hold him. He seemed to continue swimming close behind me, but I never saw him again.[69]

Heymann walked tirelessly among the shaken survivors, making sure they stood up and moved around while others gathered around the fires to get warm and dry their uniforms. On the mainland few men died once ashore, but on the little Askholmene islands the casualty rate mounted as there was limited shelter and fewer men to take care of one another. Apparently, most of the oil also drifted towards the islands adding to the difficulties for those who unknowingly swam that way.[70]

Some Norwegians, among them Anderssen from Nordre Kaholmen, later said they could hear the singing of 'Deutschland, Deutschland über alles ...', the German national anthem, as the ship went down. Few German reports mention this except Goerz, who claims it came from the non-swimmers still clinging to the propellers. Lieutenant Tewaag's account describes how he and others huddling together on Askholmene cheered three times and started singing, when the stern of Blücher rose for the last time before going under. Hauptmann Boese and Oberleutnant Eyers say the same, the latter adding that when the singing stopped, the silence was terrifying – Totenstille – likely the most reliable version.[71]

The coastline north of Drøbak is rugged and was sparsely populated in 1940. One of those living on the mainland

Rittmeister Paul Goerz looking rather uncomfortable but happy to be alive.

across from Askholmene was a fisherman called Johan Iversen. He later told of his experiences that morning:

> At 04:20 we were awakened by a mighty rumble which, as far as I could make out, came from Oscarsborg – about 4 km away. My wife woke up too and we decided to get up and find out what was going on. While we dressed, the rumbling continued, and glowing shells came flying up the fjord. We realised the fortress and the country was under attack. From enemy warships. As some of the shells fell dangerously close to our house, [the family] took shelter behind a nearby cliff.[72]

When the shooting died down Iversen went to have a look and could see thick smoke rising from a large warship coming through the mist. The ship appeared to have no steering and was burning fiercely. Then it dropped anchor and was turned completely around by the current and the wind. Many people were seen on board and after a while some of them jumped into the sea and began swimming towards the Askholmene skerries, some helped by floats others just swimming. Soon the small islands were covered by people. All the time Iversen could hear cries for help and loud moaning. He had no idea what nationality the ship was, but when it capsized and went down men in the water were shipwrecked and obviously in dire need for help. He called one of his sons and a neighbour and ran down to the quay where they took to the water, each in his own fishing boat:

> As I approached the place where the ship had gone down, I could see many men floating around, some on floats others with lifebelts. I first picked up some singles drifting away from the others, then I rowed towards a float where some officers waved at me. The float was so crowded it was well under water and I picked up some of them so it surfaced and could be rowed by those left. When the boat was full, I took them to shore, from where I pointed them to my house.[73]

One of Iversen's younger sons had meanwhile lit the oven in the house as well as one in the boathouse and while Iversen returned to the fjord to pick up more men, those who could helped the wounded and exhausted into the buildings where Iversen's wife and daughter took care of the miserable survivors. In all Iversen and the others from Digerud saved between 70 and 80 men.

Three more of Iversen's sons were on the other side of the fjord at Håøya that night. They took out a motorboat and rescued several more, including some from the edges of the burning oil.[74]

Most of the survivors from the stern, including Thannemann and Goerz of the *Weserübung* staff, struggled ashore on one of the three Askholmene islands and some nearby rocks. Goerz was not wounded and according to his own account took command, using an air mattress to try to rescue others:

> The island was some 200 metres long and 50 metres wide and consisted of snow-covered rock with a few bushes. A small wooden hut contained some old clothes that the seamen arriving first made use of [...] With a steel helmet and a spade to row, I took the mattress back towards *Blücher*, assisted by a naval petty officer, to save at least some of those still struggling in the water. [Soon] we had 8–10 people clinging on to the mattress and with the current against us were hardly making any progress at all with our primitive rowing gear. The situation was getting desperate. The mattress sank below the surface and those holding on were too cold to help us move towards land. Only after vigorous shouting were we able to make them assist us somewhat [...] Most of them had to be dragged ashore as they

The small islands of Askholmene as seen from the dorsal gun position of a He 111
heading south. In the background is Digerud on the mainland and the islands of
Aspond and Lågøya. Oslo is somewhere in the hazy background to the north.
At least three vessels are seen looking for survivors.

were not capable of hauling themselves onto the steep banks. We lit a fire
from planks laying around or torn from the hut.[75]

Goerz maintained that no one had told the soldiers below deck what was
wrong with the ship. The group where he was did not get the order to abandon
ship and when they decided on their own initiative when the list increased to
leave the compartments where they were confined, it was difficult, as they had
not been shown how to get out and nobody came to help them. He later wrote
that he struggled to open several of the hatches he had to pass on his way out.
A 'traumatic experience', he wrote, 'and the fear I experienced when I was
not sure I would be able to reach deck was dreadful.' Finally, he continues,
when they got to the after deck there was no naval officer in command and he
and his men had to evacuate the ship as best they could, throwing overboard
everything they could find to help them stay afloat.[76]

Fisherman Johan Iversen is rewarded by the Germans for saving men from *Blücher*.
In the background his sons and neighbours who also took part. To them,
all shipwrecked seamen were equal and should be saved if possible.

Løytnant Erling Carelius was guarding a nearby oil depot with thirteen soldiers when he was told that survivors were struggling ashore on the islands. He requisitioned two fishing vessels and brought as many as he could find on the shores of Askholmene to the depot where they were given dry clothes and food. During the day other Germans arrived to take care of the survivors and the Norwegian soldiers were disarmed and sent away. Løytnant Carelius was taken to Oslo with the survivors.[77]

Around 10:00, Generalmajor Engelbrecht took off in the cutter with some other officers and two or three soldiers who had managed to bring weapons along to scout to the south of the mainland group of survivors. The cutter returned after some time, with orders for the survivors to move towards three summer lodges where the general had established his headquarters and made the other cabins ready to receive the wounded. Moving along the rocky, ice-covered shoreline turned out to be no easy task, as most survivors were without shoes and improvised footwear had to be made from cut-up lifebelts.

Only around midday did the move start. One of the huts had a phone connection and Sonderführer Behrens, who spoke Norwegian, called the operator in Drøbak on Engelbrecht's orders, asking for help to be sent to the area. While the wounded were being installed in the huts, the Germans were surrounded by a group of Norwegian soldiers and ordered to continue to a farm about a mile inland. The soldiers came from 4th Guards Company whose commander, kaptein Aksel Petersson, had received orders to take his seventy men south from Oslo to take care of survivors. Behrens translated Petersson's instructions and there was little the Germans could do but comply. Leaving the most seriously wounded behind in the huts with the medical personnel until they could be picked up, what was by now a miserable crowd set out on a sluggish hour-long march through the snow towards a farm at Søndre Hallangen where as many as possible were sheltered in the farm buildings. Of the 920 men who eventually gathered at the farm, 753 were from *Blücher's* crew, including 25 officers and 180 petty officers; 167 were from the Army, 11 of them officers. The help given by the farmer at Hallangen and his family is praised in all accounts. The Norwegian soldiers were described as 'correct and polite, even friendly', in spite of Petersson forbidding all attempts to contact anybody in Oslo. A Norwegian doctor also appeared. He had limited medical supplies but started taking care of the wounded as best he could. Wounded and exhausted men were given priority for beds and floor-space in the farm-buildings while the rest took turns inside to get some heat and dry their clothes. After a while, the survivors had their first and only meal of the day: a potato each, some bread and some milk provided by the farmer.

At 18:30 Petersson approached the German officers and told them that he had received orders from Oslo to return, which he did with his men, leaving the survivors to fend for themselves. Presumably he was unaware how senior many of the captives he was freeing were. German troops were now in control of most of central Oslo and the Norwegian Army had started to establish lines of defence north of the capital. Reinforcing these was considered more important than guarding some miserable, wet seamen. Before he left, Petersson promised to find some transport for the wounded and around 22:00 two requisitioned buses left Hallangen for Oslo. The senior officers and a handful of soldiers went with the wounded. Engelbrecht, Süssmann and Kummetz thus arrived in the capital around midnight.[78]

During the night of the 9th/10th, Korvettenkapitän Förster was given the task of organising food and transport for the remaining men at Hallangen as soon as possible; this was no easy task in an occupied country, and all the more so as the survivors were stranded on a peninsula isolated from Drøbak and a significant distance from the nearest main road. Some of the men at Hallangen had to sleep outside during the night, but they all seem to have come through without further casualties. Next morning, more buses arrived and started taking the men to Oslo. Woldag stayed with his men during the night but left in one of the first buses just after daylight. Most of the remaining men followed during the day in a slow but steady shuttle. Food, cigarettes and hot drinks were brought to those remaining at the farm. The seriously wounded from the summer lodges and Hallangen were taken aboard *Emden* during the 10th.[79]

Many survivors were rescued from Askholmene, after spending a miserable day in the open. A few had to spend even the ensuing night there before being recovered; 267 survivors were picked up by *Kondor* during the evening, at least ten of them seriously wounded. Many more were rescued by *Norden* and the R-boats. About 40 bodies were also taken out of the water. In the evening, those rescued by *Kondor* were taken on board *Emden* and *Lützow*. Many of the survivors were in a bad shape with little clothing and lacking shoes or boots. Broken limbs and cuts from flying splinters were the most common injuries, but many suffered from exposure, frostbite or serious burns. Lists of the survivors were compiled, but the men were scattered over many places, including isolated skerries, and it was not easy to be sure everybody had been accounted for. The seriously wounded were forwarded to *Emden* as *Lützow*'s sick bay had been damaged. The last survivors from Askholmene were taken to Oslo by the steamer *Drøbak*, requisitioned by the Germans. At 22:00 on the 9th, a memorial ceremony was held on board the *Kondor*, over the site where *Blücher* had gone down. Kapitänleutnant Forstmann's R-boats searched the area for several days, but soon there were only bodies to be found.[80]

In the evening of the 10th a search for remaining survivors was organised using a searchlight-equipped police vessel from Oslo, but no more survivors were found.[81]

Chapter 12
Improvisations
9–10 April

Considering the Situation

While turning away from the Narrows, *Lützow* received a few brief radio-telephone signals from *Blücher*. First that her engines were out of action, then that she was anchoring. According to *Lützow*'s war diary, Kummetz added shortly after, at 04:50 Norwegian time, that *Lützow* should take command of Group *Oldenburg*. Kummetz confirmed, in his own account, that the order was given. After this, no further signals could be sent from *Blücher*, as radio communication failed and visual signals were ineffective. Thiele immediately sent to *Emden* and the ships that he, on orders from *Blücher*, was in charge. Oberleutnant Freyberg on the other hand, wrote in September 1941, that

Kapitän zur See Werner Lange on the bridge of *Emden*. This photo was taken on the morning of 9 April in Oslofjord.

Thiele asked by radio-telephone if he should assume command and was denied by Kummetz: '*Führung bleibt auf Blücher*' – 'Command will stay with *Blücher*.' In the same account, Freyberg held that Thiele turned back from the Narrows on his own initiative, unknown to Kummetz and Woldag. This was also contradicted by Kummetz, who wrote that he endorsed Thiele's decision to withdraw and that pulling the group out of harm's way after *Blücher* was hit was correct, considering the situation.

For Kapitän zur See Werner Lange on *Emden*, Thiele taking command became a challenge – most likely as Lange saw himself as senior and Thiele as a newcomer to the group. Thiele's orders were overlooked or simply ignored and in *Lützow*'s war diary, there are repeated entries about Lange's failure to follow orders: '*Befehl wird von Emden nicht ausgeführt*' – 'The order was not executed by *Emden*'. In *Emden*'s diary there is a similar number of 'suggestions' submitted to *Lützow*, including one for a renewed attempt at passing the Narrows. The situation must have been rather complex; a crisis had developed within Group *Oldenburg*.[1]

For Thiele the most important objective was to get German soldiers to the capital. Having ships in Oslo harbour was not important and it was certainly not worth risking the cruisers passing the Narrows if troops could reach the capital on land, bypassing the fortress, which could be handled in their own time. Reports from the radio room implied that the Norwegian government had refused all demands from the German representatives in Oslo and intended to fight so time appeared to be limited. Thiele decided *Emden* should go

Emden firing her guns.

to Sonsbukta and approach Moss from the north, while *Lützow* would enter Verlebukta south of Moss. Further artillery duels with Oscarsborg were out of the question until the Luftwaffe had reduced its strength significantly and going through the Drøbak Narrows was not an option at the moment. Hence, he gave orders to *Emden* and *Möwe* to land troops at Son and asked Kaptänleutnant Wilcke of *Kondor* for an update on Horten.[2]

Rau VIII preparing to offload soldiers at Son.

Lange saw things differently and stubbornly answered that in his opinion it was more important to resolve the situation at Horten than land troops on the eastern shore. Refusing to accept Thiele's authority, Lange held that he had received other orders from *Blücher*. 'This was incomprehensible,' Thiele wrote, 'Since 05:50 [German time] we had heard nothing from *Blücher*. I informed *Emden* again that *Lützow* was in command. This disruption of the chain of command created unease in the group but had in the end limited effect on the outcome of the operation.' When all was done the controversy seems to have been deliberately swept under the carpet.[3]

At one stage a signal lamp was supposedly seen aboard *Emden* apparently coming from the undamaged starboard part of the *Blücher*'s foretop. The signal, which was not seen by *Lützow*, ordered the torpedo boat *Möwe* to come to help fight the fires and take off some of the wounded. Lange ordered *Möwe* to go to *Blücher*'s assistance. The order was immediately countermanded by Thiele, and Kapitänleutnant Neuss asked: 'Which order applies, land troops or attempt to reach *Blücher*?' Thiele, who had had no contact with the flagship after the signal at 04:50 that gave him command, ordered *Möwe* to remain where she was. Who was in charge over what in Group *Oldenburg* was far from clear; not even which leaders were alive and where they might be if they were. None of the elaborate pre-operation orders, including alternatives for levels of Norwegian resistance and varying landing places, had foreseen that virtually the entire leadership of the group should be taken out in an instant, leaving everything to improvisation. While the soldiers were on board the ships, the Navy was in command. Once landed, the Army would decide for themselves what to do. But who should decide where to land, the Navy or the Army? And what should be the priority: Son and Drøbak, Horten or the outer forts? If Oslofjord was not open and safe, the transport and supply ships could not come in to Oslo and the entire Operation *Weserübung* was in jeopardy. *Lützow* and Thiele created another element of imbalance, in the naval hierarchy as well as for the Army. The 400 mountain troops on board the cruiser were not part of any plans. They should have gone to Trondheim, but at the very last moment found themselves in Oslofjord. Who would decide how they should be deployed? Generalmajor Engelbrecht, who had that authority, was not around and the situation was far from clear. One reason for the difficulties was the German dependence on VHF radio-telephone communication between ships. This was normally fine at sea as it could not be intercepted or used for direction-finding by the enemy due to its short range. In Oslofjord, however, the ships were spread out and often out of range or in a reception-shadow.

When he passed Sonsbukta, Thiele could see into the bay with his binoculars and decided the port of Son would be a suitable place for all

Rau VIII offloading soldiers at Son.

Soldiers pouring ashore from *Rau VII* at Son.

the ships to land soldiers, not least as the maps showed a rail line not far away. Hence, he abandoned his first idea of taking *Lützow* further south. The facilities at Son were rather basic, and all available smaller vessels were used, as well as the Norwegian passenger ferry *Oscarsborg I*, taken into service under the guns of men from *Lützow*. The landing of soldiers started at 06:00. Thiele and Major Hans von Poncet, CO of the *Gebirgsjäger* (2., 8., and 12./ GjR 138) on board *Lützow* agreed that some 250 of them should be landed at Son and prepare to move in the direction of Oslo. The rest would follow later. *R 18* and *R 19* were detached to land an infantry company at Moss, which was done without incident.[4] *R 19* remained in Moss harbour, while Kapitän-leutnant Forstmann returned to Son with *R 18* to receive further orders. Once there, he was told to pick up the soldiers at Moss again and move them to Son. This accomplished, both R-boats returned to the cruisers to re-fuel, after which they were ordered to assist at Rauøy and Bolærne. Meanwhile, Lange had eventually given in, and a two-company force was eventually landed from *Emden* at Son with the help of *Oscarsborg I*, *Rau VII*, *Rau VIII* and other smaller vessels. *Möwe* also landed her company at Son and later so did *Albatros* and *Kondor*, which had one company each – after the capitulation of Horten.

Around 750 German soldiers went by bus and train from Son to Oslo during the 9th. Half of the force was the mountain battalion, the rest were companies from IR 307. One unspecified unit went by vehicles to Drøbak. One company was also left behind and stayed in Son until 13 April.[5]

Shortly after 06:00 *Kondor* reported that taking Horten remained a challenge and that assistance was urgently needed. At 07:30, the situation still looked dire, and Thiele took stock. Except for a small group of soldiers landed in Horten, which was still in Norwegian hands, and those ashore at Son, none of the objectives in Oslofjord had been obtained. Confusion, indecisions, orders and counter-orders prevailed. 'The situation in Oslofjord does not look good,' he concluded with an ironic edge. The German ships were trapped in no-man's land between the Norwegian fortresses at the Drøbak Narrows and Outer Oslofjord. Norwegian aircraft and submarines were around, and British submarines might appear at any time. Only air support could make a difference and Thiele noted in his diary that unless the situation had been cleared by nightfall, he would have to take the larger ships out of the fjord.[6]

The torpedo boats and the R-boats would receive multiple orders and be given various tasks almost by the hour. Several aircraft alarms through the day, and at least one submarine alarm, added to the confusion. An air-raid alert sounded at 07:33 and a submarine alert at 07:45. *Lützow* opened fire with her 8.8-cm and 3.7-cm guns on both occasions. A counter-attack by Norwegian ships and British submarines could have created challenges for Group *Oldenburg* but, fortunately for them, it never materialised. At 08:18, Lange wrote in *Emden's* diary:

> As neither Drøbak nor Horten or Bolærne are in our hands, a critical situation has developed for the flotilla in between these strongpoints. It must be assumed that British submarines are drawn to the Oslofjord by Norwegian intelligence and the group has only limited room to manoeuvre between Horten and Filtvet […] The destruction of the

Rau VIII with *Rau VII* behind offloading at Son

batteries at Rauøy and Bolærne by gunfire from the ships is no option [as we need them for our own protection]. Intend to leave fjord at nightfall with all ships except the R-boats, *Rau VII* and *Rau VIII*, which shall remain at Horten.[7]

A little before 10:00, the first improvements in the situation appeared for the Germans. The fort at Rauøy was in German hands, Oscarsborg was being bombed, a white flag was reported over Horten, and Major von Poncet reported his *Gebirgsjäger* were ready to start moving towards Oslo in whatever trucks and buses could be commandeered. As soon as the rail line was secured, trains were also requisitioned to facilitate the transport. The railway had two stations about 4 km from Son harbour, Såner and Sonsveien but insufficient carriages so using the railway was less efficient than expected. The Norwegian forces in the area were mobilising further south under 1st Division with headquarters in Fredrikstad and did not intervene. *Lützow* and

Soldiers transferring from *Emden* to *Rau VII* to be landed at Son.

Emden remained at Son for the time being, fuelling the smaller ships and standing by to cover units on land that might need fire support. Thiele reported to the *Weserübung* staff in Hamburg that landings in Son and Moss had been completed and they were now heading for Horten to see if assistance was needed there. What had happened to *Blücher* was unclear. By lunchtime, the news from Oslo was that air-landed troops were taking control of the capital. Still, a signal from Marinegruppenkommando Ost to attempt a breakthrough during the renewed aerial bombardment was ignored as the presence of mines and the status of the torpedo battery were unclear.[8]

Between 16:00 and 16:30 several signals arrived at the *Weserübung* staff in Hamburg, summarising the situation. Marinegruppenkommando Ost reported that *Blücher* had definitely been sunk, and survivors were being take care of. Thiele was in command of the rest of the group and would take *Lützow* through to Oslo as soon as possible. Drøbak was in German hands. From Oslo, Pohlmann reported that the situation was 'normal' as far as the police and population were concerned. The anti-aircraft batteries had been taken over and public radio and phone traffic was about to be reopened – under German control. When kontreadmiral Smith-Johannsen came on board *Lützow* after Horten had been taken but before the attack on Kopås had started (*see below*), he refused to give any information on the defences in the Narrows but told Thiele that *Blücher* had gone down and that many survivors had come ashore on the islands and skerries in the fjord. At 18:32, Thiele told Lange that survivors from *Blücher* believed that the ship had been sunk by remote-controlled mines and that he had no intention of attempting to negotiate the Narrows until they were fully under German control. This decision was supported from Berlin. No German ships would appear in Oslo harbour on the 9th.[9]

Bombardment

At Oscarsborg, Eriksen had long since realised that the events of the early morning were more than a minor neutrality breach and that the intruders would likely return with a vengeance. Shortly before 08:00 kontreadmiral Smith-Johannsen called from Horten with information that he was surrendering and that the Admiral Staff had moved to Smestad. After that, Eriksen was unable to communicate with any higher authorities than general-major Jacob Hvinden Haug, the commander of 2nd Division at Akershus fortress. The sources are ambiguous as to when the two communicated but the general told Eriksen that Fornebu was lost, Oslo threatened and that several of the cities in the west had fallen. On asking Hvinden Haug to deploy troops to Hvitsten–Son to defend Oscarsborg's open flanks, Eriksen was told there were very few available, but it was agreed that a company of the King's Guard should come south by bus to handle the expected survivors from *Blücher* and try to prevent an advance towards Oslo, should infantry be landed on the eastern side of the fjord. Oberst Eriksen remained on his own.[10]

The first German bombers, 25 He 111s of III./KG 26, arrived over Oslo at dawn. Later 14 He 111s of KGr 100 also appeared. The primary role of these aircraft was to 'demonstrate' over the capital and intimidate the Norwegians into accepting the occupation. Passing up Oslofjord, they saw the burning *Blücher* beyond the Narrows and realised there would be no peaceful occupation. Indeed, some aircraft were ordered to attack Fornebu, Kjeller and Oscarsborg shortly after, while others were to bomb and strafe targets of opportunity. At 07:45 the first bombers arrived over Oscarsborg. From then on, the island was exposed to an almost continuous bombardment until dusk. Maximising the amount of fuel, the first aircraft had only a small load of 50-kg bombs. They were dropped from high altitude and those that did not fall into the sea, did little damage at the fort beyond breaking windows and creating a huge cloud of dust. After a while, however, new aircraft appeared with larger bombs attacking with higher precision from low altitude. To accommodate the request for support from Oslofjord, X Fliegerkorps in Hamburg eventually activated its reserve squadrons, KG 4 and the dive-bombers of I./StG 1. At 10:43, the first Heinkel He 111 of II./KG 4 took off from Fassberg and set course for Oslofjord loaded with 150-kg bombs. Some fifteen minutes later, 22 Ju 87 R-2 Stuka dive-bombers from I./StG 1 took off from Kiel-Holtenau; sixteen of them headed for Oscarsborg. The rest of KG 4 followed in batches from airfields in north-west Germany. At one time during the afternoon more than forty aircraft were over the fortress. The bombardment was intense, especially between 15:00 and 17:00, but a surprising number of bombs did not explode and even more dropped harmlessly into the sea.[11]

The dry moat and earthworks were made of ballast sand collected from sailing ships over a long period of time. When hit by bombs or shells, huge clouds of dust rising made the damage to the fort look dramatically worse than it was. Most of the personnel as well as officers' families, sought shelter in the deep tunnels and caverns below the fort. There they were physically safe but the bombardment, following a dramatic night, was a terrible experience. There were no casualties at Oscarsborg, either at this stage or later. Some bombs fell near the 28-cm guns, and these were sprayed with rock fragments and dirt, but suffered no harm. Other bombs fell inside the fortress where damage to buildings was extensive, even if the stone walls stood firm.

Eriksen wrote:

> It was obvious that the aircraft were aiming for the flagpole of the fortress, standing in isolation on an eight-metre-high platform. Several bombs fell nearby [...] but the flagpole and the flag remained unharmed. During the worst phase of the bombardment, when the whole island was covered in smoke and dust, the flag could be seen above the smoke. Most bombs created a disturbing, eerie sound when falling, but there was ample time to take shelter before they hit.[12]

From Kopås, the fort appeared to have been obliterated. Smoke and fire were everywhere and from each explosion earth, wood and pieces of rock were thrown about.

Løytnant Reidar Godø wrote:

Dust and smoke rising from Oscarsborg during the bombardment.

The first aircraft were observed at low altitude and well dispersed, coming from the south straight at the fortress. The first bombs were aimed at the main battery of Oscarsborg [...] Smoke and clouds of sand from the detonations made it difficult at times to see what was hit, giving an eerie impression. The regular pattern of the aircraft indicated they did not expect to be fired at by anti-aircraft guns. The bombs hit the area where we anticipated most of the people on the island had taken cover – just by the main battery. There were, however, various tunnels and cellars underground, built long before any aircraft had ever flown, that gave excellent shelter. The earthworks of the main fort made it difficult for us to see the effect of the bombing behind them.[13]

Most of the wooden buildings burned down or were damaged by blast, including Eriksen's residence at Nordre Kaholmen. At 09:00 the telephone line to Oscarsborg was severed by a bomb hit on the communication centre. No emergency connection by light or signal flag was set up and Oscarsborg was for all practical purposes isolated. To everyone's relief, Kopås, where there was hardly any shelter at all, was not bombed or shelled, merely strafed when the aircraft could find anything to aim at.

Inside one of the buildings at Oscarsborg which was hit during the German
bombing attacks.

There were two Bofors 40-mm guns and three machine guns at Seiersten
under the command of løytnant Hans Sollie. One of the 40-mm guns
malfunctioned after 22 rounds, the other fired until midday when the guns
were abandoned after intense harassment from several aircraft. The new
40-mm guns had a maximum effective range of 1,500 metres and the German
aircraft operating over Oscarsborg were out of range. Had these guns been
located at Oscarsborg or Kopås instead of at Seiersten, they might have been
vastly more effective. The equally new 7.92-mm AA machine guns of which
there were five at Kopås, four at Håøya and four on the roof of Oscarsborg
were ineffective. Hits were observed and some German crewmen, as well
as soldiers in transport aircraft on their way to Fornebu, may have been
wounded but the aircraft remained aloft in most cases.[14]

Around midday, a lull in the bombing occurred and Thiele decided to
move *Lützow* in for a long-range artillery bombardment. During the morning,
two of the three guns of turret *Anton* had been made operational and Thiele
expected gunfire would be at least as effective as the bombing. Twenty-seven
28-cm shells were fired from *Lützow* against Oscarsborg between 13:17 and
13:24. Both turrets were fired to port from around 10,700 metres and some of
the 15-cm guns were given permission to fire a salvo as well.

At Kopås, Enger was ready with his three guns and ample ammunition
but decided not to return fire due to the long range. *Lützow* was inside the

Deep craters from the bombing, but the large stone building at Oscarsborg
was still standing.

fire sector of the guns, but the orograph had a range of only 8,200 metres
and effective fire control from the command bunker would have been more
difficult. The orograph at Stjernåsen was in the vicinity of *Lützow* and could
have directed the fire but had lost its telephone connection to Kopås and
was therefore useless. There were long-range orographs with a range of over
12,000 metres at Håøya that would have been an excellent solution, but these
were not manned. In the confusion, the 'small and insignificant' German
freighter *Norden*, sent towards the Narrows to find out what had happened to
Blücher, was allowed to pass through unharmed.[15]

For the men at Kopås the artillery bombardment appeared more dangerous than the aircraft bombs, especially when *Emden* was seen to join in.
Løytnant Godø wrote:

> The formidable military force we were facing in the form of aircraft and
> ships was very intimidating [...] A landing, followed by an attack over
> land would expose our pathetic situation completely [...] The gun-crews
> were still outside the fort and the commander gave no indications that he
> intended to order the men back to the battery [...] Suddenly things started
> to happen aboard the ships. The guns of *Lützow* were elevated and turned
> in the direction of Oscarsborg. Smoke from one of the turrets, followed by
> a thunderous sound, showed us clearly that a salvo had been fired.[16]

A huge column of smoke rises above Oscarsborg.

Lützow fired ten 28-cm salvos and one 15-cm salvo. One of her aircraft was launched and gave active spotting support. The bracketing salvos landed ahead and behind the islands. One or two opening salvos splashed south of Søndre Kaholmen, and one north of Nordre Kaholmen. Then rapid salvos were fired for effect. Nordre Kaholmen, the rampart of the 28-cm battery, the old fortress and the large yard behind the fortress received hits, but dense clouds of dust from the rampart made observation impossible. Hence, it was difficult to adjust the fire and assess the damage. 'Gut ligende Salven' – 'Well-placed salvos' – was the German assessment. The men on *Lützow*'s bridge and foretop believed the bombardment was a success and Eriksen later described this part of the ordeal as the most frightening. The actual damage was limited, though, and to the surprise and relief of the Norwegians the shelling did not go on for long. *Lützow* turned away after less than ten minutes and her aircraft returned.[17]

Falkenhorst had contacted Boehm half an hour earlier asking him to find out from Marinegruppenkommando Ost in Kiel what was going on in the Narrows and if it was an option to send seaplanes with 'suitable officers' from Germany to Oslofjord to take control of events. Meanwhile, Boehm was told, Thiele and Lange should be instructed to let their ships support an advance of the troops landed at Son towards Drøbak over land. Boehm knew that *Blücher* had sunk and agreed with Falkenhorst that *Lützow* should head for Oslo as soon as possible rather than waste more time in the fjord. During the afternoon, orders came from Berlin that the *Führer* had decided not to send another large ship through the Narrows until the fortress was in German hands. As a compromise solution, a landing force to attack Kopås was prepared under the command of Oberleutnant zur see Wetjen with a mixed

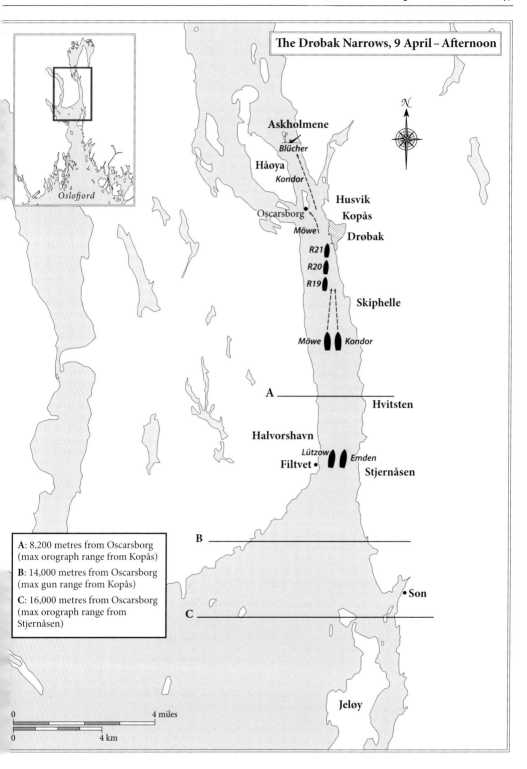

The Drøbak Narrows, 9 April – Afternoon

Oslofjord

Askholmene
Blücher
Håøya
Kondor
Husvik
Oscarsborg
Kopås
Möwe
Drøbak
R21
R20
R19
Skiphelle
Möwe *Kondor*

A —————————
Hvitsten

Halvorshavn
Lützow *Emden*
Filtvet •
Stjernåsen

B —————————

• Son

C —————————

Jeløy

A: 8,200 metres from Oscarsborg (max orograph range from Kopås)

B: 14,000 metres from Oscarsborg (max gun range from Kopås)

C: 16,000 metres from Oscarsborg (max orograph range from Stjernåsen)

0   4 miles

0   4 km

The forward turret of *Lützow*. The turret was damaged by the fire from Kopås and the central barrel was not used during the bombardment of Oscarsborg.

naval unit (*Marine Stosstrupp*) of mostly gunners from the cruisers and the torpedo boats, embarked on *R 19*, *R 20* and *R 21*. *Lützow* and *Emden* should provide heavy gun support, while *Möwe* and *Kondor* should move up the fjord to give close-range backing when the R-boats entered Drøbak and the rifle sections moved towards Kopås. *R 23* would follow with additional soldiers as soon as she was ready.[18] Around 16:30, the intensity of the bombing lessened. The reason for the pause was a new effort to break the stalemate.

Submission

After the 09:00 bomb hit that severed the phone connection to the mainland, anything that Eriksen and the Oscarsborg garrison knew about the situation in the rest of the country came from the public radio. Oslo appeared to be under German control while King Haakon and the government had left the capital. The day went by with the people on the two Kaholmens sheltering from the bombardment. Shortly after 16:30, German ships were again seen coming up the fjord. *Emden* halted north of Son, reporting a white flag over Oscarsborg, which was not correct. *Lützow* continued up the fjord, before halting and turning broadside on at about 9,000 metres. Neither ship opened fire as *Kondor*, *Möwe* and three R-boats – *R 19*, *R 20* and *R 21* – continued towards Drøbak. Enger considered the range to the cruisers too great and did not shoot. Later he claimed he would have if the cruisers had moved up the fjord to about 6,000–7,000 metres. There is no record of him trying to get in contact with Oscarsborg by light signal or boat at this stage. What happened next in the various parts of Oscarsborg Fortress has later been a source of controversy among many of the men who were there – as well as historians, investigators and authors who were not.[19]

During the lull, Eriksen risked an inspection of the battery. He found the guns covered by sand and grit from the explosions, but otherwise apparently in order. Firing the guns of the main fort would not be possible without extensive cleaning but he wished to attempt manning at least one gun. His officers advised against it, though. The men were exhausted, food had been scarce, and many were frightened by the continuous bombing and strafing. If the activity picked up, more strafing would undoubtedly follow. Reluctantly Eriksen had to accept that it would be virtually impossible to make the guns on Søndre Kaholmen operational without losses.[20]

Möwe, *Kondor* and the R-boats approached Drøbak hugging the eastern shore. *Lützow* and *Emden* remained off Filtvet, broadside on, apparently ready to open fire in support of the smaller ships if needed. Some distance up the fjord, the torpedo boats fell behind while the R-boats approached Drøbak harbour. The ships were clearly seen from Kopås. On Søndre Kaholmen Eriksen invited Anderssen, Sødem and Bexrud to express their views on what to do. Nobody came up with any firm idea. The lack of anti-aircraft guns and the main guns being in open positions made the situation extremely difficult and under the threat of continued bombing and strafing it would largely be a matter of extending negotiations as long as possible if the Germans landed at the fortress. Attempts at active resistance without proper defensive means would certainly lead

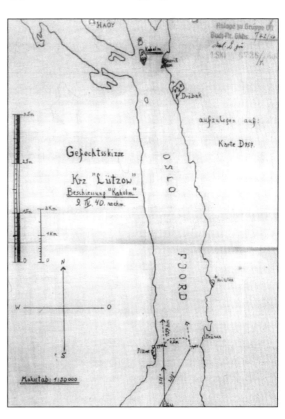

Map from *Lützow*'s War Diary showing her run-in and position when firing at Oscarsborg on the 9th.

Oscarsborg after the bombardment. The damage to parts of the fortress
is obvious and a few bomb-craters can be seen.

to pointless bloodshed. At 17:15, a signal was flashed across from Oscarsborg
to Kopås: 'Do not open fire; await further orders.' Eriksen later explained
that the signal was prompted by fear that Kopås should be shelled if the
battery fired. At this stage Eriksen had no information of any losses at Kopås
and feared the worst. There was no shelter on the landward side and he feared
there might have been casualties and that these might become substantial,
should the fort be bombarded. Eriksen did not consider the possibility that
the approaching ships were out to capture Drøbak and Kopås, he wrote some
years later. The batteries at Kopås were fully operational, but as no further
orders arrived, Enger, who did not know what was happening at the main
fort, was put in a dire situation. In his binoculars he could see that the main
guns at Kaholmen were not manned, but repeated attempts to make contact
by light signal failed. Kopås did not open fire.[21]

Landing from the R-boats with *Möwe* and *Kondor* in support, the German
soldiers secured the harbour, possibly reinforced by some of those landed at
Son. One platoon from *R 21* under Oberleutnant Wetjen headed for Husvik
in vehicles conveniently commandeered. There were no guards at the gate of
the fort and Enger, who was warned that the Germans were coming, walked
unarmed towards them. Wetjen saluted and demanded the surrender of the

Kopås batteries within twenty minutes. Otherwise the ships would open fire and the aircraft resume bombing. Oslo was in German hands according to Wetjen, who added that most of Norway was under German control and the Norwegian government had surrendered. Enger said he needed to confer with his commander at Oscarsborg and this might take some time as he had to use visual signalling due to severed telephone lines – if he could get in contact at all. Wetjen at first accepted this, but then changed his mind. Enger was kept under strict guard and not allowed to return to his bunker. Instead, he was told that there was no reason for him to hesitate. At 18:25 a signal was flashed from Kopås towards Oscarsborg. 'Kopås battery and Drøbak occupied by German forces.'

With hindsight it would have been possible to establish machine-gun positions at Drøbak harbour, even using the bunker that belonged to the searchlight at the harbour and establish guard posts covering the roads to Drøbak and Seiersten, and along the roads from Drøbak harbour to Kopås. The company-size force that Enger had at his disposal would not have lasted long, though, as they lacked transport and logistic support and would have had no possibility for tactical retreat.[22]

The 'destroyer' *Möwe* was now approaching. At 18:42, Kapitänleutnant Neuss received orders from *Lützow* to head towards Oscarsborg, showing a white flag, as a prelude to negotiations for surrender and, above all, to find out if the mine barrage really was there – '... *mit Parlamentärflagge Kaholm zur Übergabe auffordern ... und klären ob Minensperre tatsächlig liegt*'. *Möwe* was not flying the white flag when she approached Drøbak harbour about an hour earlier according to Enger, and the German war diaries confirm this. Now *Möwe* approached Søndre Kaholmen with a white pennant at the masthead. Sødem and Anderssen were sent out in a boat to talk. Kapitänleutnant Neuss demanded the two officers should surrender the fortress immediately, or an aerial bombardment would be initiated over Oslo and Drøbak. He had to accept that they could not agree to anything without their commander's consent, but they said Oscarsborg would not fire while negotiations were ongoing. The young Leutnant Döhler accompanied Sødem and Anderssen back to Oscarsborg around 19:30 with a petty officer and four seamen. Meanwhile, *Kondor* and three R-boats slipped through the Narrows to assist *Norden* in the search for survivors.[23]

At Oscarsborg, Eriksen dragged his feet, arguing over the formalities of the submission for several hours. With only the torpedo battery battle-ready and his poorly trained crews exhausted and shaken, Eriksen knew he would have to give in at some stage. The longer he could maintain the illusion of resistance, however, the better. He pointed out to Döhler that he had not shown an authorisation to negotiate and that he 'could come back tomorrow'

Two flags flying over Oscarsborg. The Norwegian flag remained for two weeks before being hauled down for the duration of the war. Today, that Norwegian flag is on display in the officers' mess at Oscarsborg.

with the proper documents. In the interim, Eriksen gave his word of honour not to fire. Surrender in the manner the Germans demanded was out of the question and the Norwegian flag would remain over the fort. Döhler went back to *Möwe* and a report was sent to Thiele on board *Lützow*. He accepted Eriksen's word of honour provided a small German guard could remain on the island to verify that the guns remained unmanned, and the Norwegian flag was taken down. That it was at sundown, but it was hoisted again next morning. The night passed with the status quo unchanged. The fort had not surrendered and there was no white flag, even if the weapons had been laid down and Döhler and his men remained on the island.[24]

On the morning of the 10th, the Norwegian flag was hoisted as normal, although the Germans, who had spent the night in the barracks, hoisted their own flag next to it. Thiele sent Kapitänleutnant Karl-Egloff von Schnurbein to conclude the procedures. Arriving at Oscarsborg shortly before 08:00, he arrogantly demanded information on all the defences in the fjord including forts, ships and minefields. Eriksen refused to give anything away, except that there were no mines in the Narrows and the rescue work could be stepped up. After further negotiations, Eriksen eventually accepted submission on the condition that ratings and civilians should be released as soon as possible while officers should remain in freedom at the fort until their status had been clarified. There was no written agreement and Eriksen did not sign a declaration of surrender, nor did he hoist a white flag. Later he claimed firmly

It's over for now. German soldiers enjoying a beer in peaceful Drøbak.

that the decision to act as he did was his own, taken without advice from anybody. Eriksen referred to the discussion with his officers in the afternoon of the 9th as 'an exchange of views', steadfastly rejecting the word 'council'.[25]

Most men and junior officers at Oscarsborg were released within a week, as were all civilians and families. The officers from the mainland forts had, according to the Germans, offered resistance and were kept in a POW camp near Oslo for several weeks. The Norwegian flag remained over Oscarsborg – next to the swastika – for some time. Kaptein Unneberg took down the flag for the last time on 21 April. He kept it safe throughout the German occupation, and it is now on display at Oscarsborg Fortress.[26]

Kapitänleutnant Bloomfield with some fifty men took control of Oscarsborg. During 14 April, they were reinforced by Kapitänleutnant Knape who came from Oslo on the steamer *Christiania*. Also aboard this ship was Oberleutnant Kühn with fifty men to take over the batteries on the Drøbak side. Admiral Boehm visited Oscarsborg on 26 April and some weeks later Großadmiral Raeder also inspected the fortress as part of his first visit to Norway. By then Eriksen had left the island.[27]

Chapter 13
War in Oslofjord
9–10 April

Horten – Group *Hameln*

The naval base at Karljohansvern had been the undisputed nerve-centre of the Norwegian Navy when Sweden was the main adversary at the turn of the century. When focus shifted towards the North Sea and the North during WW1, its importance diminished but in 1940 Karljohansvern, besides SDD1, still hosted the Naval Yard and training centre of the RNN as well as the naval aircraft factory and base for the 1st Air Wing.

On the evening of 8 April, the minesweepers *Otra* and *Rauma* were preparing to leave early next morning for western Norway to sweep the alleged British minefields off Bud and Stad. They were not ready to depart, however, and a large part of their crews had been given leave for the night. Also, the minelayer *Olav Tryggvason* was about to leave the yard, following a month-long overhaul, and return to SDD2 in Bergen. Only a few tests remained, and she was for all practical purposes fully operational. In preparation for completion and departure the next morning, she was moored at the main arsenal. Half of the crew had leave until midnight and officers with families in Horten until 07:00. The two decommissioned coast defence ships *Tordenskjold* and *Harald Haarfagre* were moored side-by-side at the quay

Commander of 1st Sea Defence District (SDD1), kontreadmiral Johannes Smith-Johannsen.

as accommodation ships for recruits, but except for a few AA guns, they were of no value to the defences of the naval base. The ancient hull of *Kong Oscar II* was also tied up at the base as an accommodation ship.

The first warning of the intruders came from outer Oslo-fjord to SDD1 at 23:10. Half an hour later, kontreadmiral Smith-Johannsen called kommandør-kaptein Briseid of *Olav Tryggvason* to his office. Briseid, who arrived at 00:10, was one of the most senior captains of the Norwegian Navy and highly respected. Now he was updated on the reports of intruders in the outer fjord, shots having been fired from Rauøy and Bolærne and the admiral's thoughts on

Trygve Sigurd Briseid of *Olav Tryggvason*.
The photo was taken after the war,
by which time he was an admiral.

the disposition of his meagre forces. Armed with four 12-cm, one 76-mm and two 20-mm guns, *Olav Tryggvason* was one of the most modern and powerful vessels in the Navy and she would have to be deployed in the defence of Horten irrespective of regular chains of command. The two officers agreed that *Olav Tryggvason* should cast off from the wharf and move to a buoy from where she could cover both the entry to Horten harbour and the Karljohans-vern docks. Smith-Johannsen later wrote he had given Briseid orders to 'open fire on unknown intruders'. Briseid later denied this, but Steen reports that Briseid confirmed Smith-Johannsen's version in a meeting with him in 1950.[1]

What was agreed was that *Olav Tryggvason*'s whaler should be sent to the half dozen merchant ships in Horten harbour ordering them to darken ship and turn off navigation lights. In addition, *Otra* and *Rauma* were to cast off as soon as they had sufficient crew on board and take positions outside the harbour, sending up red signal rockets if anything irregular was observed. As the two sweepers were not subordinated to the local command at Karljohans-vern, they had not received the order for 'increased preparedness' and both captains had allowed shore leave for some of their men. As related above, however, Smith-Johannsen later decided to send *Otra* out into the fjord, forgetting to inform Briseid of this change of plans.[2]

Just before midnight, the very limited AA defences of Horten and Karl-johansvern were ordered into position, as was the company of soldiers intended to secure the perimeter of the naval base. The AA company at Karljohansvern, under kaptein Johannessen, was equipped with four 7.5-cm Kongsberg Model 1916 guns and twelve 7.92-mm Colt machine guns. The company's assignment was exclusively an anti-air task and defence of the sea front was not included. Recruits and personnel aboard the accommodation ships were ordered ashore to safer quarters. They had no military training and Smith-Johannsen would not deploy them for combat. Electricity in the harbour and city was cut to enforce a complete black-out. The naval hospital, which also served as the civilian hospital for the area, was evacuated to Åsgårdstrand further down the coast. Civilians inside Karljohansvern were also evacuated, but the population of Horten itself was not, as the chief of police found this too complicated before daylight. The eight naval aircraft ordered to taxi on the surface to inside the Drøbak Narrows departed between 02:20 and 02:30. There was no time to load bombs onto the aircraft, even if this meant they would be unable to make any attacks later, until new bombs had been provided.

By 02:15 *Olav Tryggvason* was moored to a buoy in the inner harbour with all but a handful of the crew in place. Guns were manned and ready-use ammunition brought to the guns. Most of the men had been on board for almost a year and knew their ship well. Watches were set and kommandør-kaptein Briseid ordered coffee to be made. It would be a long night.

Otra departed on her reconnaissance mission at 02:30. She was followed shortly after by the submarine *B4* ordered to go inside the Narrows as she was unserviceable. Aboard *Olav Tryggvason* the departure of two ships was heard, but not seen in the misty darkness. Briseid assumed the ships were *Otra* and *Rauma* taking up station in the fjord as agreed. He was not told that *Otra* had been sent on a reconnaissance and that *Rauma* was still firing her boilers. Eventually, *Rauma* would not be ready until after 04:15 and thus not in the intended position outside the harbour when the German ships arrived.[3]

Kondor, *Albatros*, *R 17*, *R 21* and *Rau VIII* were detailed to capture Horten. The force commander was Kapitänleutnant Hans Wilcke, captain of *Kondor*. In most German accounts, Horten is listed as an important naval base and yard and expected to be heavily fortified, which in fact was not the case. The original German plan for the capture of Horten was to land the vanguard of the soldiers from the R-boats on the fjord-side of the Karljohansvern peninsula while the torpedo boats entered the harbour basin at dawn. The beach on the east side was too shallow, however, and the two R-boats grounded too far out. The landing was about to fall behind schedule and Wilcke, captain of *Kondor*, agreed with Kapitänleutnant (Ing.) Erich Grundmann that they would have

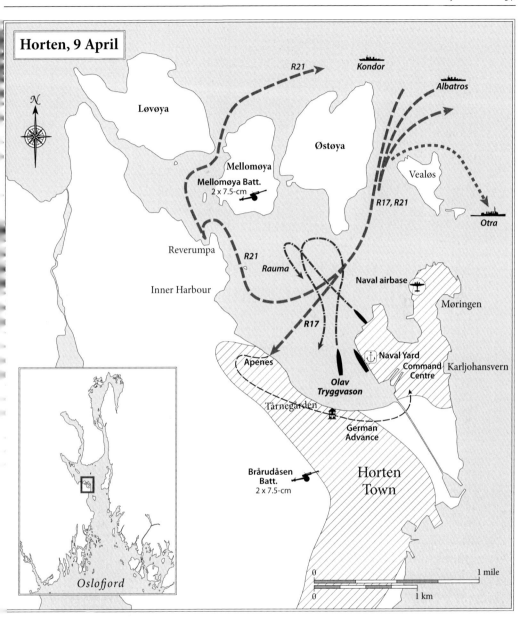

to risk a direct approach into the harbour. If they met opposition, the torpedo boats would lend gun support from the outside and go inside if necessary. Grundmann was *Flotteningenieur*, Fleet Engineer, for the R-boat flotilla but on this occasion, he was senior officer of the two R-boats and as such had the lead of the R-boats.[4]

Two attack groups, totalling some 140 men under Oberleutnant Kurt Budäus, were on board *R 17* and *R 21*. The landing force had one platoon

Horten in the late 1930s.
The Karljohansvern naval base is to
the right (east) of the central canal.

from 3. and one platoon from 4./IR 307, heavily armed with a flame thrower and several machine guns. In addition, the force included a 'Sonderkommando *Emden*' – two petty officers and ten seamen under Kapitänleutnant Werner Kimmerling – detailed from *Emden* to *R 17*, to ensure that all guns, vessels and other enemy equipment were temporarily made unserviceable, without having to destroy them. Once the harbour was under control Kimmerling was to cross the fjord in *R 17* to the expected (but non-existent) torpedo battery and submarine base at Jeløy to confirm neither was any threat to the invasion force. *Albatros* had two platoons from 3./IR 307 aboard and *Kondor* had an infantry company and men from the naval artillery. *Rau VIII* had already taken aboard a group of soldiers from *Kondor,* referred to as a *Stoßtrupp* – an attack unit. To have maximum freedom of operation, in case support was needed, Wilcke now decided to transfer all soldiers embarked on *Kondor* to *Rau VIII*.[5]

The entry beacons could be sighted even though the lights were off and at 04:35, *R 17* ran through Vealøsgapet, the entrance to Horten harbour, at high speed with *R 21* right behind. The decks of the two boats were packed, as in addition to the attack and support forces, there were naval gunners to operate the captured defensive batteries, administration personnel to look after the base and city, and communication experts to take control of the local radio station. Both boats were challenged by a light signal from the post at Østøya and illuminated by searchlights from both *Rauma* and *Olav Tryggvason*, but no shots were fired by either side at first.[6]

Rauma had finally cast off just before 04:30. Minutes later, two dark shadows were observed coming through Vealøsgapet and løytnant Ingolf Winsnes decided to check this out. Why he had not left and taken station outside as ordered, despite his ship being ready for some time, is unclear. Most likely he decided to wait for more of his liberty men to arrive as fewer than twenty were yet on board. On the bridge of *Olav Tryggvason*, *Rauma's* presence in the harbour was registered when she cast off, but before anything could be clarified, unknown vessels were reported coming through Vealøsgapet. Briseid ran towards the foredeck where his First Officer, kaptein Bernt Dingsør, and the Gunnery Officer, kaptein Hartvig Lowzow, were

Olav Tryggvason

trying to identify the incoming ships. They still believed *Otra* was patrolling outside as they had been told, and no signal rockets had been seen. The intruders were fast but did not have an obvious military look to them; they were partly obscured by the misty backdrop of the islands but their decks were seen to be crowded. Briseid was indecisive and called for a blast from the ship's whistle followed by a blank warning shot. When this had no effect, he ordered a live warning shot in front of the intruders. At this point, *R 17* passed close in front of *Olav Tryggvason* and was recognised as German by the swastika flying on her mast. Lowzow took control of the guns while Briseid headed for the bridge. It was 04:45 and time to open fire in earnest. *Olav Tryggvason* was backed off her moorings and moved into the harbour basin. Only now did *Otra*'s report 'Enemy off Karljohansvern' arrive at the bridge. It had been sent in code and by the time it had been forwarded to *Olav Tryggvason* and decoded, events were already unfolding.[7]

Sighting the jetties at Apenes ahead to port, Grundmann ordered *R 17* to steer for them and the landing force to prepare for disembarkation while *R 21* turned sharply to starboard for the headland at Reverumpa. With the bow of *R 17* scraping along the pier at Apenes, Budäus, Kimmerling and some soldiers jumped ashore, surprising the guards of the AA machine guns positioned there. The guns were hurriedly kicked into the water while the men were allowed to escape. The rest of the soldiers disembarked with their equipment just as the first shell from *Olav Tryggvason* slammed into *R 17* amidships. Stabsobersteuermann Arthur Godenau, commander of *R 17*, called for help from the torpedo boats and backed away from the pier as soon as the last soldier was off, 20-mm cannons blazing. Before he had come far, though, two more shells hit – one forward, below the bridge, and one in the engine-room. Fires from the latter spread rapidly and the doomed R-boat drifted helplessly in the harbour. At 05:20, the flames reached the depth charges on the after deck and *R 17* blew up with a mighty explosion. By then, Godenau, Grundmann and most of the men had abandoned ship. Only two men, both from the engine room, were killed from the crew of *R 17* and one man seriously wounded on deck. Onshore, however, there were several casualties among the soldiers and numerous buildings were on fire.[8]

With *R 17* duly ablaze, Briseid and Lowzow turned their attention to *R 21*. *Olav Tryggvason*'s electrical fire-control system had broken down after a few shots, and the guns had to be operated manually. *R 21* fired back with her two 20-mm guns, injuring two men that had to be taken below and replaced, while the R-boat vanished behind Reverumpa without being hit. When *R 21* escaped from *Olav Tryggvason*'s line of fire, *Rauma* gave chase, opening up with her 76-mm gun and machine guns. The R-boat was hit several times and in reply Leutnant Pommer-Esche's gunners turned their guns onto the new adversary. Fire raked the forepart of *Rauma,* and five men were wounded,

R 17 burning fiercely after being hit from *Olav Tryggvason*.

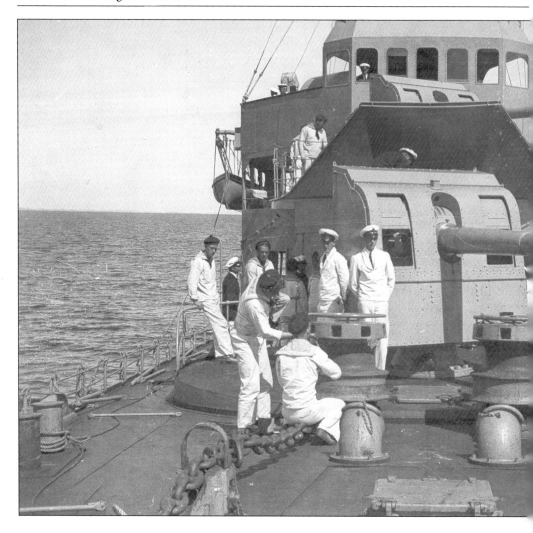

one seriously.[9] Also the bridge was hit. Løytnant Winsnes was mortally wounded, and First Officer Glattre and helmsman Peder Aalvik injured. Below deck, steam pipes were severed, reducing the pressure on the boilers and the minesweeper was temporarily out of control. Helmsman Aalvik, though wounded, steered back towards the pier as best he could to try to save the captain's life, but it was too late. Winsnes died after having been brought ashore. Behind Reverumpa, *R 21* headed for shore where she was grounded on the sandy beach, listing heavily. Some of the soldiers jumped into the water and waded ashore – others inflated a rubber dinghy. The crew of the R-boat took care of the wounded and started to get their ship afloat again. Because they had been landed quite some distance away these soldiers did not reach Karljohansvern until it was all over.[10]

The forward 12-cm guns of *Olav Tryggvason*. These, and the pair mounted at the stern, were centrally controlled and gave her the firepower of many contemporary destroyers

Wilcke's intention was that *Albatros* should be ready to follow the two R-boats into the harbour while *Kondor*, still busy transferring the remaining soldiers onto *Rau VIII*, provided fire support from outside. Within minutes, a red signal rocket from land signified trouble for the R-boats and *Albatros* was ordered into the harbour through Vealøsgapet. Halfway in, however, *Albatros* was met by precise fire from *Olav Tryggvason* as well as machine-gun fire from land. The torpedo boat was straddled repeatedly, but not hit. *Albatros* fired back from her forward gun, which was the only one that could bear, but the shots went wide. Several of *Albatros'* crew were wounded and Strelow decided this was a bit more than he was prepared for. He ordered 'full astern', backing behind Østøya, while *Olav Tryggvason* remained inside the harbour. Safely back on the outside, Strelow suggested that as soon as *Kondor* had off-loaded the soldiers, both torpedo boats should pass close by the entrance, firing full broadsides into the harbour. Wilcke fired a few test shots into the harbour, but it was difficult to see where the shells fell, and he soon discontinued. Taking the soldiers back on board *Kondor*, he called for help from *Lützow*. Thiele, however, decided that *Kondor* and *Rau VIII* should come to Sonsbukta to offload their soldiers there instead, help land troops from *Lützow* and *Emden* and act as anti-submarine guard. For now, the German soldiers in Horten would have to manage on their own, with support only from *Albatros*. Later, *Albatros* was also ordered to offload her remaining soldiers at Son.

Meanwhile, *Albatros* commenced an indiscriminate fire into the harbour; partly firing blind over the island and partly through the sounds. Shells fell randomly over Karljohansvern and the yards. Venturing too close during one

The fire at Apenes spread from *R 17* to the wooden quay which was also destroyed.

of her firing-runs around 06:30, *Albatros* took hits from a well-placed salvo from *Olav Tryggvason*. One of the shells hit near the waterline, killing one soldier and wounding another three, one of whom later died. *Olav Tryggvason* was not hit, but shrapnel sprayed her hull on a couple of occasions. The crew from *Pol III,* still aboard *Albatros,* could feel the hits and saw several wounded being brought below.[11]

Once *R 21* had completed the disembarkation of the troops and come off the ground, Leutnant Pommer-Esche headed for safety between the islands to the north. As he had reckoned, *Olav Tryggvason* could not follow, but the R-boat was hit twice before she was safe. Both shells went through the light hull without exploding and though the damage was serious, it was largely above deck. Engines and steering were not affected and no water came in so *R 21* was still operational. By now, Kapitänleutnant Strelow had had enough and pulled *Albatros* away towards the safety of the cruisers, followed by *R 21.*[12]

With the attention of *Olav Tryggvason* drawn away from the soldiers landed at Apenes, they regrouped and attended to their dead and wounded. The survivors from *R 17* joined the landing party, arming themselves with weapons from the casualties. Most of the equipment, including several machine guns, ammunition and radios had been lost. Eventually, some seventy men moved out from Apenes in the direction of Karljohansvern under the command of Grundmann and Budäus; Kimmerling and his marines made up the rear; 9 dead and 5 severely wounded were left behind with some medical personnel. Around 07:00 *Emden* took station off Horten, but she did not open fire and things remained quiet. Luckily for the Germans, none of the three old coast batteries at Karljohansvern or the fort at Vealøs had modern guns. Only Brårudåsen battery and Mellomøya had two modern 7.5-cm guns each as main weapons as part of the AA company. But the commanders had no authority to engage sea targets, only air threats.[13]

Every civilian in Horten had been woken by the gunfire and the explosion of *R17* and the streets were filled with confused and scared people, including unarmed soldiers and seamen. Reaching the first group of houses, the Germans headed for Tårnegården, a rather large house, offering good defensive positions and a view towards the harbour and Karljohansvern. From there, they attempted to reach the office of Smith-Johannsen by telephone without success. Meanwhile, the chief of police had been alerted to the presence of Germans in Tårnegården and came in his car to find out what was going on. He was brusquely pushed back into the car and Grundmann and Oberleutnant Körner jumped in and ordered him to drive to Karljohansvern. A white handkerchief was held out the window. The car arrived at the gate shortly before 07:00. In the meantime, telephone connection with the admiral's office had been established from Tårnegården and Budäus, who remained at the house with his soldiers, informed Smith-Johannsen that German officers were on their way to meet him and conclude the negotiations for ceasefire and surrender.[14]

Unknown to the Germans, two infantry platoons guarding Karljohansvern had been notified of their presence in Tårnegården and had moved in, to attack. Just as they were getting ready, though, the police car was seen leaving the house with a flag of truce and kaptein Fuglerud called off the assault, assuming the Germans were surrendering. At Karljohansvern, Grundmann and Körner were met at the gate of the yard by the chief of staff, kommandør-kaptein Paul Münster, who called kontreadmiral Smith-Johannsen. Brazenly, Grundmann stated he represented the commander of the German forces in Oslofjord and that they had come to 'help protect Norwegian neutrality from British attack'. He demanded that resistance cease immediately, or Karljohansvern and Horten would be destroyed by naval and aerial bombardment. The bombardment would start at 09:00, unless a radio signal verifying a Norwegian surrender called it off. He added that a strong German force was in position on the other side of the harbour and any resistance would be futile. Except for the fact that German aircraft had orders to start a bombardment of Horten at 09:00, unless the town had been captured, the rest was pure deception.[15]

Smith-Johannsen replied that he had no knowledge of a Norwegian request for help. Anyway, he was not authorised to make such decisions on his own and needed to consult his superiors in Oslo. Grundmann gave him fifteen minutes and continued his bluff by calling Budäus at Tårnegården from the gate and, while making sure he was duly overheard, asked him to 'hold back the bombardment as negotiations were ongoing'. Telephoning the Admiral Staff turned out to be difficult, as by this time they had left their offices in Oslo. Eventually, the call got through, but admiral Diesen was less than helpful, merely authorising Smith-Johanssen to make the decisions he considered appropriate but stressed that only Karljohansvern should be included in a ceasefire, no other forces. Smith-Johannsen had no reason to doubt Grundmann's insistence that Horten would be bombed unless he surrendered. Only a small part of the population had been evacuated and casualties would inevitably be high. There were no air defences to speak of and *Olav Tryggvason* alone could do little against several German cruisers. Smith-Johannsen decided he had little choice and called Grundmann to his office to say he was willing to surrender Karljohansvern and its forces. Any other ship or fort in the Oslofjord region would have to decide independently what to do. This was accepted and a written statement (in poor Norwegian) was signed at 07:35. Grundmann had drafted the statement in a notebook and it was typed on the spot.

Five minutes later a white flag was hoisted over Karljohansvern, and Smith-Johannsen gave the order to cease fire. The most critical command level of the RNN in eastern Norway had been neutralised through a German bluff. Kapitänleutnant Grundmann underlined that in his opinion there was no state of war between Germany and Norway and the measures taken were largely to avoid any complications or outbreak of hostilities. Thus, the ships in the harbour could keep their Norwegian flags – for the time being – as long as they were made temporarily inoperable and key parts removed from guns and radios. Most officers and men were free to move as they wished within Horten and Karljohansvern. German aircraft, not realising that Horten had been taken, dropped a dozen bombs and strafed some of the machine gun positions before a German flag could be hoisted. Four Norwegians and one German were killed, and ten others wounded. These bombs showed the seriousness of the situation, however, and the determination of the German attackers, ensuring that Norwegian soldiers or civilians did not attempt to re-take control over the situation.[16]

Smith-Johannsen immediately called Eriksen at Oscarsborg in person to make him aware of what was happening and let him know that contact with SDD1 would be severed. At the same time kommandørkaptein Tandberg-Hanssen of YOSA called Horten for a confirmation that the information

The 20-mm shells from *R 21* did great damage to the unarmoured
bridge-structure of *Rauma*.

from the staff in Horten of a cease-fire was correct. As the admiral's telephone
was busy, he was connected to acting chief of staff kaptein Knut Blich.
The two officers discussed the situation and concluded that the surrender
included the forts and ships in outer Oslofjord as well. After both telephone
conversations had been concluded, Blich repeated this to the admiral who
heatedly responded he had misunderstood and asked to be re-connected with
Tandberg-Hanssen to correct the mistake. This he was but the connection
took some minutes, and it was past 08:00 before YOSA was given the correct
information. In the meantime, Tandberg-Hanssen had issued orders for the
ships and forts of his sector to terminate resistance and, before these could be
recalled, most of the guardships were heading back to base and Rauøy Fort
had surrendered.[17]

At 08:00 *Olav Tryggvason* moored, flying a white tablecloth at the main
mast after having been ordered to do so by a courier from Smith-Johannsen.
Reports later had it that Briseid was so angered by this order 'his swearing

was heard all over the yard'. Thirty-five 20-mm hits from *R 21* were counted in the superstructure, but there was no serious damage to the ship and, except for the two gunners wounded early in the fight, there were no casualties. Fifty-five 12-cm shells had been expended. Except by wasting time in the first phase by firing warning shots, *Olav Tryggvason* and her crew had defended Horten well. *R 17* had been destroyed, *R 21* damaged and *Albatros* and *Kondor* fended off through accurate fire. Kimmerling and his men from *Emden* took command of the Norwegian minesweeper.[18]

Further German soldiers were landed at Karljohansvern from *R 22* and *R 23* later in the morning of the 9th and those from *R 21* eventually reached the town. *Albatros* and *R 21* were sent to the supposed submarine base at Tronvik on Jeløy to render the torpedo-batteries and guns believed to be there harmless and secure the radio station. A basic torpedo-test facility was all that was actually there, but the two torpedo-tubes, a generator and the radio at the control station were destroyed for good measure. Around 16:00 *Albatros* returned and dropped anchor in Horten harbour on orders from Thiele, to support the troops ashore. Nothing happened though and during the 10th, the Norwegian lower ranks were allowed to depart except those needed for the running of the base and yard, while the officers were encouraged to remain where they were and go about their business as usual. The friendly conditions lasted a few days until it was clear that Norwegian opposition was being organised.

After offloading at Son with the help of *Rau VII* and *Rau VIII*, Thiele took *Lützow* to Horten. The initial reports had included disturbing reports of cruisers taking part in the defence, and he needed to see for himself that the situation was under control. To his relief he found the town and naval base secure. The German soldiers still numbered only some 200 and a landing-party was disembarked to give support until reinforcements could be sent from Oslo.[19]

Kontreadmiral Smith-Johannsen was asked to come aboard *Lützow* for a 'conference'. He was picked up in Horten by *R 18* around 16:20 and brought to Filtvet where the two cruisers were on station, covering the ongoing operation against Kopås fort. Taken to Thiele's cabin, the admiral was greeted politely, and Thiele expressed his regrets that Germany had been compelled to invade the country. The Norwegian defences in Oslofjord had fought bravely he said, but as Narvik, Trondheim, Bergen, Stavanger and Kristiansand were all in German hands, it was time to give up and Smith-Johannsen was asked to order Oscarsborg to surrender to avoid further bloodshed. This, Smith-Johannsen declined, holding that after his surrender at Horten, the fort was no longer under his command. Thiele then urged the admiral to use his influence with the government for a general capitulation of all Norwegian forces. Somewhat bemused, Smith-Johannsen answered that unfortunately, he did not have that kind of influence with the government and as he had no knowledge of the situation in other parts of the country, he could not be expected to consider such a request. Asked whether there were further minefields in the Narrows, Smith-Johannsen refused to reply at all, and after about an hour Thiele gave up. The admiral was politely taken back to the R-boat, which returned him to Horten.[20]

Rauøy

Having cast off from *Emden* around 01:00 on the 9th, *R 20* and *R 24* headed for Rauøy with some ninety men from 1./IR 307 aboard under the command of Hauptmann Menk. The boats got lost in the fog and at the time they were supposed to have landed, an officer was sent ashore at Engelsviken to find out where they were – and where to find Rauøy. He came back with directions after talking to some locals and they proceeded, trusting their luck. By the time they approached Rauøy, the fog had started to lift. The guns of the fort turned in their direction and there was no doubt they had been sighted, even if not fired on. Leutnant Jaeger of *R 20* reckoned it would be possible to land the troops behind a headland north of the fort and eased his boat into the cove until the bow touched the bottom. The soldiers scrambled ashore in dinghies while *R 24* continued to try to find a second landing-site.

Major Enger at Rauøy knew it was not over when the unknown ships vanished northward in the fog just before midnight on the 8th. Further ships would likely follow and sooner or later those that had just passed might come back. An attack on the fort itself was possible and he ordered his men to remain at their guns while further ammunition was brought forward. Double-

R 20.

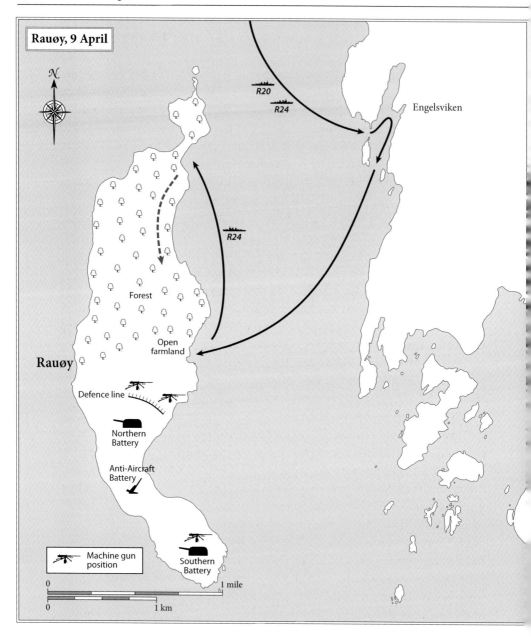

manning was arranged for all sentry posts and lookouts and the fifteen infantrymen under løytnant Andresen were told to remain vigilant. Around 04:00, Enger received a phone call from the mainland with information that a German officer had been ashore asking for directions to Rauøy. The terrain of the southern part of the island was open with sparse vegetation and easy to control from the Norwegian positions Hence, it was obvious that any landings had to take place north of the northern battery. Further infantry support was requested from the infantry regiment in Fredrikstad, but events developed too fast for this to arrive.

At 05:30, R 20 and R 24 were seen heading towards the bay behind the headland north-east of the northern battery. The cove could not be seen from the Norwegian positions, but while R 20 landed her soldiers, R 24 pulled back a little and came into the line of sight of the battery, which immediately opened fire, so that R 24 headed north behind a thick smokescreen. Between where the Germans landed from R 20 and the northern battery there was open farmland with some houses, but no Norwegian troops or military positions further north. Kaptein Eugen Sørlie at the northern battery ordered the crew of gun no. 1 forward with their rifles to a position at the battery perimeter while gun no. 2, which was the only one with an applicable firing sector, was ordered to open fire with HE shells. Sørlie positioned himself at gun no. 2, adjusting the sights himself, while løytnant Eriksen was sent forward to observe and give adjustments. The improvisations worked well. A large number of HE shells were fired at the intruders. The disembarking German soldiers were pinned down and had to spread out and take cover to limit their casualties. Leutnant zur See Jaeger backed R 20 off behind a smokescreen as soon as the last soldier was in the dinghy. Sørlie let his gun follow the boat, but no hits were scored, and she suffered only splinter damage. Return fire from the R-boat's 20-mm guns was ineffective.

Disappearing in the fog, R 20 set course northwards to join R 24, which meanwhile had landed her soldiers without any resistance on the northern part of the island. Sørlie turned the fire of his gun back to the beachhead. It is unclear if the soldiers from R 24 linked up with those landed from R 20, still under fire from the Norwegian positions. As the R-boats by now had pulled back, hiding to the north of the island, the only option for the Germans was to attack the Norwegian positions.[21] However, Enger had ordered every available man on the island, including most of the crew from the southern battery, to reinforce the defensive line on the high ground. About 100 men were in place by around 06:15 including some with Colt machine guns which were deployed further north and to the east. The Norwegian gunners were likely too inexperienced as infantry to mount a rapid counter-attack, but the Germans could not advance either and were suffering a steady attrition of their forces as cover was limited. Two Norwegian soldiers, korporal Ragnar Kongsgaard and menig Harald Johansen, lost their lives during the fighting, and some were lightly wounded. The German casualties are unknown but were most likely substantial.[22]

During the battle, the fort's 40-mm AA guns opened up on an approaching German aircraft. No hits were observed, but it later crashed north of Rauøy killing its crew. The bodies were recovered from the sea and buried at Rauøy on the 10th. The AA guns were well positioned between the two batteries.

Just before 08:00, Enger and Sørlie considered they had a firm upper hand, controlling the situation. Just then, a signal came from oberstløytnant Notland, 'Orders from Outer Oslofjord SDD. Stop all hostilities, cease firing.' Angered, Enger asked for the order to be verified, which it was, despite being a misunderstanding. Enger had no choice but to instruct his soldiers to cease fire. The Germans kept shooting, however, despite several attempts to shout to them that the Norwegians had been ordered to cease fire. No white flag could be found, but one of the soldiers had a reasonably clean shirt, which was hosted on a pole, after which the German fire died down.[23]

Hauptmann Menk, somewhat perplexed at the development, straightened his uniform and walked across to the Norwegian lines where he was met by kaptein Gullichsen and three men who told him the fort commander would like to see him. The still surprised Menk was taken to see Enger, who waited at the northern battery. Menk acted very politely towards Enger but expressed distress at being met by so much opposition when the German soldiers 'had come to help defend Norwegian neutrality'. Now, he demanded that the fort should be surrendered intact. All NCOs and soldiers should hand in their weapons and uniforms after which they were free to go home. The officers should remain and await further orders. After another conference with Notland, this was accepted. Enger was given some time to sort out 'personal matters', which he used to burn files and destroy maps and codebooks. During this, a German aircraft appeared, started strafing and dropped a bomb that did not explode. Desperate signalling from the German soldiers quickly halted the attack. In the afternoon, Enger and his officers were taken to Horten by *R 20* and *R 24* while German naval gunners occupied Rauøy. Enger later asserted that his soldiers could have maintained their opposition for a considerable time and were even capable of defeating the landing force altogether. An extensive bombing attack would have been disastrous, though, as there was only limited shelter on the island, and the outcome was inevitable as long as German air and sea superiority was total.[24]

Bolærne

Completing the embarkation of two reinforced platoons from 2./IR 307 onto *R 22* and *R 23* from *Emden*, Stabsobersteuermann Karl Rixecker set course for Bolærne around 01:00 on the 9th. The dousing of the lights in the fjord made navigation difficult in the dense fog. Shortly after 04:00, anchors were dropped off a strandline Rixecker hoped was the right one. He was far from sure, however, and decided to send a small reconnaissance force ashore to try to ascertain that they could reach Bolærne fort from the landing site.

A2 and *R 21* on 14 April. The Norwegian submarine has been towed in to Melsomvik.

Unknown to the Germans, they were off Vallø, which had no connection to Bolærne. Some twenty soldiers were disembarked to reconnoitre as dawn approached and the fog started to lift. Just as the last man jumped into the dinghy, a lookout sighted a submarine through the haze. Both R-boats raised anchor and turned towards the submarine, which started to dive. Orders were given to prepare the depth charges.

Kaptein Thorvald Fjeldstad, commander of the submarine division at Teie and captain of the submarine *A2*, had received orders from the naval staff in Oslo in the small hours of the 9th to deploy his boats at their designated operational areas in the fjord at dawn and prepare for battle. Before he set out at 04:00, additional signals confirmed that the intruders were most likely German and, as they were inside Oslo *krigshavn*, should be attacked on sight. *A3* and *A4* headed south from Teie while *A2* headed north towards a position north of the Bolærne–Rauøy line. The three submarines were of pre-WW1 vintage and considered at least as dangerous to their own crews as to anything that might venture in front of their torpedo tubes.

Entering the fjord around 05:00 kaptein Fjeldstad sighted two unknown vessels close to Vallø. Considering them too small for a torpedo he decided to dive to avoid them. The last Fjeldstad saw in the periscope when diving was both vessels approaching at high speed, obviously attacking. The R-boats were fast and *A2* was only at 25 metres when they passed overhead, dropping six or seven depth charges. Water started leaking in and the submarine was forced upwards by the explosions. The R-boats opened fire and a hail of 20-mm projectiles slammed into the conning tower as it broke surface, damaging the periscope. *A2* dived again, this time so fast that the hull touched bottom at 35 metres. The depth-charging continued, and water poured into the boat at an alarming rate. To avoid total loss, Fjeldstad decided to surface and surrender. *R 23* immediately came alongside, and the shaken crew were taken aboard at gunpoint and locked below deck. A German ensign was hoisted on *A2*, but she was left drifting in the fjord. *A3* and *A4* remained submerged all day due to 'intense aircraft activity' and returned to Teie at nightfall, having achieved nothing. The Military Investigation Committee of 1946 found the conduct of Captains Bruusgaard and Haga at fault and recommended that they were charged with neglect of duty.[25]

Having finished with *A2*, Stabsobersteuermann Rixecker realised that he could not reach Bolærne from Vallø and headed south, leaving the landed soldiers behind for the time being. On the way, the R-boats ran into the two guardships, *Oter I* and *Skudd I*, which had been sent from Tønsberg to look for them. After a few inconclusive shots, the Norwegian vessels turned away while *R 22* and *R 23* hid behind a smokescreen. The R-boats, approaching from the north, were observed from Bolærne. It was not possible to use the orographs in the command bunker as they were placed to cover the sector to the south-east and south, and not north and north-east. The battery commander, kaptein Telle, went outside and was ready to control the fire by use of his binoculars. Firing without rangefinder would be challenging but quite possible. Telle held his fire until the boats were only 1,500–2,000 metres away and when he opened up, the 15-cm shells fell close. Rixecker ordered a zigzag, but the Norwegian gunners followed skilfully. There was no way the lightly armed R-boats could fight back with any hope of success and Rixecker decided to turn back. Kaptein Fjeldstad was asked to go ashore to negotiate a ceasefire but refused and was locked up again. Heading back to Horten for help, the R-boats again passed the guardships at Vallø, which had been reinforced by *Ramoen* and *Treff*. A few shots were exchanged but, as before, the R-boats sped off behind a smokescreen. The soldiers aboard *R 22* and *R 23* were eventually landed at Åsgårdstrand to support the meagre forces at

Horten from the south. Kapitän Thiele asked the Luftwaffe to attack Bolærne. The bombing commenced in the afternoon, and everybody not strictly needed outside gathered in the tunnel just north of the 15-cm battery. Apart from chasing the gunners into shelter, the aircraft inflicted little damage. Through the following night, everything remained quiet.[26]

At 07:25 on the morning of the 10th Bolærne fired at the German transport *Curityba* entering the fjord from the south. She was originally on her way to Bergen with ammunition, petrol and Luftwaffe personnel, but had run aground north of Helsingborg on the 7th and was given assistance from Swedish tugs. SKL feared the episode should disclose the whole operation, but the master managed to hide her cargo and destination and the event seems to have hardly been registered. Once off the ground, *Curityba* was ordered to Oslo. This was how she came to be fired at on the morning of the 10th; she turned away promptly to seek protection from the trawlers of 7. Vorpostenflottille, lingering further south.[27]

Albatros hard aground and obviously badly damaged.

Major Hans Christian Ringe, former commander of Bolærne fort,
climbs onto *Rau VII* to surrender Bolærne.

Two hours later, *Kondor* was sighted coming down the eastern side of
the fjord in company with *Rau VII and Rau VIII*. After passing some minor
islands north of Rauøy, *Rau VII* and *Rau VIII* turned starboard across the
fjord, towards Bolærne to land their troops. *Kondor* remained on the eastern
side covering the boats from a distance. Again, kaptein Telle waited and only
opened fire when the Germans were about 1,000–1,500 metres from the shore.
The fire was fairly precise, and the two boats turned away. Telle then lifted his
aim towards *Kondor* which was at a range of about 9,000 metres. Telle again
controlled the shooting using his binoculars by shouted orders to the senior
officer in the command bunker. Once more, the fire was effective enough
to make *Kondor* turn around and zigzag away to the north-east. At the last
shot from Bolærne on *Kondor* she was some 10,000 metres away. During the
ten-minute artillery duel, *Kondor* fired fifteen salvos back, the last at some
12,000 metres. The torpedo boat sought shelter behind Bastøy, out of sight
and range of the Norwegian guns. The Germans familiarising themselves
with the newly captured guns at Rauøy also opened fire on Bolærne, but the
shells went wide, doing no harm.

Bolærne effectively controlled the traffic at the mouth of the Oslofjord.
The reports of Bolærne still being under Norwegian control and firing at

German ships unnerved the invaders. The Drøbak Narrows would still be closed for a few hours. Oscarsborg had not given up yet and the mouth of Oslofjord was obviously far from safe.[28]

Albatros received orders from Thiele to leave Horten, head for the mouth of Oslofjord, join up with the unfortunate transport *Curityba* and escort her past the aggressive guns at Bolærne. At the same time Kapitänleutnant Strelow should get in touch with the Germans landed at Rauøy and find out what was going on there. To avoid similar attention to *Kondor*'s recent experience, Strelow decided to take *Albatros* east of Rauøy. This succeeded well and the torpedo boat was not fired at while landing a small group of seamen there. Having completed this, Strelow continued south towards *Curityba* along the east side of the fjord at high speed. Unknown to him and the other men on the bridge of the torpedo boat, by taking a course inside the two Søster islands they were heading for the Gyren shoal where a sea mark had been broken off by the ice a few weeks earlier. Around 13:50, while at over 20 knots, they saw breakers ahead. Strelow ordered five knots, but before this took effect, *Albatros* hit the rock hard.[29]

Almost running right over the shoal, she settled with her stern well above water, heeling sharply. At least one bunker tank was opened to the sea while oil and water poured into the turbine and boiler rooms. The boilers were hastily shut down and the rooms evacuated. Parts of the electrical system fell

Rau VII aground.

Bolærne, spring 1940. German gunners have taken over.
The photo shows clearly the use of separate shells and charges.

out immediately and the rest was short-circuited within minutes. Several fires were ignited and as both steam and power had been lost, they could not be put out. Heavy smoke forced the crew on deck and the flames spread, augmented by multiple explosions. The armed trawler *V 707* and *Rau VIII* came and tried to help extinguish the flames, but it was in vain and eventually the crew were evacuated along with valuable equipment and confidential papers.[30]

Meanwhile, the air attacks on Bolærne continued. They had limited effects, though, except burning down some of the wooden buildings on the island. Strafing from low-flying aircraft was more dangerous than the bombing. The 15-cm guns of the fort could not take the extended live firing, however, and broke down one by one during the last battle. There had been some unqualified handling of the fuzes and problems with the firing tubes, which may have damaged the guns when firing. Telle discussed the status of the fort with YOSA and it was agreed around 10:00 on the 10th that further resistance was meaningless. The Norwegian flag was replaced with a white one at 12:30.[31] In total, some 60–65 shells had been fired from the three 15-cm guns. During the afternoon a group of seamen from *Kondor*, led by Oberfänrich Strauss, landed on Bolærne from *Rau VII* at a small quay on the western side of the island. To the surprise of Strauss and his men, the

Norwegians were still armed, and machine-gun positions were manned. The bombing and strafing earlier in the day had killed one Norwegian, private Hans Christian Furuseth, and wounded another and the situation was still tense. To settle matters before darkness fell, Strauss asked the Norwegians to confirm their surrender by laying down their weapons and going aboard *Rau VII* for transport to the mainland. This was done, some 15 officers and 250 men were taken prisoner and just before 20:00 the German flag was hoisted over Bolærne – almost 40 hours after *Weser*-time. During the night of the 10th/11th *Rau VII* ran aground and the Norwegians from Bolærne did not get to Horten until late in the morning of the 11th.[32]

By nightfall on 10 April, most of Oslofjord proper was in German hands. Still, few if any German transports dared venture up the fjord until the 11th, fearing submarines and mines. Håøya and Måkerøy forts only surrendered on the afternoon of the 14th.[33] In his war diary, Kapitän Thiele later described the co-operation with the torpedo boats (Senior CO Kapitänleutnant Neuss of *Möwe*) and the R-boats (Kapitänleutnant Forstmann) as 'quite outstanding'. Notably he does not mention *Emden* and Kapitän Lange at all.[34]

Chapter 14

Aftermath

First Response

In the late evening of 8 April, Halvdan Koht went for a stroll in the quiet streets of Oslo to relax and clear his mind. To his surprise, his thoughts were interrupted by air-raid sirens just after midnight and the street lights were turned off. He found a public telephone and called the front desk of the Foreign Office where he learned that warships had entered Oslofjord, and that Prime Minister Nygaardsvold had called for a Cabinet meeting at 01:30. The Foreign Minister hastened through the darkened city on foot.

The signal from SDD1 in Horten of warships in outer Oslofjord at 23:15, made sure that the Commanding Admiral, most of the Admiral Staff and the Naval Intelligence Department were in their offices in the naval wing of the Ministry of Defence around midnight. When the signal 'Rauøy and Bolærne in battle' followed at 23:50, tension rose sharply. Though not confirmed, it was believed that the intruders were German, but whether they were escaping from a superior Allied naval force in the Skagerrak, or some sort of attack was under way was unclear. Orders were issued to admiral Smith-Johannsen in Horten to prepare to lay the mines between Rauøy and Bolærne.

Shortly before 02:00, the British Naval Attaché, Captain Boyes, showed up again at the Admiral Staff, forwarding information of German ships passing through the Belts Belts and asking if there were mines in the Oslofjord. Boyes had received a signal from the Admiralty at 23:12, regarding the German activity in the Skagerrak. It stated that two groups of warships were at sea, one led by *Gneisenau* the other by *Blücher*, both heading west. There was no conclusion to the signal and no indication that any of the ships were heading for Oslo or any other Norwegian port, but Steen later added that Boyes repeated his statement that Norway could count on British naval assistance should that become necessary. He then asked if there were any mines laid in the Oslofjord. After conferring with the Commanding Admiral, Chief of Staff Corneliussen answered Boyes that there were no mines in the eastern seaways. According to Steen, there was no further discussion at this point between Boyes and the Admiral Staff regarding British ships in the Skagerrak but when the attaché left a few minutes later, Diesen and Corneliussen believed that the Royal Navy was on its way and held back any further orders to lay mines inside Norwegian territorial waters to give British ships 'full freedom of movement' should they end up in combat with German warships.[1]

Prime Minister Nygaardsvold had been wakened at 23:30 by a call from Ljungberg with information of warships in outer Oslofjord. Ljungberg called again just before midnight, this time with the news that Bolærne and Rauøy had opened fire on the ships, without being able to ascertain their nationality. Shortly after, Minister of Justice Terje Wold called, suggesting the government should assemble and Nygaardsvold agreed to meet as usual at the Foreign Office in Victoria Terrasse. He dressed and hastened from his home. Most of the other ministers had gone to bed, or were about to, when they received the call to gather. There were few taxis to be found and many had to walk. Koht arrived at 01:15 as one of the latest. The reports poured in fast, each more sinister than the last. The events escalated when SDD2 in Bergen reported at 02:06 that 'five large and two small German warships' had entered the Leads. Just before 03:00 SDD1 reported 'four large cruisers and submarines' heading up Oslofjord. Shortly after, Trøndelag SDS in Trondheim reported unidentified warships penetrating the Agdenes defences and at 04:14 SDD3 in Tromsø reported intruders off Narvik. The first report of Oscarsborg having opened fire came at 04:28 and when Kristiansand reported close to 06:00 that Odderøya Fort in Kristiansand had prevented warships entering that harbour too, there was no longer the slightest doubt that an attack on Norway was developing. This was more than an incidental breach of neutrality and Oslo was obviously a prime target for the invaders.[2]

As King Haakon was not present, there was no formal Statsråd and no minutes were taken during the night. Thus, it has been difficult to reconstruct accurately exactly what happened and who said and did what. The British note of the day before, stating that the Royal Navy would 'guard the minefields for 48 hours', made the ministers take it for granted there was an Allied fleet off the coast of Norway and that this would intercept the German warships in the west.[3] Nygaardsvold later wrote:

> It was an ominous night. I understood we were caught in a war-game between the belligerents. It was not we, but the powers at war that would fight over Norway. We, however, would pay the price. A call was made to the British Minister to find out if he had any information from his govern-ment, but he was asleep and knew nothing. England slept...[4]

Koht finally got Cecil Dormer on the phone at 02:10. He informed the British minister that foreign ships, presumably German, were approaching, but also that he believed 'the defences of Oslo might succeed in repelling them' and added 'now we are at war'. When Dormer asked if the government intended to remain in Oslo, Koht said he found it unnecessary to evacuate the capital at the moment, probably based on a statement from Commanding Admiral Diesen on 8 April that he 'believed he could guarantee Oslo would not be easily captured from the sea'.[5] A telegram summarising the information was sent to London where it arrived about an hour later, forwarded to the duty Officer at the War Cabinet, as well as the Admiralty, War Office and Air Ministry.[6]

Neither the Commanding Admiral nor Commanding General was invited to Victoria Terrasse on this morning. Neither did the commanders take any initiatives to meet with the government themselves or have any liaison officers attached to the decision-makers. All communication between the government and the military during the night would depend on Defence Minister Ljungberg. This was to be most unfortunate and lead to irreparable misunderstandings. The signal from Bergen at 02:06 that the attackers were German was central. Nygaardsvold later told the Investigating Committee that this led to the government's decision to mobilise. It is not known with certainty when the government received the information, but it may have been as early as 02:30. The issue of the mobilisation remains controversial to this day and exactly what was decided during the night remains uncertain. Ljungberg communicated with the military leaders if and how the armed forces should be mobilised in south Norway. The 6th Division in north Norway had already been partly mobilised due to the Winter War between the Soviet Union and Finland. A compromise was eventually made for a partial mobilisation of only four brigades in south Norway and calling the men by mail or telegram, which would take a minimum of three days – as Ljungberg very well knew. The Army Chief of Staff added the 5th Brigade to the mobilisation without immediately informing Ljungberg. All ministers except Ljungberg later stated that a decision for immediate, general mobilisation had been taken during the morning. When asked by the Investigating Committee the exact nature of the decision, though, the answers became more diverse. Ljungberg later claimed that a decision for general mobilisation was taken by the government between 04:30 and 05:00 – after the ultimatum from Bräuer had been rejected. He also asserted that he immediately telephoned the revised order to the General Staff. Nobody there could later recall taking such a call from the minister or be identified as the receiver. The orders were drafted during the night and hand-delivered to the telegraph office in Oslo by an officer around 05:30. As no warning had been given, the telegraph office had routinely closed the evening before. Hence, the mobilisation orders were not sent until it reopened at 08:00 on the 9th – by which time they were pointless.[7]

Except for Ljungberg, few of the ministers were familiar with the procedures and terminology for the mobilisation of the armed forces and none of them realised that even if armed and in uniform, the poorly trained soldiers of the Norwegian Army were not necessarily fit for combat on day one. Apparently, most members of the government believed they had ordered a general and immediate mobilisation sometime during the early hours of the 9th. The ministers did not have the competence to set out their intention in military terms, however, and it was never properly ascertained that Ljungberg and the General Staff understood what the government wanted – a situation of misperception and poor communication for which the responsibility rests with the government as a whole. The direct responsibility for having the government formulate clear instructions and forward them, through the Ministry of Defence, to the Commanding General, Commanding Admiral and their respective staffs, rests with Birger Ljungberg. Judging from the other ministers' accounts, it is almost inconceivable that he did not understand what Nygaardsvold, Koht, Lie, Torp and the others believed they had decided. The responsibility for making sure the government had all the information it needed and that the consequences of its orders, or lack of such, were understood rests with Laake and Diesen, who must also take responsibility for not making the government aware that their instructions were ambiguous and, as the situation developed, meaningless. The government on their side, however incompetent in military matters, must take the responsibility for failing to call the Commanding Officers or their Chief of Staffs to Victoria Terrasse to share information, ascertain that their intentions were understood and could be implemented – and if not, what alternatives existed. From the time it was known that German ships were entering more than just outer Oslofjord, nothing but a full and immediate mobilisation would do – irrespective of previous plans and concepts.[8]

The War Has Already Started

At 04:30, the German Minister Curt Bräuer was reported to be at Victoria Terrasse, insisting he see Koht. Bräuer was late. It appears he assumed the government would meet with the King at the Castle and went there first. When he arrived at Victoria Terrasse, he was shown into the library next to where the government was assembled. Appropriately for the situation, there was only candlelight due to the black-out after the air-raid alert, giving the room an eerie atmosphere. Bräuer was polite and correct as always, but there was an 'uncommonly cold tone' to his voice, Koht later wrote. Bräuer presented a nineteen-page German memorandum. It claimed that Germany, against its wish, had been drawn into a war with the Allies. As they did not dare to attack Germany on mainland Europe they had 'shifted the theatre of war to neutral territory' and Norway was neither able nor willing to oppose the Allied pressure. The German armed forces had therefore commenced 'certain military operations [to] take over the protection of the Kingdom of Norway'. The sole purpose, it was stated, was to prevent 'the intended occupation of bases in Norway by Anglo-French forces'. There were no hostile intentions, but all military installations would have to surrender, and opposition would be met with force. To avoid unnecessary bloodshed, an 'immediate military and administrative cooperation' was advised 'and information thereof sent to the armed forces, with orders to avoid friction or difficulty'. Koht listened to Bräuer's monologue, emphasising key points from the memorandum, with a sinking heart. This he had feared, but not really expected. Should the ultimatum be accepted, it would mean the end of Norway's independence and most certainly war with Britain and France. When Bräuer eventually finished, Koht, who knew that batteries had fired on the German ships and that the plan of a *fait accompli* had failed, answered that this was such an important matter it would have to be decided by the government. Bräuer said no, there was no time for that, events were unfolding too fast. Koht insisted, and as the government was only next door, Bräuer would have to wait. 'As I left', Koht later wrote, 'I quoted to him the words of his own *Führer*: a people who submissively give in to a violator, does not deserve to live.' Hearing a brief résumé of the German demands, Prime Minister Nygaardsvold and the other ministers unanimously dismissed the demands as totally unacceptable. Koht returned to Bräuer with the brief answer from the government, adding that Norway wished to maintain its independence and Germany had no right to interfere militarily. Dismayed, Bräuer answered: 'Then nothing can save you. This means war.' Koht replied: 'The war has already started.' At this stage, neither Bräuer nor any of the ministers knew that the German attack on Oslo had been halted at Oscarsborg.[9]

Bräuer hurried back to the Embassy. Too upset to use any pre-determined codes, he sent the following telegram in standard code:

> Have presented the Foreign Minister at 05:20 German time with our demands in firm, insisting manner and explained the reasons for them. Memorandum with enclosure was handed to him. The Minister withdrew for consultations with the government [...] After a few minutes he returned with the answer: We do not give in willingly; the war has already started.[10]

This telegram reached the *Weserübung* headquarters in Hamburg at 06:10 German time. The Norwegian government made several wrong or at best confused decisions during 9 April. The decision to defend Norway's independence, however, was clear and undisputed, even if this would bring the country into the war. Stortingspresident Carl Joachim Hambro had been crystal clear in the Storting on 8 April: 'The thought of Norway going to war

```
A b s c h r i f t.                                         5 2


Telegramm an A.A. Nr. 488 vom 9. April.


Habe Aussenminister um 5.20 Uhr deutscher Zeit in
fester eindringlicher Form unsere Forderungen ge-
stellt und begründet sowie Memorandum mit Anlage
übergeben. Aussenminister zog sich dann zu dem in
Aussenministerium versammelten Kabinettsrat zurück,
wobei ich unter Hinweis auf Ernst der Lage auf
schnellste Entscheidung drängte.
Nach wenigen Minuten gab er Antwort:
Wir beugen uns freiwillig nicht, der Kampf ist be-
reits im Gange.

                                          Bräuer
```

Signal from Bräuer to his superiors in Berlin, sent from Oslo shortly after 05.20,
telling them that Koht on behalf of the government had refused
the German demands and the two countries were at war.

against Great Britain is absurd.' Thus, even if Nygaardsvold and his government were unprepared and stumbled severely, they made a swift and resolute
decision when needed, which placed them firmly on the Allied side.[11]

Gudrun Hambro heard the air-raid alert just after midnight on 9 April. She
believed it was serious and decided to wake up her husband Carl. He had just
fallen asleep after a long day, and it took some time. Finally, she succeeded
and the Stortingspresident called the news agency NTB to find out what
was going on. Hearing of intruders in Oslofjord and shots having been fired,
Hambro called Nygaardsvold and Ljungberg to have the news confirmed.

The capital was an obvious target and if the intruders entered Oslo,
detaining King Haakon, the government and members of parliament,
everything would be over in a few hours. Hambro decided they would have
to evacuate to a safer place. Hamar, some 130 kilometres to the north, was
a natural choice; not too far away and with good communications back to
the capital as well as onwards, should that become necessary. On his own
initiative, he called key staff at the parliament instructing them to prepare
an evacuation of records, files and other confidential materiel. He also called
the National Railway Company, leaving instructions for a priority train to
be ready at Oslo's main station around 07:15. Then he went to the parliament

Carl Joachim Hambro was born in 1885. He was one of the most distinguished Norwegian politicians of his time and one of those who first recognised the threats from the dictatorships in Europe. As Stortingspresident, Hambro was officially the second man in the kingdom, next to the King, ranking above the Prime Minister. He was also leader of the Parliamentary Committee for Foreign Affairs, to which the Foreign Minister formally reported. He was distantly related to Charles Hambro of the British Special Operations Executive, active in Norway throughout the war.

to check the status of the preparations and verify that all 150 members were being notified of the departure before he continued to the Foreign Office. Later, after Bräuer had left the Foreign Office, Prime Minister Nygaardsvold contacted Hambro, asking him to come to Victoria Terrasse.[12]

At Victoria Terrasse, Hambro advised an immediate evacuation of the administration to Hamar. Koht was reluctant to leave the capital as he reckoned the Germans would not get past Oscarsborg and there was no report of landings yet. Hambro had it his way, though. Nygaardsvold called King Haakon to update him on the dismissal of the German ultimatum and the decision to depart. The King accepted immediately and agreed to be at the railway station with his family when the train was ready. The ministers left Victoria Terrasse between 05:30 and 06:30, most of them hurrying to their respective departments to ensure a proper evacuation after having made sure their families were aware of the situation and what to do. When the train eventually left at 07:23, King Haakon was on board with most of his family and staff, as were five of the ministers, and various MPs, civil servants and senior staff from the ministries. Members of the diplomatic corps had also been alerted and many joined the train. Civilians wishing to get out of the city were allowed aboard if they could find a place. Nobody asked for tickets. On the platform, Koht gave an interview to the press, in which he confirmed that Norway would not succumb to the German demands and that (as he believed) a general order for mobilisation had been issued. Hambro travelled by car ahead of the train to prepare for its arrival in Hamar. Prime Minister Nygaardsvold wanted to bring his family and also used a car, picking them up on the way. For those MPs who could not make it in time, a convoy of buses was set up, leaving Parliament a few hours later. At 09:00 German time, the *Weserübung* staff in Hamburg learned that King Haakon, the government and most of the Storting had left the capital and the main objectives of the operation, a peaceful, non-violent capture of the

The royal family arriving at Hamar on the morning of 9 April.
They are welcomed by Prime Minister Nygaardsvold.

country with the governing powers subserviently in place, had failed. One of the weakest armed forces in Europe would stand up to the strongest – contrary to all expectations.[13]

Finance Minister Oscar Torp and Managing Director Nicolai Rygg at Norges Bank had long since agreed that should a crisis emerge, money, bonds and gold reserves would have to be evacuated from the capital. Most of the gold reserves had already been sent to the USA and Canada in 1938–9, but some 120 million kroner remained in the vaults. Packing of this was initiated during the 8th and transport planned for next morning. During the night, Rygg was awakened by a call from one of Torp's secretaries with instructions to start moving the gold at once. Within a few hours, some 50 tons of gold and other valuables were loaded onto the trucks and just before dawn they started off for the Bank of Norway's vault in Lillehammer, one by one.[14]

The train taking the King and his government out of Oslo arrived at Hamar at 11:10. Hambro and Nygaardsvold were waiting at the platform. Nygaardsvold, according to Hambro, was deeply depressed and shaken 'as something basic in his perception of human integrity and decency had been broken'. Physically worn down after the events of the last days and by a lack of sleep, Nygaardsvold and his government recommended that a coalition government take over, and asked the king to ask Hambro to be prepared to take the responsibility. Hambro argued that this was not the time to make hasty decisions and did his best to calm 'The Old Man' down. At Hamar, a quick breakfast was served before the King, most ministers and slightly over 100 of the 150 members of the Storting gathered in Festiviteten, a local assembly building, at 12:30. Hambro chaired the meeting while Nygaardsvold and Koht recounted what had happened during the night and morning. Koht ended his account by stating that Norway was now at war with Germany. After a brief discussion, Hambro decided there was not much more to do at that point and asked the MPs to take a rest and reconvene at 18:00, hopefully with more and better information of the situation.[15]

No Ships at Oslo

While the men from *Blücher* were fighting for their lives at dawn on 9 April, naval attaché Schreiber made his way to the harbour of Oslo around 04:00. Together with Oberstleutnant Pohlmann and Hans-Wilhelm Scheidt he was to be ready to receive the ships and show Engelbrecht and his men where to find King Haakon and the government to secure a peaceful take-over. Scheidt spoke basic Norwegian and knew Oslo well and would be important as liaison for General Engelbrecht when he arrived. He had been in Berlin the week before and knew something was going on, but not the extent nor the date. On Schreiber's invitation he spent the night in the attaché's apartment and had been told the details of the invasion a few hours earlier. Schreiber himself had been informed by a coded telegram on the 5th.[16] No ships came, and the men returned to the Embassy, where nobody had any information. Schreiber and the others contacted Oberleutnant Kempf aboard *Widar* to find out what was going on. All he could say was that there appeared to be trouble at Drøbak. Schreiber then joined air attaché Spiller to head out to Fornebu. Spiller had briefly returned to the Legation to find out what was going on, without learning much. Scheidt headed for the Hotel Continental to find Hagelin and learn what knowledge he had of the situation. Aboard *Widar*, Kempf had an excellent observation platform, not least of Fornebu airfield. By 06:00, he was in communication with Abwehrstelle Hamburg, and during the next vital hours, a steady stream of some 250 signals with various observations would arrive from *Widar* and be forwarded to Falkenhorst at the Hotel Esplanade and to OKW in Berlin.[17] At 05:50 Oberstleutnant Pohlmann sent his own coded signal to Falkenhorst using the radio at the Embassy:

> No ships at Oslo, no sounds of battle to be heard. Air-raid sirens, people gather in the streets. Norwegian government declares: We will not give in. The battle has started.[18]

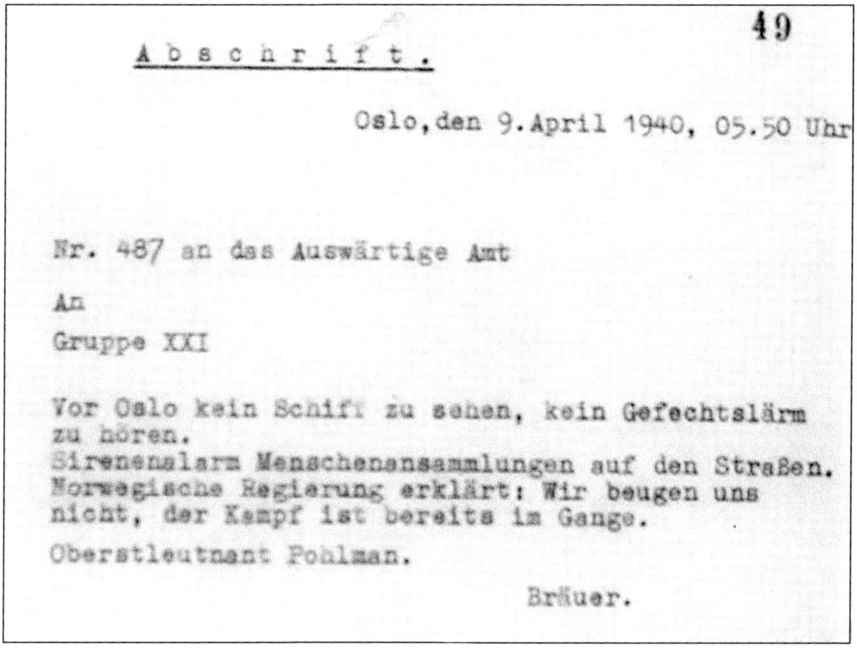

```
                                                         49
      A b s c h r i f t .

                         Oslo,den 9.April 1940, 05.50 Uhr


      Nr. 487 an das Auswärtige Amt

      An

      Gruppe XXI


      Vor Oslo kein Schiff zu sehen, kein Gefechtslärm
      zu hören.
      Sirenenalarm Menschenansammlungen auf den Straßen.
      Norwegische Regierung erklärt: Wir beugen uns
      nicht, der Kampf ist bereits im Gange.
      Oberstleutnant Pohlman.

                               Bräuer.
```

Second signal from Bräuer to his superiors in Berlin, sent from Oslo at 05:50.
No ships at Oslo ...

A Norwegian attack on the Legation was quite possible. Hence, the building was secured, and some of the staff were armed. No information came to explain what was happening, neither from Berlin nor Hamburg. Later in the morning, back from Fornebu, Schreiber again ventured outside the Legation, towards Ekeberg from where the harbour and inner fjord could be observed. This time he was wearing a civilian coat over his uniform. German aircraft were landing at Fornebu but with far fewer soldiers than anticipated and no German warships had yet appeared. Something had gone horribly wrong.[19]

Air War

Three airfields, Aalborg in northern Denmark, Sola-Stavanger and Fornebu-Oslo were considered to be of such importance for German air superiority during *Weserübung* that they would have to be captured as early as possible. Firstly, to bring in troops and supplies, secondly to use as forward bases to meet the inevitable Allied counterattack. Hence it would be critical to capture these fields in operational condition, including runways, defence installations and fuel dumps. Kjeller airfield north of Oslo was considered secondary. It would be strafed and bombed on the morning of the 9th and secured later.

A formation of Junkers Ju 52 transport aircraft flying north, across the Skagerrak.

Approaching the target. Soldiers from III./IR 159 inside a Ju 52 watching with apprehension as they near Fornebu.

Oslo was the hub of a dense network of aircraft observation posts and signal stations in south-eastern Norway. Five batteries with a total of fourteen 7.5-cm AA guns were deployed around the capital in addition to ten AA machine-gun units with in all fifty-seven guns and machine guns on rooftops or other elevated positions. These were sited to protect the city, and nobody seems to have considered the possibility of air landings at Fornebu airfield just outside on a scale that the fighters and regular defences there could not handle. Several reports of intruding aircraft were received in Oslo during the night and the air defences were alerted and ordered to man their guns at 04:17. The first German aircraft did not appear over the capital until 07:15, however.[20]

According to plan, some 340 *Fallschirmjäger* from 1st and 2nd Companies of the 1st Paratroop Regiment would jump over Fornebu in the early hours of 9 April. Once the airfield was in German hands, regular soldiers of IR 324 of 163. ID would be flown in by transport aircraft. Supplies and heavy equipment would come by sea. To achieve tactical air superiority and suppress the AA defences, eight Bf 110 heavy fighters from 1./ZG 76 were added to the first wave. These would fly independently to Oslo and fall in with the transports

Fornebu airfield on the morning of 9 April. Aircraft are spread all over the place,
illustrating the chaos that reigned. Several of the aircraft on the light taxiway seen
above the engine-cowling are civilian types commandeered for the occasion.

over Fornebu. Over the Skagerrak the transport aircraft ran into low clouds
and fog. The commander of the first wave, carrying the paratroopers, decided
to turn back and land at Aalborg, which was in German hands by then. Some
of the aircraft did not receive the order to turn, or ignored it, and continued.
The second wave also ignored the order to turn as conditions over the
Skagerrak improved rapidly.

In the spring of 1940 Oslo-Fornebu Airport was the base for the Jage-
vingen, the Fighter Wing of the Army Air Force, equipped with Gloster
Gladiator biplane fighters, seven of which were battle-ready. Around 04:00,
the alarm went off; multi-engine aircraft were reported above the fog in the
fjord. It was just light enough for two of the Gladiators to be sent up. Both

met twin-engine aircraft and fenrik Finn Thorsager opened fire on one he identified as a Dornier Do 17, establishing the intruders as German. The aircraft, probably from Fernaufklärungsgeschwader 120 (a reconnaissance unit), vanished in the clouds before it could be intercepted. A further three Gladiators took off but found nothing. All operational Gladiators took off once more but, overwhelmed by the invaders after 07:30, they could not hope to stop the German attack, only inflict maximum damage and live to fight another day. Two Bf 110s and two He 111s were shot down and others seriously damaged, against the loss of one Gladiator shot down. The rest eventually ran out of fuel and ammunition and landed wherever they could while Fornebu was under attack. Most of them were damaged and only one flew again.[21]

At least one Ju 52 transport aircraft was shot down by the AA batteries around Oslo and almost all other aircraft of the first wave took damage. Some 50–60 soldiers and crew members lay dead or seriously wounded inside the aircraft when they landed. With the Gladiators out of the way, the remaining Bf 110s began strafing the AA defences at Fornebu as planned. The machine-gun crews defended themselves as best they could, and at first kept the attackers at a distance. The Bf 110s became low on fuel, however,

Crash-landed He 111 bomber aircraft at Fornebu. The damage to the wing, next to the engine, is most likely from a Norwegian AA shell passing through without exploding, but damaging the undercarriage, resulting in a belly-landing.

and had to land somewhere, soon. To their relief, the first Ju 52s arrived over the airfield at about 08:20. To the surprise of the fighter pilots the lumbering transports started to land instead of dropping paratroopers as expected. The first Ju 52 was chased away by the Norwegian machine-gunners, but the Bf 110s were down to their last fuel reserves and were forced to land. This shocked the defenders even if at least one of the fighters crashed, and the defences started to crumble. The Ju 52s also started to come in, despite some of them being fired at as they landed, and taxied towards the control tower. Soon Hauptmann Peter Ingenhoven took charge and started to organise the disorder, assisted by a much-relieved Spiller, who could finally welcome his countrymen.[22] Seeing the German aircraft landing, the Norwegian soldiers started to flee and Fornebu airfield was captured by air-landed infantry and heavy fighters, not by paratroopers as planned.[23] During the day, most of I. and II./IR 324, a pioneer company, parts of III./IR 159 and some logistics personnel landed at Fornebu – as did Hauptmann Walther and his 2nd Paratroop Company, having temporarily landed at Aalborg. Oberst Helmuth Nickelmann, CO of IR 324, could start considering moving towards Oslo. This he did at 12:15. Until Engelbrecht arrived in the early hours of the 10th, Nickelmann was the highest-ranking German officer in Oslo.[24]

Oberstleutnant Pohlmann who had gone to Fornebu when no ships turned up in the harbour sent a telegram from the Legation:

> Just back from Fornebu. By 12:00 five companies with Oberst Nickelmann had landed. Only twelve paratroopers arrived. Eight transport machines from 6th Group made emergency landings due to ground fire. Few losses. AA machine-gun fire suppressed by landed troops. Legation secured by armed staff. Entry to Oslo by Group Nickelmann imminent. No news of the warships.[25]

Around 12:15, six Ju 87 Stuka dive-bombers from I./StG 1 led by Oberleutnant Bruno Dilley arrived over Oslo. The Stukas were equipped with two 240-litre drop tanks on the under-wing bomb racks to manage the long flight to Oslo, restricting their bomb loads to a single 500-kg bomb each, on the centre-line rack. Once over the capital, Dilley was ordered to attack Akershus Fortress in Oslo. There were many soldiers and civilians in the open courtyard of the old fort and hearing the scream of the diving Stukas, they scrambled into any archway or building believed to give protection. Luckily, Dilley's *Staffel* was not up to standard on this day, most likely as they were disturbed by dense AA fire, and three of the bombs went into the sea, one hit a nearby island and only two hit the fortress, both outside the centre courtyard. Nobody was killed, but many were wounded and those not under orders to remain evacuated rapidly.[26]

Having landed safely at Fornebu, soldiers of IR 236 gather their equipment
and prepare to march into Oslo.

When the soldiers from Fornebu arrived at Akershus not long after, they
could drive their trucks right into the fortress. Oberst Nickelmann sought
out the commander, Oberst Hans Peter Schnitler, who had stayed behind at
Akershus, demanding an immediate surrender. Schnitler managed to contact
Nygaardsvold at Hamar and received permission to surrender the city
including the AA batteries to avoid bloodshed. The capitulation was agreed
at 14:00 and half an hour later, the first German troops marched brazenly
into Oslo in columns of five. Some spectators booed, but most watched
wonderingly, trying to comprehend what was going on. From the other side
of the capital, the soldiers who had landed at Son started arriving by cars,
buses and trains. By nightfall on the 9th, however, there were fewer than
2,000 battle-ready German soldiers in Oslo, largely without heavy weapons.[27]

At Stavanger, Bergen, Trondheim and Narvik, the operations had gone
reasonably well for the Germans, but the troops were effectively isolated and
the invasion was on the verge of being repelled. In Oslo and Kristiansand,
the situation was unclear, to say the least. Falkenhorst was supposed to arrive
in Oslo on the afternoon of the 9th but delayed his transfer, later admitting
that 'the incoming reports from Oslo in particular did not give a clear
picture of the situation for quite some time'. This is an understatement and

the tension in the Hotel Esplanade must have been palpable. At Hamburg-Fuhlsbüttel airfield, Major Albrecht Philler, the most senior staff officer of 163. ID not aboard *Blücher*, was called to the phone shortly before 09:00, just as he was about to board the transport aircraft taking him to Oslo-Fornebu. On the phone was a very upset Oberstleutnant Tippelskirch from the Hotel Esplanade, telling him that things had gone badly, and he was ordered to halt his transfer to Oslo and that of all staff and support personnel. Only infantry should fly north at this stage.[28]

Falkenhorst later wrote:

> The failure of the '*Blücher*-breakthrough' was particularly painful from a command and control point of view, as this was the capital. On board the ship was a carefully selected group of important people, including General Engelbrecht, needed to occupy such a large city. The first elements of my own staff were also on board with all the material needed for an efficient take over.[29]

Tragically, neither the Norwegian government nor the military realised this and by a few hours later the situation had changed dramatically again. Oslo was in German hands, as was Kristiansand, and troops had started arriving in southern Norway. Not due to a major strategic turn, but due to individual German resolve, Norwegian hesitation and pure serendipity. At no

At Akershus fortress shortly after the capitulation at 14:00. Oberst Schnitler, who had been left behind at Akershus when the General Staff evacuated, is seen talking to German officers. The man on the left is wearing a *Fallschirmjäger* jump-suit.

time during the day did the Norwegians realise that the Germans who had landed from the warships and aircraft were lightly armed, lacking supplies, ammunition and heavy weapons.[30]

The three operational Bf 110s were refuelled from captured fuel depots and established a continuous patrol around the airfield securing the in-bound transport aircraft. During the afternoon, this was reduced to immediate readiness on the ground to conserve fuel. Around 17:30, a British Sunderland flying boat was reported over the inner Oslofjord. The Sunderland, flown by Flight Lieutenant Peter Kite of No. 210 Squadron, was ill-suited for low-level reconnaissance inland, but the mission was as improvised as most other things on the Allied side that day. The intruder was hit by AA fire over Oslo harbour, and shortly after intercepted by Oberleutnant Werner Hansen and Leutnant Helmuth Lent, who mercilessly shot it down. Of the ten-man crew, only the 21-year-old wireless operator, Sergeant Ogwyn George, survived, tumbling out of the aircraft when it broke up in mid-air and falling more than 500 metres without a parachute, landing through trees into deep snow. This episode made a great impression on the Germans and the AA guns of *Emden* were manned day and night for a long time. The British had few aircraft that could cover the distance to Oslo and back and German air superiority was virtually total in the Kattegat–Oslofjord region.[31]

Most Unexpected

At the British Legation, Minister Dormer, dressed hurriedly after Koht's first telephone call in the small hours of the 9th and gave instructions to the staff to start preparing to destroy files and documents. At 03:55, a brief telegram from Dormer arrived at the Foreign Office in London, leaving no doubt as to the seriousness of the situation: 'Am burning cyphers and archives.' It was followed within half an hour by a request no less sinister: 'Can you give me any information helpful in deciding direction of eventual evacuation from here?'[32] Dormer and French Minister de Dampierre left Oslo by car around 06:45, accompanied by their spouses and senior staff. At that hour everything in Oslo appeared normal and there was little traffic. The rest of the staff, and other British citizens alerted during the night, followed as soon as cars could be provided or headed for the railway station.[33]

In London, the British leadership strove to keep up with events during the night. Major-General Hastings Ismay, Secretary of the Military Coordination Committee, wrote:

> The phoney war ended for me in a most unexpected and dramatic way. In the very early hours of 9 April, I was wakened out of a deep sleep by the telephone bell. It was the Duty Officer at the War Cabinet Office [...] His

report was brutal in its simplicity. The Germans had seized Copenhagen, Oslo and all the main ports of Norway [...] The gathering that assembled in my office at 6.30 a.m. was not exactly inspiring. I had hoped that one or other of the Chiefs of Staff would have a plan of action, but so far as I can remember not a single constructive suggestion had been put forward by the time that we had to break up the meeting and join the War Cabinet at 10 Downing Street.[34]

During the morning the War Cabinet, which began at 08:30, decided air reconnaissance over Norway should be initiated as soon as possible to 'clarify the situation'. No bombing should commence until this had been achieved. Meanwhile, C-in-C Home Fleet should take 'all possible steps to clear Bergen and Trondheim of German forces', while the Chiefs of Staff should 'set on foot preparations for military expeditions' to recapture both cities as well as take control of Narvik. These expeditions, however, should 'not move until the naval situation had been cleared up'. The French were to be informed of these steps and asked to consider if the Chasseurs originally destined for Narvik could be redirected to Bergen or Trondheim. It was not until 10:30 in the morning that information of German landings at Narvik was received in London – through the press. At 14:00, the Admiralty issued orders to British naval authorities throughout the world that Norwegian and Danish ships were to be 'taken under British protection and detained in harbour'. Orders were also given to all ships in home waters that merchant ships approaching the Scandinavian coast should be re-routed to Kirkwall in the Orkneys.[35]

The diplomats following the Norwegian government settled at Høsbjør, a hotel some 15 kilometres outside Hamar.[36] By 12:30, British MI6 staff had rigged an aerial to a flagpole, setting up communications with London through a portable radio set brought from the Embassy. Meanwhile, Minister Dormer, Francis Foley (the local head of MI6) and Assistant Air Attaché, Wing Commander Alan Dore, went back to Hamar to find somebody from the government to learn what was going on and let them know that a line of communication to London had been established. Eventually, at 16:00, they met oberst Thomas Gullichsen, Inspector General of the Army Air Force, who brought an urgent, formal request from the government for 'immediate military and aerial assistance'.[37] The text of a telegram describing the situation at Hamar was set up, followed by an urgent request for help. Both telegrams were brought back to Høsbjør to be cyphered and transmitted over Foley's set. At 16:25, the telegram from Dormer arrived at the Foreign Office:

> Oslo has capitulated. Government is at Hamar, fifteen kilometres north of which I and several members of staff are staying [...] United States Legation has taken charge of His Majesty's Legation. Reported one

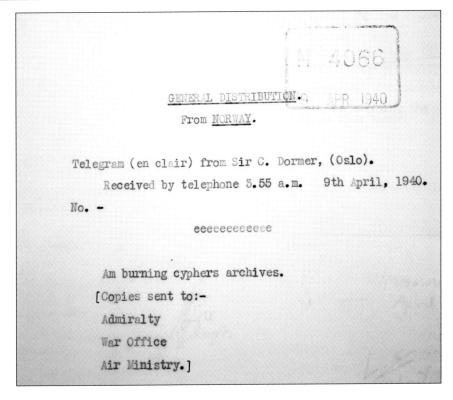

```
                                                    N 4066

        GENERAL DISTRIBUTION.        APR 1940
        From NORWAY.


   Telegram (en clair) from Sir C. Dormer, (Oslo).
        Received by telephone 3.55 a.m.   9th April, 1940.
   No. -

                eeeeeeeeeeee


        Am burning cyphers archives.
        [Copies sent to:-
        Admiralty
        War Office
        Air Ministry.]
```

One of the last signals from British envoy Dormer to the Foreign Office
while he was still in Oslo.

German ship sunk by fire from Droebak. Tonsberg, Bergen, Trondhjem, Narvik occupied […] Lillestrom bombed and in flames. French Minister and I would be grateful for any reassuring news as government anxious and are subject to strong pressure to declare a war on His Majesty's Government.

Less than half an hour later, it was followed by:

Norwegian government stress need for strong and quick assistance before Germans establish firm footing on Norwegian soil. Please reply by 6 p.m. whether strong assistance can be (?immediately) forthcoming.

And at 18:10:

German land and air forces have occupied Fornebu and Sola (Stavanger) aerodromes […] forces at Trondhjem, Egersund, Bergen and Oslo Fiord. Size and number of ships at various ports unknown at present. Information will be sent later if possible.

The British Cabinet had already decided to assist Norway. It appears that Dormer never received a telegram sent from London at 06:45, stating that 'the whole British fleet is operating in the North Sea and we are planning to re-capture the ports in German occupation'. A second telegram, originally timed 12:55, was received once Høsbjør was connected:

> You should at once assure the Norwegian Government that in view of the German invasion of their country, His Majesty's Government has decided forthwith to extend their full aid to Norway and will fight the war in full association with them. You should at the same time inform the Norwegian Government that His Majesty's Government are taking immediate measures to deal with the German occupation of Bergen and Trondjem [and] will be glad to learn what the Norwegian Government's own plans are, so that subsequent British dispositions may be in conformity with them. His Majesty's Government would in the meantime suggest that the Norwegian Government should, if possible, destroy the Stavanger aerodrome should they be unable to hold it.

This telegram reached Koht at 18:00, just before the second meeting of the Parliament.[38]

In the second meeting at Hamar, which commenced at 18:30, Nygaards-vold raised the issue of negotiations, as offered by Bräuer. Hambro argued against. The Germans would not negotiate at all in his opinion, only make demands and drag their feet. Lie, Wold, Torp and Støstad supported Hambro. Others, including Koht, held that no options should be ruled out and it was worth talking to Bräuer to see if the German terms had been modified. Eventually, it was agreed that Koht and three MPs should hear what Bräuer had to say and bring it back to the Parliament – provided the German advance was halted in the meantime. The mood of the Parliament was at an all-time low; news of landings all over the country, bombing and strafing in Oslo, loss of Norwegian lives and the confused mobilisation made the men falter in their determination.[39] A positive wave swept over the assembly, though, when Koht referred to the telegram from the British government, given to him just before the meeting, stating that London would send help forthwith.

At 19:40, the meeting was interrupted. Hambro announced that he had received information that German spearheads were only some 20 kilometres away, heading for Hamar. The train was ready at the station, and they would have to leave for Elverum at once. A scramble to depart ensued. The foreign diplomats at Høsbjør were also notified and left immediately to try to stay in touch with the government. By the time Foley, Reid and others were ready to depart, however, it was difficult to find a car and when they eventually did, the road towards Elverum was closed. Thus, they headed north towards

Lillehammer, eventually ending up in Åndalsnes the next day. The radio and its operator went with Dormer, but during the night they became separated, and Dormer lost touch with London for the moment.[40]

Contacts

Minister Bräuer had not accomplished his mission during the early morning of the 9th and found the situation deeply worrying. Nygaardsvold and Koht had decided to resist and, worst of all, the King and government had left the capital. The experienced diplomat had little else to do but start improvising. Later in the morning, Bräuer returned to the Foreign Office where he was met by Undersecretary Johannessen, the only senior civil servant remaining at Victoria Terrasse. Through him, Bräuer delivered a note to the government indicating that the terms of the ultimatum were still open and a 'peaceful' solution not yet out of reach. The note was well formulated, pointing to the situation in Denmark and arguing that resistance in the long run would cost Norway dearly. Johannessen could give no answer but called Bräuer later in the evening to confirm that the government had received the letter and an answer would follow next day.[41]

Quisling was not part of the German plans for Norway after the invasion or the occupation of the Norwegian capital, quite the contrary. There is a paragraph in the *Weserübung* orders showing clearly the German intention of maintaining the status quo:

> Once in Oslo, contacts shall be made as soon as possible with the German Minister Dr Bräuer and the Naval Attaché Korvettenkapitän Schreiber. With their help, urgent negotiations shall be initiated with the heads of the Norwegian military and government in order to secure implementation of our demands. Obstacles to these negotiations must under no circumstances delay the swift occupation of Oslo.[42]

The only reference to Quisling in Falkenhorst's papers is a note written by Major Benecke of the Abwehr in which the Norwegian is described as 'German-friendly but has no role to play. A fanatic.'[43] If King Haakon, the government and most other constitutional bodies continued with a minimum of visible changes, it was believed the Norwegian people would come to terms with the occupation. No replacement of the government was considered necessary; the iron fist inside the silken glove would suffice. In Denmark, such a system worked – for a while. In Norway King Haakon was not detained and events took a very different route.

After Scheidt and Schreiber parted company in the early morning of the 9th, Scheidt hastened towards the Hotel Continental. He knew Hagelin was at the Continental, but it is unlikely that Scheidt knew of Quisling's presence when he entered the lobby some time before 08.00. Still, no doubt guided by Hagelin, he was knocking on Quisling's door not long after. Despite the uncertainties, Scheidt gave Quisling a very positive summary of the military situation. He added, as he had learned from Bräuer before he left the Embassy, that Nygaardsvold and his government had decided to resist and asked if there was any way such a catastrophe could be avoided. Exactly which alternatives were discussed is not known, but sometime during the forenoon Quisling decided to establish a 'national government', believing he had German support to do so. In his mind the situation must have been as discussed in Berlin four months earlier – except the Germans were now in the country. Scheidt, who undoubtedly encouraged Quisling towards his decision, hurried back to the Embassy to telegraph Berlin for approval.

The timing of events that afternoon is somewhat confused, but at around 17:00, Scheidt appeared in Quisling's room once more. He was very upset, claiming Hitler was furious over the loss of *Blücher* and Koht's refusal to Bräuer. Unless there was an immediate surrender, orders would very likely be issued for the Luftwaffe to initiate a ruthless bombing of Norwegian cities. Should Quisling assume power, however, for which he had Hitler's approval Scheidt said, conditions would be different, and a solution might be found. Again, it is not known exactly what was discussed, nor has it been possible to ascertain what kind of approval Scheidt had from Berlin, though he later claimed it to be from Hitler in person. During the ensuing hour, the framework of a proclamation was set up and fine-tuned by Quisling. He also prepared a list of 'ministers' for his new 'government'. Except for Hagelin, none of them knew they were being considered for positions which would brand them as traitors for the rest of their lives.

Quisling then headed for the Radio House, accompanied by Scheidt. The last Norwegian news broadcast had been at 12:50, after which a German communication unit had occupied the house, closing it down. Scheidt, claiming he had special orders from Berlin, bluffed his way into the studios, followed by Quisling. At 19:25 the transmissions resumed with music until Quisling came on the air at 19:32 to implement his one-man *coup d'état*, unique in history. His proclamation was largely based on the leaflet issued in Oslo the day before. Following the British minelaying, to which the Nygaardsvold government had barely protested, Quisling claimed, the German government had offered 'its inoffensive assistance accompanied by a solemn assurance to respect national independence and Norwegian life and property'. After initiating a futile mobilisation, Quisling continued, the government had fled and left the population to its fate. Nasjonal Samling was the only party that could save the country from this desperate situation, and it was his 'duty and right' to take over the government with himself as prime minister and foreign minister. He then read a list of names for the other ministerial positions, most of whom were totally unknown to the public. Concluding his five-minute speech, Quisling added that opposition would be 'meaningless and equal to criminal destruction of life and property'. It was the duty of every public servant and officer to take instructions only from the new government, and denial of this would result in 'the gravest personal responsibility'.

The statement was a bombshell and when it was repeated at 22:00, the number of listeners was considerable. It created severe confusion among senior officers and some ordered their men not to fire, unless attacked, until the situation had been clarified. There was intense telephoning to reach higher authorities, which was virtually impossible. By the morning of the 10th, however, order had been restored and, in most cases, followed by bitterness over Quisling's actions, strengthening the willingness to fight. Unfortunately for Quisling, the country was not without a government and there was no parliamentary, legal or other basis for the 'National Government'. Quisling's treason was only made possible by the vacuum created by the sinking of *Blücher* and the absence of German military authority in Oslo.[44]

Against All Odds

Continuing northwards from Hamar to Elverum, the Storting and government reconvened at 21:20 in a local school. It was confirmed, against the advice of Hambro, that Koht and three MPs should meet Bräuer and hear him out. No mandate was given, and it was not clarified what the parliament or the government might be willing to accept in terms of compromises. It was clear, though, that unless Bräuer had something substantially more positive than the conditions of the first ultimatum, the decision from the early hours of the 9th would stand. If, on the other hand, the German minister had something constructive to offer, many of the MPs felt negotiations could be a positive way out of a dire situation. The content of Quisling's radio speech was known and any solution involving him would be unacceptable.[45]

Hambro realised that it would be difficult to assemble Parliament in the days and weeks ahead and suggested a constitutional *prokura* should be given to the government empowering it to 'attend to the interests of the nation and make those decisions deemed necessary [...] until such times as it is possible to convene formally again'. There was no formal vote, but nobody voiced any serious comments and Hambro declared the executive powers of the document valid. The meeting ended at 22:25 and the Norwegian Parliament would not meet again for over five years. A statement was prepared to be issued by radio the next day, confirming the Nygaardsvold government as the only legal authority in the country endorsed by the King, giving the government the legitimacy needed in the days and weeks to come, and above all later in the war, after moving to London.[46]

After the meeting, the government decided to ask Hambro to go to Stockholm to take care of Norwegian foreign affairs and other matters needing communication from neutral ground. He should also try to purchase weapons and supplies from Sweden, as direct military assistance was not expected. Hambro's political insight, administrative skills and cool head had, during the first critical hours of the crisis, used the breathing space created by Oscarsborg and Midtskogen (*see* pages 308–9) to ensure that the government and King remained in charge. Hambro left for Stockholm on the morning of the 10th.[47]

Bräuer passed through the lines early on the morning of the 10th, arriving at the small rural school building near Elverum around 15:00. King Haakon arrived too, asking that Koht and the three MPs attend the meeting.[48] Bräuer refused and insisted on seeing the King alone. King Haakon, who wanted witnesses to hear what he expected to come, told Bräuer that he, as a constitutional monarch, could not make any political decisions without his council and besides, he claimed, he did not speak German well and needed an interpreter. Outsmarted, Bräuer, who probably believed it would be possible to convince King Haakon to return, had to give in and accept that Koht would join the meeting. At first, he repeated tersely that the Germans had come as friends, forced to act through British provocations, and did not wish to change 'the prevailing dynastic situation'. He then complained bitterly that the Norwegian forces had not laid down their weapons 'as had been agreed'.[49] Nygaardsvold's government had shown itself to favour the Allied cause, he said, and as it had ordered a pointless resistance, the situation was totally changed compared to the morning of the previous day. Nygaardsvold and his government would have to go. Quisling had founded a new government, which King Haakon would have to recognise and return to the capital as soon as possible. By refusing to do so, he would personally be responsible for the inevitable loss of Norwegian lives. Rather than mellowing, the German demands were now sharper than those presented at Victoria Terrasse. King Haakon, who said very little during the meeting, did not answer directly, but stated that he could not appoint a government that did not have the confidence of the people. Bräuer answered that it might be possible to discuss some of the ministers, but Quisling remained an absolute demand. The meeting ended with a promise of a final answer within the day, and it was agreed that Bräuer should telephone Koht from Eidsvoll on his way back to Oslo.

When alone, King Haakon turned to Koht, noticeably distraught, saying that he felt terrible taking responsibility for the bloodshed that would follow from a war. He could not, however, accept 'this fellow Quisling' as prime minister and would have to abdicate if the German demands were accepted by the present administration. King Haakon continued to Nybergsund by car where he met the government and recounted the meeting with Bräuer, repeating he could not approve Quisling, 'who had no public or parliamentary support'. If the government wished to accept to avoid war, he would understand, but then have no other choice for himself than to abdicate. Minister Hjelmtveit later wrote:

> This made a great impression on us all. Clearer than ever before we could see the man behind the words: the King who had drawn a line for himself and his task, a line from which he could not deviate. We had through the five years [in government] learned to respect and appreciate our King and now, through his words, he came to us as a great man, just and forceful, a leader in these fatal times for our country.[50]

There was no discussion; the entire government, deeply moved, but also somewhat relieved, made common cause with the monarch. Koht who had remained at Elverum was informed, and when Bräuer telephoned from Eidsvoll around 20:00, the decision was made known to him. Bräuer asked if this meant that the Norwegian resistance would continue, and Koht answered in German: '*Ja, soweit wie möglich*' – as far as possible. Hitler's demand for acceptance of Quisling as Prime Minister had effectively excluded all possible options for a ceasefire.[51]

At 11:40 on 10 April, Group XXI received orders from OKW signed by both Generaloberst Keitel and Generalmajor Jodl to detain the old Norwegian government. If they would not come back to Oslo and start cooperating, they had to be 'disposed of'.[52]

A peaceful occupation was no longer an issue. Dormer later wrote to Lord Halifax:

> His Majesty and his Government were called upon to decide [on many critical issues] at a moment's notice in more or less complete unpreparedness and physical exhaustion. I was in touch with them most days, but there was no time for conversation. When they asked me to come to them it was invariably to discuss a particular question, in a crowded room, standing up; in the kind of conditions that might be described as chaos and confusion. And yet, although they had no administrative machine to work with – since everyone became scattered – they have succeeded in establishing some semblance of government in districts free of Germans.[53]

In Oslo, Quisling moved into the Parliament building during the morning of the 10th after having it cleared of German soldiers. Hagelin and Scheidt

German soldiers marching into Oslo down the main street towards the Parliament
with the Royal Palace in the background. Norwegian mounted police follow
on each side and a stunned crowd watches fearfully. The brazen bluff
succeeded, and no shots were fired.

remained close supporters. Others like Bräuer and Benecke, the Abwehr
agent, sent several critical reports on him to Berlin asserting that his self-
declared rise to head of state actually stiffened the Norwegians' resolve to
resist. At 17:00 on the 15th it was all over. Bräuer told Quisling that Hitler
had decided he would have to go. An emergency solution with a non-political
Administrative Council did not work either and, on 19 April, Hitler cut
through the mess and appointed Josef Terboven as his representative and
Reichskommissar in Norway. He would rule supreme with an iron fist in the
five years to come. All attempts at a peaceful occupation had failed. On 24
April, Admiral Boehm, the newly established Naval Commander, Norway,
reported to Raeder that, on the surface, things were quiet in the occupied
areas, but there was a 'marked stiffening of the negative attitudes of the
population and an increased passive opposition'.[54] Two days later, on the

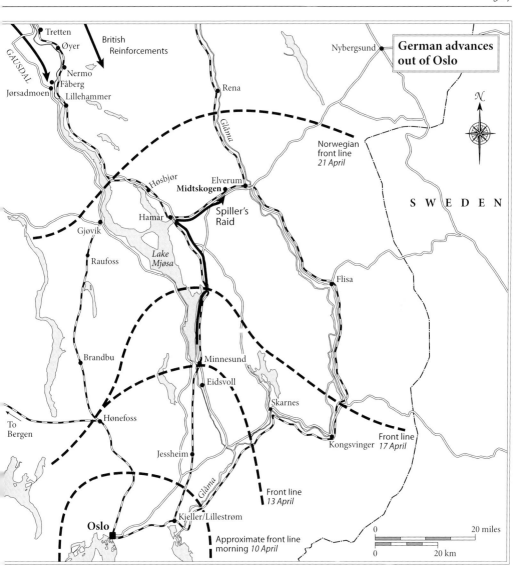

German advances out of Oslo

26th, German-controlled radio announced, if anybody was in doubt, that a state of war existed between Germany and Norway.[55]

The American journalist Leland Stowe from the *Chicago Daily News* happened to be in Oslo on his way home from Finland and Sweden. Around midday on 9 April, he stood on the balcony of his hotel watching German soldiers marching down the main street. The headline of his first report, which appeared in American and European newspapers that same day, was 'Norwegians in Oslo take the occupation calmly'. The text described passive Norwegians asking, 'When will the Brits come?' but doing nothing themselves. His next article was headed 'Betrayal of Norway' describing Norwegian traitors and German Trojan horses.[56] Stowe's articles, written without much knowledge of Norway or its political situation, were widely spread in the USA, Britain and Europe and created an impression of defeat and treason in Norway, not in line with reality. The *Daily Telegraph* in Britain printed his articles as they were, establishing a very negative image of Norwegians in general in the minds of many Brits, including military and politicians. Stowe took confusion and uncertainty among the public for indifference and, since he stayed in Oslo for only a few more days, he had no way of understanding what actually went on in the unoccupied areas. Quite the contrary, he believed Quisling was in charge and took his words and pamphlets to be true. Hence, his reports created an almost hysterical fear of fifth columnists detrimental to cooperation between Allies and Norwegians in the ensuing campaign. The damage this did skewed perceptions in America in a way that would take years to correct. The US Ambassador in Oslo, Mrs Harriman, wrote in 1941:

> I cannot help regretting that [Leland Stowe] mistook the stunned and shell-shocked attitude of the Norwegian people in the early days of the blitzkrieg for acquiescence in invasion. Journalists have to be fast, of course, but their misjudgements often require atonement, and I understand perfectly the resentment of the Norwegian people at the rumours spread by wire around the word. For, when they realised that the invasion had come, they fought with grandeur and against all odds.[57]

On the morning of 10 April, Generalmajor Jodl of OKW, issued orders on behalf of the Führer that all resistance in the Oslofjord area should be ruthlessly broken – '*rücksichtlos zu brechen*', a safe railway connection to Trondheim established and the 'old' Norwegian government arrested.[58] By then, however, Air Attaché Eberhart Spiller and Hauptmann Erich Walther, CO of the 2nd Parachute Company, had already decided to try and find King Haakon and detain him on their own. Seventy-nine paratroopers and twenty Army soldiers had been loaded into two cars, a truck and three buses and headed out of Oslo for a brazen operation behind the Norwegian lines. Bräuer later categorically denied having given Spiller any orders and Falkenhorst asserted to his interrogators in 1945, that the expedition was initiated by Spiller alone, without his approval, calling it 'Spiller's private war'.[59] There is a note in the OKW War Diary, however, saying: 'The Norwegian Government at Hamar. Paratroopers under way,' so Spiller and/or Walther had reported their departure and intentions and, one must assume, had it sanctioned by someone.[60] During the night of 9/10 April, the group ran into a company-sized Norwegian holding force at Midtskogen and the German advance was halted with half a dozen casualties, among them Spiller. The defending force was one of several established by 5th Infantry Regiment around Elverum, supported by Guardsmen and volunteers from the local rifle organisation. Hauptmann Walther found the venture too risky to continue and returned to Oslo. Spiller died in hospital the next day. In his wallet was found a note on which was written: 'King Haakon, Nygaardsvold, Hambro'. The last underlined in red. The attaché had his

German paratroopers operating behind Norwegian lines, attempting to detain King Haakon.

priorities clear. It is certain that Spiller intended to bring King Haakon back to Oslo. If the others were to be brought back or 'eliminated', is not known. Hauptmann Walther sent a laconic signal to Group XXI on the afternoon of the 10th: 'Not possible to detain Norwegian government due to strong defences.' For the second time in 24 hours, German attempts to capture King Haakon and his government had been halted. From this point on, German intentions changed to killing King Haakon and the government by repeated air-attacks. All failed.[61]

Weserübung South

In Denmark a different situation developed from that in Norway. At 04:00 on 9 April, the German envoy Cecil von Renthe-Fink, called the Danish Foreign Minister Peter Munch at home, requesting an urgent meeting with him. Twenty minutes later, Renthe-Fink told Munch that German troops were moving in to occupy Denmark and protect the country from Anglo-French aggression. Danish resistance would have to stop immediately. If not, Copenhagen would be bombed. Unknown to Munch, the first German soldiers were already ashore at Gedser while mechanised infantry units were crossing the border in southern Jutland. In addition, *Fallschirmjäger* had landed at the airfields at Aalborg, and other paratroopers had secured the Storstrøm Bridge and the fortress of Masnedø. While they were still speaking soldiers ran ashore in Copenhagen harbour from the minelayer *Hansestadt Danzig*, securing key administrative buildings as well as heading for Amalienborg Palace and King Christian X and his family. The first

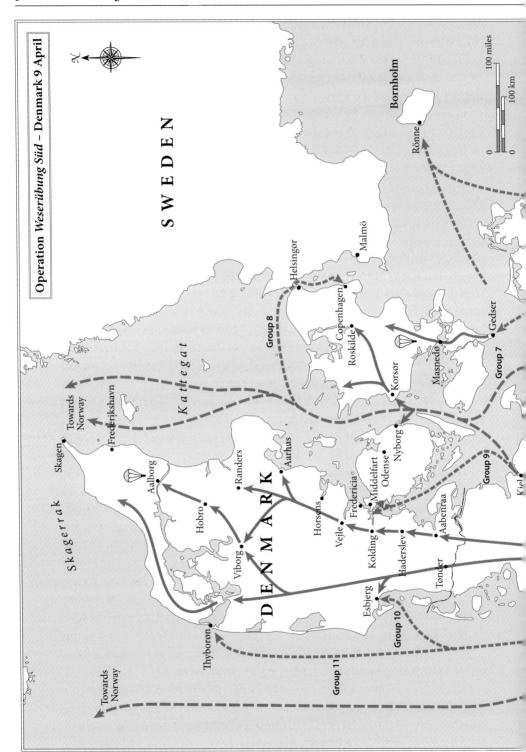

Operation *Weserübung Süd* – Denmark 9 April

N

SWEDEN

Bornholm

Rönne

Helsingor

Malmö

Copenhagen

Roskilde

Korsor

Group 8

Kattegat

Masnedo

Gedser

Group 7

Towards
Norway

Frederikshavn

Skagen

Skagerrak

Aalborg

Randers

Aarhus

Nyborg

Odense

Group 9

Kiel

Hobro

DENMARK

Horsens

Fredericia

Middelfart

Viborg

Vejle

Kolding

Haderslev

Aabenraa

Thyboron

Esbjerg

Tonder

Towards
Norway

Group 11

Group 10

100 miles

100 km

German attack on Amalienborg was repulsed by the Royal Guard. Inside the castle, the King, his government and the Supreme Commander, General William Prior, were discussing the situation. Except for Prior, who wanted to continue the resistance, all agreed that any prolonged opposition was impossible. The whole country was being overrun and the only solution was to cease fighting. At 06:00 King Christian and the Danish government decided to capitulate. A messenger was sent to deliver the Danish answer to the German ambassador while the order to stop fighting was issued. Later, the fear of Copenhagen being bombed was held as the main reason. By 07:00 all units of the Danish Army had received the order to lay down their guns.[62]

Energetic Measures

On 9 April, there were 22 British, French and Polish submarines in the North Sea, the Skagerrak and the Kattegat.[63] At 04:24, the British Admiralty issued a signal indicating that ports in south and west Norway were being invaded by German naval forces. Until this time, the submarines had only been allowed to attack 'enemy warships and transports'. Identifying which of the large numbers of merchant ships in the Kattegat and Skagerrak were German or indeed transports was virtually impossible, especially as escorts and air patrols precluded any attempt at surfacing in daylight. In the late morning of the 9th, the War Cabinet, after heavy pressure from Vice-Admiral (Submarines) Admiral Horton, agreed that all German merchant vessels in the eastern Skagerrak could be treated as warships and sunk without warning. This order was forwarded to all boats at 13:24. While the signal was decoded on board *Sunfish*, Lieutenant-Commander Jack Slaughter was focussing his periscope on the 7,129-ton *Amasis*, outside Swedish territorial waters off Lysekil. 'Just as the sights came on', he later wrote in his report, 'the last part of VA(S)'s 1324/9 was read out to me, so I fired.' One torpedo hit, and *Amasis* sank rapidly, initiating a series of successful actions by the Allied submarines.[64]

The bulk of the troops and supplies needed to sustain Operation *Weserübung* were to come through Oslo in a series of transport convoys following the initial landings. There had already been a significant attrition of the first transport group, heading for the invasion ports outside Oslo. The following groups, bringing in more than 100,000 troops and their equipment, would go to Oslo only. As the sea lanes further west were under total British dominance, connections to the other bridgeheads were planned to come via the Oslo region. This operation turned out to be not quite as easy as expected, mainly due to the one factor the Kriegsmarine had not fully prepared for: British submarines. Though not crippling, the attrition would be high enough

Generalmajor Richard Pellengahr,
commander of 196. ID.

for the set-up to be modified so that as many troops as possible were transported by air, while supplies and those that the aircraft had no room for, were shuttled between northern Denmark and various ports in and just outside the Oslofjord.

On 10 April, the Admiralty told C-in-C Home Fleet and VA(S) that they had decided that 'interference with communications in southern areas must be left mainly to submarines, air and mining, aided by intermittent sweeps when forces allow'.[65] This was a formidable upgrade of the strategic significance of the Submarine Service – probably not fully recognised at the time – creating an undreamt of opportunity for VA(S) and his submarines. At 19:56, Horton signalled his submarines that, following a Cabinet decision, any ships, merchant or otherwise, within 10 miles of the Norwegian coast, south of 61° N, and east of 6° E, could be attacked on sight; adding 'You are all doing magnificent work.' This area included all of the eastern North Sea, the Skaggerak and the Kattegat. For the first time, British submarines had been given the opportunity to wage unrestricted warfare. By now, however, air and surface activity in the Kattegat and Skagerrak had increased considerably and it was becoming difficult to find safe areas in which to charge batteries during the shortening periods of darkness. The British submarines were hunted day and night by aircraft and anti-submarine vessels and life in the Skagerrak was rapidly becoming very dangerous.[66]

At 16:35 on this day, the 10th, *Triton*, which had remained in the area off Skagen, sighted a large convoy of some fifteen ships steering north through the Kattegat, just outside Swedish territory. This was a mixed group of the first and second transport groups, heading for Oslo. On board were soldiers from 196th Infantry Division, with equipment and ammunition. Their commander, Generalmajor Richard Pellengahr, was on board *España*. When landed in Oslo, these men were intended to head for Trondheim via the valleys of eastern Norway.[67]

The transports of 2. Seetransportstaffel had sailed from Gotenhafen on the 8th at intervals and proceeded individually so as not to reveal their true purpose. Next morning, when Operation *Weserübung* had been initiated, they began forming a convoy in the Kattegat, including stragglers from 1. Seetransportstaffel, to prepare for the risky crossing of the eastern Skagerrak. A fairly large escort was also gathered to protect the valuable ships. During the night of 9/10 April some of the transports lost contact with the convoy and continued independently.[68] Pellengahr had received no information of what had happened in Norway so far during the invasion, but assumed that, as they had not been recalled, things were proceeding according to plan. As the convoy was not supposed to arrive in Oslo until next day, the ships proceeded slowly northwards just outside Swedish territory. The captain of one of the transports, *Hamm*, preferred to sail alone and was well ahead of the convoy. Just after lunch a signal was given to Pellengahr from the captain of *Hamm*: 'Attacked by submarine. Torpedo passed close aft. Torpedo-track and periscope clearly seen.' The crossing to Oslo might be even more dangerous than considered. After discussing the situation with the captain of *España* Pellengahr agreed (wrongly) that the ships ought to spread out and steer individual zigzag courses. Nothing happened, though. The commander of the escort, who presumably had received the same signal from *Hamm*, did nothing and the convoy continued unperturbed.[69]

By early afternoon, they were off Gothenburg. The sea remained glassy calm, and Lieutenant-Commander Pizey had to use his periscope sparingly to avoid detection. At 17:26 *Triton* was in position, and he fired six torpedoes

British submarine HMS *Triton*.

Friedenau hit and going down.

from about 2,000 metres. Three ships were hit: the 5,200-ton *Friedenau*, the 3,600-ton *Wigbert* and the escort *V 1507* (*Rau VI*). Total chaos broke out in the convoy. There had been no precautionary instructions and for a while it was every ship for itself. Some stopped to pick up survivors whereas others kept going. The counter-attack on *Triton* was severe. Seventy-eight depth charges were counted, but Pizey was able to get his submarine safely away within an hour. *Wigbert* sank on an even keel within about twenty minutes, while *Friedenau* remained afloat for a while longer, kept above water by her foreship. A least 384 officers and men from IR 340 perished with *Friedenau* and a similar number of men of IR 345 were lost on *Wigbert*; nineteen men went down with *V1507*. Some 800 were rescued in all, many by a Swedish destroyer that came to assist. *España* picked up 34 men and Pellengahr learned first-hand of the perils of being on board a torpedoed ship. Eventually, the transports were ushered along northwards, while a few of the escorts stayed behind to pick up the remaining survivors. When *Triton* surfaced at 21:15, Pizey set course for home as he had no more torpedoes left.[70]

A third ship of the convoy, the 2,500-ton *Antares* was stalked by *Sunfish* later in the evening and sunk off Lysekil. This caused 'considerable activity overhead' but no counter-attacks developed. *Sunfish* slipped away to charge her batteries. Later still, *Trident* and *Orzel* both missed in further attempts at decimating the convoy. The surviving transports reached Oslo on the 12th, followed by the ships of the third transport group a few days later. After this, most of the larger ships were sent to Norway in small, heavily escorted

The escort vessel *V 1501* picking up survivors. *España* is in the background.

groups. Troops who could not be carried by aircraft were taken by train to Denmark and shipped across from Frederikshavn or Aalborg to Larvik or Oslo, about 3,000 men per day.

Also on the 10th, *Tarpon* attacked what turned out to be the Q-ship *Schürbeck* (*Schiff 40*) west of Jutland. The torpedoes missed and in return *Schürbeck*, assisted by the minesweeper *M 6*, chased the submarine, dropping depth charges for about four hours. *Tarpon* was never heard from again and presumably lost with all hands in the counter-attack.[71]

On 11 April, following reports of German capital ships west of Lindesnes, Horton positioned *Severn*, *Clyde*, *Trident*, *Spearfish*, *Sunfish* and *Snapper* to cover the entrance to the Kattegat, between Lindesnes and Skagen, while *Shark* and *Seawolf* covered the German Bight. Some of the boats soon had to return to base as fuel, supplies and torpedoes were running low, but a steady number of German ships were sunk in the following days.

Lieutenant-Commander Eric Oddie took *Triad* into the Skagerrak on 11 April. He attempted to enter Oslofjord but found it too risky as the nights were short and moonlit and there were many anti-submarine (AS) patrols around. Instead, he lurked about the mouth of the fjord and sank the German transport *Ionia* after nightfall on the 11th. Afterwards, three AS trawlers searched for the submarine. They did not obtain direct contact, but 135 explosions were counted by the crew, going off at varying distances. Many of these were probably small bombs dropped as deterrents by the trawlers as well as from aircraft patrolling the outer part of the fjord.

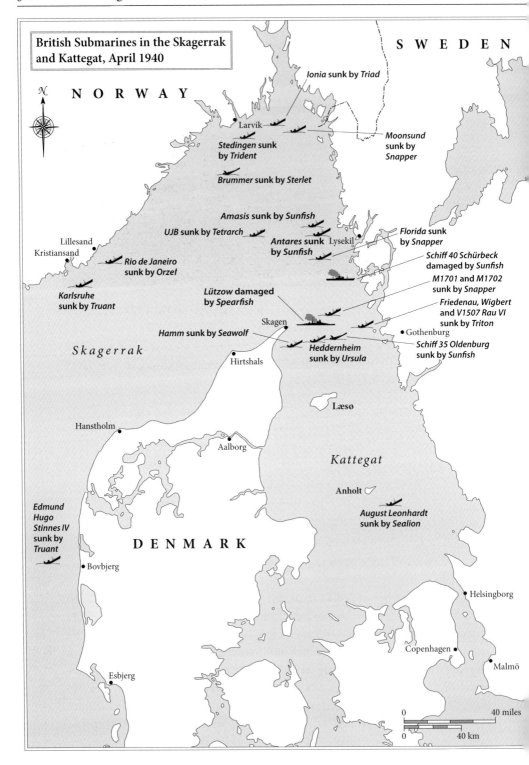

British Submarines in the Skagerrak and Kattegat, April 1940

N

S W E D E N

N O R W A Y

Ionia sunk by *Triad*

Larvik

Moonsund sunk by *Snapper*

Stedingen sunk by *Trident*

Brummer sunk by *Sterlet*

Amasis sunk by *Sunfish*

UJB sunk by *Tetrarch*

Antares sunk by *Sunfish*

Lysekil

Florida sunk by *Snapper*

Lillesand
Kristiansand

Rio de Janeiro sunk by *Orzeł*

Schiff 40 Schürbeck damaged by *Sunfish*

M1701 and *M1702* sunk by *Snapper*

Karlsruhe sunk by *Truant*

Lützow damaged by *Spearfish*

Friedenau, Wigbert and *V1507 Rau VI* sunk by *Triton*

Skagen

Gothenburg

Hamm sunk by *Seawolf*

Heddernheim sunk by *Ursula*

Schiff 35 Oldenburg sunk by *Sunfish*

S k a g e r r a k

Hirtshals

Læsø

Hanstholm

Aalborg

Kattegat

Anholt

Edmund Hugo Stinnes IV sunk by *Truant*

August Leonhardt sunk by *Sealion*

D E N M A R K

Bovbjerg

Helsingborg

Copenhagen

Malmö

Esbjerg

0		40 miles
0		40 km

Seeing their comrades perish was a shock for the survivors and many experienced
deep trauma – what today we would diagnose as PTSD.

Also on the 11th, well inside the Kattegat, *Sealion* sank *August Leonhardt*
off Anholt.[72] Lieutenant-Commander Bryant wrote:

> In the afternoon, we sighted the bridge of a ship over the horizon and
> 'grouped up' to run in to attack. Very shortly we had to slow again for an
> AS patrol and could not get in close [...] It was a longish shot, nearly 3,000
> yards and we fired two torpedoes. The AS vessels which had been troubling
> us earlier had gone off on a wild-goose chase over the horizon; and the air
> patrol had disappeared to the northward. It was one of these occasions, rare
> for a submarine, when one could wait [at periscope depth] and watch the
> shot [...] Suddenly a great column of water rose above her masts.[73]

August Leonhardt sank in very shallow water, leaving her bridge and masts
still exposed.

At midday on the 11th OKW in Berlin issued orders on behalf of the Führer
that 181. ID should be transported to Oslo by air (IR 334), by fast torpedo
boats from Frederikshavn in Denmark (IR 349) and the rest by well protected
convoys from Hamburg, along the Danish west coast, and across to southern
Norway behind the newly laid minefields. The British submarine offensive
in the Skagerrak and Kattegat complicated the transfer of troops to Norway
making room for the Allied expeditionary corps landing in mid-Norway
between 14 and 18 April. Although these were eventually pushed back and
evacuated amid a large number of faulty decisions, repeated mismanagement

Six comrades from IR 340 aboard *Friedenau*. A note on the back of the photo lists them (*left to right*) as: Kunoth – missing; Krause, Miche – missing; Lehmann, Walcher – wounded; Schadeck – missing. Three of them apparently went down with the ship.

and a general inability to cooperate with the Norwegian forces, they nevertheless prolonged the Norwegian campaign and added to the German cost.[74]

Oslo – The Centre of Gravity

It was not until 08:45 on the 10th that *Lützow*, *Emden* and *Möwe* finally passed the Drøbak Narrows behind R 21 and R 23 with sweeping gear set, partly to avoid wreckage from *Blücher*, partly in case there should be mines after all. They reached Oslo harbour at 11:00, thirty hours behind schedule. *Emden* tied up at Vippetangen pier 3 by the grain silos, while *Lützow* docked below Akershus with *Möwe* outside, near shed 38. The seriously wounded were quickly taken to hospitals around the city. The dead were temporarily gathered in a warehouse for identification and preparation for burial. Surviving officers were quartered in hotels in the city centre; men were billeted in schools, gyms and other public buildings and a search for mattresses, bedclothes and above all food was set going. By the morning of the 11th, there were around 1,000 names on the Navy's list of survivors, but

Survivors from *Friedenau* arriving in Oslo on the 11th.

confusion and uncertainty still reigned. During this day, the R-boats brought more survivors to Oslo, but also numerous bodies. Some forty bodies were recovered during the summer on the beaches of the Narrows and other remains were reclaimed along the fjord for a long time.[75]

The remaining soldiers on board the ships disembarked, more troops were flown in, and the German situation improved – somewhat. The transport ships, which should have arrived during the afternoon of the 9th, eventually turned up on the 11th and it took a week before the German forces were established in Oslo and could consider securing the rest of eastern Norway. Hauptmann Werner Boese, one of the administration officers of 163. ID later reported that in the early morning of the 10th, when he and Generalmajor Engelbrecht got to Akershus, naval attaché Schreiber showed up, very upset. He could not understand how this could have happened, according to Boese, as several reports had been sent to Berlin, confirming that the fortress at Oscarsborg would resist any attempt to pass through the Drøbak Narrows.[76]

Generalmajor Engelbrecht came aboard *Lützow* to coordinate the management of the invasion forces and to learn what had happened elsewhere in the fjord. Thiele wanted to leave as soon as possible and at 15:00 he cast off.

Sealion (left) and sister-boat *Shark* (inboard) at Portsmouth.

Hence, Lange of *Emden* became senior naval commander in Oslo and *Emden* the hub of the naval defence system in Oslofjord.

Guns, ammunition, fuel, maps and supplies were provided through her to the ships and outposts in Oslofjord until a sustainable supply line could be established. Ill and wounded men were treated in her sick bay and those who needed it prepared for transport home. In addition, the powerful radio transmitter on board became the hub for communication between Germany, Oslo, the ships in the Skagerrak and Kattegat and the isolated landing sites around the coast. The Luftwaffe and the Army also made use of *Emden*'s radio transmitter.[77]

General Falkenhorst was supposed to arrive in Oslo in the afternoon of the 9th. This was cancelled as the events unfolded, and it was not until 16:00 on the 10th that he arrived at Fornebu. Admiral Boehm, the designated Commanding Admiral Norway, landed at the same time in a separate aircraft. Buschenhagen and Krancke had arrived earlier in the morning and their aircraft almost crashed on landing. In accordance with previous decisions, Boehm continued to report to OKM and Raeder in Berlin and not to Falkenhorst. The two senior officers had strict orders, however, to communicate and collaborate.[78] In Oslo, Boehm set up a temporary headquarters in the KNA hotel and called a meeting with all senior naval staff to discuss how to run things in the unexpected situation. Next day, the 11th, he sat down with Lange and the other naval commanders to decide how to take and keep control of the country during what seemed likely to be a long and difficult campaign.[79]

Boehm asked for a hospital ship to be sent north and noted that he would ensure 'valuable specialists' were returned home as soon as possible. The rest of the *Blücher* survivors needed uniforms and weapons, for self-defence as well as taking on the tasks of administering the city. General Engelbrecht asked for the survivors to be assembled in units and used as naval infantry to support his own soldiers, but this was strongly opposed by Boehm. 'No Navy men to the Army!' he noted in his diary. The only use of the *Blücher*-men he would accept was temporarily to supplement the German garrisons at Horten, Kaholm, Drøbak and Rauøy, so that the Army personnel still there could be withdrawn. With *Emden* stuck in Oslo as headquarters, Boehm had only the remnants of 1. Räumbootsflottille, *Rau VII* and *Rau VIII* at his disposal, of which *Rau VII* was at the yard in Horten, until the surviving Norwegian naval vessels could be taken over and made operational.[80] More than twenty special commando groups led by junior or petty officers with men from *Emden* were sent out on R-boats to trace and take command of

Lützow (*right*) and *Emden* heading for Oslo on the morning of 10 April as a Heinkel He 111 bomber flies overhead.

every Norwegian naval vessel that could be found or any civilian ship that could be armed with guns and depth charges. Within a week, some fifteen ex-RNN boats were operating under the German flag. Other teams were sent ashore to help the Army to secure vital depots and systems from sabotage. On the 14th *R 18* and *R 19* returned to Germany for engine repairs that could not be made in Norway while *R 23* had been taken into a Norwegian yard the day before but was waiting for spare parts to arrive by aircraft. Hence, only four R-boats remained operational; *R 20, R 21, R 22* and *R 24.*[81]

Boehm later told Raeder that on arrival he found a degree of chaos he was not prepared for. Nobody had any overview of what was under German control and what was not. Army, Luftwaffe and Kriegsmarine personnel were deployed as they arrived and just about everything had to be improvised. Oberstleutnant Pohlmann took charge of the improvised efforts and Leutnant Kempf was ordered ashore from *Widar* to help Oberst Nickelmann secure control of key points in Oslo, including the by now abandoned AA positions. Erich Pruck, the Abwehr agent, was assigned a temporary staff for his newly established intelligence office, Abwehrstelle Norwegen (AstN) until a proper intelligence staff could be transferred from Germany. Besides organising intelligence, POW handling and communication control in the occupied areas, one of Pruck's tasks was to monitor the development of the political situation in Sweden.

Emden in Oslo harbour.

Falkenhorst and Boehm arriving at Fornebu around 16:00 on the 10th.
From right, Boehm, Falkenhorst, Bräuer and Pohlmann.

During 10 April soldiers from IR 324, III./IR 307 and III./IR 159 were still arriving at Fornebu. When Engelbrecht arrived in Oslo, his 163. ID had two infantry regiments with low operational status to consolidate the occupation of the Oslo area. Part of I./IR 307 had arrived from Son, but the battalion could not reorganise fully until the rest of its soldiers had completed their tasks in Oslofjord. II./IR 307 disintegrated when *Blücher* went down. The second regiment, IR 324, was dependent on the slow build up by air through Fornebu, still ongoing on 9 and 10 April. The third regiment, IR 310 was aboard vessels in outer Oslofjord, and had not reached Oslo harbour as planned. The 4th Battalion of Gebirgsjäger Regiment 138 from *Lützow* would soon be ready for action after arriving by train and buses from Son. At nightfall on 10 April there were some 5,000 German soldiers in Oslo. Because of the resistance from Oscarsborg and Bolærne the follow up convoys were delayed.

When *Lützow* headed down the fjord with the torpedo boats in company, the Germans left in Oslo were extremely vulnerable. None of the supply ships had arrived yet and, except for the guns of *Emden*, all defence of the capital and its approaches depended on guns taken over from the Norwegians. The Germans were in Oslo, but Oslo was not safely in German hands in the afternoon of 10 April. With the Royal Navy in command of the North Sea, west of the German minefields, the outcome of Operation *Weserübung* still

Oslo Harbour in mid-April, after the invasion.

hung in the balance. Oslo was the heart of Norway and control of the harbour and the fjord would be essential to achieve the objectives outlined by Hitler a month earlier. Control of the airspace by aircraft and anti-aircraft guns would be critical as would taking over the Norwegian coastal defences and establishing an effective anti-submarine system extending from Oslofjord through the Skagerrak towards Denmark, east of the minefield. Without a safe and effective sea-line of communication and a transport system in the air, the Germans in Norway would be extremely vulnerable once the Norwegians had regained their resolve and British and French expeditionary forces could be landed in the west. Breaking out of Oslo with the troops in the capital on the 10th was out of the question and a massive airlift operation, sufficient to bring in needed men and equipment was not realistic.

The survivors from *Blücher* were dispersed over several locations, largely as SKL insisted that Navy personnel should be given 'naval tasks' and not subordinated to the Army. After the campaign had ended Admiral Norwegen, Admiral Boehm, took stock of what he was now responsible for. On 16 June he wrote in his War Diary:

> When occupying Norway, an overall personnel plan had not been developed. What was immediately available could be used to set up a few staffs, some intelligence groups, some naval infantry units and man 4–6 of the former Norwegian batteries. All survivors from *Blücher*, *Brummer*, *R 17*, *Königsberg*, *Bremse* and the two destroyers still left in Trondheim should therefore be used to man the remaining coastal defence batteries

as well as setting up harbour-defence flotillas. The crew of the torpedo boat *Albatros* has been transferred to *Olav Tryggvason* which now is on its way to Germany. Around 200 men from *Blücher* will follow in the former Norwegian torpedo boats *Gyller* and *Odin*.[82]

Specialists and skilled technicians, now manning the forts and fortresses in Norway, could be sent to Germany when relieved by trained naval artillery personnel. Otherwise, officers and NCOs could be sent home only in special cases. This issue was to create serious disagreement, though seventy-five men were almost immediately shipped back to Germany. Based on instructions from Marinegruppenkommando Ost, it was decided to leave some 300 of *Blücher*'s survivors in Oslo, while specialists and officers not needed should accompany *Lützow* and the torpedo boats back to Germany. Of the 300, two companies of seventy-five '*Blücher*-men' each were equipped and armed from the stores of *Emden* and *Lützow* and shipped to Horten and Drøbak to bolster the meagre occupation forces there. The rest were installed aboard *Emden* or in various schools and public buildings around town and eventually employed aboard captured Norwegian naval vessels.[83]

On the 10th, Korvettenkapitän Förster, *Blücher*'s Navigation Officer was appointed Harbour Commander of Oslo (Hafenkommandant Oslo),

Everyday life has returned to Oslo. Except for a few German soldiers and some swastika flags, life appears normal – for now.

replacing the missing Korvettenkapitän Karlowa, while Kapitänleutnant Mihatsch was appointed Harbour Captain, replacing the also missing Kapitänleutnant Wulle. One of their first tasks was to take care of the survivors from *Blücher* as they were brought to Oslo, providing accommodation, food and clothes as well as medical care for the wounded. Three weeks later, on the 29th. Kapitän zur See Friedrich Rieve, former captain of the cruiser *Karlsruhe* sunk off Kristiansand by the submarine *Truant* on the afternoon of 9 April, took over as the position was upgraded to Commander of the Sea Defences of Oslo (Kommandant der Seeverteidigung Oslo). To be in the centre of his area of responsibility, and probably stay some distance away from Boehm, Rieve choose to establish himself with his staff in Horten.[84]

Eventually German control of southern Norway, including Oslo and the Oslofjord was secured and in the early morning of 7 June, the same day as King Haakon left northern Norway for Great Britain, *Emden* cast off from Oslo to return to Swinemünde.

1. Seetransportstaffel arrived with three ships (two had been sunk by torpedo) in Oslo on 11 April with the rest of 163. ID, which was IR 310 and support units. 163. ID was still securing Oslo and had no own forces available to operate outside the capital.

2. Seetransportstaffel arrived in Oslo on 11–12 April with Pellengahr's 196. ID, consisting of IR 340, IR 345, IR 362 and support units. The submarine attacks had reduced the convoy from eleven to nine ships and 20 per cent of the division was lost. By the time they landed, only IR 362 was still intact, while the other two regiments were decimated and had to reorganise. The plan for 196. ID was to launch an attack out of Oslo to the north, towards Trondheim and Åndalsnes. Due to the losses and delays, however, Falkenhorst ordered Pellengahr to secure Østfold to the south-east, towards the Swedish border, instead. This task was intended for 181. ID, but this had not arrived when the attack was launched on 11 April. Parts of 69. ID (III./IR 159 and IR 236) had landed at Fornebu and were supposed to join the rest of the division in Bergen by train. Now, they had to fight their way towards Bergen, under Engelbrecht's overall command. The westward attack was launched on 11 April. The area of responsibility between 196. ID and 163. ID was separated with a line from Kjeller to Mjøsa. Pellengahr began his operation as soon as his first troops arrived in Oslo on 11 April. 4th Gebirgsjäger Battalion was ordered to move as the spearhead towards Eidsvoll and Minnesund. The *Gebirgsjäger* battalion went by train from Oslo towards Eidsvoll but was stopped south of the small town by Norwegian forces. The planned main attack in the direction of Trondheim had at last started, but with very limited forces. Meanwhile 196. ID began its operation from Oslo harbour. IR 362 as the only battle-ready regiment of the division initiated the main operation

towards Østfold on 12 April. Companies from IR 340 began to operate further east in support of the attacks. Companies from IR 345 stayed in Oslo and secured the eastern part of the capital. There were around 15,400 German soldiers in the Oslo area at nightfall on 12 April. About a third had arrived by air with no heavy equipment.

Slowly things normalised, not least as no British or Norwegian counter-attacks developed, but only on the 13th had the 163. ID reached its goals of securing the Oslo area as far as Hønefoss, Drammen and Kongsberg North-east of the capital the *Gibirgsjäger* battalion and companies from IR 340 attacked the Norwegian infantry company at Minnesund on 13 and 14 April and the Norwegians had to retire further north.

During the 13th several aircraft left Fornebu airfield for Germany, returning the first specialists as well as a few key officers who were to convey what had happened to the SKL as well as the OKW and the Führer in Berlin. During the afternoon, however, Boehm decided enough was enough and stopped any more naval men leaving Norway. Instead, he started awarding medals to several seriously wounded men, while preparations for the burial of the dead were initiated.[85]

3. Seetransportstaffel arrived in Oslo with ten ships, after a loss of two, on 15–16 April, up to four days late, with the main body of 181. ID.[86] Horton's, Eriksen's and Færden's successes had taken a heavy toll on the German Army and delayed the offensive out of Oslo.

Except for First Officer Heymann's efforts little was done to make a systematic collection of *Blücher*'s experiences and set up a reliable account of the events. This, and the death of Woldag (described below), created unclear and contradicting stories and made a basis for later conspiracy theories.

During the preparations to abandon ship, destruction of code-lists, orders and other secret material was initiated. Standard procedure was to throw this overboard in designated weighted bags and boxes. Some of the documents did not fit into the boxes, though, and apparently there was a lack of bags in some areas. Many later reported having thrown the papers they were responsible for into the fire amidships, but it is obvious from the number of documents retrieved from the fjord that numerous sets of documents were left behind or just thrown directly into the water. At least three packages of floating documents were found by Norwegians. One (or possibly two) by civilians, one by the Guardsmen who came to intern the survivors and one at Oscarsborg by kommandørkaptein Anderssen and his men. The Germans searched for the documents, but they were well hidden and not found. Neither, however, did they reach Norwegian authorities in time to make any difference.[87]

Chapter 15
Homeward Bound

Off Skagen

For Thiele, it was urgent to take *Lützow* home to Germany as soon as possible. The risk of interference by the Royal Navy in Oslofjord or the Skagerrak was considered low but British aircraft could appear at any time. The main reason for the rush, however, was the need to reach a yard where the auxiliary engine, which had led *Lützow* to Oslo in the first place, could be repaired, as well as the newly inflicted damage from the guns at Kopås. Merchant warfare in the Atlantic remained the *raison d'être* for the cruisers of the *Deutschland* class and every week passing would shorten the length of the nights in northern waters, and thus his chances for a successful break-out into the Atlantic.

Emden and the R-boats were left behind when *Lützow* and *Möwe* headed back down the fjord at around 15:00 on the 10th. *Albatros* and *Kondor* were already operating in the outer reaches of the fjord and would join later. Kapitänleutnant Schnurbein and his men were picked up at Drøbak and replaced with survivors from *Blücher*. Further men from *Blücher* were landed at Horten on the way down the fjord.[1]

HMS *Spearfish.*

On receiving the news of *Albatros*'s grounding, Thiele detached *Möwe* to stay with *Kondor* in the fjord while *Lützow* continued alone, despite sub-marine alerts in the Kattegat. He reckoned twenty-four knots – the maximum that *Lützow* could make – would be sufficient for a safe trip home and he was not overly worried at losing his escort. As he left Oslofjord behind, the night was clear and starry with good visibility, moderate seas and a Force 4 north-easterly wind. Signals received during the day put most of the British submarine contacts near the Swedish coast. Hence, Thiele steered a westerly track in large zigzags, heading for Skagen. An hour after midnight German time, the ship's radar picked up a contact ahead, fine on the starboard bow, at a range of 11,500 metres. The echo was small and taken to be a fishing vessel, but Thiele turned to port to give it a wide berth. The range increased, and when the radar reported the echo lost, Thiele had *Lützow* turn back onto the main course. At 01:20 *Lützow* was 8 miles north-east of Skagen steering 138°.[2]

Spearfish had reached her designated patrol area in the Kattegat on the morning of 7 April. There was extensive activity in the area, both in the air and at sea, and 8 and 9 April were largely spent hiding below the surface. On the 10th, *Spearfish* was chased by a group of escorts and anti-submarine trawlers for most of the afternoon. Sixty-six depth charges were counted, causing high-pressure leaks and damage to hydrophones and periscopes. The leaks increased the pressure inside the submarine and together with the foul air made the crew exhausted and dizzy. Eventually, the hunters were shaken off and Lieutenant-Commander John Forbes could bring his boat to the surface after having been submerged for more than twenty hours.

About an hour later, the first lieutenant sighted the bow wave of a large ship on the starboard quarter at about 3,000 metres. Forbes believed it might be one of the escorts again and altered course to port to put his boat stern-on and slow down to avoid detection. Some minutes later, the vessel was seen to be very large and, later still, identified as the heavy cruiser *Admiral Scheer*, *Lützow*'s sister ship. The torpedoes were set to run at four to six metres and, with both engines stopped, Forbes fired six torpedoes, aiming from the conning tower, still on the surface. In spite of a very dark night, conditions were otherwise good, and he risked the long-range shots. Immediately after firing, *Spearfish* turned to a westerly course, still on the surface, and sent a sighting report to Submarine Command. After some minutes, a huge explosion was heard from the direction of the target.[3]

When Thiele gave the order to bring *Lützow* back on her main course, Forbes's torpedoes were running, and she almost escaped. *Lützow* was still turning to starboard when, at 01:28 GeT, a massive impact shook the cruiser aft. Nothing was seen prior to the hit, but just after a further two or three torpedo tracks were reported at an acute angle off the port side. The steering engine failed and the rudder was jammed at twenty degrees to starboard. Hence, the cruiser kept turning while speed was reduced. Nobody aft answered the telephone, and it was obvious that there was significant damage. Several compartments aft were flooded and *Lützow* settled by the stern with a slight list to port. The main engines were temporarily stopped, but the engine room reported no major damage, and they would soon be ready again. The damage-control groups quickly emptied the affected sections and closed them off and, despite severe intrusions of water, the situation appeared to be under control. Thiele gave orders for emergency steering to be arranged, but the rudder room could not be accessed and attempts to steer by the propellers had no effect; both propellers were useless. The starboard propeller was gone, the port propeller was still attached to the shaft, but all bearings and gears had been destroyed.

At 01:55 Thiele sent an urgent signal to Marinegruppenkommando Ost in Kiel, giving the estimated position, adding: 'Need immediate tug assistance,' followed some ten minutes later by: 'Probable torpedo hit aft. Engines are OK. Rudder not operational. Submarine protection is required.' And later still: 'My position is ten miles off Skagen. Ship is un-manoeuvrable. Holding water. Both propellers lost.' Eventually, the flooding was stemmed, but the three aft sections were inaccessible, including the magazines. With no propulsion or steering, *Lützow* was drifting at about two knots south-westward towards Skagen, broadside to the sea. Further submarine attacks were to be expected and in the good visibility the immobilised ship would be a sitting duck. A sharp anti-submarine watch was set, and all secondary guns manned. Thiele also ordered all crewmen to don lifebelts and the lower decks to be evacuated, except for the damage-control parties. Boats were swung out and made ready for launching. The aft turret was ordered to jettison all ammunition to help lighten the stern. At 03:08 Oberleutnant Vogler was sent off in a motor cutter towards Skagen to summon assistance from tugs and escort vessels. By 03:00 the ship's trim had been improved by pumping oil, and the main part of the hull was almost upright, even if the after deck was at an angle, partly under water. At about the same time, signals were received that 17th Anti-Submarine Flotilla, 19th Minesweeping Flotilla and 2nd S-Boat Flotilla were on their way, as were torpedo boats *Greif, Luchs* and *Seeadler,* in addition *Möwe* and *Kondor* were heading south from Oslofjord.[4]

Immediately after 03:00 German time, when he received the radio signal that *Lützow* had been hit, Kapitänleutnant Neuss of *Möwe* set course for the cruiser. *Kondor* followed but having propeller damage from hitting wreckage from *Blücher* during the rescue operation, she could only do 20 knots and lagged behind. Kapitänleutnant Wilcke wanted to retrieve Oberfähnrich

The crew of *Spearfish* coming ashore at the end of an eventful patrol.

Strauss and his men from Bolærne, but as nobody was available to relieve them it was decided to leave them where they were for the time being.[5]

During the early morning, several trawlers and minesweepers arrived and as many as possible of the ship's company were transferred to these, which thereafter took up screening positions. A temporary tow was rigged from three minesweepers to have a minimum of steerage way and keep the bow to the wind. *Möwe*, which arrived around 08:20, took charge ahead of the tow. Not long after that Oberleutnant Vogler returned from Skagen. He had not found any tugs but brought numerous fishing vessels and the Skagen lifeboat should an evacuation become necessary. At dawn, aircraft arrived overhead, reducing the danger of submarine attacks further. The RAF mercifully stayed away.

The minesweepers found handling the cruiser difficult as the wind and waves were building, but in the afternoon the ocean tugs *Wotan* and *Seeteufel* arrived to take over the job. It was feared for a while that the worsening conditions might break off the stern altogether, as it only appeared to be attached to the rest of the ship by the two propeller shafts, but the sea calmed somewhat, and the structure held. It seemed as if it might be possible to save *Lützow* after all. Still, Thiele ordered all unnecessary men off, including most of the gun crews now that a proper escort was in place. Some five hundred men were landed at Frederikshavn in Denmark, from where they were ingloriously sent home by train. Some of the men had sailed with *Lützow* for years and pleaded to be allowed to stay on board during her time of danger, but Thiele had no time for sentiment. He was trying to save his ship, so off they went.

The damage control officers eventually calculated that *Lützow* had some 1,600 tons of seawater below decks when the flooding was checked. This and the drooping stern gave her a twelve-metre draught, which became a huge problem as the Danish coastal waterways in some places are rather shallow. On the other hand, Thiele preferred to risk grounding on a sandbank to having his ship sink in deeper water. Progress down the Kattegat was slow. *Lützow* did ground on several occasions, but careful manoeuvring by the tugs and deliberate counter-flooding freed her each time. The torpedo boats were released for Kiel in the afternoon of the 13th. Eventually at 20:22 on 14 April, *Lützow* was made safe at the Deutsche Werke yard at Kiel. Fifteen men had died when the torpedo struck. Their remains were buried in Kiel with full military honours.[6]

Taken into drydock, the damage on *Lützow* was seen to be worse than feared. The crack in the after-ship was dramatic and below the waterline there was nothing but distorted steel. On the starboard side large parts of the decks above the armour-belt were shredded. Repairs would last well into 1941.[7]

Closing the Door

On 12 April, *Snapper* came across the small tanker *Moonsund* of 321 tons off Larvik. Lieutenant William King wrote in his report:

> At 03:40, as dawn was breaking, a small steamer was sighted to the north-eastwards, making for the northward. As it was getting light and aircraft were expected, it was desired to sink her quickly and two torpedoes were fired on a broad track. These missed astern. It was then seen that the steamer was smaller and nearer than at first estimated and that torpedoes were wasted on such a target as she could be chased and brought to. *Snapper* proceeded to chase and overhaul the steamer, which zigzagged and took no notice of the signal to heave to […] After a chase of seven miles, she was brought to with a shot across the bows. She then broke the German Merchant Flag. The order was shouted to abandon ship and the reply was heard, 'as you wish'. No efforts appeared to be made to get the boats out. The Lewis gun was then fired over the masts but produced no results. One round of HE was then fired into the forepeak and the cargo of aviation spirit burst into flames and the crew jumped over the side. Six out of the seven were picked up; the seventh could not be seen.[8]

In his biography King added:

Sunfish returning to port on 23 April. Part of the top of the photo
has been obscured by the wartime censor.

We nosed gently from one survivor to another, with two men hauling
them in over the saddle-tanks and lowering the exhausted, wet bodies
down the forehatch, which is about 20 ft. lower than the conning-tower
and a dangerous place for the crew to be when there is a likelihood of an
emergency dive. The last swimmer was dragged onto our casing just as the
first aircraft appeared. Deciding to abandon this one man and get the vital
forehatch closed I ordered: 'Clear the foredeck and dive.' But Geoffrey
Carew-Hunt, my third officer, begged, 'Let me get him down, sir'. Weakly I
snapped: 'Do it quick.' Looking back I think I should have been heartless.

Brummer offloading in Oslo harbour.

> The risk to my ship was unjustifiable. While perhaps fifteen seconds ticked by, Carew-Hunt bravely dragged the wet German down the steep cluttered forehatch and shut it.[9]

With everybody on board, King took *Snapper* down as quickly as he could, happy to get away from the smoking wreck that could be seen from miles away. As part of the support fleet for the German invasion forces, *Moonsund* was under way to Trondheim with aviation fuel, though the Master and Second Mate both claimed they were heading for Oslo where they were to receive orders. Two of those rescued subsequently died of shock and exposure and were buried at sea. The remaining four, including the captain, were happy to be alive and seemed to enjoy the rest of *Snapper*'s rather eventful patrol.

After Snapper had been chased most of the day by aircraft and surface vessels, things became quiet by nightfall and *Snapper* surfaced to get fresh air and charge batteries. Having released the two dead Germans to the sea after a short ceremony, King set course south to the inner parts of the Skagerrak. Anti-submarine vessels were everywhere and not being detected was hard work. Nevertheless, targets presented themselves and, on the 14 April, the 6,150-ton merchant ship *Florida* was sunk off Lysekil in Sweden. This time retribution was more accurate and persistent and depth charges exploded nearby until the pursuers were shed at nightfall. King wrote:

The German morning air patrols had recently been sent out late, so we remained on the surface to finish charging our batteries until 4 a.m. I was standing on the bridge with the officer of the watch Geoffrey Carew-Hunt and our three lookouts, peering into the misty half-light that heralded the approach of dawn when a dim shape showed in the gloom. 'Diving Stations! Night Alarm! Stand by all torpedo tubes!' [...] The tubes' bow caps were now always kept open when on the surface, with a man on watch, ready to fire them at immediate notice. Within sixty seconds of sighting the first ship, *Snapper* was ready to strike.[10]

On the 15th, *Snapper* sank the two minesweepers *M 1701 H. M. Behrens* and *M 1702 Carsten Janssen* in a surface attack north-east of Skagen. The result was the severest round of pursuit *Snapper* had experienced so far and it would take all day before they could escape, exhausted and just barely alive. Out of torpedoes, King set course for home.[11]

On 13 April, the minelaying submarine *Narwhal* laid a batch of fifty mines north of Læsø Island. Later, the German merchantman *Togo* was damaged by these mines while the minesweeper *M 1302 Schwaben* was sunk. On her return passage *Narwhal* attacked two different convoys off Denmark but was driven off in both cases by efficient escorts. In the following weeks other minefields were laid on both sides of Skagen and inside the Kattegat, but after the loss of *Seal* in May, further minelaying was focused off western Norway.[12] Next day, *Sunfish* rounded off a most successful patrol by sinking the *Oldenburg* (*Schiff 35*) off Skagen. Korvettenkapitän Selchow's trawlers of the 11th Anti-Submarine Flotilla (U-Jagd Flottille) chased her for hours

HMS *Sterlet*.

Lieutenant William King (*centre*) in the conning tower of *Snapper.*

afterwards without gaining a firm contact and no serious attack developed.[13]

On 15 April, the gunnery training ship *Brummer* sailed from Kiel to Frederikshavn where she embarked 409 soldiers for Oslo. The embarkation was swift and *Brummer* headed to sea that evening accompanied by *Jaguar*, *Falke* and *F 5*, also with soldiers on board. After reaching Oslo next morning, the soldiers and their equipment were disembarked, and the ships cast off again at 16:30, heading back to Frederikshavn for more troops. The weather was poor with fog and snow showers and Korvettenkapitän Max Gebauer ordered the other boats into line astern to avoid losing contact. There was no anti-submarine screen. At 23:07, off the island of Jomfruland, three torpedo-tracks were seen from *Brummer* which was in the van. Two of the torpedoes passed in front, but the third impacted below turret *Anton*, detonating the forward magazine. The bow was cut clean off and turret *Bruno* left pointing towards the water at a crazy angle. At first it was unclear to the other ships from which side the attack had come and *Falke* and *F 5* circled the scene, dropping depth charges and looking for a contact while *Jaguar* stayed close to *Brummer*. When it was clear that she would sink, *F 5* was ordered to approach to take off the wounded while *Jaguar* joined *Falke* searching. A submarine contact was briefly obtained and the two torpedo boats gave chase, but nothing was achieved, and the contact lost. There were twenty-five dead and at least as many wounded, largely from the foreship. Having evacuated the casualties, *F 5* set course for Frederikshavn and Gebauer, himself wounded from being thrown off the bridge by the explosion, ordered *Jaguar* alongside to take off the remaining crew. *Brummer* sank off Tvesteinen lighthouse, shortly after.[14]

The assailant was *Sterlet*. After attacking *Brummer*, however, her fate remains uncertain. No signals were ever received, and she was eventually reported overdue and lost. From the reports of the German ships, it seems likely that she escaped from *Jaguar* and *Falke*, unless she sank to her destruction unnoticed. Two days later, north-east of Skagen, a submarine fired two torpedoes unsuccessfully on a convoy just after dusk. During the attack, the boat broke surface and was heavily attacked by the escort. This was most likely *Sterlet*, and she was possibly sunk on this occasion, or so damaged that she succumbed on the way home. She may also have run into the newly laid German mines of the Skagerrak-Sperre.[15]

Finally, on the 18th, in a night attack north of Skagen, *Seawolf* sank the transport *Hamm* returning from Oslo .

The intense efforts of the German flotillas and other escorts eventually paid off, however, and by the end of the month, three submarines had been lost, *Thistle*, *Tarpon* and *Sterlet*, a heavy price to pay. During the week of

The crew of *Snapper* giving the thumbs-up after returning home safely once again.

15–21 April, the British submarines fired 21 torpedoes, sinking one escort vessel and two transports, totalling some 10,200 tons. This was perhaps not overly impressive, but adding to the heavier losses inflicted the week before, it forced the Germans to change their strategies.[16]

By the second half of April, several of the remaining submarines had been on patrol for nearly two weeks, some almost three, and one by one, the boats started heading home. Throughout April, the submarines found conditions more and more difficult in the Skagerrak. The number of anti-submarine patrols increased markedly, and low-flying patrol aircraft were everywhere, forcing them to go deep continuously. Several of the boats were bombed without warning even when submerged. By the end of April, the rapidly shortening hours of darkness and the need for re-deployment pending the expected attack in the West, forced Admiral Horton to suspend patrols in the Kattegat and the eastern Skagerrak. In early May, after the attack on France, the submarines were forced to give Norway and the Skagerrak 'a bit of a rest' altogether. Only the veteran boats *Sunfish* under Lieutenant-Commander Slaughter and *Sealion* under Lieutenant-Commander Bryant were sent past Lindesnes in early May to keep the German AS forces alert and see what could be achieved. Both found conditions extremely difficult and, despite taking many risks, only *Sealion* succeeded in getting into position for an attack, but the torpedoes missed. Both boats eventually withdrew with exhausted crews. Operations east of the Lindesnes–Skagen line were terminated, for all practical purposes leaving the supply convoys alone. The boats earned the signal sent them by the First Lord:

> Please convey to all ranks and ratings engaged in these brilliant and fruit-ful submarine operations, the admiration and regard with which their fellow countrymen follow their exploits.[17]

The successes of the Allied submarines in the Skagerrak and Kattegat in April called for active German counter-measures, draining resources needed elsewhere. Horton's tactics were so effective that some fifteen German transports and supply ships were sunk or severely damaged between 8 and 29 April, in addition to half a dozen warships. This caused a crisis at OKW and the plans for moving troops and supplies to south and west Norway had to be completely revised.[18] On 24 April, though, SKL noted in its diary that due to 'energetic' anti-submarine measures, a reduction in the threat to the convoys had become noticeable. The counter-measures included increased anti-submarine patrols at sea and in the air, timing fast convoys to cross the most dangerous areas during the nights, when the submarines had to withdraw to charge their batteries, and the laying of several anti-submarine minefields. Zigzagging was advised for the convoys and troops were to be kept on deck,

The transport of soldiers and equipment across the Skagerrak continued throughout the spring of 1940. The route remained dangerous in spite of reduced Allied activity after mid-May, and most of the soldiers are wearing lifejackets.

life vests donned, with boats and floats ready. It was also strongly emphasised that if one ship was torpedoed, the other transports should continue, leaving the rescue efforts to the escorts. The concentration of forces in the Kattegat and eastern Skagerrak left serious deficiencies in the North Sea and the Channel area, making SKL worry over the forthcoming events in the West. It also resulted in a heated discussion between Marinegruppenkommando Ost and West as to the deployment of, among other things, the S-boat flotillas.[19]

There is little doubt that the inability of the Royal Navy and the RAF to threaten – far less halt – the German supply line to Norway greatly influenced the outcome of the ensuing campaign. By being able to bring in troops and equipment, including artillery and a few tanks, in far greater amounts than the Allies were able to, the Germans tipped the outcome of the land war in Norway in their favour. In May operations east of the Lindesnes–Skagen line were generally terminated, leaving the supply convoys alone. Boats on patrol were ordered to operate in the area between south-western Norway and the declared German mine area hoping to intercept ships coming out of the Skagerrak or Heligoland Bight.

Chapter 16

Requiem

Casualties

For propaganda reasons, the German authorities preferred to withhold casualty figures from *Blücher* at the time and it has since been challenging to ascertain how many lost their lives in the incident. Some sources claim figures as high as 1,500–1,800 but the real number is most likely closer to 350, including those who went down with the ship and were listed as missing. In mid-May 1940, documents from the German naval command in Oslo listed 36 confirmed dead, 114 missing and 12 'uncertain' from the Navy in addition to 195 unspecified Army casualties – 357 altogether. The highest-ranking naval officer lost was Kapitänleutnant Pochhammer, killed inside the foretop

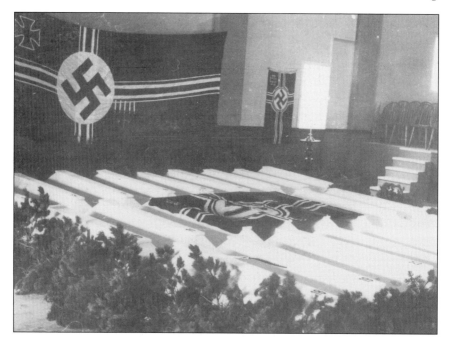

Coffins with the deceased were temporarily placed in schools and assembly halls after identification, awaiting burial.

Burial took place at Vestre Gravlund on the 16th. There are more than
a hundred coffins in this grave alone.

by the first shell from Oscarsborg. Most other casualties were petty officers,
other ranks or civilians.[1]

Jonatan Myhre Barlien and Vegard N. Toska have for several years systematically documented the Germans who died in Norway during the invasion
and subsequent campaign. Through detailed investigations of grave sites,
burial records, hospital records, archives and personal accounts in Norway
and Germany, they have arrived at confirmed numbers, including those
who died later as well as those missing. There are still some uncertainties
regarding a few individuals, but the order of magnitude is verifiable. Barlien
and Toska conclude that the total should be 133 of *Blücher*'s crew, 9 Luftwaffe
men, both aircrew and ground personnel, 168 Army soldiers, 6 propaganda
staff and reporters and 10 others. Hence, in all 326 men died when *Blücher*
went down.

In addition, another 7 died on board *Lützow* in Oslofjord, 5 seamen and
2 *Gebirgsjäger* from 8./GjR 138, plus an additional seaman who died of his
wounds on the 16th; 13 Germans died at Horten, 2 seamen, 6 Naval Artillery
men and 1 from 4./IR 307 during the landing from *R 17* and its destruction;
2 Naval Artillery men died on board *Albatros* and 2 soldiers from 4./IR 307
from friendly fire during the bomb attack on Karljohansvern. At Rauøy and
Bolærne, the German losses are highly uncertain.

In all, including soldiers and airmen at Fornebu the attack on Oslo
probably cost the Germans well over 400 dead with close to double that
number in wounded.

On 10 June, Group XXI summarised the losses of the Army during the Norway Campaign. It is assumed that the *Landser* lost aboard *Blücher* are included in 'losses during transport'. If so, the majority of the 'battle losses' occurred after 15 April. The Kriegsmarine reported the naval losses in Norway on 21 June. Most of the naval losses are from Oslofjord or Narvik, occurring between 8 and 15 April. The Luftwaffe losses are estimated to between 100 and 150 men based on the number of aircraft lost during April.[2]

German Casualties in the Norwegian Campaign			
(*Officers/other ranks*)	Dead	Missing or POW	Wounded
Army losses during transport	18 / 1,093	–	– / 64
Army battle losses	39 / 683	7 / 362	52 / 1,323
Navy losses	26 / 178	28 / 327	12 / 211
Civilians	5	5	?

Norwegian deaths around Oslofjord on 8–10 April amounted to 14: one on board *Pol III*, 2 on board *Rauma*, 2 on board *Sørland*, 4 at Horten, 2 at Rauøy, 1 at Bolærne and 2 civilians in Drøbak.

The official burial ceremony for the dead from *Blücher* was held at Vestre Gravlund near Oslo on the morning of 16 April. Falkenhorst, Boehm, Engelbrecht, Heymann and most officers and men in Oslo who could be spared were there, and seamen from *Emden* and soldiers from the Army made up the Guard of Honour. To their anger, no *Blücher*-men were allowed to attend as Boehm decided they 'were not properly dressed' – '*einheitliche Bekleidung und Ausrüstung noch nicht durchführbar*'. Later the dead were moved to individual graves at Ekeberg, east of Oslo, where a German cemetery was prepared. After the war, all German graves were moved to Alfaset further outside the city and all German memorials taken down.

Demise

Kapitän Woldag was called to Berlin to report and joined Thiele aboard *Lützow*. After she was torpedoed in the Skagerrak, Woldag was flown to Kiel in *Lützow*'s Arado, arriving on the morning of the 11th. The next day he continued to Berlin to tell his story in person to Hitler, Raeder and the SKL. Woldag was supposed to return to Norway on the 16th after a few days with his family in Kiel, but never arrived in Oslo as expected. There are several uncertainties shrouding what actually happened. Woldag's then 11-year-old son Jochen later told that he went with his father to the Kiel-Holtenau airfield and saw him off early in the morning of 16 April. The funeral of the victims

Officers of the occupation force in Oslo attended the funeral.

from *Blücher* was on that day and he wanted to be present. Fregattenkapitän Heymann in his diary writes that he and some other officers went to Fornebu to pick up the captain but he never turned up. Woldag's aircraft vanished, some say over the Baltic or the Kattegat, others over Oslofjord. On the 16th, however, a Ju 52 from KGzbv 105 vanished during a flight to Oslo. The three crew-members, Oberfeldwebel Pius Kohle, Feldwebel Ernst Maisch and Feldwebel Walter Poplow, are listed as lost by Luftwaffe, but there is no mention of any passenger.

On the 17th deputy chief of police Adamsen at Hurum received instructions from his superiors in Drammen to investigate reports of an aircraft having crashed near Ranvikholmen off Tofte, south of Filtvet. At Tofte he was met by some locals who had retrieved a jacket, a coat, a cap and some goggles from a German airman. In the jacket were the papers of Walter Poplow of Stettin. Some letters floating around had also been retrieved, but no bodies and no parts of the wreck, according to the report of Adamsen. Hence, it appears likely that the Ju 52 with Woldag on board crashed in Oslofjord, though not directly at the wreck site. Unless of course the whole thing is

It was a solemn ceremony, well documented. Note the photographer
atop the ladder at the back.

an elaborate deception and the unfortunate captain of *Blücher* was made to
disappear at the cost of three German airmen. Perhaps the Ju 52 was shot
down by friendly fire from some nervous AA gunners who misunderstood
why the aircraft came in low over the fjord. Gunners from the Navy or Army
shooting down a Luftwaffe aircraft could well have been classified a 'non-
incident' to be hidden deep under someone's carpet.

Heymann's narrative is generally very detailed, but on the issue of the
disappearance of *der Kommandant* he is surprisingly brief. He does, however,
state that on the 20th, a letter from his own wife, which Woldag was supposed
to have brought from Germany, was found floating in Oslofjord. Woldag's
wife Else had given him a small briefcase with letters from several officer's
wives to take to Oslo, but the only one retrieved was that to Heymann.

Legend has it that Woldag somehow made the Ju 52 crash near Oscarsborg, but this has never been ascertained and is very hard to believe. Jochen
Woldag later wrote that the widow of one of the crew members had been
informed that her husband had vanished, without any further details. All
investigations, according to Jochen Woldag, had been 'stopped from high
up'.[3] Still, in all likelihood, the death of Kapitän Woldag was an accident
after he asked the pilot, Oberfeldwebel Kohle, to go low over the wreck
site. The weather was poor with occasional snow and icing may well have

Many German seamen and soldiers were present, but few survivors from *Blücher*.

Later the dead were moved to individual graves in the Ekeberg Cemetery, east of Oslo, together with other deceased German soldiers from south-eastern Norway.

resulted if Kohle brought the machine down towards the fjord. Very few of the transport pilots had much experience flying over water or in snowy conditions.

The Wreck

The wreck of *Blücher* today lies upside down at 60 to 90 metres water-depth outside Drøbak. Its ownership is ambiguous but normally accepted to be held by Saga Shipping. The site is closely observed by the Department for Marine Management and Pollution Control and the Coastal Administration, Kystverket. During an operation in 1994 1,600 tons of oil were recovered, but more than a hundred tons remain. Some of these are not accessible and there is a constant leakage, though this is now slow and generally not severe. There is also a large amount of ammunition in and around the wreck. At some stage, the wreckage will collapse or break up – or both. There is a large and growing crack across the stern and the outer plates in the bottom of the ship have rusted down to about half of their original thickness, in some places more than that. When this will happen is impossible to predict, but possibly in 20–40 years or less. Due to the presumed amounts of ammunition in several parts of the wreck, it was at an early stage decided to leave the main body of *Blücher* where it is.

The three propellers were salvaged in the 1950s and two anchors have been recovered. One of these is displayed at Drøbak, the other in Oslo harbour. The remains of one of *Blücher*'s two Arado 196 aircraft were salvaged during the oil-recovery operation and are displayed at Sola Aircraft Museum.

Diving the wreck used to be popular and various artefacts have been removed over time. Some divers have even been prosecuted for removing objects. At least two divers have perished diving on the wreckage. The Norwegian Directorate of Cultural Heritage, Riksantikvaren, decided in 2016 that the wreckage should be permanently protected as a war grave and memorial of the events in April 1940. The decision is controversial as it includes a ban on diving in a zone 100 metres from the wreckage without permission and forbids removal of artefacts and objects.[4]

Oscarsborg after *Blücher*

Extensive repair and maintenance of Oscarsborg started immediately, but from 1941 onward German activities at the fortress were reduced. After the German invasion of the Soviet Union, which also included a German attack from northernmost Norway towards Murmansk and the Kola Peninsula, Oslo became less important strategically. Instead, to try and protect the entire coast from Allied invasion as well as the supply-routes to the north, 280 coastal batteries with 1,100 guns were constructed during the war.

The Askholmene memorial became a 'tourist attraction' and most Germans
visiting Oslo had themselves photographed there. A commemoration
ceremony was held at the memorial every April during the occupation.
In May 1945 the memorial was destroyed by American soldiers.

In the Skagerrak, a first line of defence was established by extending the
minefields laid on 9 April, adding powerful artillery batteries at Kristiansand
and Hanstholm in Denmark, respectively.[5] On the northern side of the
Skagerrak, several small forts were built from the Swedish border via Rauøy
and Bolærne along the coast to the south-west as a second line of defence.
Oscarsborg Fortress thus became the third line of defence, used also as centre
for training and convalescence. The three 28-cm Krupp guns of the main
battery and the torpedo battery were kept. The 12-cm Armstrong guns at
Håøya were moved to Rørvik. The howitzer battery's four 28-cm Whitworth
guns and the old battery with eight 12-cm were scrapped in 1943. The Kopås
battery's three 15-cm Armstrong guns were manned until 1944 when they
were dismantled and sent to the Baltic. On the other hand, a command
bunker was built in front of the battery to replace the simpler Norwegian
command post on the height behind it.[6]

Kaptein Thorleif Unneberg was the communications and intelligence
officer at Oscarsborg in 1940. During the occupation he became an officer
in the Norwegian underground army, Milorg. On 12 May 1945 Unneberg
took over as the first commander of the liberated Oscarsborg fortress. Birger

Oscarsborg as a training centre. Cadets during exercises at the Coast Artillery
NCO Training School in 2000. The school was the main unit at Oscarsborg
before and after the Second World War.

Eriksen was also present, playing an important ceremonial role, although he
had officially retired.

During the Cold War, Oscarsborg retained its previous peacetime
command, administration and logistics functions while the Coast Artillery
presence in the outer Oslofjord was developed. The strong Soviet naval
presence in the Baltic prompted the defence of Oslo to be maintained. The
original main battery with the three 28-cm guns at Søndre Kaholmen was
prepared for use after the war and test-fired, after which they became a
memorial. Four German 10.5-cm SKC 32 guns were installed in the Kopås
battery in 1952 and took over as the main battery. Guns 1 and 4 were in open
positions with ship-type shields, while guns 2 and 3 were in casemates. The
fire-control, located in the German-built command bunker in front of the
battery, consisted of a Zeiss optical instrument (bearing) and a vertical rangefinder. The torpedo system was modernised in 1963 with 53-cm frames and
the main weapon became the British Mk VIII torpedo. In 1961, one battery
of two 10.5-cm SKC 32 guns was installed at the southern point on Søndre
Kaholmen. These were used to train NCO cadets but could also be used in
time of crisis. The command position for the battery was established in the
ramparts by the three old 28-cm guns, later including radar, laser rangefinder
and optical systems. In addition to the guns and torpedoes, mines were laid

at the bottom of the Drøbak Narrows during the Cold War. Ships sailing to and from Oslo regularly passed over these, including cruise ships, without any incidents. The mine system could be activated and fired remotely from the command post on land. In his retirement, Birger Eriksen developed an accurate orograph for use at the minefield to make sure the right mine was set off at the optimum time. In 1974, the battery at Kopås was shut down and fire-control for the minefield moved to Oscarsborg. In the 1980s the minefield consisted of two lines with 31 US Mk 51-0 bottom mines, each of 1.6 tons, positioned 10–50 metres down. A further modernisation of the torpedo battery was completed in 1988, including better protection with fortifications and living quarters inside the rock. Fire control was improved with radar and new searchlights. In 1993, the Storting closed the fortress as a combat unit. Operational activities ceased, mines, torpedoes and live ammunition were removed and the war organisation of 400 men dispersed.[7]

In 1990 the similar minefield at Rauøy consisted of between 40 and 50 remote-controlled mines. Most of these were detonated by a lightning strike, damaging a small boat whose occupants luckily survived.

The Coast Artillery NCO Training School had been located at Hellen fort, Bergen, after the war, but was moved back to Oscarsborg in 1959. The education of gun commanders and section leaders continued as before. The main weapon for training at the school during the Cold War was the 10.5-cm SKC/32 gun, which was the most common type used in the Coast Artillery's forts and was very reliable. The live firing took place at other forts on the Norwegian coast. This strengthened preparedness as mobilisation batteries could be tested in addition to regular exercises. The NCO cadets were housed and cared for on Søndre Kaholmen. Modern guns, missiles and torpedo/mine systems were part of their education after the Cold War. The closure of the NCO Training School in 2002 was a part of downsizing the armed forces after the Cold War and of the end of the Coast Artillery in Norway.

The torpedo battery and the gun batteries were retained and today Oscarsborg is a spectacular museum, operated by the Norwegian armed forces. It displays the history of the Oscarsborg fortress as well as the Coast Artillery in Norway. At the fortress it is possible to see most of the guns that were in use at Oscarsborg and by the Coast Artillery generally since the middle of the nineteenth century, as well as the original buildings and fortifications. At Søndre Kaholmen, the main battery and its 28-cm guns are still intact, as are other guns from previous time periods. The Armstrong guns from the 1870s remain in their positions east of the main battery. At Kopås two guns are still in their casemates. Oscarsborg Fortress is open to the public, with regular boat departures from Drøbak. There is no military activity on the island any more and visitors from all over the world are welcomed.

Chapter 17
Conclusions

The sinking of *Blücher* in Oslofjord at dawn on 9 April 1940 was a fundamental event in the history of the early part of WW2. The German invasion forces, who came to take control over Norway through a coup-like invasion were halted and held back from the capital long enough for King Haakon, his government and key parts of the administration to withdraw in time to thwart Hitler's intentions. Through a remarkable series of improvisations, bluff and good luck, the Germans eventually gained control of Oslo and the approaches to the capital, but by then the concept of Operation *Weserübung* had been derailed, and due to the extended resistance from Oscarsborg and Bolærne the follow-up convoys were also delayed. The Norwegian officers of SDD1 reacted according to instructions and from *Pol III* via Rauøy, Bolærne, Horten and Filtvet, Oscarsborg Fortress was warned. Eriksen and his men were ready. Once the Norwegian guns opened fire in earnest, confusion and bewilderment spread in the German leadership. This had two critical consequences: firstly, there was a two-month campaign that would not only see the first engagements of German and British infantry since November 1918, but also result in well over 4,000 dead Allied soldiers, sailors and airmen, a major evacuation and the fall of the Chamberlain government, making way for Winston Churchill as British Prime Minister; secondly, Norway was firmly established as an Allied state with an almost intact government in London. Hence, the whole of the vast, modern merchant fleet ended up sailing for the Allied cause, while the income from this and the gold reserves were used to develop a military force that served with distinction alongside the Royal Navy, the RAF and not least the special forces of SOE, SIS and the commandos. On a longer term, it was to affect the entire five coming years of occupation. Norway was occupied, but it was to be a hard occupation consuming vast German resources.

Birger Eriksen was awarded the highest and most prestigious Norwegian decoration, the Krigskorset, by King Haakon at Oslo castle on 19 December 1945. By then he had retired from active service. During 1945 and 1946 he was subject to questioning by the Investigation Committee established by the Storting in19 45 as well as the Military Investigation Committee, in particular regarding the surrender of the fortress. Both committees concluded that all available measures of resistance had been taken and there was nothing more that could have been done. Eriksen died in 1958. Andreas Anderssen was also honoured with the Krigskorset by King Haakon on this occasion. He died one week later, 26 December 1945. Kaptein Vagn Enger was also acquitted of any wrongdoing as his hands were tied by the order from Oscarsborg not to open fire during the last attack.

At other places in south Norway the invasion went more or less as planned, but due to the non-arrival of *Blücher* and Group V in Oslo in the early morning of the 9th, little ended up as intended and new arrangements had to be organised. In Denmark, King Christian and his government remained in place and the country could be run as before – under strict German control. The same was supposed to happen in Norway, but as a direct result of Eriksen's, Enger's and Anderssen's resolve, the Storting could gather in Elverum and decide that Nygaardsvold's government, as the only legal administration, should continue to lead the country – if necessary, from abroad – until Norway could reclaim its status as a sovereign state.

On 14 April 1940 Boehm, the newly appointed Commanding Admiral Norway, concluded bluntly in a note to Raeder: 'The surprise attack has failed,' adding that the resistance at the Drøbak Narrows which led to the loss of *Blücher* and thereby the designated harbour commander and all his preparations made a large degree of improvisation necessary, which in turn led to confusion and conflict between the Army and Navy. The much-delayed arrival of the transport ships added to the difficulties. Shortly after, Admiral Boehm wrote in his diary:

> Group XXI reports 'Norway is in a state of war with Germany'. Occupation of Oslo by air-landed troops is in progress. The Navy is fighting south of Oslo […] My task as Commanding Admiral Norway did not commence as planned […] The surprise attack was not successful. The resistance at Oslo led to the loss of *Blücher* and with her the loss of the designated Harbour Commander and Harbour Captain and all the preparatory work they had made in advance. Furthermore, it also meant that the forts and batteries on the mainland and the islands could not be manned as planned but had to be improvised. Hence, the Army and the Navy were intermingled, and we lost any overview of what was under our control and by whom.[1]

A whole new management, not planned for, had to be set up in Oslo and the occupied parts of the country, as well as defence against Norwegian counter-attacks and Allied intervention. The fact that Germany was now at war with

Norway, instead of supporting and controlling an intact administrative structure was, in Boehm's opinion, a major and unwanted challenge.

The insertion of Terboven was an improvised solution when things went utterly wrong and his attitude and manner of handling his task quickly created resistance in the population. The need for a German administration frustrated all of Quisling's attempts to establish an alternative government. In fact, Quisling's manoeuvrings would not have been possible had the King and government been detained and kept as a puppet regime in Oslo. Hence the escape of the King made way for Quisling's failed attempt to seize power, which led to anger and ridicule in the population and within a short time to active resistance against the occupiers who were seen to support his treason; any powers he gained during the occupation rested entirely on German guns. On 24 April, Boehm was already reporting to Raeder that there was marked general opposition to the German regime, adding that active resistance was growing.[2]

The loss of *Blücher* made a great impression throughout the German armed forces. Senior Army officers were highly critical of the Navy, both for letting the cruiser run the gauntlet of the Drøbak Narrows as well as the handling of the ship after it had been crippled.

Boehm asked Fregattenkapitän Nieden to lead an investigation committee on the sinking. He worked meticulously and systematically, and the report was not ready until July 1941. By that time, myths and rumours about what had happened on board *Blücher* were rife, and fuelled by the disappearance of Kapitän Woldag. Most naval officers interviewed believed a smaller and less valuable ship should have been used to test the defences. *Blücher* was too new and unprepared for the task. Thiele wrote in *Lützow*'s diary on 10 April:

> Once again it has been demonstrated that against well protected and camouflaged coastal batteries, ships have slim chances of success.[3]

The Army put the blame for the failure and loss of lives directly on Woldag, particularly as he had anchored the cruiser and not beached her. Admiral Kummetz was hardly mentioned at all. Oberst Buschenhagen, Falkenhorst's second-in-command, put together a collection of accounts from Army personnel of their experiences. In particular, he wanted to clarify to what extent the soldiers had been informed of procedures in case of an emergency, what emergency equipment was available and how to use it. He also wanted to know in detail how the Army personnel had been assisted by the seamen and how the officers of the cruiser had behaved after the torpedoing to save the passengers. Few of the responses that were sent to OKH in the second half of July left the Navy with much credit. After an argument between the Captain and Generalmajor Engelbrecht the Army asserted, the general had himself organised the disembarkation and rescue of the troops. At the height of the dispute, a story spread that Engelbrecht had to take command as Woldag had done nothing. These accusations were strongly rejected by Heymann and most of the surviving naval officers, but the damage was done. The Army's conclusion was that in any future combined operation, one of their officers should be assigned the overall command and the Navy only be responsible for transport. Falkenhorst left no doubt as to his own opinion: 'The presence of torpedo batteries and their location was known [and] the commander of *Blücher* must have been well aware of the risk associated with passing through the Drøbak Narrows.' Aboard a warship, he added, the Navy was in command and therefore responsible for what happened.

On 30 July 1941, Admiral Boehm forwarded Nieden's report to SKL with the comment that as far as the disagreement between the Navy and Army commanders was concerned, Engelbrecht had, just after the event, spoken of how the conduct of the ship's crew and their efforts to rescue the soldiers had greatly impressed him. Raeder found the report unbalanced and ordered further accounts to be obtained from the surviving ship's officers. This was not easy as they were now scattered to ships and bases throughout occupied Europe, and some had since died. Kummetz was back at his Torpedo Inspectorate, Heymann was overseeing the torpedo depot in Lorient and Thannemann had been lost with *Bismarck* in the Atlantic. Others were serving in U-boats and had had other harrowing experiences, blurring the events in Oslofjord. Heymann submitted a detailed statement dismissing the Army's allegations, referring to his earlier report, but few others had much to add to the reports filed a year earlier. All that could possibly be done to save the ship and as many as possible of the men on board had been done by Woldag and his men. In one of the few written notes he made, Kummetz explained that:

> Neither Woldag nor I had any appreciation, after the hits, that the ship was lost. Hence, neither of us considered the option of grounding her [...] Anchoring seemed the right thing to do, and with all engines lost, there were few options [...] Only much later, when the fire amidships had grown disturbingly as it could not be fought with the means we had available and the 10.5-cm magazine between K1 and K2 blew up resulting in more water coming in and the list increasing, did the danger become obvious [...] 'Beaching' the ship was never an option, though, as there were no beaches nearby.[4]

Kummetz argued that from the bridge, just before they left, it looked as if the stern was close to land and Woldag had no means of adjusting this as the engines were shut down, adding that, as it was not possible to transfer men from forward to aft any more, moving any part of the ship closer to land would not have benefited those at the other end. As most floats and kapok lifebelts were destroyed by the fire, only one undamaged motorboat and some floats were available for transport of the wounded towards land, he continued, and as far as he had seen, every officer and most of the petty officers and seamen had given their inflatable vests to the soldiers. Reports of arguing or disagreements between Woldag and Engelbrecht were firmly rejected by Kummetz. Nothing untoward had happened on board the ship and after the events the general had spoken 'with respect and sincerity' of the captain, expressing 'pleasure and satisfaction' when he learned that he had also made it safely to land. Kummetz had nothing but praise for Woldag, and the way he had calmly handled his ship and taken care of his crew was 'exemplary'. Raeder and SKL appear to have been content that the honour of the Kriegsmarine had been upheld and the case was closed.[5]

Normally, when disasters occur, there is rarely a single reason for the outcome. So it was also with *Blücher* in the Drøbak Narrows. A series of direct and indirect causes can be found for the disaster: the sinking of the cruiser was the result of actions from the Norwegian side, plus construction flaws, insufficient training and direct mistakes on the German side. How the fires from the two first hits would have developed had nothing more happened, is impossible to say, but likely they would have been brought under control. The additional hits from the Kopås and Husøy batteries made the damage substantially more serious, devastating a large part of the port superstructure and interior above the armoured deck, killing many. The starboard side was less affected, though, and it was possible to move from fore to aft for a while. Most importantly the propulsion system was still operational and damage to the electrical systems and manoeuvrability was limited. Hence, the artillery fire from the fortress made *Blücher* un-battleworthy but if the ship would ever have sailed again is impossible to say. The two torpedoes probably hit in the worst possible part of the ship almost simultaneously and the whole propulsion system of the cruiser went down. Exactly where they hit and what damage they caused is not possible to reconstruct from the available sources or the wreck today. The combination of close-range artillery fire from two sides and the two torpedoes made a bad situation worse and the explosion of the 10.5-cm magazine in section VII probably sealed the ship's fate.

Ultimately the loss of *Blücher* can be ascribed to mistakes or wrong decisions made by the hierarchy from Hitler in the Reichskanzlei via SKL and Marinegruppenkommando Ost to Kummetz and Woldag. *Blücher* should not have been there in the first place – in the van of an invasion force. She was a mighty ship, but not built for the task assigned to her during Operation *Weserübung*. None of her advantages of speed, manoeuvrability or firepower could be exploited in the narrow fjord. With hindsight, the composition of Group *Oldenburg* was far from ideal. Mistakes occur at all levels in armed conflicts. The Prussian military theorist Carl von Clausewitz argued that even small delays, misunderstandings and mistakes that cannot be avoided often have a disastrous effect on the course of a battles. The more detailed the planning, the more likely it is to go wrong. Helmuth von Moltke – Chief of the Prussian and German General Staff from 1857 to 1888 – agreed. For him, officers had to be educated and trained in such a way that they were able to react correctly to unforeseen events in the chaos of war. Senior officers should not be mindless recipients of orders, but rather illustrious individuals who intuitively know what to do when things don't go as intended. The German Navy of 1940 was not quite up to these ideals. There was in general a reasonable amount of room to manoeuvre, but mistakes could have severe repercussions. Admiral Kummetz had been given an almost unprecedented opportunity and must have reflected over the amount of responsibility that had been placed on his shoulders. Whether he really was up to the task given to him is arguable. Kummetz was over-optimistic that the fortress of Oscarsborg would not offer serious resistance even after it was obvious that the Norwegians knew they were coming. Hence, he stuck to plans with devastating results.

The German invasion of Norway is brushed lightly over in most accounts of the beginning of WW2, overshadowed by events shortly to follow on the Western Front and the evacuation from Dunkirk. In addition, Operation *Weserübung* is usually held to have come as a complete surprise. Nothing could be more wrong. There were ample warnings to the Nordic countries as well as to the Allies – universally overlooked or explained away in cognitive perception. A common notion is that *Weserübung* was initiated by the Germans to protect the iron ore imports from Narvik. This was undoubtedly an element, once it was obvious that the Allies were trying to sever these, but it was far from the only underlying reason and not even the most important. During the ensuing battles in and around Narvik, the ore-loading facilities were destroyed, and no iron ore was exported to Germany through Narvik for the rest of 1940. The facilities were eventually restored but the volumes of ore sent from Sweden to Germany via Narvik in total for 1941–4 barely exceeded those for one year during 1937–9.

In a somewhat remarkable entry in its War Diary on 9 April, SKL concluded that Operation *Weserübung* had succeeded due to the boldness and decisiveness of the crews – and a good bit of luck. 'The losses we have suffered,' they wrote, 'especially the loss of the brand-new heavy cruiser *Blücher*, are painful. They are, however, absolutely within the numbers we had to expect and the risk we knew we were taking and cannot be categorised as high.' On the 11th, before the confirmed loss of ten destroyers at Narvik, the diary added:

> The torpedoing of *Lützow* is the foulest mischief that the Kriegsmarine could experience at this moment. The long-term operational loss of this ship means a weakening of surface warfare in the Atlantic, when just such a diversion would have been needed most. The inclusion of the ship in *Weserübung* and especially sending it to Oslo thus emerges as a clear strategic mistake [...] With hindsight using *Lützow* and *Blücher* against Oslo was a mistake. That has led to a severe loss of operational strength for the Kriegsmarine. Perhaps it would have been better to use a large number of smaller vessels instead (torpedo boats, escorts and similar).[6]

Having to send *Lützow* to the shipyards for a long time was a bitter disappointment to the SKL as it had fought to keep the ship away from *Weserübung* altogether and use the opportunity of the operation to let her slip unnoticed into the Atlantic. Still, the SKL concluded its lament by stating that there had been an operational need for large guns in Oslo adding that losses had to be expected as part of such a major operation.[7] During *Weserübung* and the subsequent campaign, however, the German surface fleet suffered losses that made it virtually impossible to support any amphibious operations against Britain effectively during 1940. When the accounts were made up, however, by the time the campaign in Norway finally was brought to an end, it was clear that the German Navy's surface fleet had had its back broken. Three cruisers, *Blücher*, *Karlsruhe*, *Königsberg*, were sunk as were ten destroyers, two submarines, *U 49* and *U 64*, two torpedo boats, *Albatros*, *Brummer* and a number of smaller vessels. In addition, the battleships *Scharnhorst* and *Gneisenau* were damaged as were *Lützow*, *Hipper* (one of *Blücher*'s sister-ships), and another four destroyers in addition to the decimation of the supply and support fleet.[8]

These losses wrecked Raeder's ambition of having the Kriegsmarine exploit the impact of gaining access to Norwegian ports and, in a long-term strategic context, the invasion of Norway was to have dire consequences not only for the Navy, but for the entire German war machine. When the assault on Russia commenced in June 1941, the Norwegian coast became important as a supply route for its northern flank, although there is no evidence that this was seriously considered in March 1940. For Hitler, this development would become a challenge. Norway's long and winding coastline with its narrow fjords and remote islands was difficult to defend and made tempting targets for the British who had access to an increasing number of Norwegians with local knowledge and the willingness to fight back. In March 1941, British and Norwegian commando soldiers raided the Lofoten Islands without

Großadmiral Raeder arriving in Trondheim 22 July 1940 with Admiral Boehm to inspect the harbour and discuss development of a naval base there.

the occupiers being able to counter the attack in time. For the subsequent German attack on Russia in June this demonstrated the vulnerability of the supply lines to the north and subsequent commando raids and submarine actions later in the year created a state of near panic in the Reichskanzlei. An extensive building of coastal fortifications and infrastructure followed, draining German resources and manpower that might have been used elsewhere in a more fruitful manner. After the new raids during December 1941, the building and resource-use intensified further, including transfer of the remnants of the German surface navy to northern Norway.

In January 1942 Admiral Boehm wrote that 'the campaign in Norway turned that country into a serious threat towards Britain's ability to wage war, in the same way a British occupation of Norway would have created a major danger to Germany'. Operation *Weserübung* and the ensuing occupation had opened the North Sea and the Norwegian Sea, he held, and given the German Navy an opportunity for offensive operations against Britain's seaways and supply lines. The key message in his note, however, is that the Kriegsmarine had never been able to exploit the opportunity, not having the required naval strength. Neither had the Luftwaffe been able or willing to take seriously the advantage bases in Norway had given it and Norwegian-based air-attacks on the British fleet base at Scapa Flow had been beaten off with heavy losses.

May 1940, Horten is visited by 5th R-boat Flotilla paying homage to the sad remains of *R 17*, a potent symbol of the losses endured by the Kriegsmarine in Norway.

For the Army, Boehm continued, there was no immediate gain, except the freedom of not having the British at their back when the attack on the Western Front was initiated. Boehm's main concern, though, was the lack of political acceptance in the Norwegian population of the German need for their country, its strategic geography and its resources. With very few exceptions, Admiral Norwegen concluded in January 1942, most Norwegians were pro-British – *englandfreundlich* – a problem that would only grow. In addition to guarding the coast against Allied commando raids, minelaying and naval attacks, there was a growing need for protection against sabotage, disobedience and rebellion. The head of the Kriegsmarine in Norway does not say so directly, but he is stumbling close to the conclusion that the occupation of Norway that looked so obvious two years earlier was becoming a problem.[9]

Operation *Weserübung* was far more important for the development of World War 2 in northern Europe than is usually recognised. Overshadowed by the events on the Western Front and the evacuation from Dunkirk it tends to be considered a sideshow, which it surely was not. Particularly due to the events in Oslofjord, the German objectives for the operation were not met. The Norwegian resistance and Allied help resulted in a two-month campaign – not planned for – and the combined losses to the Kriegsmarine had dramatic consequences. What would have happened if Hitler had not unleashed his dogs of war on Norway in April 1940, or if *Blücher* had not been sunk, we shall never know.

Notes

Chapter 1 – The Ship

1. Mallmann Showell, *U-Boat Commanders and Crews, 1939–1945*.
2. NA-ADM 178/137; Raeder, *Mein Leben*, vol. II. Kriegsmarine literally means 'navy of war'.
3. A metric ton is 1,000 kg whereas a long (imperial) ton is 1,016 kg (and a US 'short' ton is 907 kg). Standard displacement meant fully manned and ready for sea, including armament, ammunition, equipment, and provisions as intended to be carried in war, but without fuel or reserve boiler feed water on board.
4. Raeder, *Mein Leben* vol. II; Nolte, *Mit Anstand zu sterben verstehen*; Gray, *Hitler's Battleships*.
5. Haarr, *The Gathering Storm*.
6. The sister gun to the 10.5-cm C/33 was the 10.5-cm C/32 in single mounting. The 10.5-cm C/32 was a trusted and robust weapon, used extensively in the Norwegian Coast Artillery during the Cold War. One of the authors of this book – Melien – handled the gun as a gun commander and battery commander.
7. BA-RM 92/5087, BA-RM 92/5088, BA-RM 35/I/32, NARA PG 47493; Melien/Fjeld Private Archive; Binder and Schlünz, *Schwerer Kreutzer Blücher*; Friedman, *Naval Firepower*; Haarr, *The Gathering Storm*; Koop and Schmolke, *Heavy Cruisers of the Admiral Hipper Class*; Schmalenbach, *Die Geschichte der deutschen Schiffenartillerie*; Whitley, *German Cruisers of World War Two*; www.lexikon-der-wehrmacht.de, www.deutsches-marinearchiv.de, www.kbismarck.com and www.navweaps.com.

Chapter 2 – The Price of Neutrality

1. Harriman, *Mission to the North*.
2. The Norwegian Parliament is called the Storting. In 1940 it consisted of 150 members representing six parties.
3. Godø, *En Krigsberetning*; Hobson and Kristiansen, *Norsk Forsvarshistorie*, vol. III; and Skard, *Mennesket Halvdan Koht*.
4. Koht, *For Fred og Fridom i Krigstid*.
5. It appears Koht took Dormer's request for confidentiality seriously and he only told Nygaardsvold. In 1940, there were two main levels of representation between states, embassies (headed by an ambassador) and legations (headed by a minister). Legations had lower staff. Major powers usually had embassies in the capitals

of other major powers, and legations elsewhere – the level of the representation mutually agreed. Norway's international position at the time was such that most representations consisted of a minister running a legation.

6. Stortingsforhandlinger 1940, 6 April.
7. RA II-C-11/51, NA-FO 371/23658, NA-CAB 66/3; Koht, *Norsk Utanrikspolitikk fram til 9. April 1940*; Koht, *For Fred og Fridom i Krigstid*; and Kristiansen, *Krigsplaner og Politikk*.
8. RA-PA-1469/D/L0002/0005.
9. RA II-C-11/51; Kristiansen, *Krigsplaner og Politikk*; Haarr, *Nøytralitetens pris*.
10. RA-II-C-11/1100 and RA-PA-1469/D/L0002/0005. The underlining is in the original.
11. RA-II-C-11/1100 and RA-PA-1469/D/L0002/0005.
12. Steen, *Norges Sjøkrig*, vol. I. The guardships, called *bevoktningsfartøyer* in Norwegian, were chartered civilian ships in a great variety of sizes and types. Most were armed with an old gun on the foredeck and a few machine guns. In addition to an officer of the reserve, a few petty officers and signalmen, a large part of the original crew was drafted along with the ship. The guardships were meant to observe, challenge and report – not fight.
13. NA-FO 371/23658, Koht, *For Fred og Fridom i Krigstid*; Skodvin, 'Norwegian Neutrality and the Question of Credibility'.
14. RA-2B-061.21 and Diesen Arkivet.
15. Melien, *Vakt og Vern*.

Chapter 3 – 'Winston is Back'

1. This was the wording of a signal sent to all units from Whitehall on 3 September 1939 when Churchill was appointed First Lord of the Admiralty, a post he had held during WW1.
2. Salmon, *Churchill, the Admiralty and the Narvik Traffic*; Salmon, *Deadlock and Diversion*. The Grand Fleet frequently operated off the Norwegian coast during WW1 and for a time the British authorities considered trying to establish one or more bases in south-west Norway. Ships moving along Norway's coast often use channels between the various offshore islands and the mainland because these are partly sheltered from the rough North Atlantic seas; these shipping channels are known as the Leads and are all within Norway's territorial waters.
3. Melien, *Norges globale sjøkrig*; Thowsen, *Handelsflåten i Krig*, vol. I.
4. RA-RAFA-1924 /D/L0004/0009, RA-S-1005/Aa/L0001, NA-MT 59/1736, NA-FO 72/29421; Egeland, *Gjennom brott og brann*; Ørvik, *Norge i brennpunktet*; Pownall, *Chief of Staff*, vol. II, *1940–1944*; Churchill, *The Second World War*, vol. II; Horve, *Storbritannia og dets behov for den norske handelsflåten*.
5. NA-CAB 65/1.
6. NA-ADM 205/2, NA-ADM 199/892, NA-ADM 116/4471, NA-ADM 1/10680, NA-CAB 66/1, NA-CAB 65/1, NA-CAB 65/2, NA-FO 371/22276, NA-FO 371/23658; Butler, *Grand Strategy*, vol. II.

7. Net figures were even higher, due to the high iron content of the Swedish ore (62–66% on average).
8. NA-CAB 66/6, NA-ADM 116/4471, NA-FO 371/24821, BA-RM 7/194; Karlbom, 'Sweden's iron ore exports to Germany 1933–1944'; Bröyn, *Den svenske malmeksport fram til besettingen av Narvik i April 1940*.
9. NA-CAB 65/4.
10. Haarr, *Nøytralitetens pris*.
11. NA-CAB 65/4, NA-CAB 66/4, NA-FO 371/24820, NA-ADM 116/447; Butler, *Grand Strategy*, vol. II; Dilks, *Great Britain and Scandinavia in the 'Phoney War'*; Macleod, *Time Unguarded*.
12. NA-FO 419/34 and *Förspelet*.
13. NA-FO 371/24820, NA-ADM 199/892, NA-CAB 66/4, NA-CAB 65/11, NA-CAB 65/4; Dilks, *The Diaries of Sir Alexander Cadogan*.
14. NA-CAB 65/11, NA-ADM 116/4471; Koht, *For Fred og Fridom i Krigstid*; Skodvin, 'Norwegian Neutrality and the Question of Credibility'.
15. Colban, *Femti år*.
16. NA-CAB 65/11, *Förspelet*; Macleod, *Time Unguarded*; Churchill, *Second World War*, vol. I; Butler, *Grand Strategy*, vol. II.
17. For a full account of these events, see Haarr, *The Gathering Storm*; Haarr, *Nøytralitetens Pris*.
18. Haarr, *Nøytralitetens Pris*.
19. Colban, *Femti år*; Theien, *Fra krig til Krig*. The seamen were not only British but from many nations sailing on British ships, including the South Asian, Arab and African sailors then known as lascars.
20. NA-CAB 65/11; Gilbert, *The Churchill War Papers*.
21. NA-ADM 116/4471, NA-FO 371/24818, NA-FO 371/24802 and NA-CAB 66/5. The only partially relevant case of German use of Norwegian waters, beside *Altmark*, was the supply ship *Jan Wellem* on its way to Murmansk, where according to the Cooperation Agreement with the Soviets, the Germans could establish a submarine supply base. The British cruiser *Southampton* followed *Jan Wellem* outside the territorial boundary, but there were no confrontations. No submarines came to Murmansk, and *Jan Wellem* was eventually ordered to Narvik as a support vessel for the German destroyers sent there on 9 April.
22. NA-CAB 65/5.
23. NA-ADM 199/280, NA-FO 371/24818, NA-FO 370/2010; Colban, *Femti år*. By 8 April 1940, 2.45 million tons of Norwegian vessels were sailing under British charter – flying the Norwegian flag – of which 1.65 million tons were tankers.
24. *Förspelet*.
25. Mannerheim, *Minnen*.
26. *Förspelet*; Reynaud, *La France a sauvé l'Europe*; Kersaudy, *Norway 1940*.
27. NA-CAB 65/11, NA-CAB 65/12, NA-CAB 66/6, NA-CAB 66/5, NA-FO 371/24818; Macleod, *Time Unguarded*; Butler, *Grand Strategy*, vol. II.

28. NA-CAB 66/7, NA-ADM 116/4471, NA-WO 193/772; Butler, *Grand Strategy*, vol. II.

29. NA-CAB 65/12, NA-FO 419/34; Butler, *Grand Strategy*, vol. II; Macleod, *Time Unguarded*.

30. NA-CAB 65/12.

31. *Förspelet*.

32. NA-FO 371/24819, NA-FO 371/22283, NA-FO 371/23674, NA-CAB 66/6, NA-CAB 66/7, NA-CAB 65/12, NA-CAB 80/105, NA-WO 193/773, NA-WO 106/1969, NA-PREM 1/419 NA-ADM 199/388, NA-ADM 199/379; Dilks, *The Diaries of Sir Alexander Cadogan*; Butler, *Grand Strategy*, vol. II; Hinsley, *British Intelligence in the Second World War*; Kersaudy, *Norway 1940*.

Chapter 4 – Threat from the North

1. Raeder, *Mein Leben*, vol. II.

2. Hubatsch, *Weserübung*; Barth, *Norge og Norden i tysk strategi*; Raeder, *Mein Leben*, vol. II; Loock, *Quisling, Rosenberg und Terboven*.

3. Koht, *For Fred og Fridom i Krigstid*.

4. www.ca.nizkor.org.

5. BA-RM 7/111, BA-RM 7/180, BA-RM 7/177; Raeder, *Mein Leben* II; Jodl's diary and Rosenberg's diary.

6. BA-RM 7/180.

7. Haarr, *Nøytralitetens Pris*; Ottmer, *Weserübung*; Salewski, *Die deutsche Seekriegsleitung*, vol. I; Boehm, *Norwegen zwischen England und Deutschland*; Dönitz, *Memoirs*.

8. BA-RM 7/168; *Förspelet*.

9. BA-RM 7/891.

10. BA-RM 7/180, Assmann, *Überlegungen zur Frage der Stützpunktgewinnung für die Nordseekriegführung*.

11. Document C-66, Exhibit GB 81, Nuremberg trials, as quoted at www.nitzkor.org.

12. BA-RM 7/180, Raeder, *Mein Leben*, vol. II; *Straffesak mot Vidkun Quisling*; Hartmann, *Spillet om Norge*; Gemzell, *Raeder, Hitler und Skandinavien*; and *Lagevorträge*.

13. *Lagevorträge*.

14. *Förspelet*.

15. Haarr, *Nøytralitetens Pris*; *Lagevorträge*.

16. *Lagevorträge*. The date of the meeting varies between 13 and 16 December in different accounts. Jodl's diary, gives the 13th.

17. Stortingspresident Hambro is referred to in Raeder's minutes of the meeting as 'Juden Hambrow'. Hambro's great-grandfather had converted to Christianity in 1810, before moving to Norway from Denmark.

18. BA-RM 7/180, BA-RM 7/177, BA-N 172/14, BA-N 172/16; *Innstilling fra Undersøkelses-kommisjonen av 1945*, *Straffesak mot Vidkun Quisling*; Raeder, *Mein Leben*, vol. II; Halder, *Kriegstagebuch*; Krancke, *Norwegen Unternehmen*; Gemzell, *Raeder, Hitler und Skandinavien*.

19. BA-N 172/14.

20. Halder, *Kriegstagebuch*. Jodl tasked Hauptmann Stenburg, a Luftwaffe officer in OKW, with compiling the initial report, *Studie Nord*.

21. *Förspelet*.

22. BA-RM 7/92.

23. BA-RM 7/92 and RA-II-C-11-2150/52.

24. Jodl's diary.

25. BA-N 300/5, Gruppe XXI KTB E180-5; Halder, *Kriegstagebuch*.

26. BA-N 300/5 and Gruppe XXI KTB E180-5. Göring showed no enthusiasm, but gave in to Hitler's insistence.

27. BA-N 300/5, BA-RM 45/III/100, Gruppe XXI KTB E180-7 and NARA-PG 37848. All officers who became involved had to take a personal oath of secrecy. Falkenhorst brought a large part of his staff with him to Bendlerstrasse. Besides Buschenhagen and Pohlmann these included Hauptmann Egelhaaf (Ic), Major Treuhaupt and Major Tippelskirch. From OKW, Oberstleutnant Lossberg and Major Deyhle were involved. About a week into the work, Oberleutnant Bieler, Oberst Bäntsch, Hauptmann Michelly and Rittmeister Goerz were added, as were Oberstleutnants Schmidt, Boetzel and Bader and Hauptmann Heil, specialists in transport, signalling and intelligence, while Major Hammersen and Leutnant Johnsen spoke Norwegian. In the SKL the number of officers with knowledge of what was being planned grew quickly as the plans progressed.

28. RA-II-C-11-1200-1210, BA-N 300/5, BA-RM 7/92, BA-MSg 2/1882; Steen, *Norges Sjøkrig*, vol. I; Halder, *Kriegstagebuch*; *Lageforträge*; Scharffenberg, *Hitler's motives for the occupation*. Back in Oslo, Spiller applied for and was granted a tour of Fornebu airfield by the Ministry of Defence, against the advice of the airfield commander kaptein Munthe Dahl. What he learned from the visit – if anything – is not known.

29. BA-RM 7/92 and NARA-PG 33236.

30. BA-RM 7/180, BA-RM 7/177, BA-RM 7/1184, BA-N 300/5, NA-GFM 33/1519; Krancke, *Norwegen Unternehmen*; Jodl's diary.

31. BA-RH 24-21/23.

32. BA-RM 35 I /32, BA-RH 24-21/23, Gruppe XXI KTB E180-5; Halder, *Kriegstagebuch*. Eventually, *Gelb* was initiated 32 days after *Weserübung*.

33. BA-RM 7/92. Underlining is in the original document.

34. BA-RM 7/92. Underlining is in the original document.

35. BA-RM 7/92, MSg 2/1882; Halder, *Kriegstagebuch*; Jodl's diary; *Lagevorträge*.

36. BA-RM 7/92, BA-RM 35 I/35, BA-RM 24-21/30 and Halder, *Kriegstagebuch*.

37. BA-RM 7/92, NARA-PG 37848.

38. BA-RM 7/92, BA-RM 7/180, BA-RM 7/124, BA-RM 7/92, BA-RM 35 I/32, Gruppe XXI KTB E180-5; Halder, *Kriegstagebuch*; *Lageforträge*. It is unclear whether Hagelin had actually spoken to Diesen or if he provided second-hand information.

39. NARA-PG 37848.

40. Gruppe XXI KTB E180-07.

41. Gruppe XXI KTB E180-07.

42. Gruppe XXI KTB E180-07.

Chapter 5 – Let Slip the Dogs of War

1. In Shakespeare's *Julius Caesar*, Mark Antony laments Caesar's death and predicts that war is sure to follow: 'with a monarch's voice cry Havoc and let slip the dogs of war'.
2. BA-N 300/5
3. BA-N 300/5, BA-RM 7/92, BA-RM 35 II/35, BA-RM 7/11 and Gruppe XXI KTB E180-7.
4. Letter from Buschenhagen 31.07.57, in Hartmann, *Varslene til de Nordiske Legasjoner før den 9. April 1940.*
5. Gruppe XXI KTB E180-7.
6. BA-N 300/5 and NARA-PG 37848.
7. BA-RM 35 I/39, BA-RM 48/176, BA-RM 7/11 and Gruppe XXI KTB E180-5.
8. BA-RM 7/11.
9. BA-RM 35 II/35.
10. Dilks, *Great Britain and Scandinavia in the 'Phoney War'*; Macleod, *Time Unguarded.*
11. BA-MSg 2/1882 and Gruppe XXI KTB E180-7.
12. BA-RH 24-21/17, BA-RM 7/180, BA-N 172/1, Gruppe XXI KTB E 180-7 and E 180-11, BA-RM 7/9, BA-N 300/5; Raeder, *Mein Leben*, vol. II; Jodl's diary.
13. Gruppe XXI KTB E180-08. The note uses the term *V-männer*, short for *Vertrauens-männer*, which refers to Norwegians willing to talk to or report to German officials like Schreiber. They were sympathisers, but not necessarily agents in a modern sense. The underlining is in the original text.
14. NARA-PG 37852.
15. NARA-PG 37848 and NARA-PG 37859.
16. Koht, *Norsk Utanrikspolitikk fram til 9. April 1940*; Koht, *For Fred og Fridom i Krigstid.*
17. BA-RM 7/11 KTB SKL, BA-RM 7/180, BA-N 172/14; Hartmann, *Spillet om Norge*; Hartmann, *Quislings konferanse med den tyske overkommando*; Aspheim, *Quislings hemmelige møte i København.*
18. Pruck, 'Abwehraussenstelle Norwegen'; Hartmann, *Spillet om Norge.*
19. Gruppe XXI KTB E180-13.
20. Jodl's diary.
21. *Dagbladet* 05.04 1940 and *Norges Handels og Sjøfartstidende* 05.04.1940
22. Similar notes (in both English and French), were delivered to the Swedish Foreign Office in Stockholm as well as to the Norwegian and Swedish Embassies in London and Paris.
23. NA-FO 371/24815.
24. NA-FO 371/24815; Koht, *For Fred og Fridom i Krigstid.*
25. Harriman, *Mission to the North.*
26. Koht, *Norge neutralt och överfallet*; Kjølsen, *Optakten til den 9. April.* The film was also shown to diplomats in Berlin as well as in the German embassies in Copenhagen and Stockholm on the same day.

27. Koht, *For Fred og Fridom i Krigstid*. The note became known in Berlin during the 6th.

28. Koht, *For Fred og Fridom i Krigstid* and Lie, *Leve eller dø*.

29. BA-RM 7/11.

30. NA-Prem 1/419; Dilks, *The Diaries of Sir Alexander Cadogan*; Reynaud, *La France a sauvé l'Europe*.

31. There were mostly British troops this time, when the French and Polish did not make it back in time.

32. NA-CAB 66/6, NA-CAB 65/12, NA-PREM 1/419, NA-ADM 199/474, NA-ADM 199/393; Dilks, *The Diaries of Sir Alexander Cadogan*; Butler, *Grand Strategy*, vol. II.

33. Gruppe XXI KTB E180-07. Underlining is in the original.

34. Gruppe XXI KTB E180-07. Underlining is in the original.

35. RA II-C-11-2150/52, RA II-C-11-1200/10, BA-RM 7/11 and BA-RM 35/II-35.

36. BA-RM 7/891 and BA-RM 98/22.

37. Wesermünde was renamed Bremerhaven after the war.

38. BA-RM 92/5267 and BA-RM 92/5078.

39. BA-RM 7/11, BA-RM 92/5178, BA-RM 35/I-39, BA-RM 35/II-35, BA-RM 48/176, and BA-RM 54/30.

40. RA II-C-11-51; *Innstilling fra Undersøkeseskommisjonen av 1945*; Koht, *For Fred og Fridom i Krigstid*; Kristiansen, *Krigsplaner og Politikk*; Heradstveit, *Kongen som sa nei*.

41. Adlercreutz Arkivet.

42. NA-ADM 223/82; Hinsley, *British Intelligence in the Second World War*; Beesly, *Very Special Intelligence*.

43. NA-FO 419/34 and NA-FO 371/24815.

44. NA-ADM 116/4471, NA-CAB 65/12, NA-FO 419/34 and NA-FO 371/24815.

45. FO 371/24815. Hector Boyes had retired from the Royal Navy in 1934 with the rank of rear-admiral. In August 1939, he was recalled and appointed naval attaché in Oslo with the temporary rank of captain.

46. Jervell, *Scener fra en ambassades liv. Berlin 1905–2002*.

47. BA-RM 7/124, BA-RM 35 I/31, BA-RM 7/180; Böhme, *Underrettelser från Berlin*; *Förspelet*.

48. BA-N 300/5; Böhme, *Underrettelser från Berlin*; *Förspelet*. Falkenhorst was concerned over security issues in the Baltic ports and had rumours put about that a strengthening of the German forces in East Prussia was under way.

49. Hartmann, *Varslene til de Nordiske legasjoner før den 9. april 1940*; Koht, *Norsk Utanrikspolitikk fram til 9. april 1940*; *Innstilling fra undersøkelseskommisjonen av 1945*.

50. *Förspelet*; Steen, *Norges Sjøkrig*, vol. I.

51. Sas was killed in an accident in 1948.

52. DRA-Privatarkiv 06145; *Förspelet*; Kjølsen, *Mit livs logbog*; Kjølsen, *Optakten til den 9. April*.

53. *Innstilling fra undersøkelseskommisjonen av 1945*; *Betænkning*; Hartmann, *Varslene til de Nordiske Legasjoner før den 9. april 1940*; DRA-Privatarkiv 06145.

54. BA-RM 7/11.

55. DRA-Privatarkiv 06145; *Betænkning*; Kjølsen, *Optakten til den 9. April*; Kjølsen, *Mit livs logbog*.
56. RA-II-C-11-52.2/52.6; Steen, *Norges Sjøkrig*, vol. I.
57. RA-II-C-11-51 and *Innstilling fra undersøkelseskommisjonen av 1945*.
58. *Förspelet* and Adlercreutz Arkivet.
59. *Betænkning*; *Förspelet*; Kjølsen, *Optakten til den 9. April*; Kjølsen, *Mit livs logbog*; Diesen Arkivet and Adlercreutz Arkivet.
60. DRA-Privatarkiv 06145, *Betænkning*; *Innstilling fra Undersøkelseskommisjonen av 1945*.
61. RA-II-C-11-51 and *Innstilling fra Undersøkelseskommisjonen av 1945*.
62. RA-II-C-11-52.2/52.6; Diesen Arkivet; Jervell, *Scener fra en ambassades liv*; *Aftenposten* 20.06.2005.
63. *Innstilling fra Undersøkelses-kommisjonen av 1945*; Kjølsen, *Mit livs logbog*.
64. RA-II-C-11-52.2/52.6; Willoch Papers; Steen, *Norges Sjøkrig*, vol. I; G. Ræder, *De uunnværlig flinke*. Gudrun Martius figures in many documents as Gudrun Ræder, but she did not marry Johan Ræder until late 1940, in London. Martius's version of the events of 7 April were put on paper in November 1941 at the request of Trygve Lie, who had replaced Koht as Foreign Minister in the Norwegian Government-in-Exile in London in November 1940. Koht played down the whole episode.
65. RA-II-C-11-51; *Innstilling fra Undersøkelseskommisjonen av 1945*.

Chapter 6 – No Way Back

1. NA-CAB 66/7, NA-ADM 116/4471, NA-WO 193/772, Butler, *Grand Strategy*, vol. II.
2. NARA-PG 378484
3. BA-RM 7/92 and Gruppe XXI KTB E180-7.
4. BA-RM 92/5087 and NARA-PG 37848. The supply ship *Nordmark* was assigned to accompany *Lützow* into the Atlantic.
5. BA-RM 92/5269, BA-RM 92/5087 and BA-RM 92/5088.
6. BA-RM 7/194. Oskar Kummetz was born in East Prussia in 1891. He joined the Navy as a cadet in 1910 and rose to *Oberleutnant* during WW1, when he mainly served on board torpedo boats. By 1934 he was C-in-C Torpedo Boats and by the outbreak of WW2 he was Chief of Staff at the Fleet. Shortly after, he was made inspector of torpedo weapons from where he was temporarily assigned to lead Group V.
7. Whitley, *German Cruisers of World War Two* and Melien/Fjeld Private Archive.
8. BA-RM 92/5087, BA-RM 92/5088, BA-RM 134/271, Gruppe XXI KTB E180-05 and Herzog, *Drei Kriegsschiffe Blücher*.
9. BA-RM 92/5097.
10. BA-RM 48/176, BA-RM 7/92, BA-RM 92/5267, BA-RM 92/5097, BA-RM 92/5223 and BA-RM 92/5097.
11. Hauptman Boese's report in the Melien/Fjeld Private Archive.
12. BA-RM 92/5087, BA-RM 92/5088 BA-RM 134/271, NARA-PG47493 and Gruppe XXI KTB E180-05. *Landser* is an old term for German infantry soldiers, still commonly used during WW2.

13. NARA-PG 73159 and BA-RM 102/3893.
14. BA-RM 72/73. The ships were *Widar, Schlewig Holstein, Luise Leonhard, Olga Siemers, Klara L. M. Russ, Kleopatra, Viola, Kepler* and *Reinhard L. M. Russ.*
15. Denham, *Inside the Nazi Ring.*
16. NA-ADM 223/126 and Denham, *Inside the Nazi Ring.*
17. Jodl's diary.
18. BA-RM 54/30, BA-RM 48/176, BA-RM 7/92, BA-RM 92/5178 and BA-RM 92/5267.
19. BA-RM 92/5257, BA-RM 96/667, BA-N 300/5 and Gruppe XXI KTB E180-5.
20. Denham, *Inside the Nazi Ring*; Roskill, *Churchill and the Admirals.* All aircraft returned safely.
21. NA-AT 1259/7, NA-FO 371/24815 and NA-ADM 199/3.
22. Denham, *Inside the Nazi Ring.*
23. NA-AIR-22/8, NA-ADM 223/126, NA-ADM 223/82, NA-AIR 14/669, NA-ADM 199/393, BA-RM 92/5245 and Brown, *Naval Operations of the Campaign in Norway.*
24. NA-ADM 199/393, NA-ADM 199/385, NA-ADM 223/126, NA-ADM 267/126, NA-ADM 199/479. NA-ADM 199/361, NA-ADM 199/2202, NA-ADM 199/388 and NA-ADM 199/474.
25. See Haarr, *No Room for Mistakes.*
26. Hezlet, *British and Allied Submarine operations in WWII*; Bryant, *One Man Band.*
27. NA-ADM 199/288 and NA-ADM 199/373.
28. Bryant, *One Man Band.*
29. NA-ADM 234/380, NA-ADM 199/373, BA-RM 7/11, BA-RM 35/II-35 and Simpson, *Periscope View.*

Chapter 7 – Towards Oslo

1. BA-RM 92/5087.
2. NARA-PG 37855.
3. BA-RM 69/108. The obsolete battleship *Schleswig-Holstein* ingloriously went aground, but damage was small.
4. *Generalrapport; Begivenheterne omkring den 9'April 1940; Bjerg, Dansk Orlogshistorie 1510–2010.*
5. BA-RM 92/5087, DRA-Privatarkiv 06145 and *Begivenhederne omkring den 9' april 1940.*
6. Rechnitzer, *Admiral Rechnitzers maritime og politiske erindringer 1905–1940.*
7. *Begivenhederne omkring den 9' april 1940* and BA-RM 72/73. The Danish submarine fleet consisted of three modern boats, well designed for operations in the shallow waters of the Kattegat, based at Aarhus.
8. DRA-Privatarkiv 06145; Rechnitzer, *Admiral Rechnitzers maritime og politiske erindringer 1905–1940; Begivenhederne omkring den 9' april 1940.*
9. DRA-Privatarkiv 06145; *Begivenhederne omkring den 9' april 1940*; Rechnitzer; *Fra neutralitet til besættelse.*
10. NARA-PG 73159 and BA-RM 102/3893.

11. These were the patrol vessel *Ingolf*, torpedo boats *Glenten* and *Høgen*, minesweepers *Søløven*, *Søridderen* and *Støren*, minelayer *Lossen* and four patrol cutters.
12. BA-RM 92/5087, BA-RM 92/5097 and NARA-PG 47493.
13. *Begivenhederne omkring den 9' april 1940*.
14. BA-RM 24-21/30.
15. BA-RM 24-21/30, BA-RM 134/271 and BA-RM 92/5097.
16. DRA-Privatarkiv 06145.
17. BA-RM 134/271, BA-RM 8/1152 and *Begivenhederne omkring den 9' april 1940*.
18. NA-ADM 199/286.
19. NA-ADM 199/373, NA-ADM 223/126 and NA-ADM 199/288. See also www.marinehist.dk.

Chapter 8 – A Day of Highest Tension

1. NA-ADM 223/126, NA-ADM 199/474, RA-II-C-11-52, RA-II-C-11-940, AE 2913/2, NA-FO 419/34 and The Willoch Papers.
2. BA-RM 35/II-35 and Halder, *Kriegstagebuch*.
3. NA-ADM 199/2202, NA-ADM 53/113071, NA-ADM 199/474, NA-ADM 199/323, NA-ADM 199/361, NA-ADM 223/126. BA-RM 35/II/35, BA-RM 92/5267, BA-RM 54/30, BA-RM 48/176, BA-RM 48/176, BA-RM 92/5178, BA-RM 54/30, BA-RM 57/93, BA-RM 92/5257, BA-RM 7/11, BA-RM 35/I/39 and BA-RM 57/125. For a full account of these events, see Haarr, *The German Invasion of Norway*.
4. NA-ADM 199/361, NA-ADM 199/393, NA-ADM 223/126, NA-ADM 199/388, NA-ADM 199/2202, NA-ADM 199/385, NA-ADM 199/474, NA-ADM 199/379 and Roskill, *Churchill and the Admirals*.
5. *Orzeł* had escaped the German invasion in September 1939 and arrived in Britain after an adventurous journey – see Haarr, *No Room for Mistakes*.
6. NA-ADM 199/285.
7. Gruppe XXI KTB E180-9b and the Haarr Archives.
8. NA-ADM 199/285 and the Haarr Archives.
9. NA-ADM 199/285, NA-ADM 199/1853; Sopocko, *Orzeł's Patrol*; Steen, *Norges Sjøkrig*, vol. II. *Orzeł* was lost with all hands in early June 1940, possibly in a British minefield. The wreck has not been found.
10. 'Army this side. Navy that side.' Leutnant Voss was from the regimental staff of IR 159.
11. RA-II-C-11-52, RA 1256-3/10 and RA FKA Ec, 0125.
12. NA-ADM 223/126 and NA-ADM 199/278.
13. NA-ADM 199/286.
14. RA-II-C-11-1103. *Stedingen* was ordered from the Bremen Vulkan yard by the British Anglo-Saxon Petroleum Co. When the war broke out, she was taken over by Nordwestdeutsche Tankschiff Reederei, before being requisitioned by the military in January 1940. Two months later she was assigned to the Tankerstaffel for Operation *Weserübung*.

15. RA-II-C-11/52, RA-FKA-II-C-11/1103, RA-II-C-11/1122, AE 2958/41 and BA-RM 35/II-35.
16. Diesen Arkivet and Steen, *Norges Sjøkrig*, vol. I.
17. RA-II-C-11-1100 boks 180, RA-PA-1469/D/L0002/0005 and Diesen Arkivet.
18. RA-II-C-11-1200, RA-II-C-11-52, RA-PA-1469/D/L0002/0005, Diesen Arkivet, Steen, *Norges Sjøkrig*, vol. I; and *Innstilling fra Undersøkelseskommisjonen av 1945.*
19. RA-II-C-11-1100, DRA-Privatarkiv 06145 and *Generalrapport.* Danish naval authorities informed the German naval attaché in Copenhagen of the mines, asking if this would result in actions against Norway or Denmark, without having any answer.
20. RA-II-C-11-1100 and Steen, *Norges Sjøkrig*, vol. I.
21. Adlercreutz Arkivet.
22. BA-RM 7/92.
23. Steen, *Norges Sjøkrig 1940-45*, vol. I.
24. BA-RM 7/92, BA-RM 12/II/167 and Steen, *Norges Sjøkrig*, vol. II.
25. MMU-privatarkiv 36 and Steen, *Norges Sjøkrig*, vol. I.
26. RA-II-C-11/1100 and MMU-privatarkiv 36.
27. RA-II-C-11-1100 and RA-II-C-11-2020.
28. RA-II-C-11/2010, DRA-Privatarkiv 06145, and *Generalrapport.* Pontoppidan uses the name *Poseidon* for *Stedingen* and says he was told that *Kreta* had also been torpedoed and sunk.
29. RA-II-C-11/2010, Diesen Arkivet and Haarr, *The German Invasion of Norway.*
30. RA-1256-3/10 and Jervell, *Scener fra en ambassades liv.*
31. RA-II-C-11/1200-1210, Diesen Arkivet and Koht, *Frå skanse til skanse.*
32. RA-D/L0002-0009. *See* Chapter 13 and Hegland, *Sjøforsvarets minevesen 1870–1970.* Of the Norwegian minesweepers only *Otra* and *Rauma* were large enough to operate in the area.
33. RA-II-C-11-1200-1210; Hambro, *Historiske Dokumenter;* Heradstveit *Kongen som sa nei;* Koht, *For Fred og Fridom i Krigstid;* Koht, *Norsk Utanrikspolitikk fram til 9. April 1940;* Lie, *Leve eller dø; Innstilling fra Undersøkelseskomiteen av 1945.* Not until 1941 in London did the Ministers become aware of the full set of incoming documents.
34. *Förspelet.*
35. RA-1256-3/10, Koht, *Frå skanse til skanse;* Koht, *Norsk Utanrikspolitikk fram til 9. April 1940.*
36. Hambro, *De første måneder* and *Innstilling fra Undersøkelseskommisjonen av 1945*
37. RA-1256-3/10 and RA-II-C-11-51.
38. RA-Pa-1469/D/L0002/0005; *Innstilling fra Undersøkelseskomiteen av 1945; Betænkning.*
39. RA-II-C-11-1200/1210, RA-PA-1469/D/L0002/0005; *Undersøkelseskommisjonen av 1945;* Lie, *Leve eller dø.*
40. RA-II-C-11-1100 and RA-II-C-11-1103. By midnight, the news of the lighthouses in southern Norway being shut down was made international by the news agency Ritzaus Bureau.
41. Skard, *Mennesket Halvdan Koht.*

42. Koht, *For Fred og Fridom i Krigstid*; Koht, *Norsk Utanrikspolitikk fram til 9. April 1940*

43. BA-RM 7/11, BA-RM 7/180, BA-N 172/14; Hartmann, *Spillet om Norge*; *Straffesak mot Vidkun Quisling*; Knudsen, *Jeg var Quislings sekretær.*

44. Guhnfeldt, *Fornebu 9. april.* Most of the invited officers had excused themselves but some turned up, having had their attendance approved by the Commanding General.

45. NA-GFM 33/1111, BA-N 172/14; Pruck, 'Abwehraussenstelle Norwegen'; Hartmann, *Spillet om Norge*; *Innstilling fra Undersøkelseskommisjonen av 1945.*

46. BA-N 300/5. Falkenhorst apparently never met directly with air attaché Spiller.

47. BA-RM 7/92, BA-RM 12/II/167, NA-GFM 33/1111, E 278-02a; Pruck, *Abwehraussenstelle Norwegen.*

48. DRA-Privatarkiv 06145. Pontoppidan's diaries say the call was made *ca.* 22.30, The Norwegian log has the call received at 22:10.

49. *M 6, M 10, M 11* and *M 12* from Cuxhaven.

50. NARA-PG 73854.

51. Andersen, *Skagerrak-Sperre*

52. BA-RM 7/92, BA-RM 7/11, BA-RM 35/II-35, and BA-RM 12/II-167.

53. BA-N 300/5.

54. '*Tag höchster Spannungen*' – Springenschmid, *Die Männer von Narvik.*

Chapter 9 – *The Guns of Oscarsborg*

1. RA-II-C-11-1100.

2. RA-II-C-11-1100 and Fjeld, *Klar til Strid.* Orographs could be used as a combined rangefinder and director: The guns would receive range and bearing data which made indirect firing possible, though indirect fire was not used by the Norwegian Coast Artillery in 1940.

3. In 1940 Drøbak had a population of *ca.* 2,100 people.

4. RA-II-C-11/1100 and Melien/Fjeld Private Archive.

5. RA-II-C-11/1100, RA-II-C-11/2010; Fjeld, *Klar til Strid.*

6. RA-II-C-11/1100, RA-II-C-11/2010; Godø, *En Krigsberetning.*

7. RA-II-C-11/1100, RA-II-C-11/2010, RA-PA-1469/D/0002/0005 and Fjeld, *Klar til Strid.*

8. RA-II-C-11/1100, RA-II-C-11/2010 and RA II-C-11/2012.

9. RA-II-C-11/1100 and RA-II-C-11/2017.

10. RA-II-C-11/2010 and Fjeld, *Klar til Strid.*

11. RA-II-C-11/1100 and Melien/Fjeld Private Archive.

12. RA-II-C-11/1100.

13. Fjeld and Kolstad, *Oslofjord Festnings Historikk 1916–1962*; Fjeld, *Klar til Strid.*

14. RA-II-C-11/1100.

15. RA-II-C-11/1100 and Fjeld and Kolstad, *Oslofjord Festnings Historikk 1916–1962.* Men for the 12-cm battery were called during the evening of 8 April, but they arrived too late to make any difference.

16. Fjeld and Kolstad, *Oslofjord Festnings Historikk 1916–1962*; Fjeld, *Klar til Strid.*

17. RA-II-C-11/1100.

Chapter 10 – Trespassing

1. BA-RM 92/5097, BA-RM 57/93, BA-RM 8/1152 and BA-RM 134/271.

2. BA-RM 24-21/30.

3. BA-RM 92/5097.

4. BA-RM 92/5223, BA-RM 92/5259, BA-RM 92/5097, BA-RM 92/5088, BA-RM 57/93, BA-RM 8/1152, and BA-RH 24-21/30. From now on all times are Norwegian unless specified otherwise.

5. RA-II-C-11/1122. During the afternoon of the 8th, at least five merchant ships did so, including the German *Reinhard L. M. Russ*.

6. RA-II-C-11/1100, RA-II-C-11/1120 and MMU 55830/948.181. Nine guardships, in three groups of three each, shared the duty of patrolling the southern boundary of Oslo *krigshavn*. Most of them were requisitioned whalers with minimal armament. *Pol III* usually had a seventeen-man crew, but on this night, two were ashore sick. Welding-Olsen had been diagnosed with colour blindness a short time before and was about to be dismissed from the service altogether.

7. RA-II-C-11/1100. The order to shut down the lighthouses had first been given at the end of the regular seven o'clock news bulletin.

8. The Watch Commander this night, sersjant Warstad, later held that the signal arrived at 23:03, in which case *Pol III* must have heard the engines of Gruppe *Oldenburg* earlier than 23:06. RA-II-C-11/2023.

9. RA-II-C-11/1100, RA-II-C-11/1102, RA-II-C-11/1120, RA-D/L0002-0009 and MMU 55830/948.181.

10. RA-II-C-11-1122 and BA-RM 134/271.

11. RA-II-C-11-1122, MMU 55830/948.181 and BA-RM 57/93.

12. RA-II-C-11/1120, RA-II-C-11/1122, MMU 55830/848.1818, Diesen Arkivet and BA-RM 57/93.

13. RA-II-C-11/1100, RA-II-C-11/1122 and BA-RM 57/93.

14. RA-II-C-11/1100, RA-II-C-11/1122, MMU 55830/948.181 and BA-RM 57/93.

15. RA-II-C-11/1100, RA-II-C-11/2020 and RA-II-C-11/2022.

16. RA-II-C-11/1100 and RA-II-C-11/2020. The men in the southern battery at Rauøy insisted that they heard sounds indicating that one of the first shots had been a hit. There are no German reports to verify this, though.

17. RA-II-C-11/1100 and RA-II-C-11/2022. The mines and their detonators were susceptible to ice and the mines were stored in magazines on land during winter.

18. RA-II-C-11-1120 and RA-II-C-11/2022.

19. First Officer Heymann re-recorded and reconstructed *Blücher*'s war diary based on his own experiences and interviews with others, mostly officers or petty officers. Chief Engineer Fregattenkapitän Karl Thannemann made a similar record of events for the engine-room areas as did Gunnery Officer Kurt-Eduard Engelmann for the artillery and fire-control sections.

20. BA-RM 92/5087 and BA-RM 92/5088.

21. BA-RM 92/5269 and BA-RM 92/5088.

22. BA-RM 92/5088 and BA-RM 134/271 and Herzog, *Drei Kriegsschiffe Blücher.*
23. BA-RM 8/1152, BA-RM 134/271, BA-RM 24-21/30 and BA-RM 92/5097.
24. NARA-PG 73159, BA-RM 102/3893 and BA-RM 102/3893.
25. BA-RM 92/5223, BA-RM 92/5087 BA-RM 102/3894, BA-RM 92/5088 and the Haarr Archives.
26. BA-RM 72/73.
27. RA-II-C-11-1100, RA-II-C-11-51, RA-II-C-11-52; The Willoch Papers; and Steen, *Norges sjøkrig 1940–45*, vol. II.
28. This was *Kondor, Albatros, R 17, R 21,* and *Rau VIII.*
29. RA-II-C-11-1100, RA-II-C-11-1102, BA-RM 102/3894 and BA-RM 57/93. The crew abandoned *Otra* at Filtvet. During the afternoon, men from *Kondor* came aboard to immobilise her and disable the guns.

Chapter 11 – Intruders

1. BA-RM 92/5087. Signalman Fritz Limbach on the bridge of *Blücher* later held that a civilian merchant master from Neptun-Reederei was present to assist in the navigation. He had allegedly sailed between Germany and southern Norway for years before the war and knew the Oslofjord well. This man's name is unknown and even his presence cannot be confirmed.
2. RA-II-C-11 1100 and MMU Privatarkiv 36.ld
3. Koop and Schmolke, *Heavy Cruisers of the Admiral Hipper Class.*
4. BA-RM 92/5088 and BA-RM 92/5097.
5. RA-II-C-11-1100, RA-RAFA-2017/Y/Ye/L0193, RA-PA-1469/D/0002/0005; Fjeld, *Klar til Strid.* The main battery at Oscarsborg had a maximum range of 20,900 metres and Kopås of 14,000 metres, although the practical range for both batteries was somewhat shorter.
6. RA-II-C-11-2012, RA-II-C-11-2016 and Steen, *Norges Sjøkrig, 1940-1945*, vol. II.
7. BA-RM 92/5097. He was appointed Kommandant der Befestigungen der Pommerschen Küste on 30 March 1939. He left the post on 5 October 1939. By then his position was renamed Küstenbefehlshaber Pommern.
8. BA-RM 71/5, NARA-PG 33238 and Gruppe XXI KTB E180-07.
9. BA-N 300/5.
10. BA-N 300/5.
11. NA-ADM 234/427, BA-RM 70/1, BA-RM 92/5259, BA-RM 92/5087, BA-RM 92/5088, BA-RM 92/VM855/47900-910, BA-RM 92/5223, BA-N 300/5 and Pruck, *Abwehraussenstelle Norwegen.*
12. RA-II-C-11/2010 and RA-II-C-11/2020.
13. RA-II-C-11/1100, RA-RAFA-2017/Y/Ye/L0193, RA-PA-1469/D/0002/0005; Melien/ Fjeld Private Archive and *Regulations for 28 cm Krupp gun.*
14. RA-FKA-2B.072.42.
15. RA-II-C-11/1100 and RA-II-C-11/2012.

16. RA-II-C-11/1100, RA-RAFA-2017/Y/Ye/L0193, RA-PA-1469/D/0002/0005 and Fjeld, *Klar til Strid.*
17. RA-II-C-11/2014. The permitted arc of fire from Nesset was strictly limited to avoid hitting Drøbak.
18. RA-II-C-11/1103 and BA-RM 92/5088.
19. RA-II-C-11/2010.
20. RA-II-C-11/1100, RA-RAFA-2017/Y/Ye/L0193 and RA-II-C-11/2010.
21. RA-FKA-2B.072.42 and Melien/Fjeld Private Archive.
22. RA-II-C-11/1100, RA-II-C-11/2017, RA-II-C-11/2010 and Melien/Fjeld Private Archive. The underlining is in the original journal.
23. Melien/Fjeld Private Archive.
24. RA-RAFA-2017/Y/Ye/L0193 and Melien/Fjeld Private Archive.
25. RA-II-C-11/2012, RA-RAFA-2017/Y/Ye/L0193, RA-FKA-2B.072.42 and Melien/Fjeld Private Archive.
26. RA-II-C-11/1100, RA-II-C-11-1102/1110, RA-RAFA-2017/Y/Ye/L0193, RA-FKA-2B.072.42 and BA-RH 24-21/30. In other reports, the time varies between 04:19 and 04:25. Most German reports use 05:19 German time, i.e. 04:19 Norwegian time.
27. RA-II-C-11/2014 and BA-RM 134/271.
28. BA-RM 92/5087, BA-RM 92/5088, BA-RM 92/5223, BA-RM 134/271, BA-RM 92/5097, BA-RH 24-21/30 and RA-FKA-II-C-11-1103.
29. BA-RM 92/5087 and BA-RM 92/5088.
30. BA-RM 92/5088 and Melien/Fjeld Private Archive. Some Norwegian sources report the hits in the opposite order, but all reports from on board *Blücher* have the hit on the foretop happening first.
31. RA-II-C-11/2012 and RA FKA-2B.072.42.
32. NARA-PG 47493 and Binder and Schlünz, *Schwerer Kreutzer Blücher.*
33. BA-RM 92/5088, BA-RM 92/5269, RA-II-C-11/2012 and Melien/Fjeld Private Archive.
34. BA-RM 92/5087, BA-RM 92/5269, BA-MA III M 35/1, BA-RM 92/5088 and Melien/Fjeld Private Archive.
35. RA-II-C-11/2012 and RA-FKA-2B.072.42.
36. BA-RM 92/5088.
37. RA-II-C-11/1100, BA-RM 92/5087 and BA-RM 92/5088.
38. BA-RM 92/5088.
39. NARA-PG 47493.
40. Melien/Fjeld Private Archive
41. RA-II-C-11-1100 and RA-II-C-11-2017.
42. BA-RM 92/5088 and BA-RH 24-21/30
43. BA-RM 92/5088 and RA-FKA-II-C-11/1103. The three aircraft that escaped were all damaged or destroyed during the ensuing campaign. Some of the pilots ended up in the UK, serving in the Norwegian Air-Force.
44. BA-RM 92/5269, BA-RM 92/5087 and BA-RM 92/5088.

45. BA-RM 92/5087, BA-RM 92/5088, BA-RM 92/5269 and NARA-PG 47493.
46. BA-RM 92/5087 and BA-RM 92/5088.
47. BA-RM 92/5223 and BA-RM 92/5097.
48. BA-RM 92/5097.
49. BA-RM 92/5097.
50. BA-RM 92/5097.
51. BA-RM 7/11, BA-RM 92/5088, BA-RM 92/5259, BA-RM 92/5223 and BA-RM 92/5097.
52. BA-RM 134/271.
53. BA-RM 70/1; Steen, *Norges Sjøkrig*, vol. II; Hovland, *Bli med til Oscarsborg*; Bud Sogelag. The fire was seen from Kopås, probably giving rise to the misunderstanding that an additional German ship had been sunk. For many years, the training ship *Brummer* was listed as sunk by Norwegian sources. This was not the case, however, as she was not even in the Narrows at the time. *See* Chapter 15.
54. BA-RM 92/5088, BA-RM 92/5269 and Boese's report in Melien/Fjeld Private Archive.
55. BA-RM 92/5088 and BA-RM 92/5269.
56. BA-RM 92/5088.
57. RA-II-C-11/2010, RA-PA-1469/D/L0002/0005 and RA-RAFA-2017/Y/Ye/L0193.
58. RA-II-C-11/2010 and RA-RAFA-2017/Y/Ye/L0193.
59. BA-RM 92/5087 and BA-RM 92/5088.
60. BA-RM 92/5088 and BA-RM 92/5269.
61. BA-RM 24-21/30.
62. SKL 23685/41 in Herzog, *Drei Kriegsschiffe Blücher*; BA-RM 92/5088, BA-RM24-21/30, BA-RM 92/5269 and Melien/Fjeld Private Archive.
63. BA-RM 92/5088 and BA-RM 24-21/30.
64. BA-RM 134/91 and BA-RM 24/21/30.
65. BA-RM 92/5269, BA-RM 92/5223, BA-RM 92/5087, BA-RM 92/5088, BA-RH 24-21/30 and Melien/Fjeld Private Archive.
66. BA-RM 134/91, BA-RM 24/21/30, BA-RM 92/5088 and BA-RM 92/5269.
67. Zöpfel, in Hase, *Die Kriegsmarine erobert Norwegens Fjorde*.
68. BA-RM 24-21/30.
69. BA-RM 24-21/30.
70. BA-RM 134/91, BA-RM 24-21/30, BA-RM 92/5088 and BA-RM 92/5269.
71. BA-RM 92/5088, BA-RM 24-21/30, BA-RM 92/5269 and Boese's report in Melien/Fjeld Private Archive.
72. RA-II-C-11/2000.
73. RA-II-C-11/2000.
74. RA-II-C-11/2000.
75. BA-RH 24-21/30. Several details in Goerz's account are obvious misunderstandings and his perception of what happened is not always in line with Heymann's and Thannemann's stories. Goerz had with him a camera and film in watertight bags and

took some of the photos shown here. He also had money from the funds he had been given to kickstart his job as a supply officer. Some of the money was later given to officer friends who lacked everything from underwear to boots and overcoats. When Falkenhorst learned of this, he confiscated the remaining cash.

76. BA-RH 24-21/30 and SKL 44094/41 in Herzog, *Drei Kriegsschiffe Blücher*.

77. BA-RM 134/91.

78. BA-RM 134/91 and Boese's report in Melien/Fjeld Private Archive.

79. BA-RM 134/91, BA-RM 92/5088, BA-RH 24-21/30 and *Die erobert Norwegens Fjorde*.

80. BA-RM 134/91, BA-RM 57/93, BA-RM 24-21/30. During the rescue operation *Kondor*'s propeller was damaged from hitting some wreckage and she could no longer make maximum speed. The small German steamer *Norden* was not part of the *Weserübung* forces. On regular civilian traffic, she happened to come by Son on the morning of the 9th and the master immediately volunteered to assist in the search for *Blücher* and her survivors. A petty officer and a radio operator from *Lützow* were sent on board, but she was not armed.

81. BA-RM 45/III/119.

Chapter 12 – Improvisations

1. BA-RM 7/11, BA-RM 92/5088, BA-RM 92/5259, BA-RM 92/5223, BA-RM 92/5097, BA-RM 92/VM855/47900-910 and the Haarr archives.

2. BA-RM 92/5223, BA-RM 92/5097, BA-RM 92/5259, BA-RM 57/93, BA-RM 70/1 and BA-RH 24-21/17.

3. BA-RM 134/271 and BA-RM 92/5097.

4. 5./IR 307 or a company from IV./GJR 138.

5. BA-RM 92/5097, BA-RM 92/5088, BA-RM 57/93 and BA-RM 134/271.

6. BA-RM 92/5097.

7. BA-RM 134/271.

8. BA-RM 92/5097, BA-RM 134/271 and E 278-02a.

9. BA-RM 134/271 and E 278-02a.

10. RA-II-C-11/1100 and RA-II-C-11/2010. The sources diverge from 05:45 to after 08:00, but there is no doubt that Eriksen and Hvinden Haug had a telephone conference that morning.

11. Hafsten et al., *Flyalarm*; Guhnfeldt, *Fornebu 9. April*; Haarr, *The German Invasion of Norway*. The Heinkels of KG 4 came from Delmenhorst (II./KG4), Fassberg (II./KG4) and Perlberg (I./KG4) in north-west Germany. Aircraft from other units also participated.

12. Evensen, *Oscarsborg forteller historie*.

13. Godø, *En Krigsberetning*.

14. RA-II-C-11-2010, RA-FKA-2 B.072.42; Godø, *En Krigsberetning*; Melien/Fjeld Private Archive.

15. RA-II-C-11/2012, RA-FKA-2 B.072.42; Godø, *En Krigsberetning*.

16. Godø, *En Krigsberetning*.

17. RA-II-C-11/1100, RA-II-C-11/2012, RA-FKA-2B.072.42, BA-RM 92/5097 and Melien/ Fjeld Private Archive.
18. BA-RM 45/III/100.
19. RA-FKA-2B.072.42. and NARA-PG 73159.
20. RA-II-C-11/2010.
21. RA-RAFA-2017/Y/Ye/L0193, RA-II-C-11/2010 and Melien/Fjeld Private Archive.
22. RA-II-C-11/1100, RA-II-C-11/2010, RA-FKA-2B.072.42, BA-RM 57/93, BA-RM 92/5259; Godø, *En Krigsberetning*. Later in the evening *R 23* joined the group of R-boats in Drøbak.
23. RA-II-C-11/2017, BA-RM 92/5097 and BA-RM 134/271.
24. BA-RM 134/271.
25. RA-II-C-11/2010, BA-RM 134/271 and Melien/Fjeld Private Archive.
26. RA-II-C-11/1100, RA-II-C-11/2017, BA-RM 57/93, BA-RM 92/5097 and BA-RM 92/5223.
27. RA-II-C-11/2010.

Chapter 13 – War in Oslofjord

1. RA-II-C-11-1102.
2. RA-II-C-11-1100, RA-II-C-11-1102 and Steen, *Norges Sjøkrig*, vol. II.
3. RA-II-C-11/1100, RA-II-C-11/1102 and Steen, *Norges Sjøkrig*, vol. II.
4. MMU 948.181.2, RA-II-C-11-1102, RA-II-C-11-1100 and NARA-PG 73159.
5. BA-RM 134/271, BA-RM 57/93 and BA-RM 102/3894.
6. BA-RM 134/271 and BA-RM 57/93.
7. RA-II-C-11/1100, RA-II-C-11/1102 and Steen, *Norges Sjøkrig*, vol. II.
8. MMU 948.181.2, BA-RM 134/271, BA-RM 102/3894, BA-RM 7/486, BA-RM 70/1 and NARA-PG 73159.
9. Gunner Erik Jevanord later died in hospital.
10. RA-II-C-11-1102, RM 70/1, BA-RM 134/271, BA-RM 102/3894, BA-RM 7/486 and NARA-PG 73159.
11. RA-II-C-11-1102, BA-RM 57/93, BA-RM 102/3894 and Steen, *Norges Sjøkrig*, vol. II.
12. BA-RM 70/1 and BA-RM 92/5223.
13. BA-RM 70/1, MMU 948.181.2, BA-RM 134/271 and BA-RM 92/5223.
14. NARA-PG 47514.
15. RA-II-C-11/1100, MMU 948.181.2, MMU Privatarkiv 36, BA-RM 134/271 and BA-RM 92/5259.
16. RA-II-C-11/1100, RA-II-C-11/1102, MMU 948.181.2, BA-RM 70/1 and BA-RM 134/271.
17. RA-II-C-11/1100 and MMU privatarkiv 36.
18. RA-II-C-11/1102 and BA-RM 134/271.
19. RA-II-C-11/1100 and BA-RM 70/1.
20. RA-II-C-11/1100, BA-RM 92/5097, BA-RM 92/5223 and BA-RM 92/5259.
21. The men on the island could not communicate with the R-boats as nobody had realised they were on different radio frequencies.

22. RA-II-C-11/1100 and BA-RM 70/1.
23. RA-II-C-11/1100.
24. RA-II-C-11/1100, BA-RM 70/1 and BA-RM 92/5332
25. BA-RM 70/1 and RA-II-C-11/1100. *A2* was used as a target before finally being scrapped at Lübeck. *A3* and *A4* were salvaged and scrapped after the war. Knutsen, *Tilstede og Usynlig.*
26. RA-II-C-11/1100, RA-II-C-11/1122 and BA-RM 70/1. Stabsobersteuermann Karl Rixecker was awarded the Knight's Cross for the capture of *A2*, in spite of failing to secure Bolærne. Kapitänleutnant (Ing.) Erich Grundmann, Oberleutnant Kurt Budäus and Stabsobersteuermann Arthur Godenau were also awarded the Knight's Cross for their achievements and initiatives.
27. *Curityba* was eventually escorted past the forts and reached Oslo on 11 April.
28. BA-RM 57/93. RA-II-C-11/2022.
29. BA-RM 92/5223.
30. BA-RM 92/5223, BA-RM 57/93 and BA-RM 7/1475.
31. Later, there was some discussion over who gave the order to hoist the white flag, but this was never fully clarified. Rumour had it that it was hoisted by a soldier terrified by the strafing and bombing, but it made no practical difference.
32. BA-RM 57/93 and RA-FKA-2B.072.42.
33. BA-RM 70/1 and RA-II-C-11-1100.
34. BA-RM 92/522, BA-RM 92/5259 and BA-RM 57/93.

Chapter 14 – Aftermath

1. RA-II-C-11-1100, NA-ADM 223/126; Diesen Arkivet, MMU privatarkiv 36 and Steen, *Norges Sjøkrig*, vol. II.
2. RA-II-C-11-52,2/52,6, RA-II-C-11-1100 and E 279-01.
3. The Statsråd or 'Council of State' was the name for a formal meeting of the Norwegian government led by the King. Beside the eleven government ministers, Undersecretary Jens Bull of the Foreign Office was present at Victoria Terrasse.
4. Nygaardsvold, *Norge i krig 9. April– 7. Juni 1940.*
5. Diesen Arkivet.
6. NA-FO 419/34, NA-FO 371/24829, IWM 67/25/1; Koht, *Frå skanse til skanse*; Lie, *Leve eller dø.* Koht wrote that he 'believed in Oscarsborg' and never considered it would be possible to transport sufficient troops by aircraft to threaten Oslo.
7. RA-II-C-11-51, RA-PA-1469/D/L0002/0005; *Innstilling fra Undersøkelseskommisjonen av 1945*; Koht, *Frå skanse til skanse*; Lie, *Leve eller dø*; Hjelmtveit, *Vekstår og vargtid*; Munthe-Kaas, *Aprildagene 1940*; Grimnes, *Veien inn i krigen.* Parts of 6th Division had already been mobilised and deployed in north Norway, reinforced with one battalion from south Norway.
8. RA-II-C-11-51, RA-PA-1469/D/L0002/0005; *Innstilling fra Undersøkelseskommisjonen av 1945*; Faye, *Krigen i Norge 1940.* Koht later maintained that all southern Norway had

been mobilised. A few hours later he told a journalist that 'full mobilisation' had been ordered and at Hamar he told the assembly that mobilisation had commenced.

9. RA-FKA-Ya II-C-11-00; Koht, *For Fred og Fridom i Krigstid*; Koht, *Frå skanse til skanse*; Lie, *Leve eller dø*.

10. E 279-01. An hour later, at 06:17 GeT, Group III in Bergen received a signal from Kiel: 'To all: Norwegian government has decided full resistance.'

11. E 278.02a.

12. Hambro, *C J Hambro Liv og drøm*.

13. RA-FKA-Ya II-C-11-00, E 278-02a and Hambro, *De første måneder*.

14. Øksendal, *Gulltransporten*.

15. Hambro, *De første måneder*; Hambro, *C J Hambro liv og drøm*; Lie, *Leve eller dø*.

16. Scheidt returned to Oslo on 5 or 6 April.

17. E 278-02a and E 279-01.

18. E 279-01.

19. BA-RM 7/92.

20. Zeiner-Gundersen, *Norsk artilleri gjennom 300 år*.

21. Guhnfeldt, *Fornebu 9. April*; Haarr, *The German Invasion of Norway*. All seven Gladiator pilots survived, later to serve in the RAF or the re-established Norwegian Air Force, operationally or as instructors.

22. Hauptmann Ingenhoven was later awarded the Knight's Cross for this.

23. Guhnfeldt, *Fornebu 9. April*; Haarr, *The German Invasion of Norway*.

24. E 288-01, E 279-01 and Haarr, *The German Invasion of Norway*.

25. E 288-01. By the time Nickelmann left Fornebu for Oslo, he had seventeen paratroopers with him.

26. Guhnfeldt, *Fornebu 9. April*; Haarr, *The German Invasion of Norway*.

27. E 279-01 and Haarr, *The German Invasion of Norway*.

28. Philler was told *Blücher* had been sunk with a great loss of life, including most of the divisional staff. Group XXI had no knowledge of the fate of General Engelbrecht at this stage.

29. BA-N 300/5.

30. NA-GFM 33/1111, BA-N 172/14, BA-N 300/5, BA-RM 12/II/167, BA-RM 7/92, BA-RM 48/176, RA-II-C-11-2150/52; Pruck, *Abwehraussenstelle Norwegen*; Skodvin, *Striden om okkupasjonsstyret i Norge*.

31. Haarr, *The German Invasion of Norway*. George survived and spent the rest of the war as a POW. The remaining crewmen rest at Sylling Churchyard west of Oslo.

32. NA-FO 371/24834. The answer was an instruction to try to stay with the Norwegian government, while 'all redundant staff' should head for Sweden as soon as convenient.

33. NA-FO 371/24832 and NA-FO 419/34.

34. *The Memoirs of General the Lord Ismay*.

35. NA-ADM 234/380, NA-ADM 116/4471, NA-FO 419/34 and Churchill, *Second World War*, vol. I.

36. By midday, most of the British and French Embassy personnel had arrived, as had the US Ambassador Mrs Harriman. She had originally planned to stay in Oslo, but was encouraged by Koht to follow the government, which was also her instruction from Washington.

37. Colonel Gullichsen was one of the few high-ranking officers who was a member of the Labour Party and probably chosen because Koht and Nygaardsvold knew and trusted him.

38. NA-FO 419/34, NA-FO 371/24832, NA-FO 371/24834 and NA-FO 371/24829. Justice Minister Wold later wrote that he found it ironic that the British Minister now assisted by way of an illegal radio transmitter, which he had previously denied any knowledge of. Francis Edward Foley had arrived in Oslo on 28 August 1939 with his secretary Margaret Grant Reid, see Haarr *The German Invasion of Norway.*

39. In the meeting, Nygaardsvold brought up the issue of a coalition government. Hambro and the opposition leaders held that this was not the time for major changes and suggested instead that the government was enlarged by consultative ministers from the other parties. This was agreed.

40. NA-FO 419/34, Nygaardsvold, *Norge i krig 9. April–7. Juni 1940*; Lie, *Leve eller dø*; Hjelmtveit, *Vekstår og vargtid*; and Margaret Reid's diary. Characteristically for the chaotic situation, Prime Minister Nygaardsvold missed the train out of Hamar. He would have been in dire trouble had it not been for a helpful businessman who placed his car at the Prime Minister's disposal.

41. BA-RH 24-21/24.

42. BA-RH 24-21/17.

43. Hubatsch, *Weserübung.*

44. BA-N 172/14; *Innstilling fra Undersøkelseskommisjonen av 1945*; *Betænkning, Straffesak mot Vidkun Quisling*; Knudsen, *Jeg var Quislings sekretær*; Heradstveit, *Quisling hvem var han?*

45. Grimnes, *Norge i Krig*, vol. 1. Nygaardsvold later claimed the news of Quisling's coup 'stiffened him up'.

46. Nygaardsvold, *Beretning om den Norske Regjerings virksomhet fra 9. April 1940 til 25. Juni 1945*; Hambro, *De første måneder*; Lie, *Leve eller dø*. The legal basis of the *prokura* has been questioned as there was no formal vote, just a common consent. The Investigation Committee concluded after the war that the *prokura* established clarity in a situation not provided for in the constitution.

47. Princess Märtha and her three children also crossed into Sweden during the 10th.

48. In a conversation with the journalist and author Per Øyvind Heradstveit in 1979, the former Crown Prince Olav, by then King of Norway, explained that King Haakon had decided Olav should stay away, and be prepared to take over, in case there was foul play involved and the Germans planned to kill or kidnap him. Heradstveit, *Kongen som sa nei.*

49. Nothing had been agreed, and the Germans had certainly not ceased firing, far less halted their advance.

50. Hjelmtveit, *Vekstår og vargtid*.

51. Koht, *Frå skanse til skanse*; Heradstveit, *Kongen som sa nei*.

52. BA-RH 24-21/24.

53. NA-FO 419/34.

54. BA-RM/6-87.

55. There has been a curious debate at times whether Norway was at war with Germany or not. Already at 13:25 on the 9th, however, there is a note in the war diary of Admiral Boehm, designated Commanding Admiral Norway: 'Group XXI informs Group East and West: Norway is at war with Germany.'

56. www.vg.no 11.04.05.

57. Harriman, *Mission to the North*.

58. E 278-02a.

59. '*Privatkrieg von Spiller*', BA-N 300/5.

60. Frau Spiller later suggested that the expedition had been approved by Bräuer 'to convince the King to return'.

61. BA-RH 24-21/24 and Heradstveit, *Kongen som sa nei*. Walther and his men returned to Germany on the 18th.

62. DRA-Privatarkiv 06145. Danish casualties on 9 April amounted to 11 soldiers, 3 frontier guards and 2 airmen killed; 20 soldiers were wounded. German losses are unknown but were probably somewhat higher.

63. Hezlet, *British and Allied Submarine Operations in WWII*.

64. NA-ADM 199/288, NA-ADM 199/373, NA-ADM 234/380, NA-ADM 234/52 and NA-ADM 199/1843.

65. NA-ADM 186/798.

66. NA-ADM 199/1853 and NA-ADM 199/373.

67. NA-ADM 199/286. The convoy consisted of *Scharhörn, Tucuman, Itauri, España, Friedenau, Hamm, Antares, Muansa* and *Wigbert*, escorted by *V 1501, V 1505, V 1506, V 1507, V 1508, V 1509* supported by T-boats and submarine chasers.

68. *Hanau, Kellerwald, Rosario, Wolfram* and *Wandsbek*.

69. MMU 948.181.1. *Hamm* was torpedoed and sunk on her way home.

70. NA-ADM 199/1847, NA-ADM 199/286, BA-RM 69/108 and BA-RM 72/169. *Triton* was lost with all hands in the Adriatic in December 1940. By then, Lt-Cdr G. Watkins had taken command.

71. NA-ADM 199/288.

72. NA-ADM 199/288 and NA-ADM 199/1847.

73. Bryant, *One Man Band*.

74. E 278-02a; Kiszely, *Anatomy of a Campaign*; Haarr, *The Battle for Norway*.

75. BA-RM 134/91, BA-RM 134/271, BA-RM 70/1 and BA-RM 24-21/30.

76. Boese's report in Melien/Fjeld Private Archive

77. BA-RM 8/1152 and BA-RM 134/271.

78. BA-RM 45/III/100 and *Trial of Nikolaus von Falkenhorst*. This changed in July 1940, when Falkenhorst was promoted to *Generaloberst* and made supreme commander in

Norway, Wehrmachtsbefehlshaber Norwegen. Boehm was recalled from Norway in March 1943. Falkenhorst remained until December 1944.

79. BA-RM 8/1152 and BA-RM 134/271.
80. Several of the Norwegian vessels remained with the Norwegian forces and some of them ended up in UK at the end of the campaign, serving with the Royal Navy.
81. BA-RM 134/91, BA-RM 134/271, BA-RM 45/III/100, BA-RM 92/5088, BA-RH 24-21/30, and NARA-PG 73159.
82. BA-RM 45/III/100.
83. BA-RM 92/5088.
84. BA-RM 45/III/119, BA-RM 92/5257 and BA-RM 57/93. On 21 August, Rieve was promoted to *Konteradmiral* and appointed Chief of Staff at the North Sea Naval Command in Wilhelmshaven. His replacement in Horten was Kapitän Ruhfus of the cruiser *Königsberg*, sunk at Bergen by British Skua dive-bombers.
85. BA-RM 92/5259, BA-RM 7/92, BA-RM 12/II/167 and BA-RM 48/176.
86. Faye, *Krigen i Norge i 1940. Operasjonene i Østfold*; Munthe-Kaas, *Krigen i Norge i 1940. Operasjonene gjennom Romerike-Hedemarken-Gudbrandsdalen-Romsdalen*, bind 1.
87. BA-RM 92/5088.

Chapter 15 – Homeward Bound

1. BA-RM 57/93.
2. BA-RM 92/5223 and BA-RM 92/5097.
3. RNSM-A1994/95, NA-ADM 199/1843 and NA-ADM 199/294.
4. BA-RM 92/5097.
5. BA-RM 57/93 and BA-RM 92/5097.
6. BA-RM 92/5097.
7. BA-RM 48/176 and BA-RM 6/87.
8. NA-ADM 199/288. In all eight men perished when *Moonsund* sank, plus two who later died aboard *Snapper*.
9. King, *The Stick and the Stars*.
10. King, *The Stick and the Stars*.
11. King, *The Stick and the Stars*. Throughout these events, the German survivors from *Moonsund* were stuffed away in various corners of the boat enduring the same ordeal as the crew.
12. *Seal* was captured off Denmark in May; see Haarr, *No Room for Mistakes*.
13. NA-ADM 199/288, NA-ADM 199/1847 and BA-RM 74/7.
14. BA-RM 57/93 and BA-RM 102/3622.
15. Haarr, *No Room for Mistakes*; Andresen, *Skagerrak-Sperre*.
16. Haarr, *No Room for Mistakes*. In all, thirteen Allied submarines were lost from 1 April to 1 August 1940.
17. A-ADM 234/380.

18. NA-ADM 234/52, NA-ADM 199/1843; Chalmers, *Max Horton and the Western Approaches*; Haarr; *The German Invasion of Norway*.
19. BA-RM 7/92. The SKL had ambitions to develop operations in the North Sea and decided to keep 2nd S-boat Flotilla in the west, for the time being, with the depot ship *Tsingtau* stationed in Kristiansand.

Chapter 16 – Requiem

1. BA-RM 92/VM855/47900-910, BA-RM 45/III/101 and BA-N 300/5.
2. BA-RM 7/797 and BA-RM 8/1152.
3. BA-RH 24-21/30, BA-RM 92/5088; Herzog, *Drei Kriegsschiffe Blücher*.
4. Dykking 5/94.
5. Three 38-cm SKC/34 guns were set up at Møvik near Kristiansand. Together with four 40.6-cm SKC/34 at Hanstholm, these powerful long-range batteries, in combination with the minefields, closed the Skagerrak.
6. Fjeld, *Klar til strid*. At least six people were executed by the Germans at Håøya during the war.
7. Fjell, *Klar til Strid*; Terjesen, *Kystartilleriet*; Ness, *Befalsskolen for kystartilleriet*; and interview with Gunnar S. Jensen, last inspector of the underwater branch in the Norwegian Coast Artillery.

Chapter 17 – Conclusions

1. NARA-PG 46853a.
2. BA-RM 7/92 and BA-RM 6/87.
3. BA-RM 92/5097
4. SKL 23685/41 in Herzog, *Drei Kriegsschiffe Blücher*.
5. BA-RM 92/VM855/47900-910, BA-RM 45/III/101, BA-N 300/5; Herzog, *Drei Kriegsschiffe Blücher*.
6. NARA-PG 32028.
7. NARA-PG 32028.
8. For a full account of the losses, see Haarr, *The German Invasion of Norway*; Haarr, *The Battle for Norway*; and Haarr, *No Room for Mistakes*.
9. BA-RM 7/127.

Equivalent Ranks
By Service and Nationality, 1940

Norwegian Coast Artillery	Royal Norwegian Navy	Royal Navy	Kriegsmarine
Menig	Menig	Ordinary Seaman	Matrose
Visekorporal		Able Seaman	Matrosengefreiter
Korporal		Leading Seaman	Matrosenobergefreiter
			Matrosenhauptgefreiter
			Matrosenstabsgefreiter
			Matrosenstabsobergefreiter
		Petty Officer	-maat*
		Chief Petty Officer	-obermaat
	Kvartermester	Boatswain	Bootsmann Steuermann
Sersjant	Kanoner	Coxswain	Stabsbootsmann Stabssteuermann
	Minør	Warrant Officer	Oberbootsmann Obersteuermann
			Stabsoberbootmann Stabsobersteuermann
Kadett	Kadett	Midshipman	Fähnrich zur See
			Oberfähnrich zur See
Fenrik	Fenrik	Sub-Lieutenant	Leutnant zur See
Løytnant	Løytnant	Lieutenant	Oberleutnant zur See
Kaptein	Kaptein	Lieutenant-Commander	Kapitänleutnant
Major		Commander	Korvettenkapitän

			Fregattenkapitän
Oberstløytnant	Kommandørkaptein	Captain	Kapitän zur See
Oberst	Kommandør		Kommodore
		Commodore	Konteradmiral
	Kontreadmiral	Rear-Admiral	Vizeadmiral
	Viseadmiral	Vice-Admiral	Admiral
	Admiral	Admiral	Generaladmiral
		Admiral of the Fleet	Großadmiral

The comparison is not exact but gives a fair idea of the relationship between ranks in the different services. Behind each navy's ladder of ranks was a multitude of branch and trade subdivisions not shown here.

* A man's trade would prefix the word -*maat* such as *Funkermaat* for a radio petty officer or a *Bootsmannsmaat* for a sailor petty officer.

Norwegian Forces

Headquarters and 1st Sea Defence District, April 1940

Admiral Staff

Kommanderende Admiral	*Kontreadmiral Diesen*
Chief of the Admiral Staff	*Kommandør Corneliussen*
	Kommandørkaptein Danielsen
Staff Officer Coast Artillery	*Major Hoel*
Liaison and Intelligence Officer	*Kaptein Steen*
C-in-C Naval Air Force	*Kommandørkaptein Lützow-Holm*
C-in-C Coast Artillery	*Oberst Hammerstad*

1. Sjøforsvarsdistrikt　　　*Kontreadmiral Smith-Johannsen*
[1st Sea Defence District – SDD1]

Responsible for the area from the Swedish border to Jærens Rev, south of Stavanger. Headquarters at Karljohansvern, Horten.

Sea Defence Staff	*Kommandørkaptein Hovdenak*
Karljohansvern Sea Defence Area	*Kommandørkaptein Münster*
Oscarsborg Sea Defence Sector	*Oberst Eriksen*
Outer Oslofjord Sea Defence Sector	*Kommandør Tandberg-Hanssen*
Kristiansand Sea Defence Sector	*Kommandør Wigers*
3rd Destroyer Division	*Kaptein Gunvaldsen*

Subordinated both to Commanding Admiral and SDD1. In Kristiansand on 8 April.

3rd Torpedoboat Division	*Løytnant Holthe*

Area Stavern-Homborsund.

1st Minelayer Division	*Kaptein Schramm*
1st Air Wing	*Kaptein Wendelbo*

Norwegian Navy Support Organisations in Oslofjord

Located in Karljohansvern, Horten.

The Naval Yard

The Aircraft Factory

The Accumulator Factory

The Naval Hospital

Technical departments: ship control, artillery, mines, navigation, communication, construction service, and administration

The Submarine Inspection

Education units: Naval Academy, Naval NCO Training School, Basic Training Unit, Naval Flying School, Signal School, Artillery School and schools for torpedo, mine and engineering personnel

Other locations: Melsomvik depot;

Vestre Bolærne mine depot;

Teie submarine base, Tønsberg

Army Units assigned to Karljohansvern Sea Defence Area		
Unit/CO	*Location*	*Strength*
3. landvernkompani, Vestoppland Infanteriregiment nr 6 *Kaptein Fuglerud*	Horten/Karljohansvern	9 officers, 125 men
	Melsomvik	1 officer, 14 men
2. landvernkompani, Akershus Infanteriregiment nr 4, *Kaptein Ramm*	Torød	9 officers, 73 men
Anti-Aircraft Artillery Company, *Kaptein Johannessen*	Horten/Karljohansvern	130 men
Sub-units	*Equipment*	*Location*
1 battery	2 × 7.5-cm Kongsberg M1916	Brårudåsen
1 battery	2 × 7.5-cm Kongsberg M1916	Mellomøya; Horten
	3 × searchlights	
	3 × 7.92-mm Colt M1929	Fyllingen
	3 × 7.92-mm Colt M1929	Møringen
	3 × 7.92-mm Colt M1929	Møringen fort
	3 × 7.92-mm Colt M1929	Apenes, Horten

Outer Oslofjord Sea Defence Sector *Kommandør Tandberg-Hanssen*
    Chief of Staff *Kaptein Stamsø*
    Oslofjord Guardship Unit *Kommandørkaptein Finborud*
    6th Guardship Division *Kommandørkaptein Finborud*
    8th Guardship Division *Kaptein Godager*
    1st Submarine Division *Kaptein Fjeldstad*
    1st Minesweeper Division *Løytnant Apold*
    3rd Minesweeper Division *Kaptein Dæhli*
    Coast Watch Posts: Vikertangen, Torbjørnskjær, Færder, Kirkehavn, Sogndal
    Communication centres: Sarpsborg, Skien and Arendal.

Outer Oslofjord Fortress *Oberstløytnant Notland*
    Rauøy Fort, Bolærne Fort, Måkerøy Fort, Håøy Fort

Oscarsborg Sea Defence Sector *Oberst Eriksen*
    Communication Officer *Kaptein Unneberg*
    Oscarsborg Guardship Division *Kommandørkaptein Anderssen*
    Oscarsborg Fortress *Oberst Eriksen*
    Recruit Battalion *Kaptein Vagn Enger*
    Coast Artillery NCO School *Kaptein Nesse*

Ships of SDD1

1st Minelayer division – *Kaptein Schramm*					
	Built	Tonnage	Speed (knots)	Armament	Crew
Glommen Kaptein Coucheron-Aamot	1917	351	9.5	2 × 7.6-cm, 120 mines	39
Laugen Kaptein Schramm	1918	351	9.5	2 × 7.6-cm, 120 mines	39
Nor Løytnant Monsen	1878	250	8.5	1 × 12-cm, 1 × 47-mm, 2 × 37-mm, 50 mines	31
Vidar Løytnant Knudtzen	1882	250	9.5	1 × 12-cm, 1 × 47-mm, 2 × 37-mm, 50 mines	31

The division reported both to the Commanding Admiral and SDD1. Ships operated from Jarlsøy, Tønsberg and West Bolærne.

Outer Oslofjord Sea Defence Sector

6th Guardship Division – *Kommandørkaptein Finborud*

	Built	Tonnage	Speed (kt)	Armament	Crew
Farm *Kaptein Amundsen*	1900	424	10	2 × 6.5-cm	32
Pol III *Kaptein Welding Olsen*	1926	214	11	1 × 7.6-cm	15
Skudd I *Kaptein Bendixen*	1929	247	12	1 × 7.6-cm	15
Skudd II *Løytnant Johansen*	1929	247	12	1 × 7.6-cm	15
Oter I *Kaptein Marthiesen*	1929	251	12	1 × 7.6-cm	15
Treff *Løytnant Heggemsnes*	1925	204	11	1 × 7.6-cm	14
Ramoen *Fenrik Stensholt*[†]	1907	299	10.5	1 × 7.6-cm	15

Based at Tonsberg. *Hval II* and *Hval III* were at Karljohansvern for maintenance. [†]Stensholt was acting CO, replacing Kaptein Tveten.

8th Guardship Division – *Kaptein Godager*

	Built	Tonnage	Speed (kt)	Armament	Crew
Sætre *Kaptein Godager*	1925	172	11.5	1 × 7.6-cm	**14**

Based at Tonsberg. *Beta* was at Karljohansvern for maintenance.

1st Submarine Division – *Kaptein Fjeldstad*

	Built	Tonnage	Speed (kt)	Armament	Crew
A2 *Kaptein Fjeldstad*	1913	268	9/14.5[*]	1 × 7.6-cm, 3 × 45-cm torpedo	16
A3 *Kaptein Bruusgaard*	1913	268	9/14.5[*]	1 × 7.6 cm, 3 × 45-cm torpedo	16
A4 *Kaptein Haga*	1913	268	9/14.5[*]	1 × 7.6-cm, 3 × 45-cm torpedo	16
Sarpen (Support vessel)	1860	190			

Based at Teie submarine base, Tønsberg. [*]Top speed submerged/surfaced.

1st Minesweeper Division – *Løytnant Apold*					
	Built	*Tonnage*	*Speed (kt)*	*Armament*	*Crew*
Hvas *Løytnant Strøm*	1900	73	19	2 × 37-mm	14
Falk *Løytnant Paulsen*	1902	73	20.5	2 × 37-mm	14
Kjæk *Løytnant Kraft*	1900	73	19	2 × 37-mm	14

Hauk was at Karljohansvern for maintenance. *Hvas* and *Kjæk* were ordered to Bergen on 9 April.

Karljohansvern Sea Defence					
Olav Tryggvason *Kommandørkaptein Briseid*	1932	1,596	20	4 × 12-cm, 1 × 7.6-cm, 2 × 12.7-mm, 280 mines	175

Olav Tryggvason was at the end of a maintenance visit to the Horten yard.

3rd Minesweeper Division – *Kaptein Dæhli*					
Otra *Kaptein Dæhli*	1939	355	9	1 × 7.6-cm	25
Rauma *Løytnant Winsnes*	1939	355	15	1 × 7.6-cm	25

Otra and *Rauma* were in Horten on 8 April being readied to sail on the 9th to clear the supposed British minefields at Bud and Stadlandet.

Other Ships

Several vessels were in the yard for maintenance or repair on the evening of 8 April:

Guardships	*Hval II, Hval III, Beta*
Submarine	*B4*
Torpedoboats	*Ørn, Lom*
Minesweeper	*Hauk*

Aviation Units

1. Flyavdeling   *Kaptein Wendelbo*

Marinens Flystasjon, Karljohansvern, Horten

1 × MF.10B	Trainer	Serial no. F. 202
5 × MF.11	Reconnaissance	Serial nos. F.304, F.306, F.308, F.334, F.348
2 × DT-2B/C	Torpedo bombers	Serial nos. F.84 and F.86

(plus 4 × Breda 28 at maintenance)

Marinens Flystasjon, Oslo (provisional)

1 × Ju 52/3m   Not operational.

Naval Flying School, Karljohansvern

3 × MF.8B   Trainers   Only two operational.

Plus aircraft undergoing maintenance at the Naval Aircraft Factory, Karljohansvern

Coast Artillery of SDD1

Outer Oslofjord Fortress   *Oberstløytnant Notland*
Reporting to: 1. Sjøforsvarsdistrikt
Headquarters: Håøy fort/Vetan, Nøtterøy

Bolærne Fort   *Major Færden*   17 officers, 148 men
15-cm battery   *Kaptein Telle* (2IC: *Løytnant Eieland*)
2 × orograph; 3 × 15-cm L/50 Bofors M1919; 1 × 150-cm searchlight
(Garnholmen), 1 × 90-cm searchlight (Ramsholmen); 6 × 7.92-mm
AA MG; 1 officer, 20 men of IR 4
Gun commanders: 1 *Sersjant Antonsen*; 2 *Korporal Høiseth, Korporal Eide*;
3 *Sersjant Bakke*

Not manned at Bolærne Fort
12-cm battery: 4 × 12-cm Cockerel Nordenfeldt L/44 M1896 (2 inside
the tunnel, 2 in open position); 1 × 90-cm searchlight (Skarvesete)

Rauøy Fort   *Major Enger*   23 officers, 210 men
Southern battery   *Kaptein Gullichsen* (2IC: *Løytnant Halvorsen*)
1 × orograph, 2 × 15-cm L/50 Bofors M1919
Gun commanders: *Sersjant Gatås, Korporal Magnussen*
Northern battery   *Kaptein Sørlie*
1 × orograph, 2 × 15-cm L/50 Bofors M1919; 1 × 150-cm searchlight,
1 × 110-cm searchlight
AA battery   *Løytnant Rønning*
2 × 40-mm L/60 Bofors M1936; 6 × 7.92-mm MG; 1 officer, 15 men of IR 4
Reporting to Rauøy Fort: Søndre Missingen Coast Watch Post;
1 × orograph

Not manned at Rauøy Fort

12-cm battery

4 × 12-cm L/25 gun M1885, 2 × 6.5-cm gun, 1 × searchlight; 3 × 7.92-mm
AA MG; 1 × 110-cm searchlight at Sondre Missingen

Planned minefield between Rauøy and Bolærne; 3 mine lines with a
length of 7000 m

Håøya Fort   *Kaptein Aas*   10 officers, 90 men

21-cm battery

1 × orograph, 2 × 21-cm L/45 Armstrong M1896, 1 × 90-cm searchlight;
3 × 7.92-mm AA MG; 1 officer, 15 men of IR 4

Not manned at Håøya Fort

12-cm battery

2 × 12-cm L 43.9 Armstrong M1897; 4 × 6.5-cm; 1 × searchlight;
3 × 7.92-mm AA MG

Reporting to Håøya Fort   Sundåsen

2 × 15-cm L/25.6 Krupp; 1 × 12-cm L/25 Krupp (all unmanned)

Måkerøy Fort   *Kaptein Wølner*   10 officers, 79 men

Howitzer battery

2 × 30.5-cm L/30 M1916, 1 × orograph (temporary – forward orograph at
Torås not ready)

Not manned at Måkerøy Fort

2 × searchlights; 3 × 7.98-mm AA MG.

Torås Fort under construction with 15-cm L/50 Bofors M1919.

Oscarsborg Fortress	*Oberst Eriksen*	
Reporting to:	1. Sjøforsvarsdistrikt	
Headquarters:	Oscarsborg/Søndre Kaholmen	
Full artillery complement:	154 officers, 1,191 men	
On duty 9 April:	unknown	
Recruit Battalion, acting CO:	*Kaptein Vagn Enger*	430 recruits
	replacing *Oberstløytnant Ullmann*	
Coast Artillery NCO School:	*Kaptein Nesse*	7 officers, 52 cadets (at Husvik)
Guardship Division	*Kommandørkaptein Anderssen*	
Alpha	*Kaptein Bøhmer*	Filtvet, 1 × 7.6-cm gun
Furu	*Løytnant Jensen*	Filtvet, 1 × 7.6-cm gun
Signal station at Filtvet		
Kranfartøy 2	*Overingeniør Bakke*	Drøbak habour

Søndre Kaholmen main battery   *Kaptein Sødem (2IC: Løytnant Bonsak)*
1x orograph, 3 × 28-cm L/40 Krupp M1889; 4 × 7.92-mm AA MG
Gun commanders: 1 – *Sersjant Rækken*; 2 – *Sersjant Strøm*, 3 – not manned
1 company, Recruit Battalion

Nordre Kaholmen Torpedo battery   *Kommandørkaptein Anderssen*
9 × 45-cm Whitworth torpedoes, 3 underwater firing sites

Håøya
1 company, Recruit Battalion; 4 × 7.92-mm AA MG

Not in action at Søndre and Nordre Kaholmen: Remote-controlled minefield not in position; a number of 5.7-cm guns unmanned.

Not manned at Håøya: Fortress Headquarters and command bunkers with orographs; 12-cm battery (2 × L/43.9 Armstrong M1897); howitzer battery (4 × 28-cm Whitworth M1892); 12-cm battery (8 × L/38 guns)

Kopås and Husvik Area   *Kaptein Vagn Enger*
    Kopås battery   *Kaptein Vagn Enger (2IC: Kaptein Hjelvik)*
    1 × orograph, 3 × 15-cm L/47.5 Armstrong M1899; 5 × 7.92-mm AA MG
    Gun commanders: 1 – *Løytnant Gjerberg*; 2 – *Cadet Jørgensen*; 3 – *Sersjant Knudsen (?Skår)*

    Reporting to Kopås   Stjernåsen fire control
    1 × orograph   *Fenrik Reitan*
    (Elton orograph not manned.)

Husvik
    Husvik battery   *Løytnant Bertelsen*   2 × 5.7-cm
    2 × searchlights (not manned)

Drøbak
    3 × searchlights (partly under maintenance);
    1 company, Recruit Battalion.

    Nesset battery   *Løytnant Strand*
    3 × 5.7-cm gun and 2 × searchlights;
    1 × platoon IR 6   2 officers, 37 men

    Seiersten AA battery   *Løytnant H. Sollie*
    2 × 40-mm L/60 Bofors M1936; 3 × 7.92-mm AA MG
    Skiphelle
    1 × platoon IR 4   2 officers, 36 men

Appendix C
German Forces
Norway, April 1940

The German Naval forces for Operation Weserübung were grouped into several task groups or *Kampfgruppen*. These would carry the troops for the first wave of the invasion. Heavy equipment, vehicles, horses and fuel would come in transports and tankers once the invasion ports were safe. The first ships sailed towards Norway on 3 April. Between 9 April and 15 June, more than 105,000 men, 16,100 horses, 20,000 vehicles and 110,000 tons of supplies were brought in.

The surface ships were assigned to the two Naval Command Groups:

Marinegruppenkommando West Wilhelmshaven	*Generaladmiral Alfred Saalwächter* Groups I, II, III, IV, VI, X and XII Covering Forces
Marinegruppenkommando Ost Kiel	*Admiral Rolf Carls* Groups V, VII, VIII and IX Support ships and anti-submarine forces in Kattegat

Covering forces

Battle fleet led by acting Flottenchef Vizeadmiral Günther Lütjens (deputising for Admiral Marschall, on sick leave). The battleships *Gneisenau* (flag), Kapitän zur See Harald Netzbandt, and *Scharnhorst*, Kapitän zur See Kurt Caesar Hoffmann, would act as covering force for Groups I and II on their exposed 1,100-mile journey and return home. During the landings, they were to patrol into the Norwegian Sea and then rejoin the forces from Narvik and Trondheim on their way home after unloading and refuelling.

A series of U-boat groups were deployed in early April in support of the invasion, partly off the invasion ports, partly off the British fleet anchorage at Scapa Flow and in the North Sea and the Shetland Narrows. These were (as usual) under the direct command of BdU Konteradmiral Dönitz.

Kampfgruppe I   *Kapitän zur See Friedrich Bonte*
Narvik

    1st Destroyer Flotilla: *Georg Thiele, Wilhelm Heidkamp*
    3rd Destroyer Flotilla: *Hans Lüdemann, Hermann Künne, Diether von Roeder, Anton Schmitt*
    4th Destroyer Flotilla: *Wolfgang Zenker, Bernd von Arnim, Erich Giese, Erich Koellner*

All destroyers carrying troops for Narvik. Bonte on board *Z-21 Wilhelm Heidkamp*. Departure from Wesermünde 23:00, 6 April.

Troops:

Mountain troops of Gebirgsjäger Regiment 139 of 3. Gebirgsjägerdivision. Division commander Generalleutnant Edouard Dietl and his staff were also on board as well as naval artillerymen and communication personnel. In all, 2000 men.

Support:

Tankers: *Jan Wellem, Kattegat* of Tankerstaffel
Support ships: *Rauenfels, Alster, Bärenfels* of Ausfuhrstaffel

All ten destroyers and the submarines *U 49* and *U 64* were sunk. See tables below for the fates of transport ships in all groups.

Kampfgruppe II   *Kapitän zur See Hellmuth Heye*
Trondheim

    Heavy cruiser   *Admiral Hipper* (Heye)
    2nd Destroyer Flotilla: *Paul Jacobi, Bruno Heinemann, Theodor Riedel, Friedrich Eckoldt.*

All carrying troops for Trondheim. Left Cuxhaven 22:00, 6 April.

Troops:

Mountain troops of I. and III. Gebirgsjäger Regiment 138 of 3. Gebirgsjägerdivision plus mountain artillery and support troops. Oberst Weiss in command. 1,700 men.

II./GjR 138 and one artillery battery went to Oslo aboard *Lützow*.

Support:

Tankers: *Skagerrak, Moonsund* of the Tankerstaffel
Support ships: *São Paolo, Levante, Main* of Ausfuhrstaffel.

Kampfgruppe III   *Konteradmiral Hubert Schmundt*
Bergen

Light cruisers *Köln* (flag) and *Königsberg*, gunnery training ship *Bremse*, torpedo boats *Leopard* and *Wolf*, and 1. S-bootflottille (5 boats), with depot ship *Carl Peters*.

The larger vessels sailed from Wilhelmshaven and Cuxhaven 00:40, 8 April. The S-boats set out from Heligoland on the morning of the 8th.

Troops:

I./ and II./IR 159 of 69. ID (Generalmajor Hermann Tittel). 1,900 men
The rest of 69. ID would arrive in Bergen, Stavanger and Oslo later.

Stavanger: Two battalions from IR 193 would land at Sola after the airport
had been secured by paratroops. The rest of IR 193 would come by
transport aircraft.

Support:

Belt of the Tankerstaffel. *Marie Leonhardt*, *Curityba* and *Rio de Janeiro* of
1. Seetransportstaffel. No warships went to Stavanger on 9 April. *Roda*
of the Ausfuhrstaffel, *Tübingen*, *Tijuca* and *Mendoza* of 1. Seetransportstaffel and tanker *Stedingen* carried troops, supplies and fuel to support
the air landings.

Königsberg was sunk by British air attack in Bergen harbour on the 10th.

Kampfgruppe IV   *Kapitän zur See Friedrich Rieve*
Kristiansand and Arendal

Light cruiser *Karlsruhe* (Rieve), torpedo boats *Luchs*, *Seeadler*, *Greif* and
2. S-bootflottille (7 boats), with depot ship *Tsingtau*.
Left Wesermünde 05:30, 8 April.

Troops:

I./IR 310 plus one additional company and M.A. personnel to
Kristiansand. Bicycle Squadron 234 of 163. ID aboard torpedo boat *Greif*
would occupy Arendal. In all 1,100 men.

Support:

Wiegand, *Westsee*, *Kreta* and *August Leonhardt* of 1. Seetransportstaffel
were all heading for Kristiansand.

Karlsruhe was sunk by the British submarne *Truant* on 9 April.

Kampfgruppe V   *Konteradmiral Oskar Kummetz*
Oslo
Departure from Kiel 03:00, 8 April.

Blücher (flag)	*Kapitän zur See Heinrich Woldag*
Lützow	*Kapitän zur See August Thiele*
Emden	*Kapitän zur See Werner Lange*
Möwe	*Kapitänleutnant Helmut Neuss*
Albatros	*Kapitänleutnant Siegfried Strelow*
Kondor	*Kapitänleutnant Hans Wilcke*
1. Raumboot Flottille	*Kapitänleutnant Gustav Forstmann*

R 17 (*Stabsobersteuermann Godenau*); R 18 (*Kapitänleutnant Gustav
Forstmann*); R 19 (*Obersteuermann Wels*); R 20 (*Leutnant zur See Jaeger*);

R 21 (*Leutnant zur See von Pommer Esche*); R 22 (*Stabsobersteuermann Scheurer*);
R 23 (*Stabsobersteuermann Rixecker*); R 24 (*Stabsobersteuermann Deters*)
Two armed whaleboats *Rau VII* and *Rau VIII.*

Troops:
The majority of the soldiers on board the ships, except *Lützow*, came from
I./ and II./IR 307. In addition, there were staff personnel from Group
XXI and 163. ID as well as naval gunners, communication personnel,
pioneers, war correspondents, miscellaneous Navy and Coastal Artillery
personnel and ground crew for the Luftwaffe units to be stationed at
Oslo-Fornebu. In total almost 2,200 men. In addition, III./IR 307 and
IR 324 plus one pioneer company would come by air to Fornebu. The rest
of 163. ID would land in Oslo by transport ship in the days following.
(One paratroop company and troops from 69. ID began arriving at
Fornebu simultaneously.)

Blücher
Elements of HQ Group XXI and forward command officers
(Army and Luftwaffe), inc. Generalmajor Wilhelm Süssmann   62 men
Staff personnel of 163. ID, inc. Generalmajor Erwin Engelbrecht   50 men
Staff personnel of IR 307 (inc. brass band), Oberst Karl Blomeyer   80 men
II./IR 307, Hauptmann Ludwig Telthörster   600 men
Personnel to run the Norwegian mail and broadcasting services   20 men
War correspondents, Propaganda Company Army/Navy   10 men
   Total   822 men

Lützow
Part IV./GjR 138 and 50 Luftwaffe ground crew,
   intended for Trondheim   450 men

Emden
I./IR 307 (minus ⅔ of 3. Kompanie) and naval artillery (M.A.)   610 men

Albatros
Two-thirds of 3./IR 307 and naval artillery (M.A.)   96 men

Kondor   95 men

Möwe: 5 officers, 109 other ranks

7. Vorpostenflottille
V 702, V 703, V 705, V 706, V 707, V 708, V 709 (Kapitänleutnant Brauns).
These vessels guarded the entrance to Oslofjord from the morning of
9 April, but were not part of the invasion force proper.

Warship losses:
Blücher, Albatros and *Brummer* were sunk, as described in the main text
above, together with a number of transport vessels.

Support ships:

The support fleet destined for Oslo was extensive. The first transport ships, *Antares, Ionia, Muansa, Itauri* and *Neidenfels* of 1. Seetransportstaffel, left Stettin in convoy at 02:00 on the 7th. The soldiers were mainly from 163. ID (Engelbrecht): IR 310 (Wachsmuth) and AR 234. In all the ships carried 2,000 tons of equipment and aviation fuel, 500 vehicles, 250 horses and 1,250 men. Following were 11 ships of 2. Seetransportstaffel carrying the main body of 196. ID (Pellengahr): IR 340 (Fischer), IR 345 (Ländle), IR 362 (Shaller) and AR 223 (8,500 men); plus some 2,170 tons of equipment, 1,250 vehicles and 1,000 horses. Ships of 3. Staffel would join in later.

Transport Ships, Oslo First Wave – 1. Seetransportstaffel			
Ship	*Tonnage*	*Departure port/time*	*Fate*
Antares	2,592	Stettin, 02:00, 7 April	Sunk by *Sunfish* on 10 April, 6 miles off Lysekil.
Ionia	3,102	Stettin, 02:00, 7 April	Torpedoed by *Triad* on 9 April in Oslofjord. Capsized and sank 12 April.
Muansa	5,472	Stettin, 02:00, 7 April	Arrived Oslo, early morning of 12 April.
Itauri	6,837	Stettin, 02:00, 7 April	Arrived Oslo, early morning of 12 April.
Neidenfels	7,838	Stettin, 02:00, 7 April	Arrived Oslo, early morning of 12 April.
Transport Ships, Oslo First Wave – 2. Seetransportstaffel			
Friedenau	5,219	Gotenhafen, 16:00, 8 April	Sunk in Kattegat by *Triton*, 10 April.
Kellerwald	5,032	Gotenhafen, 16:00, 8 April	Arrived Oslo, 11 April.
Hamm	5,874	Gotenhafen, 16:00, 8 April	Arrived Oslo, 11 April. Sunk by *Seawolf* on 18 April, during return to Germany.
Wigbert	3,647	Gotenhafen, 16:00, 8 April	Sunk in Kattegat by *Triton*, 10 April.
España	7,465	Gotenhafen, 16:00, 8 April	Arrived Oslo, 11 April.
Rosario	6,079	Gotenhafen, 16:00, 8 April	Arrived Oslo, 11 April.
Tucuman	4,621	Gotenhafen, 16:00, 8 April	Arrived Oslo, 11 April.
Hanau	5,892	Gotenhafen, 16:00, 8 April	Arrived Oslo, 11 April.
Wolfram	3,648	Gotenhafen, 16:00, 8 April	Arrived Oslo, 11 April.
Wandsbek	2,388	Gotenhafen, 16:00, 8 April	Arrived Oslo, 11 April.
Scharhörn	2,643	Königsberg, 16:00, 8 April	Diverted to Fredrikshavn.

In addition, the tankers *Senator* and *Euroland* of the Tankerstaffel would head for Oslo. A large number of ships would follow in the weeks after *Wesertag*, with a shuttle service to be established as soon as possible.

Kampfgruppe VI   **Egersund**

Four *Minensuchtboote*, *M 1*, *M 2*, *M 9*, *M 13* of 2nd Minesweeping Flotilla under the command of Korvettenkapitän Kurt Thoma of *M 9*, were deployed to capture Egersund.

Departure from Cuxhaven in the evening of 7 April, but with orders to wait outside the mouth of the Elbe until 04:45 on the 8th.

Troops:

150 men of the Bicycle Squadron of 169. Reconnaissance Battalion from 69. ID.

Kampfgruppe VII   **Korsör/Nyborg**
Schleswig-Holstein   *Kapitän zur See Gustav Kleikamp*
Claus von Bevern
Nautilus
Pelikan
S-8, S-17, S-30, S-31, S-32, S-33
8 transport ships
Some 500 men, mostly from 198. ID

Kampfgruppe VIII   **Copenhagen**
Hansestadt Danzig   *Korvettenkapitän Wilhelm Schröder*
Stettin
1,000 men, I./IR 308

Kampfgruppe IX   **Middelfart**
Rugard   *Kapitän zur See Helmuth Leissner*
Otto Braun, Arkona, Monsun, Passat
M 103, V 102, R 6, R 7
Unterseebootjäger 172
400 men, MG Stoßtrupp, 3./IR 399, one *Zug* 13./399

Kampfgruppe X   **Esbjerg**
Königin Luise   *Kapitän zur See Friedrich Ruge*
12. M-Flottille
150 men, Marinetruppen

Kampfgruppe XI   **Limfjord, Thyborön**
Von der Gröben   *Kapitän zur See Walter Berger*
4. M-Flottille
4. R-Flottille
100 men, Marinetruppen

Support Ships
Three Transport Groups were organised.

Ausfuhrstaffel
The Ausfuhrstaffel (literally 'Export Echelon') consisted of seven large transports, which were to travel ahead of the invasion fleet (disguised as normal merchantmen) to the more distant invasion ports of Trondheim and Narvik (one would go to Stavanger). The ships would bring heavy weapons and supplies vital for sustaining the operations of the initial assault groups. Of these ships, only two would survive the invasion.

Ships of the Ausfuhrstaffel				
Ship	*Tonnage*	*Departure port/time*	*Destination*	*Fate*
Bärenfels	7,569	Brunsbüttel, 02:00, 3 April	Narvik	Severely damaged and partly sunk by British aircraft in Bergen on 14 April after being delayed and diverted.
Rauenfels	8,460	Brunsbüttel, 02:00, 3 April	Narvik	Delayed. Reached Ofotfjord on 10 April. Sunk by *Havoc* in later stages of first British attack on Narvik.
Alster	8,570	Brunsbüttel, 02:00, 3 April	Narvik	Delayed. Captured by *Icarus* on 10 April outside Bodø.
São Paulo	4,977	Brunsbüttel, 21:00, 4 April	Trondheim	Delayed and redirected to Bergen where she struck a mine and sank late on 9 April.
Levante	4,768	Brunsbüttel, 02:00, 5 April	Trondheim	Arrived on 12 April, three days late.
Main	7,624	Brunsbüttel, 02:00, 5 April	Trondheim	Captured by *Draug* near Haugesund and sunk by own crew on 9 April when being taken to Britain.
Roda	6,780	Brunsbüttel, 02:00, 7 April	Stavanger	Sunk off Stavanger on 9 April by *Æger*.

Tankerstaffel
Three large and several smaller tankers would head for the main ports disguised as merchant ships. These would be essential for delivering oil for the return of the Navy ships, few of which could carry enough fuel to complete a round trip. Some of the tankers also carried aviation fuel to be supplied to the airfields that were to be captured. It was therefore essential

that the tankers were in the invasion harbours shortly after or in some cases prior to '*Weserzeit*', as after this, the Royal Navy would certainly be about looking for them – as was proven by events. Several smaller ships would follow with supplements in the days following the invasion.

Ships of the Tankerstaffel				
Ship	*Tonnage*	*Departure port/date*	*Destination*	*Fate*
Kattegat	6,044	Wilhelmshaven, 3 April	Narvik	Scuttled by own crew off Ørnes, 9 April, when intercepted by *Nordkapp*.
Skagerrak	6,044	Wilhelmshaven, 4 April	Trondheim	Redirected to position offshore. Scuttled by own crew when intercepted by *Sheffield*, 14 April.
Jan Wellem	12,000	Basis Nord, Murmansk, 08:00, 6 April	Narvik	Arrived Narvik on 8 April as planned. Sunk by own crew, 28 April.
Moonsund	322	Brunsbüttel, 9 April	Trondheim	Sunk by British submarine *Snapper* outside Larvik, 12 April
Euroland	860	Hamburg, 13 April	Oslo	Arrived Oslo as planned.
Senator	845	Hamburg, 12:00, 6 April	Oslo	Arrived Oslo as planned.
Belt	322	Brunsbüttel, 9 April	Bergen	Arrived Bergen as planned.
Dollart	280	Brunsbüttel, 9 April	Stavanger	Arrived in Stavanger 28 April (2nd trip?).
Stedingen	8,036		Stavanger	Sunk off Stavern by British submarine *Trident* on 8 April.
Karl Meyer			Kristiansand	Diverted to Stavanger.
Rolshoven			Bergen	Arrived as planned on the morning of 9 April.
Bernhard von Tschirschky			Bergen	Arrived as planned on the morning of 9 April.

Seetransportstaffeln

The Seetransporstaffeln would bring in the bulk of the troops and supplies for the invasion of the Oslo region. 1. Staffel would go in four groups, to Oslo, Kristiansand, Stavanger and Bergen. It consisted of 15 ships and carried some 3,800 troops, 675 horses, more than 1,300 vehicles and 6,000 tons of supplies. 2. Staffel would go to the Oslo area to secure the break-out from the initial landing area and link up with the other landing sites. This would consist of 11 ships.

No follow-up transport ships would go to the western ports for fear of British interception. It was believed that the route to Oslo would be relatively safe from British surface ships and planes and easier to defend than the North Sea.

After completing their first trips, most ships would return to Germany and then enter a shuttle service until the invasion was complete. The inner route to Oslofjord was considered safer and less vulnerable to British attack. As it turned out this was not quite correct. After relatively high losses in 1. and 2. Staffeln, the transports were rearranged, however, so that most personnel were transported by air, or by a modified shuttle of small ships in fast convoys between northern Denmark and Oslo, which also took care of important equipment.

3. Staffel consisted of *Entre Rios, Campinas, Leuna, Buenos Aires, Cordoba, Moltkefels, Köln, Dessau, Philipp Heineken, Thetis, Hohenhörn* and *Utlandshörn* plus three reserve ships. The first five were temporarily assigned to 1. Staffel; the rest were eventually loaded with horses, vehicles and other heavy equipment and attached to subsequent transport convoys composed from returning ships on an ad hoc basis.

Ships of 1. Seetransportstaffel				
Ship	*Tonnage*	*Departure port/time*	*Destination*	*Fate*
Antares	2,592	Stettin, 02:00, 7 April	Oslo	Torpedoed and sunk by *Sunfish* on 10 April, 6 miles off Lysekil.
Ionia	3,102	Stettin, 02:00, 7 April	Oslo	Torpedoed by *Triad* in Oslofjord on 9 April. Capsized and sank, 12 April.
Muansa	5,472	Stettin, 02:00, 7 April	Oslo	Sank after hitting mine, 10 April.
Itauri	6,837	Stettin, 02:00, 7 April	Oslo	Arrived in Oslo early morning of 11 April, two days late.
Neidenfels	7,838	Stettin, 02:00, 7 April	Oslo	Arrived in Oslo early morning of 11 April, two days late.

Ship	Tonnage	Departure port/time	Destination	Fate
Wiegand	5,869	Stettin, 17:00 6 April	Kristiansand	Arrived as planned, 9 April.
Westsee	5,911	Stettin, 17:00 6 April	Kristiansand	Arrived as planned, 9 April.
Kreta	2,359	Stettin, 04:00, 6 April	Kristiansand	Abandoned by crew after gunfire from *Trident*, 9 April. Later repaired.
August Leonhardt	2,593	Stettin, 04:00, 6 April	Kristiansand	Torpedoed and sunk by *Sealion* south of Anholt, 11 April.
Tübingen	5,453	Stettin, 04:00, 6 April	Stavanger	Arrived as planned, 9 April. Left Stavanger on 1 May.
Tijuca	5,918	Stettin, 04:00, 6 April	Stavanger	Arrived as planned, 9 April. Left Stavanger on 4 May.
Mendoza	5193	Stettin, 04:00, 6 April	Stavanger	Arrived as planned, 9 April. Left Stavanger on 22 May.
Marie Leonhardt	2,594	Stettin, 04:00, 6 April	Bergen	Arrived 10 April, one day late.
Curityba	4,968	Stettin, 04:00, 6 April	Bergen	Ran aground north of Helsingborg on 7 April and was redirected to Oslo. Arrived there on 11 April.
Rio de Janeiro	5,261	Stettin, 04:00, 6 April	Bergen	Sunk by *Orzel* off Lillesand, 8 April.
Ships of 2. Seetransportstaffel				
Friedenau	5,219	Gotenhafen, 16:00, 8 April	Oslo	Torpedoed and sunk in Kattegat by *Triton* on 10 April.
Kellerwald	5,032	Gotenhafen, 16:00, 8 April	Oslo	Arrived Oslo on 11 April, two days late.
Hamm	5,874	Gotenhafen, 16:00, 8 April	Oslo	Arrived Oslo on 11 April, two days late.
Wigbert	3,647	Gotenhafen, 16:00, 8 April	Oslo	Torpedoed and sunk in Kattegat by *Triton* on 10 April.
España	7,500	Gotenhafen, 16:00, 8 April	Oslo	Arrived Oslo on 11 April, two days late.

Ship	Tonnage	Departure port/time	Destination	Fate
Rosario	6,079	Gotenhafen, 16:00, 8 April	Oslo	Arrived Oslo on 11 April, two days late.
Tucuman	4,621	Gotenhafen, 16:00, 8 April	Oslo	Arrived Oslo on 11 April, two days late.
Hanau	5,892	Gotenhafen, 16:00, 8 April	Oslo	Arrived Oslo on 11 April, two days late.
Wolfram	3,648	Gotenhafen, 16:00, 8 April	Oslo	Arrived Oslo on 11 April, two days late.
Wandsbek	2,400	Gotenhafen, 16:00, 8 April	Oslo	Arrived Oslo on 11 April, two days late.
Scharhörn	2,643	Königsberg, 16:00, 8 April		Diverted to Fredrikshavn.

Bibliography

Primary Documents from Public Archives

The National Archives, Kew
NA- FO 419/34, NA-ADM 1/10680, NA-ADM 116/447, NA-ADM 116/4471, NA-ADM 178/137, NA-ADM 186/798, NA-ADM 199/1843, NA-ADM 199/1847, NA-ADM 199/1853, NA-ADM 199/2202, NA-ADM 199/278, NA-ADM 199/280, NA-ADM 199/285, NA-ADM 199/286, NA-ADM 199/288, NA-ADM 199/294, NA-ADM 199/3, NA-ADM 199/323, NA-ADM 199/361, NA-ADM 199/373, NA-ADM 199/379, NA-ADM 199/385, NA-ADM 199/388, NA-ADM 199/393, NA-ADM 199/474, NA-ADM 199/393, NA-ADM 199/479, NA-ADM 199/892, NA-ADM 205/2, NA-ADM 223/126, NA-ADM 223/82, NA-ADM 234/380, NA-ADM 234/427, NA-ADM 234/52, NA-ADM 267/126, NA-ADM 53/113071, NA-AIR 14/669, NA-AIR-22/8, NA-AT 1259/7, NA-CAB 65/1, NA-CAB 65/11, NA-CAB 65/12, NA-CAB 65/2, NA-CAB 65/4, NA-CAB 65/5, NA-CAB 66/1, NA-CAB 66/3, NA-CAB 66/4, NA-CAB 66/5, NA-CAB 66/6, NA-CAB 66/7, NA-CAB 80/105, NA-FO 370/2010, NA-FO 371/22276, NA-FO 371/22283, NA-FO 371/23658, NA-FO 371/23674, NA-FO 371/24802, NA-FO 371/24815. NA-FO 371/24818, NA-FO 371/24819, NA-FO 371/24820, NA-FO 371/24821, NA-FO 371/24829, NA-FO 371/24832, NA-FO 371/24834, NA-FO 419/34, NA-FO 72/29421, NA-GFM 33/1111, NA-GFM 33/1519, NA-MT 59/1736, NA-PREM 1/419, NA-WO 106/1969, NA-WO 193/772, NA-WO 193/773.

Forsvarsmuseet, Oslo
Regulations for Orograph, Regulations for 15-cm Armstrong gun, Regulations for 28-cm Krupp gun, Regulations for 40-mm AA gun.

Imperial War Museum, London
IWM 67/25/1.

Royal Navy Submarine Museum, Gosport
RNSM-A1994/95.

Riksarkivet, Oslo
RA-1256-3/10, RA-2B-061.21, RA-D/L0002–0009, RA-D/L0002–0009, RA-FKA Ec, 0125, RA-FKA-2B.072.42, RA-FKA-2B.072.42, RA-FKA-Ya II-C-11-00, RA-II-C-11-1100, RA-II-C-11-2016, RA-II-C-11-2017, RA-II-C-11-2020, RA-II-C-11-2150/52, RA-II-C-11-940, RA-II-C-11/1100, RA-II-C-11/1102, RA-II-C-11/1103, RA-II-C-11/1120, RA-II-C-11/1122, RA-II-C-11/1200, RA-II-C-11/2000, RA-II-C-11/2010, RA-II-C-11/2012, RA-II-C-11/2014,

RA-II-C-11/2022, RA-II-C-11/2023, RA-II-C-11/51, RA-II-C-11/52, RA-RAFA-1469/D/L0002/0005, RA-RAFA-1924 /D/L0004/0009, RA-RAFA-2017/Y/Ye/L0193, RA-S-1005/Aa/L0001.

Rigsarkivet, Copenhagen
DRA-Privatarkiv 06145.

Marinemuseet, Horten
MMU 55830/848.1818, MMU 55830/948.181, MMU-948.181.1, MMU-948.181.2, MMU-privatarkiv 36.

Bundesarchiv, Freiburg
BA-MA III M 35/, BA-MSg 2/1882, BA-N 172/1, BA-N 172/14, BA-N 172/16, BA-N 300/5, BA-RA 57/93, BA-RH 24-21/17, BA-RH 24-21/23, BA-RH 24-21/24, BA-RH 24-21/30, BA-RM 102/3622, BA-RM 102/3893, BA-RM 102/3894, BA-RM 12/II-167, BA-RM 134/271, BA-RM 134/91, BA-RM 24-21/30, BA-RM 35 I/31, BA-RM 35 I/32, BA-RM 35 I/35, BA-RM 35/I/39, BA-RM 35/II-35, BA-RM 45/III/100, BA-RM 45/III/101, BA-RM 45/III/119, BA-RM 48/176, BA-RM 54/30, BA-RM 57/125, BA-RM 57/93, BA-RM 6/87, BA-RM 69/108, BA-RM 7/11, BA-RM 7/111, BA-RM 7/1184, BA-RM 7/124, BA-RM 7/127, BA-RM 7/1475, BA-RM 7/168, BA-RM 7/177, BA-RM 7/180, BA-RM 7/194, BA-RM 7/486, BA-RM 7/797, BA-RM 7/891, BA-RM 7/9, BA-RM 7/92, BA-RM 70/1, BA-RM 71/5, BA-RM 48/176 BA-RM 72/169, BA-RM 72/73, BA-RM 74/7, BA-RM 8/1152, BA-RM 92/5078, BA-RM 92/5087, BA-RM 92/5088, BA-RM 92/5097, BA-RM 92/5178, BA-RM 92/522, BA-RM 92/5223, BA-RM 92/5245, BA-RM 92/5257, BA-RM 92/5259, BA-RM 92/5267, BA-RM 92/5269, BA-RM 92/5332, BA-RM 92/VM855/47900-910, BA-RM 96/667, BA-RM 98/22, BA-RM/6-87, BA-RM24-21/30, BA-RM92/5097.

US National Archives, NARA, Washington DC
NARA-E 278-02a, NARA-E 279-01a, NARA *Gruppe XXI KTB E 180-11*, NARA *Gruppe XXI KTB E180-13*, NARA *Gruppe XXI KTB E180-5*, NARA *Gruppe XXI KTB E180-7*, NARA *Gruppe XXI KTB E180-9b*, NARA-KTB SKL, NARA-PG 37859, NARA-PG 33238, NARA-PG 47493, NARA-PG 73159, NARA-PG 32028, NARA-PG 33236, NARA-PG 37848, NARA-PG 37852, NARA-PG 37855, NARA-PG 47493, NARA-PG 47514, NARA-PG 73159, NARA-PG 73854, NARA-PG 46853a, NARA-PG 7493; AE 2913/2, AE 2958/41.

Websites

www.ca.nizkor.org
www.deutsches-marinearchiv.de
www.kbismarck.com
www.lexikon-der-wehrmacht.de
www.marinehist.dk
www.navweaps.com
www.festningsverk.no
www.storting.no

Private Archives and Memoirs

A number of private archives have been made available to us. The contents of these have been scrutinised thoroughly and used with caution:

The Willoch Papers.
Adlercreutz Arkivet.
Margaret Reid: *Diary*
Rosenberg's diary.
The Haarr Archives.
Melien/Fjeld Private Archive.

Newspapers and Magazines

Dykking May 1994
Aftenposten 20 June 2005,
Dagbladet. Various issues used, 1–10 April 1940.
Norges Handels og Sjøfartstidende. Various issues used, 1–10 April 1940.

Miscellaneous Published and Unpublished Documents

Assmann, H., *Überlegungen zur Frage der Stützpunktgewinnung für die Nordseekriegführung*, in Salewski, *Die Deutsche Seekriegsleitung*.
Begivenhederne omkring den 9' april 1940.
Betænkning til Folketinget, Bilag 1. Copenhagen. JH Schultz, 1945. Cited as *Betænkning*.
Böhme, *Underrettelser från Berlin*
Bud Sogelag.
Förspelet till det Tyska angreppet på Danmark och Norge, Stockholm. PA Norstedt, 1947. Cited as *Förspelet*.
Fra Neutralitet til Besættelse, Viceadmiral H. Rechnitzers dagbok om flådens virke 1939–40. Udgivet og kommenteret af Hans Christian Bjerg. Selskabet for utgivelse af Kilder til Dansk Historie. København, 2000.
Generalrapport for Sikringsstyrken 1939/1940, Copenhagen 1943. Cited as *Generalrapport*.
Herzog, P., *Drei Kriegsschiffe Blücher*. Marinekameradschaft SKrz. Blücher im Deutschen Marinebund.
Horve, T., *Storbritannia og dets behov for den norske handelsflåten*. Privat 18 May 1971
Innstilling fra Undersøkelseskommisjonen av 1945. Stortinget. Oslo, 1946
Jervell, S., *Scener fra en ambassades liv. Berlin 1905–2002*. Kartonisert utgave, Deichmanske bibliotek.
Kriegstagebuch der Seekriegsleitung 1939–1945, Teil A. Bd. 1–71. W. Rahn, G. Schreiber & H. Maierhöfer (ed.). Berlin/Bonn/Hamburg 1988–1997. Cited as KTB SKL.
Lagevorträge des Oberbefehlshabers der Kriegsmarine vor Hitler 1939–1945. Cited as *Lageforträge*.

Militære undersøkelseskommisjon 1946. Oktober forlag. Oslo 1978

Ness, A., *Befalsskolen for kystartilleriet* (Unpublished)

Stortingsforhandlinger 1940 6 April – Downloaded from *stortinget.no*

Straffesak mot Vidkun Abraham Lauritz Jonssøn Quisling. Oslo, 1946

Secondary Works

Andresen, J., *Skagerrak-Sperre, den tyske Minesperring.* Historisk Årbog for Thy og Vester Han Herred, 2017.

Arndt, P., *Deutsche SperrbrecheR-1914–1945.* Bernard und Graefe Verlag. Bonn, 2005.

Aspheim, O. V., 'Quislings hemmelige møte i København'. *Aftenposten*, 17 July 1987.

Barth, B., *Norge og Norden i tysk strategi, 1914–1945,* in Simensen, J. (ed.) *Tyskland – Norge, den lange historien.* Tano Aschehoug. Oslo 1999.

Beesly, P., *Very Special Intelligence.* Chatham Publishing. London, 1977.

Binder, F., and H. H. Schlünz, *Schwerer Kreutzer Blücher.* Koehlers Verlagsgesellschaft. Hamburg, 1991.

Bjerg, H. C., *Dansk Orlogshistorie 1510–2010.* København, 2010.

Boehm, H., *Norwegen zwischen England und Deutschland.* Klosterhaus Verlag. Leinen, 1956.

Brown, D., *Naval Operations of the Campaign in Norway* Frank Cass. Oxford, 2000.

Bryant, B., *One Man Band.* Kimber. London, 1958.

Bröyn, P., *Den svenske malmeksport fram til besetingen av Narvik i April 1940.* University of Oslo, 1964.

Butler, J., *Grand Strategy,* vol. II, *September 1939–June 1941.* HMSO, London, 1970.

Chalmers, W. S., *Max Horton and the Western Approaches.* Hodder & Stoughton, London, 1954.

Churchill, W. S., *The Second World War,* vols I and II. Cassell. London, 1949.

Colban, E., *Femti år.* Aschehoug, Oslo, 1952.

Denham, H., *Inside the Nazi Ring.* John Murray. London, 1984.

Dilks, D. (ed.), *The Diaries of Sir Alexander Cadogan.* Cassel. London, 1971.

Dilks, D., 'Great Britain and Scandinavia in the "Phoney War"'. *Scandinavian Journal of History*, 2:1–2 (1977).

Dönitz, K., *Memoirs: Ten Years and Twenty Days.* Greenhill Books. London, 1959.

Egeland, J., *Gjennom brott og brann.* Aschehoug. Oslo, 1968.

Evensen, K., *Oscarsborg forteller historie.* Boksenteret. Drøbak, 1992.

Faye, W., *Krigen i Norge i 1940. Operasjonene i Østfold.* Gyldendal Forlag. Oslo, 1963.

Fjeld, O. T. (ed.), *Klar til strid.* Kystartilleriets Offisersforening. Oslo, 1999.

Fjeld, O. T., and H. P. Kolstad, *Oslofjord Festnings Historikk 1916–1962.* Kolbotn, 2019.

Friedman, N., *Naval Firepower*. Seaforth. London, 2013.

Gemzell, C.-A., *Raeder, Hitler und Skandinavien*. Gleerup. Lund, 1965.
Gilbert, M., *The Churchill War Papers*. Norton & Co. London, 1993.
Godø, R. L., *En Krigsberetning fra Invasjonen i Norge 1940*, Godøytunmuseet, 1995.
Gray, E., *Hitler's Battleships*. Pen & Sword. London 1993.
Grimnes, O. K., *Norge i Krig*, vol. 1. Aschehoug. Oslo, 1984.
Grimnes, O. K., *Veien inn i krigen*. Aschehoug. Oslo, 1987.
Guhnfeldt, C., *Fornebu 9. April*. Wings. Oslo, 1990.

Haarr, G. H., *The German Invasion of Norway April 1940*. Seaforth. London, 2009.
——, *The Battle for Norway, April–June 1940*. Seaforth. London, 2010.
——, *The Gathering Storm*, Seaforth Publishing. Barnsley, 2013.
——, *No Room for Mistakes*. Seaforth. London, 2014.
——., *Nøytralitetens pris, Altmark-saken februar 1940 og den betydning for Norges nøytralitet*, Commentum. Stavanger, 2018.
Hafsten, Bjørn, and Bjørn Olsen, *Flyalarm*. Sem & Stenersen. Oslo, 2005.
Halder, F., *Kriegstagebuch*. Kohlhammer. Stuttgart 1962.
Hambro, C. J., *De første måneder*. Aschehoug. Oslo, 1945.
——. (ed.), *7.Juni – 9. April–7. Juni Historiske Dokumenter*. Gyldendal. Oslo, 1956.
Hambro, J., *C J Hambro, liv og drøm*. Aschehoug. Oslo, 1984.
Harriman, F. J., *Mission to the North*. Lippincott. New York, 1941.
Hartmann, S., *Quislings konferanse med den tyske overkommando*, vol. 5. Samtiden. Oslo, 1956.
——., *Spillet om Norge*. Mortensen. Oslo, 1958.
——., *Varslene til de Nordiske Legasjoner før den 9. april 1940*. Universitetsforlaget. Aarhus, 1958
Hase, G., *Die Kriegsmarine erobert Norwegens Fjorde*. Hase & Koehler-Verlag. Leipzig, 1940.
Hegland, J. R., *Sjøforsvarets minevesen 1870–1970*. Bergen, 1970.
Heradstveit, P. Ø., *Quisling hvem var han?* Hjemmets Forlag. Oslo, 1976.
——, *Kongen som sa nei*. Hjemmets Forlag. Oslo, 1979.
Hezlet, A., *British and Allied Submarine Operations in World War II*. Royal Navy Submarine Museum. Gosport, 2001.
Hinsley, H., *British Intelligence in the Second World War*. HMSO. London, 1993.
Hjelmtveit, N., *Vekstår og Vargtid*. Aschehoug. Oslo, 1969.
Hobson, R., and T. Kristiansen, *Norsk Forsvarshistorie*, vol. III. Eide. Bergen, 2001
Hovland, T., *Bli med til Oscarsborg*. Kolofon. Oslo, 2005.
Hubatsch, W., *Weserübung, Die deutsche Besetzung von Dänemark und Norwegen 1940*. Musterschmidt. 1952.

Ismay, H., *The Memoirs of General the Lord Ismay*. Heinemann. London, 1960.

Karlbom, R., 'Sweden's iron ore exports to Germany 1933–1944'. *Scandinavian Economic History Review*, 13:1–2 (1965).

Kersaudy, F., *Norway 1940*. Collins. London, 1990.

King, W., *The Stick and the Stars*. Hutchinson. London, 1958.

Kiszely, J., *Anatomy of a Camp*aign. Cambridge Univerity Press. Cambridge, 2017.

Kjølsen, F. H., *Optakten til den 9. april*. Hagerup. Copenhagen, 1945.

——., *Mit livs logbog*. Berlingske. Copenhagen, 1957.

Knudsen, Aa., *Tilstede og usynlig i 100 år. Ubåtvåpenet 1909–2009*. Bodoni. Bergen, 2009.

Knudsen, H. F., *Jeg var Quislings sekretær*. Eget Forlag. Copenhagen, 1951

Koht, H., *Norge neutralt och överfallet*. Natur och Kultur. Stockholm, 1941.

——, *Frå skanse til skanse*. Tiden. Oslo, 1947.

——, *Norsk Utanrikspolitikk fram til 9.April 1940*. Tiden. Oslo, 1947.

——, *For Fred og Fridom i Krigstid 1939–1940*. Tiden. Oslo, 1957.

Koop, G., and K.-P. Schmolke, *Heavy Cruisers of the Admiral Hipper Class*. Greenhill. London, 2001.

Krancke, T., 'Norwegen Unternehmen'. *AW* 5 (1965) 6.

Kristiansen, T., *Krigsplaner og Politikk i mellomkrigstiden*. Institutt for forsvarsstudier. Oslo, 2004.

Lie, T., *Leve eller dø*. Tiden. Oslo, 1955.

Loock, H. D., *Quisling, Rosenberg og Terboven*. Gyldendahl. Oslo, 1972.

Lossberg, B., *Im Wehrmacht Führungsstab*. Nölke. Leinen, 1949.

Macleod, R. (ed.), *Time Unguarded, The Ironside Diaries 1937–1939*. Greenwood Press. London, 1974.

Mallmann-Showell, J. P., *U-Boat Commanders and Crews 1939–1945*. Crowood Press. Ramsbury, 1998.

Mannerheim, G., *Minnen*. Schildts. Stockholm, 1952.

Melien, T. J., 'Vakt og Vern. Marinen og Kystartilleriet 1914–1918'. *Defense Studies*, Jan. 1995.

——, *Norges globale sjøkrig. Skipsfartsberedskap fra 1914 til i dag*. Scandinavian Academic Press. Oslo, 2020.

Mispelkamp P. K., 'Avoidable Loss: The Saga of the *Blücher*'. *The Northern Mariner*, VI, No.3, June 1996.

Munthe-Kaas, O., *Krigen i Norge i 1940. Operasjonene gjennom Romerrike – Hedemarken – Gudbrandsdalen – Romsdalen*, vol. 1. Gyldendal. Oslo, 1955.

——, 'Aprildagene 1940'. *Norsk Militært Tidsskrift*. June 1978.

Nolte, M., *Mit Anstand zu sterben verstehen*. Der Andere Verlag. Tönning, 2005.

Nygaardsvold, J., *Norge i krig 9. April–7. Juni 1940*. Tiden. Oslo, 1982.

Øksendal, A., *Gulltransporten*. Aschehoug. Oslo, 1974.

Ørvik, N., *Norge i brennpunktet*, vol. I. Grundt Tanum Forlag. Oslo, 1953.

Ørvik, N., *Sikkerhetspolitikken*, 2 vols. Grundt Tanum Forlag. Oslo, 1960.

Ottmer, H. M., *Weserübung.* Oldenbourg Verlag. Munich, 1994.

Pownall, H., *Chief of Staff,* vol. II: *1940–1944.* Leo Cooper. London, 1972.

Pruck, E., 'Abwehraussenstelle Norwegen'. *Marine Rundschau,* no. 4, 1956.

Raeder, E, *Mein Leben,* 2 vols. Verlag Fritz Schlichtenmayer. Tübingen, 1957.

Ræder, G., *De uunnværlig flinke.* Gyldendahl. Oslo 1975.

Rechnitzer, H., *Admiral Rechnitzers Maritime og politiske erindringer 1905–1940.* Udgivet og kommenteret af Hans Christian Bjerg. Gyldendal. København, 2003.

Reynaud, P., *La France a sauvé l'Europe.* Editions Flammarion. Paris, 1947.

Roskill, S. W., *Churchill and the Admirals.* Collins. London, 1977.

Salewski, M., *Die deutsche Seekriegsleitung,* vol. I. Bernard & Graefe. Frankfurt am Main, 1970.

Salmon, P., 'Churchill, the Admiralty and the Narvik Traffic, September–November 1939'. *Scandinavian Journal of History,* 4:1–4, 305–26 (1979).

Salmon, P., *Deadlock and Diversion.* Bremerhaven 2012.

Schmalenbach, P., *Die Geschichte der deutschen Schiffenartillerie.* Koehler. Berlin, 1993.

Simpson, G. W., *Periscope View.* Seaforth. London, 2010.

Skard, S., *Mennesket Halvdan Koht.* Det Norske Samlaget. Oslo, 1982.

Skodvin, M., *Striden om okkupasjonsstyret i Norge.* Det Norske Samlaget. Oslo, 1956.

Skodvin, M., 'Norwegian Neutrality and the Question of Credibility'. *Scandinavian Journal of History,* 2 (1977)

Sopocko, E. K. S., *Orzel's Patrol, The Story of the Polish Submarine.* Methuen. London, 1942.

Springenschmid, K., *Die Männer von Narvik.* Ullstein. 1968.

Steen, E. A., *Norges Sjøkrig 1940–45,* vols I & II. Gyldendal. Oslo 1954.

Stevens, E. H. (ed.), *The Trial of Nikolaus Falkenhorst.* London, 1949.

Terjesen, B., *Kystartilleriets undervannsforsvar 100 år.* Kystartilleri-inspektoratet. Bergen, 2000.

Theien, I., *Fra krig til krig.* Spartacus. Oslo, 2015.

Thowsen, A., *Handelsflåten i krig, 1939–1945.* Grøndahl. Oslo, 1992.

Whitley, M. J., *German Cruisers of World War Two.* US Naval Institute Press. 1987.

——, *Destroyers! German Destroyers in World War II,* US Naval Institute Press. 1992.

Zeiner-Gundersen, H. F., *Norsk artilleri gjennom 300 år.* Agdin. Arendal, 1986.

Index

Page number in *italics* indicate an illustration or photograph.

Persons

Aalvik, Peder, rormann 262

Adamsen; deputy chief of Police 343

Adlercreutz, Carlos; Överste 98, 147

Amundsen, Gustav; kaptein 179

Anderssen, Andreas; kommandørkaptein 198, *199*, 201, 209, 115, 225, 227, 249, 251, 327, 351

Andresen, Rudolf Kristian; løytnant 270

Assmann, Kurt; Admiral 53

Audet, Sylvestre-Gérard; Général 44

Auphan, Gabriel Adrien Joseph Paul; Admiral 43

Bakke, Sophus Michael; signalør 200, 201

Behrens, Willi; Sonderführer 174, 231

Benecke, Berthold; Major 65, 158, 301, 306

Bergan, Hans; overkanoner 177

Bertelsen, Rolf Thorleif; løytnant 198, 204, 207, 209, 218

Bertelsmann, Hans-Joachim; Leutnant 212

Bexrud, Sigurd Monrad Lorang; minør 199, 209, 249

Blich, Knut Nergård; kaptein 267

Blomeyer, Karl; Oberst 80

Boehm, Hermann; Generaladmiral 3, 64, 246, 253, 306, 320–2, 323, 324, 326, 327, 342, 351–3, 357, 358

Boese, Werner; Hauptmann 227, 319

Bøhmer, Kristian Nikolai; kaptein 192, 200

Bonsak, Johan August; løytnant 195, 197

Boyes, Hector; Captain 91, 132, 148, 280

Brauchitsch, Walter von; Generaloberst 62, 75

Bräuer, Curt; German Minister to Norway 58, 59, 63, 71, 76, 79, 81, 158, 159, 190, 282–6, 289, 300–6, 308, 323

Brinchmann; korporal 200

Briseid, Trygve Sigurd; kommandørkaptein 255, 256, 259–61, 267

Bruusgaard, Reidar Gram; kaptein 274

Bryant, Benjamin; Lieutenant Commander 114, 317, 338

Budäus, Kurt; Oberleutnant 257, 260, 265, 266

Bull, Jens; undersecretary 97, 109

Buschenhagen, Erich; Oberst 64, 72, 76, 78, 320, 352

Canaris, Wilhelm; Admiral 54, 78, 79, 94

Carelius, Erling; løytnant 230

Carls, Rolf; Generaladmiral 2, 3, 53, 54, 73, 75, 104

Chamberlain, Neville; Prime Minister 35, 37, 38, 40, 44, 44–6, 60, 83, 84, 137, 350

Christian X, King of Denmark 309

Churchill, Winston; First Lord of the Admiralty 28–30, *29*, 34, 35, 37, 39, 40, 41, 45, 46, 48, 61, 74, 83, 96, 103, 109, 111, 112, 135, 137, 350

Clausen, Frits; Danish Nazi leader 78

Colban, Erik; Norwegian Minister to Britain 33, 37, 38, 40, 41, 77

Collier, Laurence; Counsellor Foreign Office 38, 91

Corbin, Charles; French Minister to Britain 38, 83

Corneliussen, Elias; kommandør 91, 145, 146, 148, 150, 151, 152, 280

Czygan, Werner; Korvettenkapitän 17, 212, 222, 224

d'Arzur, Albert Christophe Marie; Capitaine de Frégate 132

Dæhli, Arne; kaptein 188

Daladier, Édouard; Prime Minister 34, 38, 44, 46

Dampierre, Comte de; French Minister to Norway 80, 132, 297

Denham, Henry; Naval Attaché 109, 109

Diesen, Henry; admiral 24, 25, 39, 69, 71, 99, 132, 145, 146, 148–51, 152, 155, 266, 280, 282, 283

Dietl, Eduard Wohlrath Christian; Generalmajor 79

Dilley, Bruno; Oberleutnant 294

Dingsør, Bernt Teodor; kaptein 259

Döhler; Leutnant 251, 252

Dönitz, Karl; Konteradmiral 3, 53, 86

Dore, Alan; Wing Commander 298

Dormer, Sir Cecil; British Minister to Norway 21, 28, 29, 45, 80, 81, 132, 157, 281, 297–301, 305

Douglas, Carl; Chargé d'affaires 153

Edwards, Ralph; Captain 109, 111, 112

Engelbrecht, Erwin; Generalmajor 107, 113, 160, 174, 176, 190, 203, 221, 225, 230, 231, 237, 288, 294, 296, 319, 321, 323, 326, 342, 352–4

Engelhardt-Bergeshof; Kapitänleutnant 17

Engelmann; Kurt-Eduard; Korvetten-kapitän 17, 185, 207, 221

Enger, Hersleb Adler; major 172, 180, 182, 269, 270–2

Enger, Vagn Jul; kaptein 172, 197, 198, 200–2, 204, 205, 218, 244, 248, 250, 251, 351

Eriksen, Birger Kristian; oberst, ii, 166, 168–70, 182, 194, 195, 197–204, 218, 224, 225, 241–3, 246, 248–53, 266, 271, 327, 348–51

Esmarch, August; Norwegian Minister to Denmark 97, 150, 153

Evans, Edward R.; Admiral 44

Færden, Fredrik Wilhelm; major 173, 198, 327

Falkenhorst, Nicolaus von; General der Infanterie 62, 64, 65, 66, 68, 71, 72, 75, 76, 85, 107, 111, 160, 161, 194, 246, 289, 295, 296, 301, 308, 320, 323, 326, 342, 353

Findahl, Theo; journalist 98

Foley, Francis (Frank) Edward; intelligence officer 298, 300

Forbes, Charles Morton; Admiral of the Fleet 112, 113

Forbes, John; Commander 329

Forshell, Anders; Kommendörkapten 55, 93, 92–7

Förster, Hugo; Korvettenkapitän 17, 189, 190, 203, 221, 231, 325

Forstmann, Gustav; Kapitänleutnant 108, 116, 124, 232, 238, 279

Freyberg; Walter Eisneberg-Allmendingen; Oberleutnant zur See 17, 105, 193, 233, 234

Frisnes, Hans; båtsmann 216

Fuglerud; kaptein 265

Gebauer, Max, Korvettenkapitän 336, 337

George VI, King of United Kingdom 37

George, Ogwyn Francis; Sergeant 297

Gjerberg Lars Fredrik; fenrik 197

Glattre, Sigurd Odd; løytnant 262

Godenau, Arthur; Stabsobersteuermann 260, 261

Godø, Reidar Lauritz; løytnant 242, 245

Goerz, Paul; Rittmeister 105, 129 225, *227*, 228, 229

Göring, Hermann; Generalfeldmarschall 72, 75

Gotås; Sersjant 180

Gripenberg, Georg Achates; Finnish envoy to London 40

Grudzinski, Jan; Lieutenant-Commander 139–42, *141*, 144

Grundmann, Erich; Kapitänleutnant (Ing.) 256, 257, 260, 261, 265, 266

Gullichsen, Thomas; kaptein 180, 272

Gullichsen, Thomas Hartvig; oberst 298

Günther, Christian; Swedish Foreign Minister 42, 151

Gutsche; Mechanikersmaat 208

Haakon VII, King of Norway 37, 70, 71, 76, 158, 179, 248, 281, 285–8, *287*, 301, 304, 305, 308, 309, 326, 350, 351,

Haga, Rolf; kaptein 274

Hagelin, Albert Viljam; Norwegian NS member 55–8, 60, 65, 68, 69, 77, 289, 301, 302, 305

Hagene, Georg; Kapitänleutnant 17, 185, 207

Halder, Franz; Generaloberst 51, 59, 60, 62, 66, 67

Halifax, Earl of (Edward Frederick Lindley Wood); Foreign Secretary 35, 37, 38, 40–2, *45*, 48, 305

Hambro, Carl Joachim; stortingspresident 40, 57, 83, 154, 284–8, *286*, 300, 303, 304, 309

Hambro, Gudrun 285

Hamilton, Carl; Swedish Minister to Denmark 97

Hammerstad, Hans Oscar; oberst 145

Hansen, Anette 207

Hansen, Werner; Oberleutnant 297

Harriman, Florence Jaffray; US Minister to Norway 18, 81, 308

Hassel, Ulrich; Special Envoy 49

Heitmann; Gefreiter 224

Heye, Hellmuth Guido Alexander; Kapitän zur See 87, 88

Heymann, Erich; Fregattenkapitän 17, *103*, 183, 210–12, 216, 217, 221, 222, 225, 226, 327, 342–4, 353,

Hindenburg, Paul Ludwig Hans Anton von; German President 1

Hitler, Adolf; German *Führer* 1, 6, 7, 22, 30, 49–63, *50*, 66–72, 75, 76, 94, 96, 106, 112, 302, 305, 306, 324, 342, 354, 356, 358

Hjelmtveit Nils; minister 305

Hjelvik Peder Edvard; kaptein 197

Høie, Kristen; fenrik 197, 202

Hore-Belisha, Leslie, War (Army) Minister 57

Horton, Max; Vice-Admiral (Submarines) 114, 115, 131, 311, 312, 315, 338

Hovdenak, Gunnar; kaptein 188

Hvinden Haug, Jacob; generalmajor 241

Ingenhoven, Peter; Hauptmann 294

Ironside, Edmund; General 30, 46, 48

Jacobs, Ian; Lieutenant-General 135

Jaeger; Leutnant zur See 269, 271

Jamvold, Peter Krefting; doctor 143

Jodl, Alfred; Generalmajor 1, 58, 60, 62, 66, 75, 78, 79, 111, 161, 305, 308

Johannessen, Haakon; kaptein 256

Johannessen, William Malthe; ekspedisjonssjef 301

Johansen, Harald; menig 271

Johnsen, K.; leutnant 226

Jørgensen; NCO cadet 197

Kaaveland, Bjarne; kaptein 132

Karlowa, Otto; Korvettenkapitän 130, 326

Karlsen, Albert Elias; overminør 199

Keitel, Wilhelm Bodewin Johann Gustav; Generaloberst 1, 60, 66, 72, 75, 76, 305

Kempf, Hermann; Oberleutnant 160, 289, 322

Kermarrec; Lieutenant de Vaisseau 68

Kimmerling, Werner; Kapitänleutnant 258, 260, 265, 268

King; William Donald; Lieutenant 332, 336

Kite, Peter William Hansford; Lieutenant 297

Kjølsen, Frits Hammer; Kommandør-kaptajn 93, 94–6, 98

Knape; Kapitänleutnant 253

Knauss, Robert; Oberst 64

Knutsen; sersjant 197

Kohle, Pius; Oberfeldwebel 343, 344, 346

Koht, Halvdan; Foreign Minister 19–22, 20, 29, 37, 41, 49, 76, 77, 79, 80–3, 82, 89, 92, 93, 96–9, 145, 146, 150–6, 158, 280–4, 286–8, 300, 301, 303–5

Kongsgaard, Ragnar; korporal 271

Körner; Oberleutnant 265

Kraft, Knut; løytnant 183

Krancke, Theodor; Kapitän zur See 60, 64, 66, 320

Kühn; Oberleutnant 253

Kummetz, Oscar; Konteradmiral 104, 105, 107, 108, 127, 128, 130, 174, 176, 179, 183, 185–7, 189, 190, 192–4, 203, 204, 206, 212, 221, 225, 231, 233, 234, 252–5

Laake, Kristian Kristiansen; general 81, 155, 283

Lange, Werner; Kapitän zur See 105, 130, 185, 186, 215, 233, 234, 236, 238, 239, 241, 246, 279, 320, 333

Langkau Mechanikergefreiter 208

Laporte, Walter de; Major 78, 157

Lent, Helmuth; Leutnant 297

Lie, Trygve Halvdan; Minister of Trade and Supply 155, 283, 300

Liebe, Heinrich; Kapitänleutnant 34

Linder, Sven; Kommendörkapten 90, 146

Ljungberg, Birger; Minister of Defence 22, 23, 77, 82, 83, 89, 96, 98, 99, 144–6, 148, 149, 151, 154–6, 179, 281–3, 285

Löblich, Hans-Joachim; Oberfähnrich 208

Lowzow, Hartvig; kaptein 259–61

Lütjens, Günther; Vizeadmiral 106

Magnussen; corporal 180

Maisch, Ernst; Feldwebel 343

Mannerheim, Carl Gustav; Field Marshal 34, 43

Markworth, Friedrich; Oberleutnant zur See 17

Marschall, Wilhelm; Admiral 3

Martinsen, Asbjørn; skipper 216

Martius, Gudrun; secretary 98, 99

Menk; Hauptmann 269, 272

Mihatsch, Karl; Kapitänleutnant 217, 326

Munch, Peter Rochegune; Danish Foreign Minister 309

Nesse, Klaus; kaptein 197, 198, 201

Neuss, Helmut; Kapitänleutnant 236, 251, 279, 330

Nickelmann, Helmuth; Oberst 294, 295, 322

Nieden; Fregattenkapitän 352, 353

Noel-Baker, Philip; MP 77

Notland, Kristian; oberstløytnant 171, 179, 272,

Nygaardsvold, Johan; Prime Minister 18, 19, 22, 49, 77, 82, 83, 93, 99, 146, 150, 151, 155, 156, 158, 280–8, 287, 295, 300–4, 309, 351

Nyhus, Olaug 207

Onsrud, Nils; police officer 142–4

Oster, Hans; Oberst 94, 95, 99

Pellengahr, Richard; Generalmajor 312, 313, 314, 326

Perleberg, Rüdiger; Obersteuermann 189

Petersson, Aksel; kaptein 231

Philler, Albrecht; Major 296

Phillips, Tom Spencer Vaughan; (Acting) Vice-Admiral 91, 112, 113, 153, 154,

Piekenbrock, Hans; Oberst 77, 78, 157

Pinckernelle; Sonderführer 226

Pizey, Edward Fowle; Lieutenant-Commander 130, 131, 313, 314

Pochhammer, Hans-Erik; Kapitänleutnant 17, 185, 204, 340

Pohlman, Hartwig; Oberstleutnant 64, 78, 157–9, 241, 288, 289, 294, 322, 323,

Pommer-Esche, Gerd von; Leutnant 261, 264

Pommerehne, Walter; Kapitänleutnant 17

Poncet, Hans von; Major 238, 240

Pontoppidan, Fredrik Carl; Kommandør-kaptajn 147, 147–9, 160

Poplow, Walter; Feldwebel 343

Pound, Alfred Dudley Pickman Roger; Admiral of the Fleet–First Sea Lord 28, 29, 91, 122

Prior, William; General 311

Pruck, Erick; Major 65, 78, 79, 158, 322

Prytz, Björn; Swedish envoy to London 42

Quisling, Vidkun Abraham Jønsson; Norwegian NS leader 55–9, 56, 61, 64, 68, 69, 74, 77, 78, 91, 157, 301–6, 308, 352

Raeder, Erich; Großadmiral 1–5, 2, 49–58, 50, 52, 60–2, 64, 67–70, 72–6, 106, 124, 159, 194, 253, 306, 320, 322, 342, 351–4, 357

Rækken, Ragnvald; sersjant 197, 202

Ramm; Korvettenkapitän 17

Rechnitzer, Hjalmar; Viceadmiral 122, 124, 147

Reid, Margaret Grant; secretary 300

Renthe-Fink, Cecil von; German envoy to Copenhagen 309

Reynaud, Paul; Prime Minister 43, 46, 74, 83

Ribbentrop, Joachim von; Foreign Minister 58, 158

Richert, Arvid; Swedish Minister to Germany 93, 94, 96, 97

Rieve, Friedrich; Kapitän zur See 326

Ringe, H. Chr.; Major 276

Rixecker, Karl Jakob; Stabsobersteuer-mann 272, 274

Rognlien, Eivind Randers; Undersecretary of State 143, 144

Rosenberg, Alfred; Reichsleiter 55, 57, 58, 61, 68, 74

Rygg, Nicolai; MD Bank of Norway 288

Saalwächter, Alfred; Generaladmiral 2, 3, 75, 104, 133, 161,

Sahm, Heinrich; German envoy to Norway 49

Sas, Gijsbertus Jacobus 'Bart'; Major 94–6, 99

Schäfer; Kapitän 144

Scheel, Arne; Norwegian Minister to Germany 92, 93, 95–9

Scheidt, Hans-Wilhelm, Amtsleiter 57, 57–9, 65, 71, 288, 289, 301, 302, 305

Schniewind, Otto; Konteradmiral 2, 3, 4, 51

Schnitler, Hans Peter Krag; oberst 295, 296

Schnurbein, Karl-Egloff von; Kapitän-leutnant 252, 328

Schramm, Ernst Wilhelm; kaptein 173

Schreiber, Richard; Korvettenkapitän 64, 65, 148, 158–60, 194, 288–90, 301, 319

Schulte-Mönting, Erich, Fregattenkapitän 55, 56, 92–4

Schürdt, Heinrich Wilhelm; Oberleutnant zur See 17, 204

Seale, Alan George Luscombe; Lieutenant-Commander 144, 145

Selchow; Korvettenkapitän 335

Slaughter, Jack; Lieutenant-Commander 311, 338

Smith-Johannsen, Johannes; kontre-
    admiral 147, 148, 162, 188, 195, 241, 254, 255,
    256, 265–9, 292
Smith-Kielland, Ingvald; Vice-consul 153
Sødem, Magnus; kaptein 168, 195, 197,
    200–2, 208, 249, 251
Sollie, Hans; løytnant 244
Sørlie, Eugen Holm; kaptein 271, 272
Spiller, Eberhardt; Hauptmann 64, 158, 289,
    294, 308, 309
Stamsø, Trond; kaptein 171
Stang, Ulrich; Vice-consul 92, 95, 96, 98, 99
Steen, Erik Anker; kaptein 89, 90, 99, 147,
    148, 255, 280
Steensen-Leth, Vincens de; Under-
    secretary 95
Stosch, Richard von; Kapitän 193
Stowe, Leland; journalist 307, 308
Strand, Hans; løytnant 198
Strauss; Oberfänrich 278, 279, 331
Strecker, Karl; Major 64
Strelow, Siegfried; Kapitänleutnant 178–80,
    188, 263, 264, 277
Strøm, Ø.; sersjant 197
Sundlo, Konrad Bertram Holm; oberst 68
Süssmann, Wilhelm; Generalmajor 176,
    225, 231
Sutton-Pratt, Reginald; Lieutenant-
    Colonel 91

Tandberg-Hanssen, Einar Andreas;
    Kommandørkaptein 171, 179, 266, 267
Telle, Knut; kaptein 173, 181, 274, 276, 278
Terboven, Josef; Reichskommissar 306, 352
Tewaag, Carl Otto; Leutnant 129, 223
Thannemann, Karl; Fregattenkapitän
    (Ing) 17, 104, 185, 210–12, 222, 223, 228, 353
Thiele, August; Kapitän zur See 102, 106,
    174, 185, 192, 212–14, 233, 234, 236–41, 244,
    246, 252, 263, 268, 269, 275, 277, 279, 319,
    328–32, 342, 352

Thommessen, Roald Juel; løytnant 144
Thorsager, Finn; fenrik 293
Tippelskirch, Eyk von; Oberstleutnant 296
Tornes, Ole; 216
Torp, Oscar; Finance Minister 82, 283, 288,
    300

Unneberg, Thorleif Dagfinn; kaptein 195,
    197, 253, 347

Vian, Philip Louis; Captain 39, 40
Vogler, Oberleutnant 330, 331
Voigt, Rudolf; Kapitän 140
Voss, Hermann; Leutnant 142

Walther, Erich; Hauptmann 294, 308, 309
Warburton-Lee, Bernard; Captain 85
Warlimont, Walter; Oberst 64, 75
Wegener; Korvettenkapitän 87
Welding-Olsen, Leif; kaptein 177–80, 178
Wendelbo, Gøsta Harald; kaptein 198
Wetjen; Oberleutnant 246, 250, 251
Whitworth, William; Vice-Admiral 85, 113
Wilcke, Hans; Kapitänleutnant 235, 256,
    258, 263, 330
Willoch, Håkon Isaachsen; kaptein 98, 99,
    132
Winsnes, Ingolf; løytnant 259, 262
Wold, Terje; Minister of Justice 281, 300
Woldag, Heinrich; Kapitän zur See 9, 17,
    103, 105, 126, 174, 176, 183, 185, 189, 190, 194,
    203, 206, 212, 216, 217, 221, 222, 232, 234,
    327, 342–4, 352–4
Wrede-Holm, Harald; Oberstløytnant 89,
    98, 147
Wulle; Kapitänleutnant 326

Zahle, Herluf; Danish Minister to
    Germany 95
Zöpfel, Kurt; Korvettenkapitän 17, 225

Ships

Br = British; D = Danish; G = German; N = Norwegian; P = Polish

A2 (N) 273, 274

A3 (N) 273, 274

A4 (N) 273, 274

Admiral Graf Spee (G) 5, 6, 39

Admiral Hipper (G) 6, 7, 87, 88, 112, 133, 134, 138, 139, 356

Admiral Scheer (G) 5, 6, 60, 329

Agder II (N) 141

Albatros (G) 106, *108*, 116, 122, 130, 131, *176*, 178–80, 183, 187, 188, 238, 256, 258, 263, 264, 268, *275*, 277, 325, 328, 329, 341, 356

Alpha (N) 167, 190, 200

Alster (G) 86

Altmark (G) 38, 39, 41–2, *42*, 43, 61, 62–4, *63*, 66–8, 74, 76, 119, 160

Amasis (G) 311

Antares (G) 314

August Leonhardt (G) *88*, 317

B4 (N) 198, 256

Bärenfels (G) 86

Berlin (G) 26, 27

Bismarck (G) 5, 6, 353

Blücher (G) *iii*, 6–10, *8*, 12–17, *12*, *14–15*, 102–11, *107*, 116, 120, 125, 127, 129, 131, 174–6, 183–7, 190, 194, 201, 203, 204, 209–10, *210–11*, 211–32, *214*, 216, 233–6, 241, 280, 296, 302, 303, 318, 321, 323, 324, 325, 327, 328, 340–7, 350–6, 358

Bremse (G) 324

Brummer (G) 334, 336, 337, 356

Clyde (Br) 315

Cobra (G) 161

Curityba (G) 275, 277

Deptford (Br) 33, 34, *36*

Deutschland (G), see *Lützow*

Dragen (D) 129

Emden (G) 4–6, *5*, 17, 70, *104*, 105, 106, 108, 116, 121, 122, 131, 146, 147, 180, *182*, 185–8, 195, 214, 215, 218, 232–6, *233*, 235, 238–40, 245, 248, 249, 258, 263, 265, 268, 269, 272, 279, 297, 318, 320–3, *321*, 322, 325, 326, 328, 342

Esk (Br) 85

España (G) 313, 314, *315*

F 5 (G) 336, 337

Falke (G) 336, 337

Farm (N) 176, 179

Florida (G) 334

Friedenau (G) 314

Furious (Br) 113

Furu (N) 167, 190, 192

Garoufalia (Gr) 33, 34

Glommen (N) 148, 173, 183

Glowworm (Br) 133, 134, *137*, 139

Gneisenau (G) 5, 6, 87, 88, 106, 122, 131, 134, 146, 147, 280, 356

Graf Zeppelin (G) 6

Greif (G) *108*, 330

Hamm (G) 313, 337

Hansestadt Danzig (G) 309

Harald Haarfagre (N) 254

Hardy (Br) 85

Havock (Br) 85

Hotspur (Br) 85

Hunter (Br) 85
Hvalen (D) 129
Hvas (N) 149

Icarus (Br) 85
Impulsive (Br) 85
Ionia (G) 315
Ivanhoe (Br) 85

Jaguar (G) 336, 337
Jenny (N) 140, 141

Karlsruhe (G) 6, 111, 326, 356
Kattegat (G) 86
Kjæk (N) 176, 183
Köln (G) 6, 7, 111
Kondor (G) 106, 116, 185, 187, 188, 232, 235, 238, 248–51, 256, 258, 263, 268, 276, 278, 328–30
Königin Louise (G) 161
Königsberg (G) 6, 69, 70, 111, 324, 356
Kranfartøy Nr.2 (N) 167, 198, 200, 201, 203, 204
Kreta (G) 88, 128, 145

Laugen (N) 148, 173, 183
Laxen (D) 129
Leipzig (G) 6, 122, 131, 147
Levante (G) 86
Lindebø (N) 140, 141
Luchs (G) 330
Lützow (G) 6, 69, 70, 100, 101, 106, 107, 109, 116, 122, 127, 128, 130, 131, 160, 174, 185, 187, 188, 192, 212–15, 218, 232–41, 244–9, 248, 251, 252, 263, 268, 318, 319, 321, 323, 325, 328–32, 341, 342, 352, 356

M 6 (G) 315
M 1302 (G) 335
M 1701 (G) 335
M 1702 (G) 335
Main (G) 86

Mira (N) 79, 80, 82
Moonsund (G) 332, 334,
Möwe (G) 5, 106, 108, 116, 187, 194, 215, 216, 235, 236, 238, 248–52, 279, 318, 328–31

Narwhal (Br) 335
Navarra (N) 137
Nor (N) 148, 173, 183
Norden (G) 232, 245, 251
Nürnberg (G) 6, 131

Odin (N) 141, 142, 325
Olav Tryggvason (N) 23, 254–64, 260, 262, 266–8, 325
Oldenburg (*Schiff 35*) (G) 335
Orzeł (Pl) 114, 131, 139–42, 140, 314
Oscarsborg I (N) 238
Oter I (N) 274
Otra (N) 152, 188, 254–6, 260

Peder Skram (D) 129
Penelope (Br) 113, 133
Pol III (N) 176–82, 177, 179, 180, 182, 188, 264, 342, 350
Posidonia see *Stedingen*
Preußen (G) 161
Prinz Eugen (G) 6

R 17 (G) 107, 187, 256, 257, 258, 260, 261, 264, 265, 268, 324, 341, 358
R 18 (G) 107, 117, 187, 215, 216, 238, 268, 322
R 19 (G) 107, 117, 187, 216, 238, 248, 322
R 20 (G) 107, 187, 248, 269, 271, 272, 322
R 21 (G) 108, 187, 248, 250, 256–8, 260–2, 264, 268, 273, 318, 322
R 22 (G) 108, 187, 268, 272, 274, 322
R 23 (G) 108, 187, 248, 268, 272, 274, 318, 322
R 24 (G) 108, 187, 269, 271, 272
Ramoen (N) 274
Rau VI (G) 314
Rau VII (G) 108, 116, 124, 186, 187, 211, 238–40, 268, 276–9, 277, 321

Rau VIII (G) 108, 116, 124, 186, 187, 236, 237, 238, 239, 240, 256, 258, 263, 268, 276, 278, 321

Rauenfels (G) 86

Rauma (N) 152, 254–9, 261, 267, 342

Ravn (N) 149

Renown (Br) 85, 113, 133, 134

Repulse (Br) 113, 133

Rio de Janeiro (G) 115, 139–44, 142, 149, 150, 154, 156, 157, 161, 174

Roda (G) 86

Rodney (Br) 113

Roland (G) 161

São Paolo (G) 86

Scharnhorst (G) 2, 5, 6, 87, 88, 106, 134, 356

Schlesien (G) 6

Schleswig-Holstein (G) 6, 103

Schürbeck (*Schiff 40*) (G) 315

Seal (Br) 335

Sealion (Br) 114, 317, 338

Seawolf (Br) 315, 337

Seeadler (G) 330

Seeteufel (G) 331

Severn (Br) 315

Shark (Br) 315, 320

Skagerrak (G) 86

Skudd I (N) 274

Skudd II (N) 145, 176

Snapper (Br) 315, 332, 334, 335, 336, 337

Sørland (N) 215, 216, 342

Spearfish (Br) 315, 328, 329, 331

Sperrbrecher X (G) (ex *Vigo*) 193

Sperrbrecher XI (G) (ex *Petropolis*) 193

Stedingen (G) 144, 149, 156

Sunfish (Br) 114, 131, 311, 314, 315, 333, 335, 338

Swordfish (Br) 114

Tarpon (Br) 315, 337

Teviotbank (Br) 84, 113

Thistle (Br) 337

Thomas Walton (Br) 33, 34

Tirpitz (G) 5, 6

Togo (G) 335

Tordenskjold (N) 254

Treff (N) 274

Triad (Br) 315

Trident (Br) 114, 131, 144, 145, 314, 315

Triton (Br) 114, 130, 131, 312, 313, 314

Truant (Br) 326

Unity (Br) 114

V 1501 (G) 315

V 1507 (G) 314

Valiant (Br) 113

Vidar (N) 148, 173, 183

Widar (G) 160, 289, 322

Wiegand (G) 88

Wigbert (G) 314

Wotan (G) 331